Media And Cultural Theory

Media & Cultural Theory brings together leading international scholars to address key issues and debates within media and cultural studies including:

- Media representations of the new woman in contemporary society
- The creation of self in lifestyle media
- The nature of cultural globalisation
- The rise of digital actors and media

These subjects are analysed through the use of contemporary media and film texts such as Bridget Jones and The Lord of the Rings trilogy as well as case studies of the US and UK after 9/11.

Contributors: Asu Aksoy; Lisa Blackman; Jonathan Burston; Nick Couldry; James Curran; Aeron Davis; Des Freedman; Christine Geraghty; Janet Harbord; Sarah Kember; James Lull; Angela McRobbie; Ted Magder; David Morley; Keith Negus; John Durham Peters; Arvind Rajagopal; Kevin Robins; Bill Schwarz; Gareth Stanton.

Editors: James Curran and David Morley are both Professors of Communications at Goldsmiths College, University of London.

James Curran's publications include, with others, *Culture Wars* (2005), *Mass Media & Society* (4th edition, 2005), *Power without Responsibility* (6th edition, 2003) and *Media and Power* (2002).

David Morley's publications include *Home Territories* (2000), *Television Audiences and Cultural Studies* (1992) and *Family Television* (1986).

Media and Cultural Theory

Edited by James Curran and
David Morley

Routledge
Taylor & Francis Group

LONDON AND NEW YORK

First published 2006
by Routledge
2 Park Square, Milton Park, Abingdon, Oxon, OX14 4RN

Simultaneously published in the USA and Canada
by Routledge
270 Madison Ave, New York, NY 10016

Transferred to digital printing 2009

Routledge is an imprint of the Taylor & Francis Group

Typeset in Perpetua and GillSans by Taylor & Francis Books
Printed and bound in Great Britain by
CPI Antony Rowe, Chippenham, Wiltshire

British Library Cataloguing in Publication Data
A catalogue record for this book is available from the British Library

Library of Congress Cataloging in Publication Data
Media & cultural theory : edited by james curran and david
morley.
    p. cm.
  Includes bibliographical references and index.
  ISBN 0-415-31704-5 (hardback : alk. paper) -- ISBN 0-415-
31705-3 (pbk. : alk. paper) 1. Mass media and culture. 2.
Intercultural communication. I. Title: Media and cultural theory. II.
Curran, James. III. Morley, David, 1949-
  P94.6.M4 2005
  302.23--dc22

                                   2005006413

ISBN10: 0–415–31704–5   ISBN13: 978-0-415-31704-7 (hbk)
ISBN10: 0–415–31705–3   ISBN13: 978-0-415-31705-4 (pbk)

T&F informa

Taylor & Francis Group is the Academic Division of T&F Informa plc.

Contents

Contributors

Asu Aksoy is a Research Associate in the Department of Media and Communications, Goldsmiths College. She is presently working on an EU Fifth Framework project, Changing City Spaces: New Challenges for Cultural Policy in Europe.

Lisa Blackman is a Senior Lecturer in critical psychology and cultural studies in the Department of Media and Communications at Goldsmiths College. She has published in the area of embodiment, selfhood and cultural processes in a joint publication with Professor Valerie Walkerdine, *Mass Hysteria: Critical Psychology and Media Studies* (Palgrave, 2001). She has also published work on embodiment and voice hearing: *Hearing Voices: Embodiment and Experience* (Free Association Books, 2001) She is currently working on a new book, *Embodying the Psychological* (Palgrave), which develops these interests in relation to nineteenth-century and contemporary cultures of self-help.

Jonathan Burston is Assistant Professor at the Faculty of Information and Media Studies, University of Western Ontario. His recent work is on performing bodies in the digital space and time of the military–industrial–media complex. His book, *Corporate Broadway: Media, Megamusicals and the Theatre*, is forthcoming from Duke University Press.

Nick Couldry is Senior Lecturer in Media and Communications at the London School of Economics and Political Science, where he is co-director of the Masters Programme in Culture and Society. He is the author of *The Place of Media Power* (Routledge, 2000), *Inside Culture* (Sage, 2000) and *Media Rituals: A Critical Approach* (Routledge, 2003), and co-editor, with James Curran, of *Contesting Media Power* (Rowman & Littlefield, 2003) and with Anna McCarthy, *MediaSpace* (Routledge, 2004). He was a founder member of the *OurMedia Nuestros Medios* network of activists and theorists of alternative media.

James Curran is Professor of Communications at Goldsmiths College, London. He has published over 18 books, including *Culture Wars: The Media and British*

Left (with Ivor Gaber and Julian Petley) (Edinburgh University Press, 2005), *Power without Responsibility* (with Jean Seaton), 6th edition (Routledge, 2003), *Mass Media and Society* (ed. with Michael Gurevitch), 4th edition (Arnold, 2005) and Media and Power (Routledge, 2002).

Aeron Davis is Lecturer in Sociology and Director of the MA in Political Communications and Society at City University. He has published widely on aspects of political communication, media sociology and promotional culture, and is the author of *Public Relations Democracy* (Manchester University Press, 2002). He is currently researching the impact of promotional culture on markets and how media and culture influence elite networks.

Des Freedman is Senior Lecturer in Communications and Cultural Studies in the Department of Media and Communications at Goldsmiths College, University of London. He is on the management committee of the European Science Foundation's COST Action examining 'The impact of the internet on the mass media in Europe' and has recently completed ESRC-funded research on the dynamics of media policy-making. He is the author of *The Television Policies of the British Labour Party: 1951–2001* (Frank Cass, 2003) and co-editor of *War and the Media: Reporting Conflict 24/7* (Sage, 2003).

Christine Geraghty is Professor of Film and Television Studies at the University of Glasgow and has written extensively on film and television. She is the author of *Women and Soap Opera* (Polity, 1991) and *British Cinema in the Fifties: Gender, Genre and the 'New Look'* (Routledge, 2000), and co-editor of *The Television Studies Book* (Arnold, 1998). Her contextual study of the British film *My Beautiful Laundrette* was published by I.B. Taurus in 2004 and she is currently working on a book on screen adaptations.

Janet Harbord lectures in film studies at Goldsmiths College. She is author of *Film Cultures* (Sage, 2002) and *Gathering Film: Film Studies for the Twenty-first Century* (Polity, 2005, forthcoming) and co-editor, with Jan Campbell, of *Temporalities: Autobiography and Everyday Life* (Manchester University Press, 2002). She is currently researching the philosophy and practice of digital editing.

Sarah Kember is a Reader in New Technologies of Communication at Goldsmiths. She is the author of *Virtual Anxiety: Photography, New Technologies and Subjectivity* (Manchester University Press, 1998) and *Cyberfeminism and Artificial Life* (Routledge 2002). A co-edited issue (with Mariam Fraser and Celia Lury) of *Theory, Culture and Society*, entitled 'Lure for Life: Towards a New Vitalism' was published in 2005.

James Lull is Professor Emeritus of Communication Studies at San José State University, California, specialising in media and cultural studies. He holds an honorary doctorate in social sciences from the University of Helsinki, Finland. He regularly teaches and conducts research in Mexico and South America. His publications include *Media, Communication, Culture: A Global Approach* (Polity, 2002) and the edited collection *Culture in the Communication Age* (Routledge, 2001).

Angela McRobbie is Professor of Communications at Goldsmiths College. Her most recent book is *The Uses of Cultural Studies* (Sage, 2005). She is also currently completing a book *Post-feminism and the Displacement of Sexual Politics* (Sage, 2006).

Ted Magder is an Associate Professor and Chair of the Department of Culture and Communication at New York University. His publications include *Canada's Hollywood: Feature Films and the Canadian State* (University of Toronto, 1993) and *Franchising the Candy Store: Split-Run Magazines and a New International Regime for Trade in Culture* (1998). Magder is also the academic advisor to the Center for Communication in New York City and co-director of the Coordinating Council for Culture, Communication, Journalism and Media Studies at NYU. In 2003, he was a visiting scholar at the University of Amsterdam's School of Communication Research.

David Morley is Professor of Communications at Goldsmiths College. Among his publications are *Television, Audiences and Cultural Studies* (Routledge, 1992) and *Spaces of Identity* (with Kevin Robins) (Routledge, 1996). His most recent book is *Home Territories: Media, Mobility and Identity* (Routledge, 2000).

Keith Negus is Professor in Musicology at Goldsmiths College. His books include *Producing Pop* (Arnold, 1992), *Popular Music in Theory* (Polity Press, 1996), *Music Genres and Corporate Cultures* (Routledge, 1999) and *Creativity, Communication and Cultural Value* (Sage, 2004) (co-authored with Michael Pickering). He is joint co-ordinating editor of the journal *Popular Music*.

John Durham Peters, F. Wendell Miller Distinguished Professor of Communication Studies, University of Iowa, is the author of *Speaking into the Air: A History of the Idea of Communication* (1999) and *Courting the Abyss: Free Speech and the Liberal Tradition* (2005) (both University of Chicago Press), and co-editor of *Canonic Texts in Media Studies* (Polity Press, 2003) and *Mass Communication and American Social Thought: Key Texts, 1919–1968* (Rowman & Littlefield, 2004). He is the recipient of a Fulbright Fellowship to Greece, National Endowment for the Humanities Fellowship, and Leverhulme Trust Fellowship to Goldsmiths College.

Arvind Rajagopal is an Associate Professor in media studies at New York University. His book, *Politics after Television: Hindu Nationalism and the Reshaping of the Public in India* (Cambridge, 2001), won the Ananda K. Coomaraswamy

Prize from the Association of Asian Studies in 2003. He has recently guest edited a special issue of *Interventions* 'America and Its Others: Cosmopolitan Terror as Globalization' (6(3), November 2004).

Kevin Robins is currently Professor of Sociology at City University, London, and was formerly Professor of Communications at Goldsmiths College.

Bill Schwarz is Reader in English and Drama, Queen Mary College, London. He is on the editorial boards of *History Workshop Journal*, *New Formations* and *Visual Culture in Britain*.

Gareth Stanton has a doctorate in anthropology and has conducted fieldwork in North Africa and the British colony of Gibraltar. His research interests include North African fiction, postcolonial theory and media histories. His articles have appeared in a variety of international journals. He is currently Head of the Media and Communications Department at Goldsmiths College.

Acknowledgement

The editors would like to acknowledge all the valuable administrative and technical assistance they have received from Richard Smith in the long process of this book's gestation – without which the project could not have been brought to fruition.

Editors' introduction

James Curran and David Morley

In the years since the publication of our previous volume *Cultural Studies and Communications* in 1996[1] much has changed in the fields of media and cultural studies. Like that volume, this one represents the specific, hybrid combination of these disciplines that has been developed by past and present members of our own department, in collaboration with a group of scholars in other institutions with whom we have worked increasingly closely in recent years.[2] The intellectual centre of gravity of our project could probably best be mapped as falling along the fault lines of media and cultural studies, as conventionally defined. This is no mishap, but rather, betokens an intellectual choice to inhabit this 'intermediate zone', in the conviction that it is at the point where the productive tensions between these fields are at their strongest that the most interesting work is to be done. Certainly, these fields have themselves changed since 1996 and it may now even be hard (not to mention unprofitable) to attempt to disentangle them – to the extent that the field of investigation of this book could perhaps be defined as that of media-studies-after-the-impact-of-cultural-studies.

Nowadays, some of the debates that characterised this field in the 1990s – many of which were plainly visible in our previous volume – such as that between political economy and reception studies, concerning whether the Holy Grail was to be found in the institutional structure of the media or in the conditions of their reception – do (happily) seem to have worn themselves out.[3] Now we see scholars on both sides of that debate more readily granting intellectual recognition to the claims of the other. The business in hand is then how better to articulate the insights produced by these different perspectives, rather than how to adjudicate their relative importance in the theology of the field (a sign of an increasing maturity – but we hope not sclerosis – in the field).[4]

The central thread that defines the contributions to this volume is the attempt to take stock of where our field has got to – and where it is going. In that endeavour, our contributors were encouraged to produce a critical intellectual 'audit' of what are now established as the taken-for-granted wisdoms of the field as it currently stands. To this extent, although in a different spirit, this volume shares some of the concerns of Katz *et al.*'s recent volume[5] in critically addressing many of the canonical texts, established theoretical frameworks and conceptual models now dominant in our field. Our concern is to see how much these theories and models have to offer us in understanding the contemporary field of communication and culture, in the context of the political, economic, cultural and technological transformations that we see all around us. Thus, we also see this volume as (hopefully) following in the footsteps of the issue of the *Journal of Communications*[6] that took as its title 'Ferment in the Field'. If the critiques and revisions to contemporary wisdoms that these essays offer can produce another round of fundamental debate, we shall have achieved our main objective.

An intellectual audit: gains and losses

At a time when media studies is (once again) under sustained attack in Britain, it is worth registering some of its successes. In the first place, its academic study has increased critical understanding of the media. New forms of audience research have rightly undermined widely held views about the omnipotent power of the media.[7] Media sociology has highlighted the pivotal role of sources in news production, encouraging a more discerning approach to consuming the news.[8] Media history has revealed how the industrialisation of the press limited freedom of expression, legitimating a movement for press reform that has been especially influential in the USA.[9]

Media studies' intellectual twin – cultural studies – has also profoundly influenced contemporary understandings of culture. In 1960, the 'cultural' section of the British national press was largely confined to arts reviews (books, theatre, classical music and art exhibitions). This reflected the traditional notion of a fixed hierarchy of cultural value, with High Culture of transcendent value at the peak, and 'trivial' forms of popular culture at the bottom. This traditional view was challenged by cultural studies, which showed that understandings of cultural value changed over time, were strongly influenced by self-serving struggles for prestige and status, and were distorted by geography and unequal dispositions of power.[10] A second strand of work, concerned with cultural consumption, showed that cultural judgements were also linked to symbolic forms of protest and to the expression of social identity, and were strongly influenced by class and educational background.[11] This body of iconoclastic research made it impossible to think about culture in the simplifying, canonical terms that had seemed axiomatic to schoolteachers of English and newspaper editors only half a century ago. In Britain and elsewhere, its effect was to encourage an enormous expansion in the range of cultural experience that was felt to be worthy of being subjected to critical scrutiny in the media – an approach that Christine Geraghty's analysis of UK

soap opera in this volume exemplifies. It also influenced how culture was examined, in a cumulative way that is currently subverting even those previous bastions
of conservative tradition, the fashion and travel sections of the press. Ironically,
we see, in this instance, it was not so much journalism studies as cultural studies
that changed the face of journalism.

The academic study of the media has certainly proved to be enormously
popular. Pioneered some eighty year ago in countries like Finland and the USA, it
really took off during the last quarter of the twentieth century. Thus, while in
Britain, media and cultural studies were only first introduced as an undergraduate
degree subjects in the 1970s and 1980s, by 2004 they were both taught at most
British universities. The subjects' expansion in the UK broadly coincided with
their diffusion throughout much of Europe, Latin America, Africa, Australasia and
Asia (with China now representing one of the fastest areas of growth). Media and
cultural studies have thus become truly global phenomena: as subjects now well-
established at universities around the world, despite the insistent sniping at their
intellectual value by the would-be guardians of intellectual 'standards' in the
British media and in UK educational politics.

Their creation has established a new intellectual space in which different disciplines have been brought together to shed light on a new subject. This has
generated a range of new insights and perspectives, some of which have subsequently been re-exported to the parent disciplines from which media and cultural
studies themselves originally derived. Numerous examples can be cited of the
influence of cultural studies on the recent development of history, anthropology
and sociology – not least the much-lauded 'cultural turn' in all these disciplines in
recent years. For instance, the leading eighteenth-century historian John Brewer
presented his last work as a 'new' type of history (Brewer 2004). In fact it is the
clearly recognisable product of a cultural studies tradition (centring on the telling
and retelling of sex scandals in public life) if a very good instance of that genre.

Regrettably, in recent years, under the strictures of the new forms of academic
performance management and all the pressures they produce towards institutional respectability, media and cultural studies have paid a price for their success,
by tending to become somewhat inured behind new, departmental walls. This has
encouraged a narrowing of focus in an increasingly self-referential, repetitive
form. However, work in the field now seems to be breaking out into a variety of
new specialist areas and this is encouraging researchers to re-engage with a
broader range of literatures and debates beyond the boundaries of media and
cultural studies themselves. This process is prompting current research to address
new questions in relation to a wide range of issues such as transnationalism,
ethnicity, gender, sexuality, communications technology, the sociology of new
social movements, global political economy, the new 'e-economy', area studies,
cultural history and much else besides. Green shoots are once again appearing.

Media and cultural studies have thus been illuminating, popular and academically influential, and the field is currently undergoing a process of renewal. However, not everything about these developments is cause for celebration. Indeed critics of cultural studies would claim that, in squaring up to traditional cultural elitism, and in assailing an earlier tradition of radical fundamentalism, it is now perhaps in danger of entering a Panglossian phase, where everything is portrayed as being for the best in the best of all possible worlds. Cultural studies has introduced valuable insights into the pleasures of media consumption and how these connect in rich and varied ways to the personal lives of audiences, but having exposed the limitations of traditional cultural critiques, it has sometimes proved reticent about how we should conceptualise 'cultural value' in more useful ways. Here, this challenge is taken up by Christine Geraghty's essay, among others, in her insistence on the need for careful aesthetic analysis of the forms of popular drama. In this conceptual move, Geraghty builds on the earlier work of authors such as Charlotte Brunsdon and Simon Frith on questions of 'quality' in popular culture (cf. Brunsdon 1990 and Frith 1991)

Similarly, in recent years, a new wave of cultural studies research has seemed to confound earlier fears that we are moving towards ever greater, global homogeneity. This work has offered reassuring evidence of multidirectional flows of global communication, the humbling of global media giants and their need for local media partnerships, and above all the power and resilience of local audiences and the rich resources they draw upon in making diverse sense of globally distributed media products. These are certainly useful insights that have undermined simplistic notions of growing global uniformity. But they do not lay to rest continuing concerns: that cultural globalisation is, in part, promoting the rise of the informal empire of the USA and tending to support the growing neo-liberal hegemony of our times. These issues have not always been adequately addressed by contemporary work on international communications and transnational culture – a deficiency that David Morley's essay here attempts to make good, in its reconsideration of the now neglected work of Herbert Schiller on media and cultural imperialism, from a cultural studies perspective.

More reassurance in relation to simplistic theories of media power has come from revisionist feminism. Fundamentalist claims that women were straightforwardly indoctrinated by the media into acceptance of a subordinate position were confounded by research highlighting the subversive ambiguity, liberating aspects or increasing diversity of media representations of women. The claim of some pioneer feminist analysts to speak on behalf of women was rebuffed by revisionists pointing to differences of experience and preference among women – most especially in the writings of those involved in second-wave feminism, who felt compelled to address the complications of how 'outmoded' that approach could appear to a younger generation of women (cf. Brunsdon 1991 and McRobbie

1999). Nonetheless, important questions remain about how best to make sense of media 'post-feminism' at a time when inequalities of pay, life chances, power and domestic responsibilities between men and women persist. For this reason, it is perhaps now worth returning to some of the original questions of feminist analysis as to how the media represent, and influence, the gender order. The essays by McRobbie and Blackman here both address (from different perspectives) these questions, in relation to the growing influence of post-feminist discourse not only within the academy, but also within the realm of popular culture itself

There are certainly some who are concerned by what they see as a narrowing of political perspective within cultural studies in so far as, from their point of view, much of this work has come, increasingly, to think of politics only in its personal dimension; and to conceive of redistribution solely in terms of recognition and inclusion, the right to be heard, understood and respected. Thus, such critics would argue, while these things are important, they also leave out much that ought to be included – sidelining more structural understandings of redistribution in terms of wealth, resources, life chances and space. They would also claim that, in practice, such overly personalised approaches tend to exclude consideration of the state and other agencies of redistribution – and to pay insufficient attention to the democratic processes that authorise social transfers.

However, in trying to understand such structural forms of determination and power there is little to be gained by rejecting the contribution of cultural studies work to this field, even if some of it can be argued to be vitiated by its overly personalised and relentlessly micro-perspective. To seek salvation in the (supposedly) eternal verities of political economy will avail us nothing. For one thing, those 'verities' are themselves now quite transformed by the extent to which the nation state, while still important, finds itself operating in a newly (if unevenly) globalised environment. Moreover, some of the most innovative work in cultural studies in recent years – on questions of 'cultural economy' (cf. du Gay and Pryke 2000; Negus and Pickering 2004; and Negus this volume) has taken economics itself as its object of study and has begun to address the ways in which economies themselves inevitably operate through cultural forms. This is not to pose cultural analysis as an 'alternative' to that of the economic but to enquire as to the modes of their articulation. In this approach, culture is not some kind of 'optional extra' or 'add-on' to the Real World of economics and politics – and consumption itself is not to be seen as merely derivative of, or supplementary to, the field of production – not least because production, as Marx argued, must be itself understood as motivated by and for consumption (cf. Marx 1973; Hall 1974; du Gay et al. 1997).

While there have been many exciting new developments in the fields of both media and cultural studies, there are also areas where an element of predictability has set in. It is sometimes now possible to anticipate (even without the benefit of an abstract) from the beginning of an essay, in books and journals in these fields, how an argument is going to develop, and to have a pretty good idea what its eventual conclusion will be. When a field begins to resemble the opening gambits of a chess game, it is time to move on. That is why we have sought in this book to break some new ground in search of more challenging answers – or perhaps, of some better questions.

The logic of the book

Starting from these premises, the book has been designed to offer a set of new perspectives and paradigms that can transcend the sterile debate between cultural studies and those associated with the political economy tradition. Fundamental questions of media and cultural theory are addressed here in an open-minded spirit and issues of political control of the media, their ownership and regulation are integrated with the analysis of issues of consumption, identity and taste – questions that are usually the preserve of a quite separate 'sphericule' of intellectual debate.

It is patently absurd that investigations of the different institutions of the cultural and communications industries (and their products) should continue to be conducted separately, at a time when all these industries are themselves going through a variety of modes of technologically (and economically) driven convergence, in the wake of digitalisation. To take but one example, while the realms of media fiction and media journalism have tended to become the subject of separate traditions of inquiry, both are now influenced by many of the same forces and both raise common questions (from how to make judgements about 'quality', to the role of both fiction and journalism in mediating public debate). As editors, our aim has been to encourage the production of analyses that will enable readers to see, in practice, how these dichotomies can be transcended and these debates most productively carried forward in a more catholic spirit. We have thus been concerned to move beyond a position where, as still often happens, cultural identity is taken to be the subject of one analytical tradition, while political power is debated separately in another. To preserve these divisions would be to miss the opportunity to explore the rich possible interconnections that the essays here strive to make, across these entrenched intellectual divisions. The collection aims to utilise perspectives and pose questions primarily developed in one area of study to issues more usually addressed in another. We thus present culturalist approaches alongside more sociologically and institutionally informed perspectives, which span the realms of production and consumption, which also strive to situate their analyses in relation to the changing technological frameworks of the media and cultural industries.

Among our other concerns has also been that of transcending the narrowly national frame within which studies of the media have historically been locked.

Thus, while we would not want to be seen to subscribe to any simplistic notion that questions of nation and nationality are somehow *passé*, in the (supposedly new) age of globalisation, the perspective of the book is necessarily informed by contemporary concerns with issues that do transcend the national – questions to do with new media technologies and their regulation, and with transnational broadcasting (see, in particular, the contributions by Lull, Magder, Morley, Robins and Aksoy). Many of the essays also address fundamental issues in media and cultural theory that are of concern across the field internationally – questions of disciplinarity, power and identity (Schwarz, Curran, McRobbie). Our authors also focus on a variety of particular issues at the hub of contemporary media theory – issues of community at national, transnational and local levels (Ragagopal, Robins and Aksoy, Peters and Stanton), the power-geometry of the media (Couldry), promotional culture (Davis), identity (Blackman), issues of cultural value and aesthetics (Geraghty) and of cultural production and 'new' communications technologies (Negus, Kember, Burston, Harbord and Freedman).

The book's materials are thus organised as contributions to what we have identified as five key debates concerned with: 1) media, modernity and globalisation; 2) media, community and dialogue; 3) media power, ideology and markets; 4) cultural production, consumption and aesthetics; and 5) new technologies and cultural forms.

Key themes

The material in Section I on 'Media, modernity and globalisation' reviews the relationship of media and culture to broad processes of social, political, economic and cultural change. These processes are represented by modernity, and its various 'posts' – principally, in this context, postmodernism, postcolonialism and post-feminism.

The section begins with Bill Schwarz's meditation on the history and development of media and communications studies as a discipline, which poses important questions about the philosophical limitations of the dominant literatures in these fields. David Morley broadens the frame by revisiting theories about the relationship of the media to the claims of contemporary globalisation theory that we are now living through a new epoch characterised principally by flux and change, mobile social identities, accelerated globalisation and the postmodern repudiation of meta-narratives. He argues that contemporary debates on this topic still need to be informed by earlier (and now often disregarded) critiques of cultural/media imperialism, if globalisation is to be understood in its concrete manifestations, rather than as an abstract universal process. Addressing the same contradictory dynamics of the globalised forms of contemporary culture but from another angle, James Lull offers a perspective on how questions of identity and consumption are to be understood within the dynamics of what he calls the 'push and pull' of global culture, in relation to the complex matrices of individual and collective fetishes and fears, in the new context of the postmodern forms of global communication. Angela McRobbie addresses the question of another 'post' – the development in recent years of ideas of 'post-feminism'. Like Lull, she also draws on recent sociological theory about individualisation, as represented by the work of Giddens, Bauman and Beck on intimacy, 'Liquid Modernity' and individualisation. However, McRobbie's more particular focus is to examine how these concepts might be applied to a range of key post-feminist texts in the realm of popular culture. Her approach is later echoed in Lisa Blackman's analysis of the contemporary forms of 'self-help' culture – where Blackman also draws critically on the work of Beck and Bauman.

Thus, we hope that our readers will find here both an attempt to critically review some of the philosophical presumptions and foundations of our field (or absences of such, in any explicitly declared form) in combination with a set of arguments that encourage the reader to reconsider what it is that we think we know that is 'new' about the contemporary forms of globalisation – and what their consequences are for the contradictory field of postmodern and post-feminist identities

The second section 'Media, community and dialogue' takes a fresh look at debates about the relationship of the media to community, focusing on how the media support and reconstruct 'imagined communities', shape communities' principal conversations and produce understandings of what constitutes a community, and what its boundaries are. Thus, from a transnational perspective, Arvind Ragagopal looks at the role of the media in the process of dramatically redrawing both national and internal boundaries in the USA, in the wake of the terrorist attack on New York, and within the broader context of the need to rethink media studies in the post-Cold War era. Kevin Robins and Asu Aksoy, drawing on their research with migrants and transnational communities in the UK, attempt to move beyond what they call the 'national imagination' and also critique many of the established wisdoms of diasporic media theory to address the ambivalence that their respondents feel towards the racial and ethnic communities to which they are often still presumed to 'belong' (here Robins and Aksoy also make a valuable contribution to the study of transnational media audiences). Moving from the transnational to the local level, Gareth Stanton offers a 'thick description' (cf. Geertz 1973) of the complex and rapidly changing dynamics of community in a particular multicultural area of Inner London – demonstrating how the long tendrils of the global and the diasporic are articulated within the context of understandings of the local and its history. Finally, in this section, John Durham Peters offers a critical examination of the trend towards a more conversational style of journalism, and of the sometimes uncritical championing of this tradition within cultural studies, arguing that such perspectives, while valuable in themselves, nonetheless perhaps pay insufficient attention to the continuing need for knowledge and expertise as key elements of a democratic conversation (cf. also Nick Couldry's consideration of this issue in Section III). In this particular case, a striking index of the growing centrality of these issues is provided by the proceedings of the conference on 'Public Proofs: Science, Technology and Democracy' organised by Bruno Latour and his colleagues at the Centre de Sociologie de l'Innovation, Ecole des Mines de Paris, in August 2004. The conference was designed to address the problem of the crisis of 'Public Proofs' in an age of growing suspicion of all forms of expertise and of the deification of the vernacular forms of 'experience', and thus brought into focus many of the pressing problems with which Peters is concerned in his essay.[12]

In this section we thus retrace some of the threads that underlay Raymond Williams's argument[13] that the very concept of 'community' could only be understood if one pays due attention to the significance of its etymological roots in the concept of communication – in so far as communities are not to be understood as entities that exist and then, in some secondary sense, happen to communicate – but rather as only being created, sustained and changed through the variable dynamics of communication. The institutions, forms, patterns and styles through which communication then occurs thus, by definition, give rise to very different understandings of what – and where – communities are, and of who is deemed to belong to, or be excluded from them.

The following section on 'Media power, ideology and markets' re-examines the contribution of perspectives on media in relation to processes of control, coordination and conflict in society, and also raises questions about how the now widely disregarded conception of the media as ideological agencies might be rehabilitated. The central issues here include how society is represented by the media, how this reflects and affects the disposition of power and reward in the society, how the media enter and influence people's lives, and how media power is regulated through market and democratic structures. Also now at issue are the questions of whether the 'new media' do, as is often now claimed, give more effective expression to dissent, and whether our repertoire of understandings of the role of the media in society takes adequate account of comparative difference at a time when globalisation encourages a less parochial view of the world. Thus James Curran offers a rereading of the supposed gains of recent cultural theory, focusing on the high price that has been paid for its supposed theoretical gains, in terms of the now widespread neglect in our field of issues such as the continuing inequalities of class and the deeply problematic effects of the supposedly liberating global markets, which are so much lauded in the discourse (or, perhaps, to reinvoke that now largely neglected term 'ideology') of liberal capitalism. For Curran, despite its advances, too much 'culturalist' work is, in effect, too often still complicit with this ideology.

Aeron Davis opens up a largely under-researched area in our field, by investigating the contradictions of the 'promotional cultures' that have now become so central to both the commercial and the political cultures of our age. Like James Curran, he questions the validity of market liberal culturalist accounts, challenging the adequacy of conceptions of promotion as a tool of empowerment and reciprocal communication. Ted Magder turns a questioning eye on another neglected topic, international regulation, and at the same time extends the debate about globalisation broached in Section I. In order to set contemporary debates about the 'regulation of global conversation' in better historical perspective – one sadly lacking from much contemporary debate about globalisation – he traces the story of how legislation in this field has developed through the last two centuries, from the creation of the International Telegraph Union in 1865 to today's attempts to police and control the field of international communication. Nick Couldry offers a substantial revision of some of the central presumptions of contemporary theory, in so far as it rests on a set of unexamined – and in Couldry's view unsustainable – assumptions about the necessary centrality of the established media in the lives of those who consume them.

In Section IV, the focus shifts to questions of 'Cultural production, consumption and aesthetics'. Keith Negus revisits the work of Frankfurt School authors, such as Adorno, from a new perspective, drawing also on Becker and Bourdieu, to offer a critical commentary on recent debates about the role of the creative and cultural industries in the contemporary economy, and taking a sceptical position in relation to much of the recent celebratory writing on this topic. Moving from production to consumption and revisiting, from a different angle, some of the concerns of Angela McRobbie's contribution to Section I, in relation to the discourse of post-feminism, Lisa Blackman draws on the work of authors such as Michael Billig and Richard Sennett[14] in an analysis of the complex forms of situated autonomy of social subjects or agents that shares much with Robins's and Aksoy's analysis in Section II. Blackman thus explores the cultural and psychological significance of the new models of selfhood, gender and subjectivity being articulated by contemporary lifestyle magazines, from the perspectives of both cultural studies and critical psychology, in a way that offers us a rather different perspective on the culture of personalisation and conversationalisation critiqued by Peters earlier in the book. Christine Geraghty examines the contradictions and complexities that have beset critical vocabularies for the definition of 'quality' in various areas of popular culture. Taking her main case study from the realms of popular television soap opera, in the form of the BBC's influential *EastEnders*, Geraghty poses important questions about the value of the aesthetic discourse of melodrama for our understanding of such popular cultural forms. Here we see analyses of the changing modalities of the production and consumption of media texts combined with a type of detailed and aesthetically informed textual analysis more commonly associated with other disciplines, such as English or film studies, but sadly often absent from contemporary forms of media and cultural studies.

The last section revisits key issues to do with 'New Technologies and Cultural Forms' in the study of the media and popular culture. In recent years the field of 'new media studies' (a.k.a. 'cyberstudies' or 'Web-studies') has taken off in leaps and bounds in the wake of the technological developments surrounding digitalisation, media convergence, the growth of the Internet and cyberspace. Despite the evident importance of these new developments, it is nonetheless clear that much of this field has itself been caught up in the very techno-hype that it has claimed to analyse. Taking the argument forward into the development of research in the field of 'intelligent media' technologies, Sarah Kember offers a philosophical framework for the development of new media studies that also draws on the more developed theoretical discourses of science and technology studies. She examines how we might best pursue the urgent task of addressing the particularities – and materialities – of these new technologies without falling back into a form of born-again McLuhanite technological determinism. In a similar spirit, Jonathan Burston addresses the significance of new CGI techniques in the film industry, whose principal actors are now no longer necessarily human. Here Burston develops his ongoing work on the political economy of virtual technologies of cultural production, in his analysis of the significance of what he calls 'synthespianism' in the new digital entertainment economy, focusing on the role of new technologies in the transformation of the dynamics of production in the creative and cultural industries.

Janet Harbord also explores the terrain opened up by Burston's essay, addressing the new technologies of digitalisation in the realm of film and asking how these technologies are influencing both the aesthetics of production and the structure of the text in different industrial sectors, from that of European 'art house' film production to that of the new Hollywood epics of the post-*Gladiator* era. Des Freedman examines the impact of the Internet on the media industries with a sceptical eye and looks closely at the extent to which particular media sectors are in fact being transformed by the 'network logic' of the Internet, in terms of its impact on copyright and regulatory structures. He also examines the various ways in which the 'old media' have already come to achieve forms of symbiosis with the new technologies and offers a critical reassessment of the widespread claims that the Internet is, in fact, likely to usher in radical and necessarily liberating changes in media ownership, content, distribution and consumption.

Thus, overall, the essays in this final section aim to recognise the irreducibility of technology, while attempting to avoid the seductions of the hype surrounding the 'new media'. They offer some important challenges to the humanism of the intellectual traditions of media and cultural studies – and also to established positions such as Williams's canonical denunciation of technological determinism[15] by paying close attention to the ways in which new technologies reshape the overall field of cultural possibility, enabling new options as well as reinflecting pre-existing tendencies in the fields of both cultural production and consumption.

Notes

1 J. Curran, D. Morley and V. Walkerdine (eds) *Cultural Studies and Communications*, London: Arnold, 1996.
2 These include members of the Department of Culture and Communications at New York University (Magder and Ragagopal); scholars who our department has had the pleasure of hosting as Visiting Fellows (Peters from Iowa, Lull from San José State University, California); and those with whom we have ongoing research collaborations of one kind or another (Burston, now at University of Western Ontario; Couldry, now at London School of Economics; Davis, now at City University; Geraghty, now at the University of Glasgow; Schwarz, now at Queen Mary College, London).
3 Larry Grossberg made another version of this point some time ago, in his essay 'Cultural studies versus political economy: is anyone else bored with this debate?' *Critical Studies in Mass Communications* 12, March 1995.
4 In another version of his essay printed here, Schwarz makes a series of important observations on the difference between debates in history and debates in this field, with scholars in the former less inclined to argue that only one particular perspective or approach has any value – see Schwarz (2000).
5 Cf. E. Katz, J. Durham Peters, T. Liebes and A. Orloff (eds) *Canonic Texts in Media Research*, Cambridge: Polity Press, 2003.
6 See *Journal of Communications*, special issue, 'Ferment in the Field', summer 1983, 33(3).
7 For an especially useful overview see Tulloch (2000).
8 The insights from this research should be part of the core school curriculum. For a useful, critical overview of the news source literature, see Manning (2001).
9 This is a key argument framing the historic Hutchins report (1947), the manifesto of the professional responsibility reform movement in the US media industries. For a British version of the argument see Curran and Seaton (2003).
10 Classic studies include Bourdieu (1993), Carey (1992) and DiMaggio (1986), each coming from a different tradition.
11 Landmark studies are Hebdige (1979) and Bourdieu (1984) with Thornton and Gelder (1996) providing a good collection.
12 For details of the papers and debates at the conference see :
www.csi.ensmp.fr/csi/4S/index.php?pagepublic_proof.
13 Williams (1962) on community/communication – in the book that Schwarz (this volume) cites as still foundational for the field.
14 Cf. Billig (1997) and Sennett (1977).
15 Cf. Williams (1974).

References

Billig, M. (1997) 'Cultural studies, discourse and society', in M Ferguson and P. Golding (eds) *Cultural Studies in Question*, London: Sage.
Bourdieu, P. (1984) *Distinction*, London: Routledge.

—— (1993) *The Field of Cultural Production*, Cambridge: Polity Press.

Brewer, J. (2004) *Sentimental Murder*, London: Harper Collins.

Brunsdon, C. (1990) 'Problems with quality', *Screen* 31(1).

—— (1991) 'Pedagogies of the feminine: feminist teaching and women's genres', *Screen* 32(4).

Carey, J. (1992) *The Intellectuals and the Masses*, London: Faber & Faber.

Curran, J., Morley, D. and Walkerdine, V. (eds) (1996) *Cultural Studies and Communications*, London: Arnold.

Curran, J. and Seaton, J. (2003) *Power without Responsibility*, 6th edn, London: Routledge.

DiMaggio, P. (1986) 'Cultural entrepreneurship in nineteenth century Boston: the creation of an organisational base for High Culture in America', in R. Collins, J. Curran, N. Garnham, P. Scannell, P. Schlesinger and C. Sparks (eds) *Media, Culture and Society: A Critical Reader*, London: Sage.

du Gay, P. and Pryke, M. (eds) (2000) *Cultural Economy*, London: Sage.

du Gay, P., Hall, S., Janes, L., Mackay, H. and Negus, K. (1997) *Doing Cultural Studies: The Story of the Sony Walkman*, London: Sage.

Frith, S. (1991) 'The good, the bad and the indifferent: saving popular culture from the populists', *Diacritics* 21(4).

Geertz, C. (1973) *The Interpretation of Cultures*, New York: Basic Books.

Grossberg, L. (1995) 'Cultural studies versus political economy is anyone elso bored with this debate?' *Critical Studies in Mass Communication*, 12.

Hall, S. (1974) 'Marx's notes on method – a reading of the "1857 Introduction"', *Working Papers in Cultural Studies* 6.

Hebdige, D. (1979) *Subcultures*, London: Methuen.

Hutchins Report (1947) *A Free and Responsible Press*, Chicago: Chicago University Press.

Kaz, C., Peters, J.D., Liebes, T. and Orloff, A. (eds) (2003) *Canonic Texts in Media Research*, Cambridge: Polity Press.

McRobbie, A. (1999) 'Feminism versus the TV Blondes', Inaugural Lecture, Goldsmiths College, London, October 1999.

Manning, P. (2001) *News and News Sources*, London: Sage.

Marx, K. (1973) *Grundrisse: Introduction to the Critique of Political Economy*, Harmondsworth: Penguin.

Negus, K. and Pickering M. (2004) *Creativity, Communication and Cultural Value*, London: Sage.

Schwarz, B. (2000) 'Poetics', in J. Pacecho (ed.) *Theory and Culture: Essays in the Sociology of Culture*, Lund, Sweden: University of Lund Press.

Sennett, R. (1977) 'Destructive Gemeinschaft', in N. Birnbaum (ed.) *Beyond the Crisis*, Oxford: Oxford University Press.

Thornton, S. and Gelder, K. (1996) *The Subcultures Reader*, London: Routledge.

Tulloch, J. (2000) *Watching Television Audiences*, London: Arnold.

Williams, R. (1962) *Communications*, Harmondsworth: Penguin.

Williams, R. (1974) *Television, Technology and Cultural Form*, London: Fontana.

Section I

Media, modernity and globalisation

This section begins with some theoretical considerations on the philosophical and ethical foundations of media studies, in the shape of Bill Schwarz's self-reflexive meditation on the intellectual and institutional development of the discipline. His reflections on its specificity are informed both by his personal experience of moving between disciplines (those of history, English, cultural studies, and media and communications studies) – as well as by that of his own children, in encountering media studies as it is now institutionalised, in a rather mechanical form, in the UK school system. One of his central questions concerns the relative absence in our field of foundational texts – apart from Raymond Williams's canonical *Communications* (1962) – with a comparable status to that of books like E.H. Carr's *What is History?* (1969) or C. Wright Mill's *The Sociological Imagination* (1970) in the disciplines of history and sociology. In this connection, he offers a critical review of a series of recent attempts to make good this absence in our field. However, he argues, on the whole, media studies still lacks a coherent philosophical foundation that would address the broader (and in part 'imaginative') questions concerning the philosophy and history of the concept of communication, which would be the proper concern of a poetics or ethics of the field (a topic also pursued by Nick Couldry in Part III).

The following chapters in this part all address the 'posts' (postmodernism, postcolonialism and post-feminism) of our contemporary 'globalised' world. David Morley reviews recent debates about the political and cultural consequences of globalisation, so as to produce a synthetic account of the central dynamics involved in this contradictory process. His essay attempts to articulate the critique of some of the more mechanistic theses about the homogenising effects of globalisation with 'revisionist' arguments that globalisation is as much a political (and largely US) project, as an inevitable historical process. This recognition takes us back to the questions posed by writers such as Herb Schiller, in his insistent equation of globalisation with the idea of US cultural imperialism. Morley's position is that for too long debates about the media have oscillated unproductively between a political economy of the global media that sees everything else as a forgone conclusion, and an over-optimistic cultural studies critique of this model ('don't worry, they've indigenised it') that sidelines the question of power. The issue is how to understand the contradictions at the heart of this process. Thus the chapter focuses on the tensions between the control of media flows, the development of new technologies, the opportunities afforded by these technologies for the articulation and adoption of new identities, and the extent to which global power relations still dictate that many people have to live within the confines of identities ascribed to them by others. The chapter shares with others in the book an insistence on the necessity of a historical dimension of analysis. In this respect, its concerns resonate closely with those of Magder and Freedman (in relation to technology, power and regulation) just as they do with those of Lull and Ragagopal (in relation to the new global configurations of cultural power).

James Lull's chapter discusses culture in a global context that, he argues, is characterised by the dynamic interaction of an unprecedented degree of 'symbolic abundance' in cultural forms; the rapid development of personal communications technologies and their integration into common sense and everyday life; and extraordinary patterns of human migrations and mobility. Lull argues that 'human expressive needs' are exercised with increased facility under the conditions of contemporary cultural globalisation, and the consequent expansion of 'communicational space'. For him, this explosion of symbolic and technological resources encourages expressive creativity through intensive personal involvement with media, information technology and popular culture. He argues that, in this process, individuals become 'cultural programmers' who construct personal 'supercultures' that transcend cultural traditions and boundaries. In Lull's argument, these 'individualising' cultural tendencies (the 'pull' aspects) are then contrasted theoretically with the force of culture as an enduring collective project (the 'push' dimension), especially in light of recent geopolitical events.

Lull's argument here about the 'expansion' and transformation of cultural spaces also foreshadows some of the concerns of Kevin Robins's and Asu Aksoy's article in Section II with questions of how transnational cultures are lived out at an individual level. Both Lull and McRobbie (along with Blackman and Geraghty in different ways, later in the book) consider the significance of Ulrich Beck's work on the process of 'individualisation' in the 'Risk Societies' of our age. While for Lull, on balance, this is to be seen as a largely positive process, for McRobbie, Blackman and Geraghty the negative dimensions of the process of the disembedding of individual lives from community and cultural frameworks are seen as a more contradictory 'blessing'.

Angela McRobbie's particular focus is on the question of how the term 'post-feminist' has been used in recent years. Her analysis entails a detailed review of the various accounts of post-feminism in both the wider field of women's writing and journalism, and in cultural and media studies. She looks beyond these perspectives to also consider how concepts in contemporary sociological writing might be useful in pursuing these issues (although, as she notes, they remain under-developed in relation to both gender and media theory). In this connection she reviews the relevance of Anthony Giddens's work on 'intimacy' and the 'project of the self', of Zygmunt Bauman's theorisation of 'Liquid Modernity' and of Ulrich Beck's work on 'individualisation'. Following a critique of this work for its inattention to political antagonisms and to the specific role of feminism, she argues that Judith Butler's work provides a better model for fully engaging with post-feminism. Here feminism has a 'haunting existence', and for McRobbie, Butler's figure of 'Antigone' embodies how feminism has become an 'impossible object'. This work then provides the theoretical framework for McRobbie's detailed exploration of the significance of key post-feminist texts including *Bridget Jones's Diary* and TV series such as *Sex in the City* and *Ally McBeal*. Her focus links closely with Lisa Blackman's later analysis of the contradictions of 'self-made' femininity in Section IV.

Chapter 1

The 'poetics' of communication

Bill Schwarz

Academic disciplines represent a distribution of knowledge that owes more to historical circumstance than to over-arching philosophical truth. We know this, but in the bustle of everyday institutional life, we don't always remember that it is so. For the most part less grandiose concerns intrude. We know too that when a particular dimension of human knowledge crosses the threshold and stakes out its claim to be a legitimate academic discipline, strange things happen. The term itself – discipline – is apt: it invokes a degree of ordering, in which that which was previously informal or inchoate assumes a new and sharper form. In the recent past this is something that has come to be increasingly transparent. Quality controls, the itemisation of teaching objectives, the formulation of curricula, the devising of appropriate modes of assessment, the writing of research monographs and textbooks – all take place in institutional locations that carry a distinct and often strict conception of what academic knowledge is and what it should do. Indeed, in Britain and elsewhere this is, if indirectly, a matter of state regulation. This would seem to confirm the Foucauldian hypothesis about the proximity between knowledge and the more popular meaning of discipline, in which the locations of knowledge profoundly shape, maybe even determine, what can and cannot be said within any particular discourse. The classic Foucauldian formulations were, in their earliest manifestations, uncompromising in this respect. Yet one doesn't have to be a card-carrying Foucauldian to recognise that all institutional forms of knowledge allow some things to be said more readily than others. This has to be so. All academic disciplines, whether we're conscious of it or not, contain elements that, within the norms they have generated, are unspeakable. A crisis in a discipline occurs when attempts are made to render speakable, within the protocols of the discipline itself, what previously had been unspeakable, and much excitable speech follows.

However, this is only a partial picture, which emphasises structure over human agency. Any academic discipline is also the consequence of an enormous complex of intellectual production, with its own social division of labour, drawing in administrators and professors, archivists and schoolteachers, students and amateurs, and many more. Each curriculum produced, or lecture delivered or essay written, at the same time it is a curriculum, lecture or essay, is also a means for determining what the respective discipline is. Each works to define its boundaries. Sociology, say, or philosophy is in effect the sum of this divergent, contested multitude of intellectual practices – although not all of them are invested with equal power. To think in these terms places agency rather than structure at the centre of things. From this perspective, an academic discipline is less the codified system of knowledge that its most esteemed practitioners profess and more a mode of thought that is in a state of perpetual, if often imperceptible, renovation and rejuvenation.

These are general reflections. They are prompted by my own move from one disciplinary location to another. Until recently, I worked in a department of media and communications. I worked with colleagues of great intellectual vitality, who had all arrived at media studies from a variety of different disciplinary and professional backgrounds. All possessed different intellectual dispositions and different projects, but were bound together by an appreciation of the deep necessity of comprehending the media in order to understand contemporary life. At the same time, my children were first encountering media studies in a different sector of the state education system. They were, it seems, less fortunate. They were habitually asked to discuss media representations, drawing on adverts in popular magazines. For some reason, this required reviving the nursery-school skills of (non-electronic) cutting and pasting. More often than not they found themselves having to consider the representation of women, or of non-white peoples. I favoured this, at least in the first instance. Given that they devote considerable amounts of time to watching television, and given too the ever-increasing quantity of commercials shown on television, to reflect on what they are watching, to develop interpretative skills, and to be alerted to the power relations in play, all to my mind are valuable lessons. More worrying, however, was the sense they picked up that this *was* media studies. They quickly learned, once they had grasped the basic principles, that work produced one year could be handily recycled the next year, and the year that followed. This may have eased their progression through school, but did little to enhance their understanding of the media, or their intellectual commitment to media studies.

Media studies, in its recognisable, contemporary form, has a history spanning less than fifty years. The speed of this transformation is staggering. Yet it is astounding, so far as the UK is concerned, that no history of this development has been written, for it would raise important questions about the intellectual organisation of the post-war epoch, as well as about the shifting sociology of professional life. Why there is no such standard history is itself a question that is worth pondering. But nor, as I discovered when I was quizzed by my children, did there exist an imaginative popular primer that makes the case for media studies, not only as an academic or intellectual activity, but also as a deeper human endeavour – on the model, perhaps, of texts that served a previous generation in the fields of history or sociology: E.H. Carr's *What Is History?* for example, or C. Wright Mills's *The Sociological Imagination*.

Given the profusion of media textbooks for students, which reproduce the key authorities, or endlessly summarise the key arguments, the absence of a work simultaneously more synthetic and more wide-ranging, or of a general intellectual history, is surprising. When pressed, I often cite as a founding text Raymond Williams's *Communications*. This was written nearly half a century ago, just at a moment when such a thing as media studies first came to be conceivable. It derived from a trade union conference, a fact that is unimaginable today: the National Union of Teachers' discussion, in 1960, of 'Popular Culture and Personal Responsibility'. It is written, consequently, as an accessible book for a lay reader, and is barely concerned with academic issues at all. Most of all, Williams was prepared to conduct general theoretical arguments in simple prose, beginning with what he called society rather than with any putative discipline. In the very first pages he maintained that 'society is a form of communication'. He went on:

> Many people seem to assume as a matter of course that there is, first, reality, and then, second, communication about it. We degrade art and learning by supposing that they are always second-hand activities: that there is life, and then afterwards there are these accounts of it. Our commonest political error is the assumption that power – the capacity to govern other men – is the reality of the whole social process, and so the only context of politics. ... The struggle is not begun, at second-hand, after reality has occurred. It is, in itself, a major way in which reality is continually formed and changed.
>
> (Williams 1976: 10–11)

This was Williams writing in an idiom that he made his own. Yet it represents what might be taken as a semiotic theory of society, in which narrative forms constitute the real, and in which the material world cannot be thought outside its discursive or symbolic forms. With a deceptive ease of expression it offers the reader a sense of conceptual *possibility*. Indeed, in both form and content it affirms the sovereignty of the imagination.

It's this largeness of vision, driven by a commitment to a democratic intellectual practice, which is attractive, and which seems so difficult to reproduce in the field of media studies in our own times. We can grasp this contrast from a number of perspectives. Around the time that Williams was working on what became *Communications*, in the US Mills was drafting his introduction to sociology. This too carries that same sense of imaginative and human possibility:

The very shaping of history now outpaces the ability of men to orient themselves in accordance with cherished values. And which values? Even when
they do not panic, men often sense that older ways of feeling and thinking
have collapsed and that newer beginnings are ambiguous to the point of
moral stasis. Is it any wonder that ordinary men feel they cannot cope with
the larger worlds with which they are so suddenly confronted? … That – in
defense of selfhood – they become morally insensible, trying to remain altogether private men?

Neither facts alone, he argues, nor even the capacity to reason is sufficient. The
'moral energy' required was encapsulated in what he determined to call 'the sociological imagination'. It was this which

enables its possessor to understand the larger historical scene in terms of its
meaning for the inner life and the external career of a variety of individuals.
It enables him to take into account how individuals, in the welter of their
daily experience, often become falsely conscious of their social positions. …
By such means the personal uneasiness of individuals is focused upon explicit
troubles and the indifference of publics is transformed into involvement with
public issues.
   The first fruits of this imagination … is the idea that the individual can
understand his own experience, and gauge his own fate only by locating
himself within his period, that he can know his own chances in life only by
becoming aware of those of all individuals in his circumstances. In many ways
it is a terrible lesson; in many ways a magnificent one.

(Mills 1959: 4–5)[1]

There is a humanity to this writing that is compelling.
   Or to take another perspective, it is common for those general principles that
arise from my own home discipline – history – to invoke not merely the importance
of knowing the past, but of learning its meanings for the present. This impinges too
on mortal time, and on the workings of the inner life. Even a historian of such
eminently Victorian sensibilities as G.M. Trevelyan, once the doyen of national historians, thought in these terms. There occurs a famous passage in his *Autobiography*:

The poetry of history lies in the quasi-miraculous fact that once, on this
earth, once, on this familiar spot of ground, walked other men and women,
as actual as we are today, thinking their own thoughts, swayed by their own
passions, but now all gone, one generation vanishing into another, gone as
utterly as we ourselves shall shortly be gone, like ghosts at cockcrow.

(Trevelyan 1949: 13)

As Trevelyan's great admirer, J.H. Plumb, was quick to recognise, this was a historical imagination underwritten by the knowledge that 'each historical fact is implicit with our doom' (Plumb 1988: 184). A more contemporary instance can be found in the Boyer lectures – Australia's equivalent of the BBC's Reith lectures – delivered in 1976 by the radical, nationalist historian Manning Clark:

> Everything a historian writes should be a celebration of life, a hymn to the praise of life. It should come up from inside a man who knows all about the horror of the darkness when a man returns to the dust from whence he came, a man who has looked into the heart of that great darkness, but has both a tenderness for everyone, and yet, paradoxically, a melancholy, a sadness, and a compassion because what matters most in life is never likely to happen.
>
> (Clark 1976: 12)

Perhaps prose of this sort is too purple, smacking too much of sentiment, for a relatively new academic discipline, with half an eye on the harder, social-scientific requirements from which, quite properly, it also draws inspiration. We don't read many media studies monographs that proclaim themselves as hymns 'to the praise of life'. Yet it is strange that what might appear eccentric in media studies is the norm in history. History is a more intellectually conservative and cautious endeavour than media studies. Its ties to an older positivist tradition are more visible and its rituals more entrenched. Induction into the mysteries of its practices continues to instil very tight conventions about the correct modes of historical inquiry. Yet even the most casual introduction to historiography will refer, at some point, to the historical imagination. Such a notion is used without embarrassment, as a legitimate dimension of historical thought, and has a very long pedigree even in the empiricist intellectual culture of English historiography. For all the desire to codify the practices of history, in all their technicalities, there is a moment when the primers concede that the imagination comes into play, and when positivist instruction is subsumed by quite contrary imperatives. Most often, recourse to the idea of the historical imagination remains untheorised, and works according to the unacknowledged concepts bequeathed by an older aesthetic embedded in Romantic idealism. It is often alluded to, in metaphorical terms, as the poetic dimension of historical practice. But the fact that it can be spoken, and is regarded as part of the overall enterprise, is I believe a matter of significance.[2]

Indeed, I'm struck by the absence of these or cognate terms in contemporary media studies, with the notable exception of the sub-branch concerned with cinema studies.[3] Despite the tradition of Dilthey in the cultural sciences, there is no easy way in English of referring to the media studies imagination, as there is of calling upon the historical imagination.[4] Yet arguably the intellectual practices in each case are no so far removed. Maybe there would be a virtue in considering what would compose the specifically 'imaginative' or poetic properties of media studies.

Poetics, though, is a difficult, compacted term, whose meanings are always on the move. In the British traditions of historiography it serves two distinct purposes. On the one hand it refers to narrative style, championing a form of writing that is self-consciously lively and non-academic, as a counter to the 'dry as dust' image of the professional historian writing only for his or her kind. On the other hand it refers to a way of devising the object of historical inquiry itself. In particular, to narrate history poetically is to get as close as one can to the texture of human experience. This is to capture the domain of the human emotions, and of the inner life. It is alive, as we saw in both Trevelyan and in Clark, to apprehensions of mortality. In some historians, this commitment to grasp the specifically human – love, fear, dignity and so on – was also part of a political populism, in which history-writing was at the service of the dispossessed and voiceless.[5]

There is, though, a more contemporary meaning attached to the idea of poetics. In the Anglophone academic world of the 1970s and 1980s high theory took hold of the humanities and social sciences. The first phase of this conceptual revolution was conducted in the name of various stucturalisms. These were ways of thought that were hostile to a theoretical humanism, that is, to modes of analysis in which human consciousness and will were understood to function in their own terms, transparently, as if the social world were simply a consequence of the sum of individual intention. Structuralism sought to uncover those deeper forces that organised human life, but which remained unseen, beyond the everyday world of empirical observation: whether in the social relations of production (as in Marxism), or in the unconscious (in psychoanalysis), or in language, narrative and ritual (in linguistics and anthropology). While this paid many dividends, there was at the same time much that this way of thinking didn't, or couldn't adequately, address, especially in the domain of lived experience. As structuralism transmuted into post-structuralism and its derivatives, the problem of experience re-emerged in many different guises, as an unresolved problem. Indeed, the reaction to high theory – 'after theory' – produced, as one of its manifestations, something resembling a new poetics, seeking to recover the lived, or 'human', attributes of love, fear, dignity, et cetera. One can see this intellectual transformation dramatised in the figure of Terry Eagleton. Once long ago a pioneer of high structuralism, and something too of an unforgiving cadre in its ranks, Eagleton now, in a book which takes for its title the explicit term, *After Theory*, has swung back – if not to a theoretical humanism – to a more urgent concern with the lived qualities of human life. If the tone of the volume is unnecessarily repentant for past theoretical sins, it nonetheless marks an important intellectual shift, which is not Eagleton's alone (Eagleton 2004).

Of course, it's possible to track similar developments within the field of media studies. An early indication of this larger shift can be discerned in an article published many years ago by Paddy Scannell, which served as a defence of public-sector broadcasting (Scannell 1992). Its purpose was to break from the structuralist-inspired paradigm in which questions of state, ideology and domination prevailed. Its significance, so far as I'm concerned here, lies in the fact that Scannell himself had – uneasily or not – earlier subscribed to these interpretative devices. To this degree, this was also an intervention that carried an unnecessary, and an unpersuasive, recantation of an entire previous way of thinking. Scannell himself effectively moved back to pre-structuralist positions, alighting upon the enthnomethodology of social interactionism as practised by Garfinkel, Schutz and Goffman. But in doing so, one could see at the time that he was attempting to find a means of opening up areas of social life for scrutiny – especially the texture of lived experience – which had been peremptorily closed down in an early enthusiasm for structuralism. His later recourse to phenomenology, in its bid to get close to the experience, consciousness and sensuousness of human life, is – methodologically – close to what the historian's primers call a poetics (Scannell 1996).[6]

In this respect Roger Silverstone's 1999 publication *Why Study the Media?* is of great interest. This was conceived as a 'manifesto', presumably as a reaction to the British pastime, beloved of journalists, politicians and assorted punditry, of – every so often, when other targets lose their allure – savaging media studies. 'I wanted,' Silverstone explained, 'to define a space. To engage with those outside my own discourse, elsewhere in the academy and in the world beyond. It was time, I thought, to take the media seriously' (Silverstone 1999: ix). In intention, one can see that Silverstone was setting out to write the kind of intellectually open, expansive survey of the field that I've been describing here in which the media in all their dimensions, not media studies, take precedence. Yet maybe as a result of the crazed over-production of academic textbooks it hasn't achieved the prominence such an intervention might properly expect. For my tastes, however, the mix of prose styles doesn't do him many favours. His enthusiasm for abolishing verbs, and for producing quickfire tabloid sentences, is just too breathless and portentous, testament to an ersatz hip that has nowhere to go. 'Yes,' he tells us in a single paragraph, 'but psychoanalysis is big trouble' (Silverstone 1999: 10). Knowing statements such as these sit with fine passages, full of insight. That this is so demonstrates how difficult it is, I think, to create a language both capable of explaining complex ideas, without falling into academicism, and which is also able to speak to a wider constituency, without falling into too easy a populism. As much as Silverstone's book is to be welcomed, it is also symptomatic of a difficulty with which we all have to contend.

Yet what's also intriguing is the degree to which Silverstone aims to integrate the poetic or human dimensions of the media, explicitly drawing on these terms, with more orthodox sociological and economic analysis. The structure of the book combines classical philosophical concerns (rhetoric, poetics) with the staples of contemporary media studies (house and home, community, globe) and with rather more intangible, but arguably necessary, phenomena that we would normally associate with an exploration of subjective life (trust, memory, the other). In one instance, he specifically coins the notion of a 'media poetics', though he restricts this to the issue of narrative (Silverstone 1999: 43). Indeed in a theoretical move that has been curiously unnoticed, he opens his 'manifesto' with the category of experience. He does this by referring to Isaiah Berlin, which certainly has the virtue of taking one by surprise. His appropriation of Berlin, he says, is 'related to moral and aesthetic analysis', and then – quoting Berlin – the passage continues:

> in so far as it presupposes conceiving of human beings not merely as organisms in space, the regularities of whose behaviour can be described and locked in labour saving formulae, but as active beings, pursuing ends, shaping their own and others' lives, feeling, reflecting, imagining, creating in constant interaction and intercommunication with other human beings; in short engaged in all forms of experience that we understand because we share them, and do not view them purely as external observers.
>
> (Silverstone 1999: 3)

There is though, I think, a formalism about the argumentation here. Silverstone places on the agenda, as definitive categories for the analysis of the media, moral and aesthetic questions, or what I have called, more abstractly, poetics. As I've been arguing, one can see from this – formally – how the given curriculum of media studies might, as a consequence, be opened up to new domains of thought. I'm less convinced, though, that this occurs, at least in this book. My own sense is that once these issues have been announced, with all due fanfares, the substance of what comes after is a good deal more conventional than at first appears.

But intellectual exploration holds many surprises. As I've explained, my own relatively brief institutional encounter with media studies occurred in a department whose formal title was given as the Department of Media and Communications. Raymond Williams notwithstanding, I never took much notice of the 'communications' part. There were, I know, obligatory undergraduate classes on different aspects of communication theory, but I fear they never really touched me. Indeed, the most public formal acknowledgement of the department's commitments to communications took place when the office administrators answered the phone. In identifying to the caller which part of the college they'd reached, the crisp if uncannily enigmatic utterance came: 'Communications', with a peculiar lilting emphasis on the second syllable. In my ignorance I had always supposed that communications theory was in thrall to US psychologistic functionalism, and of no earthly use to any but the most redoubtable utilitarian. Yet maybe classic laws of combined and uneven development, not now much in fashion, still pertain, for it has been precisely out of communications theory that there has emerged what I find to be the most elegant and thoughtful consideration of what studying the media – or communications – might involve. I'm referring to John Durham Peters's *Speaking into the Air* (1999).[7]

For Peters, communication theory should stake its claim as 'the natural history of our talkative species' (Peters 1999: 9). His is a book about the history of the concept of communication, encompassing not only the prescribed texts within the field, but also philosophy and literature, from classical times to the post-modern present. Communication, he argues, has become both a public and private compulsion *and* an impossibility. In a startling proposition, he suggests that it was only in the late nineteenth century (at the moment when telegraphy and photography unleashed their 'metaphysical mischief') that people began to define themselves by their capacity to communicate, one with another. In this sense, the media made communication possible. 'Communication as a person-to-person activity became thinkable only in the shadow of mediated communication' (Peters 1999: 6). Yet the moment it came to be thinkable, it also came to be troubling. He argues for the historical interconnection of the invention of the terms solipsism (1874) and telepathy (1882): the one proposing an absolute divide between the inner life and the external world, the other the complete collapse between the two. These polarised positions, he says, have come to define the ways in which we have imagined communication, and by extension the mass media, in the intervening years and up to the present period. Critical in this regard are the impediments to communicating. For communication, both face-to-face and in its mediated forms, is not just in the habit of breaking down, but is essentially dysfunctional. Peters has the poet's eye for communicative failure, relishing the mishaps and ironies brought about by 'lost letters, wrong numbers, dubious signals from the dead, downed wires, and missed deliveries' (Peters 1999: 6). He acknowledges as well the lived forms of these dysfunctions: 'Only moderns could be facing each other and be worried about "communicating" as if they were thousands of miles apart' (Peters 1999: 2). In repudiating the fantasy of unsullied communication, of communication where the message from A to B glides through the air untouched by its own journey, Peters displays an unusually tough, modernist sensibility, in which the profanities of communication – its misdirections, anxieties, inhibitions, collapses and disturbances – are all that we can hope for. 'That we can never communicate like the angels is a tragic fact, but also a blessed one' (Peters 1999: 29). To abjure the dream of instant, unperilous communication is not at all, he insists, to be driven back into the nightmare of solitude. Communication, in all its fractures and mediations, is all we have: it is, he hints, that which makes us modern, perhaps even, human. Communication, in this view, acts as 'a registry of modern longings' (Peters 1999: 2).

> Distance and death have always been the two great obstacles to love and the two great stimulants of desire. Great obstacles excite great passions; since eros, as Socrates argues in the *Symposium*, consists not in possession but in wanting, what could stimulate eros more than distance and especially death, itself the ultimate distance. Eros seeks to span the miles, reach into the grave, and bridge all the chasms.
>
> (Peters 1999: 137)

So too human communications.

Speaking into the Air is a book rich in thought. It represents what I understand to be a rigorous poetics, with the potential to transform the conventions of the discipline. (The discipline that reveals the 'registry of modern longings'?) In form, it is distant from the kind of engaging, expansive introductory text that could enliven a new generation of students coming to investigate the media, in the ever-proliferating media studies courses in the universities. But maybe, if that elusive window of opportunity presented itself, Peters – or if, as I suspect, he has fans, one of their number – could be prevailed upon to write such a book. In the meantime, more cohorts of British schoolchildren will once more, I fear, be reaching for the scissors and glue.

Notes

1   For a wonderful contemporary development of these foundational sociological themes, see Stanley Cohen (2001) *States of Denial: Knowing about Atrocities and Suffering*, Polity: Cambridge.
2   I'm drawing here from Bill Schwarz (2000) 'Poetics?' in José Pacheco (ed.) *Theory and Culture: Essays in the Sociology of Culture*, University of Lund Press: Lund.
3   I wonder if the exception of cinema studies may not be accounted for by the fact that both cinema, and many of the most important early interpretations of cinema, were self-consciously allied to the sensibilities of high modernism.
4   See especially Wilhelm Dilthey (1962) *Pattern and Meaning in History*, New York: Harper, for an elaboration of his theory of hermeneutics. This is shadowed by an explicit humanism: 'Understanding is a rediscovery of the I in the Thou', p. 67.
5   Much of the inspiration for this intellectual tradition can be found in Wordsworth's 1800 'Preface' to his and Coleridge's *The Lyrical Ballads*.
6   I have discussed these themes more fully in Bill Schwarz (2004) 'Media times/ historical times' *Screen* 45(2).
7   And see too the chapter in this volume: 'Media and conversation, conversation as media'. Some of the more immediately political consequences, developing the insights of Benedict Anderson, can be found in Depew and Peters (2001).

References

Carr, E.H. (1969) *What is History?* Harmondsworth: Penguin.
Clark, Manning (1976) *A Discovery of Australia*, Sydney: Australian Broadcasting Commission.

Cohen, Stanley (2001) *States of Denial: Knowing about Atrocities and Suffering*, Cambridge: Polity.

Depew, David and Peters, John Durham (2001) 'Community and communications: the conceptual background', in Gregory Shepherd and Eric Rothenbuhler (eds) *Communication and Community*, Mahwah, NJ: Lawrence Erlbaum.

Eagleton, Terry (2004) *After Theory*, Harmondsworth: Penguin.

Mills, C. Wright (1959) *The Sociological Imagination*, New York: Oxford University Press.

Peters, John Durham (1999) *Speaking into the Air: A History of the Idea of Communication*, Chicago: University of Chicago Press.

Plumb, J.H. (1988) *The Collected Essays of J.H. Plumb*, Vol. I, *The Making of an Historian*, Brighton: Harvester Wheatsheaf.

Scannell, Paddy (1992) 'Public service broadcasting and modern public life', in Paddy Scannell, Philip Schlesinger and Colin Sparks (eds) *Culture and Power: A 'Media, Culture and Society' Reader*, London: Sage.

——(1996) *Radio, Television and Modern Life: A Phenomenological Approach*, Oxford: Blackwell.

Schwarz, Bill (2000) 'Poetics?' in Jose Pacheco (ed.) *Theory and Culture: Essays in the Sociology of Culture*, Lund: University of Lund Press.

——(2004) 'Media Times / Historical Times', *Screen* 45(2).

Silverstone, Roger (1999) *Why Study the Media?*, London: Sage.

Trevelyan, G.M. (1949) *Autobiography and Other Essays*, London: Longman.

Williams, Raymond (1976) [1962] *Communications*, Harmondsworth: Penguin.

Chapter 2

Globalisation and cultural imperialism reconsidered

Old questions in new guises

David Morley

We are often told that nowadays, under the impact of the new technologies of our postmodern age, we live in an increasingly globalised world, characterised by the experience of time–space compression brought about by an increase in the speed and reach of communications. However, these questions about postmodernity and globalisation are often presented in a rather abstract and ahistorical manner. In this essay I want to look back at some of the roots of these concerns in earlier debates within media and cultural studies, concerning the question of what used to be called media (or cultural) imperialism.[1] In these debates, we find some important questions still lurking, and still unanswered, which may provide us with the historical perspective we need if we are able to properly grasp the issues facing us today, as we discuss globalisation. To that extent, as my title implies, I think we today confront 'old questions in new guises'.

Globalisation and Americanisation – the history of a problem

Nowadays, it has come to seem natural, in many parts of the world, that television should be not only in colour and in stereo, but also in English. However, while English may have become the dominant international language in many areas of the world, we also see many flourishing forms of its indigenisation – such as its local transformation into hybrid languages, such as 'Hinglish' and 'Singlish'. This dispersal of English into a variety of regional forms may perhaps be best understood as the inevitable price it pays for its global hegemony. As Stuart Hall puts it, today, if much of the world speaks English, it speaks it as an 'international' language, in a variety of 'broken forms' – 'English as it has been invaded, and as it has hegemonised a variety of other languages, without being able to exclude them' (Hall 1991: 28).

However, some scholars claim that, nowadays, the percentage of the world population speaking English is actually in decline – and has been for some considerable time.[2] In this connection we might also point to the increasing number of websites on the Internet in languages other than English. Certainly, English is far from being the only language in play in the world of international communications. A few years ago a Brazilian friend reported to me that she had noticed, when visiting Portugal, that people there now understood her Brazilian-inflected version of that language far better than when she had visited the country in the previous decade. She (probably rightly) attributed this to their greater familiarity with Brazilian Portuguese, as a result of the increasing popularity of exported Brazilian *telenovelas* in Portugal.

In this essay I aim to trace some of the roots of contemporary debates about globalisation in an older discourse, which spoke of the problems of media imperialism, the free flow of information, the possibilities for a 'New World Information Order' and the dangers of what used to be described as Americanisation. We have been told for some time now (cf. Fukuyama 1992) that in the new era of globalisation 'we' (whoever that is) stand at the 'End of History'. The key question here is who is at the end of which history, and how they (or 'we') got there (cf. Clarke 1991: 39). In this endeavour I will trace out some of the themes of the classical debate about cultural imperialism. I will then consider the various critiques of this approach, and identify some problems with it, in order to end by posing some more questions about where all this leaves us now, in relation to the current state of taken-for-granted wisdom on these issues, within media and cultural studies.

Centrally, I wish to offer a reassessment of the continuing significance of the work of the late North American political economist, Herb Schiller, following on from the comments made in this book's introduction about the recent neglect of his work. If the 'optimistic' school of cultural studies audience theory seems to claim that, in the postmodern world of active audiences, living in a 'semiotic democracy' (Fiske 1986), we need not worry about the question of media power, still, the fact that many political economists have an inadequate model of audience consumption means just that: it does not mean that they are wrong about everything else as well (cf. Morley 1992).

It is undoubtedly true that we need to add serious questions about the audience to the questions that political economy poses; but that does not mean that we should simply substitute the one set of questions for the other. Rather, we need to develop a perspective that can deal with both sorts of issues, and how they can be understood in their complex relations to each other. While there are strengths to both sides of this argument, for too long this debate has oscillated unproductively between a political economy of the global media that sees everything else as a foregone conclusion, and an over-optimistic cultural studies critique of this model ('don't worry, they've indigenised it') that sidelines the question of media power. The issue is how to understand the contradictions at the heart of this process (cf. Harindrath 2003 and Sreberny-Mohammadi 1991).

To clarify my point, let me offer an analogy to a comparable argument in another field. When Derrida says that we must recognise that philosophy, as a form of writing, involves figures of rhetoric, to which we must pay attention in ways that philosophers have not always done before, he does not conclude that philosophy is therefore reducible to rhetoric, or that it is only rhetoric. Rather, he argues, we must adopt a 'bi-focal' perspective, in which we have to look both at and through the rhetoric of philosophy, in assessing the truth claims it makes. In a similar sense, to suggest that political economy has an inadequate analysis of the media audience is not to conclude that we should necessarily thus abandon all the truths of political economy in favour of those of audience scholars but, rather, following Derrida, to argue that we should adopt a similarly bi-focal perspective, which will allow us to understand these different registers of truth in their articulation with each other.

Mass communication and American empire

Having previously discussed Schiller's work at some length, I will only rehearse the bare outlines of his position here (see Morley 1994 and Morley and Robins 1996: ch. 10). To quickly 'recap', the basic proposition of his classic *Mass Communication and American Empire* (1969) was that, in effect, the 'media are American' (by which he meant, of course, North American). In the book, he traces the long history of American dominance of a series of different media. He also traces the role of the US government is supporting this dominance, right from the moment when Herbert Hoover, as President of the Board of Trade in the 1920s, spotted the potential of Hollywood as a form of export-led advertising for US consumer products (and the 'American way of life') abroad. From that point on, Schiller traces the thread that takes us from Hoover, to Henry Luce who, when head of the *Time Life* magazine conglomerate in the 1940s, wrote his book *The American Century* (Luce 1941) in which he argued that the USA's potential to influence, if not control, imagery and opinion overseas was, in fact, the new quintessence of power. President Truman was quick to pick up Luce's point, and to dress it up as a crusade for 'Free Trade' – in goods and information. Schiller traces the trajectory of all this through to the point, in the later period, when the US government also came to recognise that communications should no longer be seen as a mere 'support' to foreign policy, but as a direct instrument of it. In Schiller's vision, this is still a world of principally one-way media flow; where America still dominates international trade in film and television; where key areas of the media – such as news – are still controlled by a small number of Anglo-American agencies; and where, through the export of formats as much as contents, America has, in effect, written the grammar of TV production world-wide.[3]

If it be objected that this is an old story and that 1969 is now a long time ago, the fact remains that when Schiller revised his text for republication, in the 1990s, he painted an even darker picture than before – of a world where not only the poorer countries of the world, but also now the industrialised areas of Europe, were increasingly dominated by US media imports. This, of course, was also the period when President Mitterand famously defined a 'European' as someone who watches American soap opera on a Japanese television. In his essay 'Not yet the post-imperial era' Schiller argues that the key change is that today 'national (largely American) media-cultural power has been largely (though not fully) subordinated to transnational corporate authority' so that if 'American *national* power no longer is an exclusive determinant of cultural domination' and if it is 'transnational corporate cultural domination' that is now the key issue, nonetheless, that domination still bears a 'marked American input' (Schiller 1991: 13, 15). To that extent, he writes, today's world market economy 'has evolved from, but retains the central characteristics of, the original American pattern' (Schiller 1992: 39).

Unfashionable as it has become in some circles, it may still be that we should take Schiller's argument for the continuing existence of North American cultural imperialism very seriously. Just in case his concerns should seem nowadays outmoded, we might, for instance, consider the speed with which, after the invasion of Iraq in 2003, the US government set up the prototype channel 'Iraq and the World'. This channel was initially beamed into Iraq from a US Air Force plane, and later instituted as the *Al-Hurra* satellite channel broadcasting throughout the Middle East, in order to counter the influence of *Al-Jazeera* in the region.

Here we might also think back to the North American 'modernisation theory' of the 1960s (cf. Rostow 1960 and Lerner 1964) which was premised on the belief that all that was holding back successful modernisation in the Middle East was the remaining prevalence of backward-looking 'traditional attitudes'. The proposed solution was to get transistor radios, broadcasting US radio stations, into the fields where the peasants worked. Somewhat simplistically, it was presumed (on the basis of a hypodermic-effects model of communications) that this 'input' would automatically transform the problematic attitudes in the desired way. In the Middle East today, Samer Shehata argues that the US government has been obsessed with the idea that *Al-Jazeera* was 'indoctrinating' a whole new generation of viewers with anti-Americanism. As Shehata puts it: just 'think about the assumption involved in that – that the Arabs just sit in front of television sets and *Al-Jazeera* just pumps this information into them'. As he points out, the operation was premised on the belief that the 'primary (solution) to the hackneyed question "why do people hate (America)?" is that "they" just don't understand us' – so the solution must be better propaganda (Burkeman 2003).

As for the 'American Century', it now seems, if anything, to be reborn with new vigour. Not so long ago, when the neo-conservatives who now dominate US foreign policy were still a marginal force operating through a variety of think tanks, the US Army War College quarterly journal *Parameters* published an article by (Retired) Major Ralph Peters (Summer 1997) in which he argued that anyone who has not yet learnt to do so, must now adapt to the 'New American Century'. Peters describes with pride and admiration the two-pronged US assault (by the military and mass-produced popular culture) on those who have not learned how to properly navigate this new geopolitical landscape – among whom he lists 'the Taliban militiaman', 'the American blue collar worker' and the 'traditional intellectual elites'. He is quite explicit about the role of US popular culture in softening up 'regressive' populations world-wide, for economic and military assault, in an alliance, as he puts it, of 'culture with killing power'. In this context he proudly claims that

> Contemporary American culture is the most powerful in history. ... The 'genius', the secret weapon of American culture, is the essence that the (liberal) elites despise: ours is the first 'genuine people's culture'. It stresses comfort and convenience – and ease – and it generates pleasure for the masses. ... We are Karl Marx's dream, and his nightmare. ... There will be no peace ... the 'de facto' role of the US armed forces will be to keep the world safe for our economy and open to our cultural assault.[4]

Of course, we need not take Major Peters's bumptious declarations at face value. As Immanuel Wallerstein reminds us, this kind of assertion can also be read symptomatically, as an index of anxiety about US claims on power. As he puts it 'We [Americans – DM] have spent the last 30 years insisting very loudly that we are still hegemonic and that everyone needs to continue to acknowledge it. But if one is truly hegemonic, one does not need to make such a request' (Wallerstein 2003: 213). However, Major Peters's chilling statements aside, we must now turn to the main critiques made in recent years of the work on cultural imperialism, which point to its limitations, its over-simplification and blind spots. We shall, however, also need to attend to the blind spots of these critiques themselves.

The cultural imperialism thesis and its limits

There are four main issues to consider here:

1   The way the original model oversimplifies the complex nature of flows in international communications.
2   Its failure to address the more recent strategies of 'glocalisation' adopted by many of the key media producers.
3   The problems that follow from the policies of 'cultural protectionism' to which this model of media imperialism seems to lead.
4   The inadequacies of the simple 'hypodermic' model of the media's supposed effects on their audiences, which underlies the original theory of media imperialism.

Let me say a little about each of these, in turn. I will deal with the first two points in brief and the others at more length

The complexities of flow (and counter-flow) in international communication

The original model of cultural imperialism can certainly be criticised for concentrating as exclusively as it does on instances of one-way flow from the USA to the rest of the world. It also ignores the importance of the counter-flows generated by burgeoning regional television exporters in various other parts of the world, e.g. the Brazilian TV Globo, along with Mexico, as exporters of *telenovelas* throughout Latin America, Southern (Catholic) Europe and elsewhere; India, in film; and now Japan (especially in the world of TV cartoons) and South Korea in different parts of Southeast Asia. These forms of regional counter-flow (cf. Mattelart *et al.* 1984) certainly complicate the picture painted by Schiller and we need to address the complexities they introduce. However, it remains to be demonstrated that these new developments totally change the overall picture (cf. Sreberny-Mohammadi op. cit.). In fact, world trade in TV and film is still largely dominated by Anglo-American producers. Hollywood continues to dominate the import markets of Europe, Asia and Latin America, and now has a significant presence in Africa – and besides the USA, only India and China are *net* exporters of film. While the USA controls 80 per cent of the European film market, Europe only gets 2 per cent of the US market. In fact, world trade in TV and film is still largely dominated by producers only one of whom – Sony – is neither Anglo-American nor European.

Glocalisation

One of the limitations of the original model of cultural imperialism is that it takes no account of the strategies of 'glocalisation' of their products now frequently adopted by cultural exporters. Here we might recall the moment, some time back now, when Coca Cola announced that it was no longer a 'multi-national' but rather a 'multi-local' company. Or we might consider the graphic description in the opening scene of Quentin Tarantino's film *Pulp Fiction* of how different a 'Big Mac' is, in Amsterdam, from its North American cousin. We might also recall the speed with which MTV realised it had to regionalise and diversify its programming into a series of 'localised' variants, in order to find success in the global market, adapting its products to local tastes, rather than attempting to sell a standardised product in the same way, world-wide (cf. Hujic 1999).

Anyone who has travelled through Heathrow Airport in recent years cannot help having been struck by the extensive advertising campaign orchestrated by

HSBC, which now describes itself as 'the world's local bank', under the campaign slogan 'never underestimate the importance of local knowledge'. The point of the campaign is to establish the bank's credentials as a business that is thoroughly sensitive to matters of cultural difference – just as do its local adverts, in areas of the UK with large Muslim populations, which now declare that its bank loans are 'offered in accordance with *Shariah* [Law]'. This is, indeed, an issue of real complexity that we need to address and which the basic model of media imperialism ignores. However, the problem with this critique is that all these variegated products can still be argued to be versions of a template originally designed in North America. In relation to the issues of the export of formats, rather than contents, there may now be regional versions of *Blind Date* or *Who Wants to Be a Millionaire?* all over the world – but they are all modelled, in the first instance, on Anglo-American formats.

Cultural protectionism and cultural identities

The basic cultural imperialism thesis also seems to lead fairly directly to policies of cultural protectionism – designed to defend indigenous cultures against their corruption, 'pollution' or destruction by foreign elements. Evidently, the problem here is how one is to define what constitutes the original, indigenous, culturally pure forms that are to be defended, without falling into an essentialist position. How far back in history do you have to go to find the pure elements to be defended? To take the British case – how would you ever define the 'pure' British culture that is to be defended? Could it possibly exclude the cultures of post-war immigrant groups? And if so, should it also exclude all Norman, or Scandinavian or Roman elements, as themselves originally foreign to the Anglo-Saxons who lived in the primeval forests?

The further question, of course, is that of who would define that culture? In Britain, as in most cultures, the national culture has in fact largely been defined by a very particular class-based metropolitan elite – whose own culture is, in fact, quite foreign to other groups within the society. As I have argued elsewhere (Morley 1994) the question of what is foreign to who may not necessarily be, primarily, a matter of nationality – it can be a matter of ethnicity, class, region, gender or generation. It is only by grasping that issue that we can understand why imported forms of North American culture have, at various points, seemed *less* foreign (and thus more appealing) to British working-class media audiences than the class-based forms of their own national culture. In this connection, besides the well-known work of Dick Hebdige (1988) and Ken Worpole (1983) on the popularity of US cultural products among British working class consumers, we should also consider this commentary on his cultural preferences, by a Welshman, quoted by Gill Branston in her recent essay on cinema and 'Welsh Heritage':

America was what I admired … because really for Britain … you had the damn class system, All you could look up to was Kenneth More, patches on his jacket, like, cap and all that. … Bloody brogue shoes, give me a break! So it was America that was classless, America [that] was cool. I remember thinking it would be great to drink Coca-Cola, and … going to Cardiff market and … drinking it from the bottle and thinking, this is fabulous, this is like being at some drive-in or somewhere.

(Branston, forthcoming)

The problem with the politics of cultural protectionism is that it is, of course, premised on a notion that there are pure, authentic, cultural spaces, unsullied by cultural imperialism, which must be defended. As a number of anthropologists and cultural studies scholars have pointed out (cf. Clifford 1997: ch. 1) this pre-lapsarian fantasy depends on the inaccurate presumption that cultural mixing is a new and recent phenomenon – whereas, in fact, all cultures (if to different degrees) have routinely absorbed and indigenised elements from other sources, throughout history, so that it is, rather, a question of 'hybridity all the way down'- and, indeed, all the way round. As Piot's work (1999) shows us, notionally tradi-tional or primitive cultures are routinely replete with modern elements – and vice versa – as Bausinger (1990) demonstrates in his analysis of the prevalence of traditional elements in modern cultures.

To this extent, it is clear that we must acknowledge the complexity of inter-cultural flows and the ambivalence of their signification, when imported into new contexts. Thus, as Hebdige has rightly argued

American popular culture [among other sources – DM] … offers a rich iconography … which can be assembled and re-assembled by different groups in a literally limitless number of combinations. And the meaning of each selection is transformed as individual objects … are taken out of their original historical and cultural contexts and juxtaposed against signs from other sources.

(Hebdige, op. cit.)

This important insight is also one of the motors of James Lull's argument in the following chapter about the 'push and pull' of cultural influence. However, there are complexities here. Within any one society, different consumers have variable amounts of cultural capital with which to create their own identities, through the sort of '*bricollage*' that Hebdige describes. The same point applies in terms of inter-cultural communications, at a transnational level. Some countries, to put it simply, are more powerful than others, and better placed to make their own iden-tity, rather than to have to live through imagery supplied to them by others. To this extent, these issues cannot be resolved at an abstract level, but, rather, must be analysed conjuncturally.

The story of the current international popularity of West African music is instructive in this respect. The international success of musicians like Youssou N'Dour and Orchestra Baobab from Senegal, within the category of what is now understood as 'world music', is often used as an example of the dispersed and decentred nature of contemporary cultural flows. Certainly, this music represents an extremely rich mix of hybridised cultural influences, combining as it does an adapted form of Western electric guitar playing, Cuban-derived brass sounds and traditional African rhythms. From a positive perspective, all of this can be understood as an index of the productivity of complex cultural flows. In this case, if these transatlantic flows originated in slavery (cf. Gilroy 1993) they now operate in both directions, from the Caribbean to West Africa and back, and in the music of the region they are also mixed with North African (and Islamic) cultural influences.

However it is well attested that, in the 1950s and 1960s, the indigenous music of West Africa was all but defunct, at least in many urban areas – where US popular music and Cuban dance bands almost totally dominated the local cultural scene. As Orchestra Baobab's guitarist, Bartholemy Atisso, put it 'When I arrived in Senegal in 1968, there was only Cuban music' (Hudson 2003). It was only the intervention, in that period, of politicians such as Sekou Toure in Guinea, Leopold Senghor in Senegal and the now disgraced President Mobutu of the (then) Congo, with their campaigns of 'cultural protectionism' (through state subsidies to 'authentic cultural producers') and for the 'indigenisation' (cf. *Negritude*) of West African music and culture, which laid the groundwork for the contemporary flowering of the hybridised musical forms that now characterise the region. Without the state subsidies that allowed these artists to practise and develop their music for a long period, before it found an audience, all the subsequently influential musicians, such as Mory Kante and Salif Keita, who began their careers in the Super Rail Band of Bamako, would have had no 'academy' in which to learn their skills – and the subsequent forms of world music would have had no local cultural basis from which to develop.

These matters must, then, be assessed conjuncturally. If policies of cultural protectionism and cultural subsidy are always problematic, nonetheless, there are circumstances in which they may be both necessary and wise. However, to return to my central argument, if the foreign can undermine traditional industries and hierarchies, and is thus not necessarily a Bad Thing, to be kept out, that is still only an abstract concept of the foreign. The problem is that in fact, in many places in the world, the forms of foreignness primarily available for importation are still mainly, if no longer exclusively, Anglo-American.

Let me turn, lastly, to the question of the audience for imported media products.

The problem of the audience

There is a very serious problem with the basic cultural imperialism thesis, as developed by Schiller and others, in so far as it tends to assume that the media necessarily have straightforward, predictable and automatic ('hypodermic') effects on their audiences. This is a model of the audience that has largely been discredited in recent years, as it has come to be recognised that audiences are active in various ways, as they select from and reinterpret, for their own purposes, the media materials that they consume. There is an array of (now canonical) work in our field (cf. Ang 1985; Silj 1988; Liebes and Katz 1991; Gripsrud 1995) offering studies of cross-cultural differences in the decoding of North American television programmes like *Dallas* and *Dynasty*, which demonstrates how globally distributed media forms are often reinterpreted by audiences through their own local and particular cultural frameworks. The work of Eric Michaels (1994) is perhaps the most striking, in demonstrating just how radically audiences can reinterpret the texts they consume. In his case, he shows how Australian Aboriginal communities reinterpret narrative patterns in *Dallas* through their own, very different, understanding of kinship relations and obligations. However, to take the particular example of Michaels's work, the problem is that of its subsequent extrapolation by others in the field. The fact that particular Australian Aboriginal communities reinterpret *Dallas* in ways radically different from those intended by the programme's producers provides no intellectual warrant for the unseemly generalisation of this one, detailed ethnographic example, to provide a general theory of some supposed tendency for audiences world-wide to always make 'oppositional' readings of the media materials they consume.

I have argued elsewhere (Morley 1992) against the regrettable tendency, in much recent audience studies work, towards what can only be called the romanticisation of the power (and supposed freedom) of media consumers to reinterpret texts at will, as if they were all relentlessly engaged in some form of 'semiotic guerrilla warfare' with the media (cf. Eco 1972). To follow that route is to risk falling into the trap acerbically identified by the editors of the critical North American magazine, *The Baffler*, of believing that the 'noble consumer' always and necessarily 'uses the dross with which he or she is bombarded to fashion little talismans of rebellion and subversion'.[5] This is also to be potentially complicit, as Thomas Frank has rightly argued, with the key tenets of the discourses of consumer sovereignty, which lie at the heart of what he calls 'market populism' (Frank 2003). Of course, there is another way of looking at all this, which takes a perspective of what we might call 'glocalisation from below'. This view is well-represented by Ulf Hannerz, among others, who argues that, in many places, 'local cultural entrepreneurs have ... (now) ... mastered the alien cultural forms which reach them through the transnational commodity flow' and are busy 'taking them apart, [and] tampering with them ... [so] ... that the resulting new forms are more responsive to, and ... in part outgrowths of, local everyday life' (Hannerz 1991: 124). The question is how we balance these two perspectives and how we discriminate between empirical situations where one or the other is more applicable, without presuming that either tells the whole truth, for all places and all times.

Conclusion

Where does all that leave us? We live, we are told, in a new era of complex globalisation, in which old models of imperialism will not serve us well and it is certainly the case that those old models have real limitations. However, among all the excited talk of cultural hybridity, bricollage, creolisation and 'transculturation', Hannerz (1996) rightly argues the need for what he calls 'some unexciting caution'. He recognises, of course, that the world of international communications and media flows is now more complex than it was – that there is more than one 'centre', in relation to which a whole variety of different cultural peripheries are constituted. Furthermore, he recognises that not all cultural flows run, automatically, in the same uniform direction, from Hollywood (or from the World Bank) to the rest of the world. However, for Hannerz, this does not mean that we are now somehow 'beyond' centre–periphery models of cultural flow – even if those models must now take account of a variety of different regional centres – and their varying peripheries. This is, not least, because those peripheries 'out there in distant territory' are still, as he notes, predominantly the 'takers, rather than the givers of meaning' (Hannerz 1991: 107). It is for exactly these reasons that we must insist on the continuing importance of questions of what Doreen Massey (1994) has called the 'power-geometry' of culture, and of cultural imperialisms of various sorts.

Thus, when Arjun Appadurai claims that 'the United States is no longer the "puppeteer" of a world system of images, but is only one node of a complex transnational construction of imaginary landscapes' (Appadurai 1996: 31) we should remember that it is still the most powerful single 'node' in that complex. Similarly, when Hardt and Negri claim that 'Empire presents a superficial world, the virtual centre of which can be accessed immediately from any point across the surface' (Hardt and Negri 2000: 53) we might bear in mind how difficult it still is to get from Dakar to Brazzaville without passing through Paris. As Goran Therborn acerbically notes, however 'globalised' the world may now be, some parts of it are still much closer ... than ... others' (Therborn 2002: 295). Despite the popularity of Deleuze and Guattari's metaphor of the 'rhizome' in many academic circles, the fact remains that globalisation has simply not produced a planet in which all points are connected in a reticular network. And it is for this reason that the development of transversal forms of communication and travel, across the poor 'South' of the world, remains such a political priority.[6]

In this context it is, of course, crucial to relativise the story of globalisation, as told (as it usually is) from the perspective of the West. 'History' itself is often equated with the history of the West, and the story of modernisation is hard to disentangle from the story of Westernisation, and, in the twentieth century, from the story of Americanisation (cf. Wolf 1982). Rather than try to answer Frances Fukuyama's presumptuous question about whether or not 'we' (whoever that is) stand, as he claimed, at the 'End of History', we might perhaps better ask, with John Clarke (op. cit.), who is at the 'end' of which history, and how they got there – and what the continuing role is of the Anglo-American media in the constitution of the story of that history. We may live in a globalised world, but in most places global time still ticks to the clock of CNN, and we may do well to recognise the extent to which the Anglo-American media continue to provide, for many people, the constitutive horizons of what has been called the 'Global Familiar' of our times.[7]

Notes

1   Here I develop a set of arguments first outlined in Morley (1994), which will be further explored in one of the chapters in a forthcoming book of essays – see Morley, forthcoming. To avoid duplication, in the rest of this essay I shall use the broader term 'cultural imperialism' to include processes of media imperialism.

2   Cf. Huntingdon (1996).

3   Cf. Therborn, 2002 for some recent statistics on international media flows.

4   Major Peters's comments were quoted in a post to the Cultstuds email list on 28 April 2003 by Beth Ogden; Media/Cultural Studies, Hampshire College, Amherst, MA 01002; bjoCC@helios.hampshire.edu.

5   Cf. *The Baffler* website, www.thebaffler.com/onemarket.html. *The Baffler*, PO Box 378293, Chicago Ill 60637; see also Paul McEwan posting on 25 July 2002 to the CultStuds email list at www.cultstud-1@lists.acomp.usf.edu.

6   To give but one important example, one might cite here the work of projects like the *Inter-Asia Cultural Studies Journal*, in developing such transversal links throughout and across East and South Asia.

7   My thanks are due to Paul Giles of Linacre College, Oxford, for alerting me to the quotes by Appadurai, Hardt and Negri, and Wallerstein used earlier.

References

Ang, I. (1985) *Watching Dallas*, London: Methuen.

Appadurai, A. (1996) *Modernity at Large*, Minneapolis: University of Minnesota Press.

Bausinger, H. (1990) *Folk Culture in a World of Technology*, Bloomington: Indiana University Press.

Branston, G. (forthcoming) 'What a difference a Bay makes: cinema and Welsh heritage', in J. Littler and R. Naidoo (eds) *The Politics of Heritage*, London: Routledge.

Burkeman, O. (2003) 'Arab world now faces invasion by American TV', The *Guardian*, 24 April 2003.

Clarke, J. (1991) *New Times and Old Enemies*, London: Harper Collins.

Clifford, J. (1997) *Routes*, Harvard: Harvard University Press.

Denselow, R. (2003) 'Sound politics', The *Guardian*, 3 July 2003.

Eco, U. (1972) 'Towards a semiotic enquiry into the TV message', *Working Papers in Cultural Studies* 3.

Fiske, J. (1986) 'Polysemy and popularity', *Critical Studies in Mass Communications* 3.

Frank, T. (2003) *One Market under God*, New York: Doubleday.

Fukuyama, F. (1992) *The End of History and the Last Man*, Harmondsworth: Penguin.

Gilroy, P. (1993) *The Black Atlantic*, London: Verso.

Gripsrud, J. (1995) *The Dynasty Years: Hollywood, Television and Critical Media Studies*, London: Routledge.

Hall, S. (1991) 'The local and the global', in A. King (ed.) *Culture, Globalisation and the World System*, London: Macmillan.

Hannerz, U. (1991) 'Scenarios for peripheral cultures', in A. King (ed.) *Culture, Globalisation and the World System*, London: Macmillan.

—— (1996) 'Flows, borders and hybrids', unpublished paper to Department of Anthropology, University of Stockholm Workshop, Lund, October 1996.

Hardt, M. and Negri, A. (2000) *Empire*, Harvard: Harvard University Press.

Harindrath, R. (2003) 'Reviving cultural imperialism', in S. Kumar and L. Parks (eds) *Planet TV*, New York: New York University Press.

Hebdige, D. (1988) 'Towards a cartography of taste', in *Hiding in the Light*, London: Routledge.

Hudson, M. (2003) 'Their roots are growing', The *Observer*, October 2003.

Hujic, A. (1999) *MTV Europe: A Study of Programming and Marketing Strategies*, unpublished Ph.D. thesis, Goldsmiths College, University of London.

Huntingdon, S. (1996) *The Clash of Civilisations*, New York: Simon & Schuster.

Lerner, D. (1964) *The Passing of Traditional Society*, Glencoe, IL: Free Press.

Liebes, T and Katz, E. (1991) *The Export of Meaning*, Oxford: Oxford University Press.

Luce, H. (1941) *The American Century*, New York: Farrar & Reinhart.

Massey, D. (1994) *Space, Place and Gender*, Cambridge: Polity Press.

Mattelart, A., Delacourt, X. and Mattelart, M. (1986) International Image Markets, London: Comedia.

Michaels, E. (1994) *Bad Aboriginal Art and Other Essays*, Minneapolis: University of Minnesota Press.

Morley, D. (1992) *Television, Audiences and Cultural Studies*, London: Routledge.

—— (1994) 'Postmodernism: the highest stage of cultural imperialism?' in M. Perryman (ed.) *Altered States*, London: Lawrence & Wishart.

—— (forthcoming) *Questions of Culture, Media and Technology*, London: Routledge.

Morley, D. and Robins, K. (1996) *Spaces of Identity*, London: Routledge.

Piot, C. (1999) *Remotely Global*, Chicago: University of Chicago Press.

Rostow, W.W. (1960) *The Stages of Economic Growth*, Cambridge: Cambridge University Press.

Schiller, H. (1969) (2nd edn 1992) *Mass Communications and American Empire*, New York: Beacon Press.

—— (1991) 'Not yet the post-imperial era', in *Critical Studies in Mass Communications* 8.

Silj, A. (1988) *East of Dallas: The European Challenge to American Television*, London: British Film Institute.

Sreberny-Mohammadi, A. (1991) 'The global and the local in international communications', in J. Curran and M. Gurevitch (eds) *Mass Media and Society*, London: Edward Arnold.

Therborn, G. (2002) 'Asia and Europe in the world – locations in the global dynamics', *Inter-Asia Cultural Studies* 3(2).

Wallerstein, I. (2003) *The Decline of American Power*, New York: New Press.

Wolf, E. (1982) *Europe and the People without History*, Berkeley: University of California Press.

Worpole, K. (1983) *Dockers and Detectives*, London: Verso.

Chapter 3

The push and pull of global culture

James Lull

September 11 and its violent aftermath have motivated people everywhere to reflect intensely on the meanings and implications of their cultural realities and futures. This reflection takes place at a time in history when 'Culture' as a normative social force that inscribes values and regulates behavior is being confronted by the pervasive decentralization of life experience and the dramatic rise of the individual as a personal cultural decision-maker.[1] As Ulrich Beck has pointed out:

> The ethic of individual self-fulfillment and achievement is the most powerful current in modern society. The choosing, deciding, shaping human being who aspires to be author of his or her own life, the creator of individual identity, is the central character of our time.
>
> (Beck 2000: 165)

Processes of individualization that emerged as cultural characteristics in Western societies have intensified greatly in the current era and the trend is spreading rapidly elsewhere. The diversity and amount of cultural information to which people have access today encourages unprecedented personal cultural experimentation and self-reliance. But a seemingly contrasting development – cultural retrenchment – is also taking place. The remarkable rise of the individual in globalization has changed but not erased the role of collective Culture as a stable, guiding source of belonging-ness, security, and identity. So at the same time individuals the world over put an ever-increasing array of cultural resources to work for innumerable personal purposes, groups of persons who identify with and are affiliated by nation, religion, ethnicity, tribe, and race confront today's uncertain and threatening times by displaying their collective will and cultural capital as well.

These seemingly antithetical tendencies in contemporary cultural experience represent the classic 'dichotomy between the autonomous agent and the social-ized self' (Agre 2001: 6) and make up what I call the 'push and pull' of culture. This expression – push and pull – has many uses in the English language and Western culture. In the present context 'push' refers to those cultural influences that become part of our cultural lives more or less implicitly and not necessarily with our knowledge or consent. Many push aspects of culture are inherited: primary languages, religious or spiritual orientations and practices, basic social values, types of food, and so on. They are the non-volitional elements of our dominant cultural consciousness and praxis – features of life over which we originally had little control, whose contours make up our basic orientation to the world, provide primordial stability, and whose influence can never be completely extinguished, no matter how hard we may try later in life (Lull 2000: 132–3). The product of these influences is the acculturated individual and the societies in which they live.

The 'pull' side of culture, on the other hand, refers to the dynamic nature of contemporary communication and the role of the self as an active agent of cultural construction – the do-it-yourself cultural programmer. Pull represents the volitional side of cultural formation and is characterized by the 'flexible self' (Willis 2000) who actively seeks increased personalization of cultural experience through individual creativity and choice. Pull culture is more space than place, more dynamic than static, more engaged than removed. Pull represents the provisional self under constant construction.

The push and pull dichotomy directs attention to the precarious balance between collective and individual needs, both of which have been sharpened considerably by the profusion, contrasts, and contradictions of the Communication Age. I have appropriated the specific meanings of the associated terms 'push' and 'pull' from the world of information technology and marketing. The relationship between information/culture providers and users exemplifies broader cultural tendencies. 'Push' refers in part to the idea that certain events can be introduced into the awareness of people without their asking or consent. In terms of the internet, for example, junk email and unwanted pop-up ads on a home computer are push intrusions. So is the channeling of a search engine request to a sponsored link or a telemarketing call received at home.[2]

'Pull' signifies the user-driven side of the model. In technology and marketing, the user tells the browser what information he or she wants to retrieve from the digital environment in a pull experience. The user actively sets preferences and then searches, selects, and socializes according to his or her own schedule and priorities. Indeed, in today's cultural landscape information technology and telecommunications devices offer 'not only the feeling of being able to control the complexities of modern life, but also a real possibility to do so' (Kopomaa 2000: 5).

Overall, the locus of much cultural activity today is shifting from structure and tradition (push) to individual persons and their chosen networks that are composed of varying degrees of proximity and mediation (pull). The technological advances brought on by modernity and globalization make the speed and efficiency of the pull side of cultural activity extremely attractive and rewarding for individuals, and, in many respects, for the societies in which they live. The personal cultural freedoms that individuals enjoy today clearly have 'liberated inventive and entrepreneurial talents and accelerated [further development of the same] technological innovations' that helped open or widen the creative spaces in the first place (Soros 2002: 4).

Certainly not all prominent contemporary thinkers are as pleased as George Soros is with current developments, and in truth Soros himself has no pollyannaish position on this issue either. Warning signs about the cultural consequences of globalization appear everywhere. Globalization creates tremendous uncertainty and trepidation, especially for those who believe they have been victimized or abandoned by it. Some observers fear the severe degradation of cultural integrity and the breakdown of community. Zygmunt Bauman, for example, argues that the uncertainties of the present day have become 'a powerful individualizing force [so that] the idea of "common interests" grows ever more nebulous and loses all pragmatic value' (Bauman 2000: 148). Even Ulrich Beck, whose generally evenhanded analysis of individualization will be discussed later suggests that 'God, nature, and the social system are being progressively replaced, in greater and lesser steps, by the individual – confused, astray, helpless, and at a loss' (Beck and Beck-Gernsheim 2002: 8).

We live in Cultures but we initiate 'cultural experiences' and we lead 'cultural lives' that don't just reflect our primary cultural locations. The push and pull refers to the dynamic and dialectical nexus between Culture and culture, between the cultural life of the group and that of the individual. The key contrasts are summarized as follows:

Push	Pull
Culture	culture
collective	individual
non-volitional	volitional
security	risk
slow-paced	fast-paced
gradual change	rapid and flexible
macro	micro
closed	open
community	habitat
uniformity	diversity
social norms	personal wants and needs
production	consumption
coherent	fragmented

The push of Culture

Individual persons today chase their dreams with unprecedented energy and latitude but they still need to connect, communicate, and commune with others. From birth the human organism gravitates toward the safety and stability provided by a relatively predictable, orderly, and constant flow of everyday life. As Abraham Maslow pointed out more than sixty years ago, when infants and young children are confronted with 'new, unfamiliar, strange, unmanageable stimuli or situations' (such as new faces, new contexts, new voices, new objects) they 'frequently [exhibit] a danger or terror reaction' (Maslow 1943: 378). This basic instinct never disappears. Adults also depend on predictable structures, norms, and behavior for survival and stability, especially when they believe their individual or collective living situations have become abnormally uncertain, threatening, or uncontrollable.

Familiar cultural structures and traits act as commodious resources for physical survival, psychological stability, and identity. These primordial elements include ancestry, nation, ethnicity, tribe, race, religion, everyday customs, rituals, language, core values, geographic territory, and trusted institutions – 'blood and belief, faith and family' (Huntington 1996: 126). People rely on the 'push' side of culture to maintain the integrity and viability of the familiar in an increasingly incomprehensible and dangerous world. In this sense, Culture can be said to represent the general interests of an entire group. That's why Culture never functions solely as an unwanted, dominating, limiting force that is imposed on individual persons. To the contrary, most people depend on Culture for great comfort, even for survival.

Although uncertainty and threat greatly sharpen allegiances and dependencies on Culture, the less chaotic and treacherous activities and routines of everyday life are likewise patterned according to the expectations and sanctions of ideological orthodoxy. As David Chaney points out, even the most familiar cultural structures 'tell us that there is a distinctive way of doing things [that is] imbued with moral force' (Chaney 2002: 8). The ongoing, shared life of cultural groups (the *durée* of social activity: see Giddens 1984) reinforces and shapes the idea that Culture has ethical qualities, long-term viability, and practical utility. Moreover, 'these ways of doing things persist through generations; they will generally hold without discussion or question, and they display a level of group life that precedes individual experience' (Chaney 2002: 8). Cultural institutions introduce, reinforce, and perpetuate the group's characteristic values, rituals, and patterns of behavior as normal and expected. These cultural values, practices, styles, and identities are contained within and emerge from a collective memory system – an empirically elusive cognitive architecture that is widely sensed by cultural members. While not hard-wired into the genetic composition of human being, and not historically invariable or determined, these 'internal cultural patterns' nonetheless migrate across time and space from generation to generation (Sowell 1994: 229; see also Lull 2000: 152–5).

One consequence of today's patterns of intense global migration is the creation of multicultural societies composed of groups representing very different cultural histories, values, and practices. In many respects nations and economies that embrace and encourage multiculturalism, even in circumstances where dissimilar ethnic and religious groups co-mingle, can reap tremendous economic and cultural benefits from the energy, creativity, and productivity that diversity gener-ates, especially in this era of technological development and heightened global economic competition (e.g. Cowen 2002; Zachary 2000). Waves of technological innovation and subsequent economic prosperity for many decades in northern California's Silicon Valley may still best exemplify how cultural diversity has led to impressive economic productivity in the USA. In such complicated situations, however, the culturally disparate groups must be held together by an effective over-arching push structure.

The push tendencies of culture have multiple and contradictory consequences. The push side offers cultural members safety, security, identity, and a sense of belonging. It supplies a ready stockpile of material and symbolic resources, and a general framework for interpreting the world. But powerful cultural systems can also inculcate rigid, divisive, non-cosmopolitan values among cultural members and be used as pretexts for severe racial, ethnic, religious, political, or cultural discrimination against others inside and outside national borders. As Phil Agre succinctly points out, 'people understand new things through the prism of what they know, and the distortions introduced by the prism are often severe' (Agre 2001: 6). So while the push of Culture organizes life and offers certain stabilizing influences and other benefits, it also limits freedom, opportunities, and well-being – consequences that have become especially relevant as human beings move around the planet in such great numbers.

Culture and nation are frequently equated. But as Terry Eagleton points out in *The Idea of Culture*, 'people who belong to the same place ... do not thereby form a culture; they do so only when they begin to share speech habits, folklore, ways of proceeding, frames of value, a collective self-image' (Eagleton 2000: 37). Culture, he rightly argues, is not the same as synchronous living. The fixity, shared understanding, and appreciation of Culture, especially National Culture, have become less stable than ever before in a globalized world of international busi-ness, tourism, foreign employment, legal and illegal immigration, military interventionism, nation-building, and increased privatization of the public sphere. Cultural loyalties, customs, rituals, and identities have become less and less confined to or determined by geographical territory or human surroundings. The conditions that inscribe and reinforce the foundations of most national cultures –

common languages, religions, histories, and relations with other nation states – have become far less taken-for-granted. National Cultures today are held together more by their capacity to effectively expose people to common symbolic referents than by their ability to exact social compliance. The push of culture therefore increasingly refers to *the shared experience of particular signs in a crowded and highly competitive symbolic environment.*

The pull of culture

In his comprehensive treatise on the origins of human emotions, Jonathan H. Turner (2000) shows how the propensity toward individualism, autonomy, freedom, and mobility observable in contemporary human behavior is clearly evident throughout the evolutionary history of apes and humans dating back to the hominids, our last common ancestors. Individualism, autonomy, freedom, and mobility comprise the dynamic essence of the 'pull' side of contemporary cultural experience. Strong and natural human tendencies toward gratification of individual physical and psychological needs, the flexible pursuit of differentiating personal interests and preferences, and the making of increasingly diverse cultural choices constitute the core processes of individual cultural programming and the creation of personal supercultures (Lull 2001).

The trend toward greater individualism, autonomy, freedom, and mobility in contemporary societies is associated with core Western values, and with capitalism and commercialism, all of which have greatly permeated and shaped the multifarious processes of modernization and globalization. The impact of these ideological and cultural influences increased significantly in the late twentieth century even within traditional societies. Consequently, many basic cultural orientations and practices, including those related to the most intimate sensibilities and expressive outlets of the culturally situated human body, are changing. Millions of young urban Chinese, for instance, are more likely now than ever before to exercise autonomy from family and state to determine their sexual partners, preferences, and activities. The popularity of arranged marriages in the Far East and South Asia is declining overall. Individual fashion and style – such as Chinese women's liberation from androgynous Maoist uniformity, the hip-hop look of modern urban youth in Manila, and the 'tea hair' fad among today's individually expressive Japanese youth – have found highly symbolic cultural places in contemporary Asian cultures. Cultural changes that appear on the human body are never just cosmetic; they disrupt tradition, open up cultural options, and eventually create new cultural norms and social practices.

The scope and scale of cultural resources available for personal use and the concomitant degree of cultural variety and flexibility they produce have expanded tremendously in Western cultural settings. In the West individual cultural entrepreneurship is itself a cultural value. People creatively appropriate, person-alize, and indigenize cultural materials ranging from the abstract to the didactic for reasons determined largely by them. When people have more material and symbolic resources to work with they have greater capacity to 'pull' what they need or want. The expanded and improved range of available resources and options has facilitated more cultural freedom overall, established new cultural precedents, and encouraged greater acceptance of diverse lifestyles. Some of the cultural choices made by inhabitants of Western countries in the relatively free-wheeling spaces of modernity and postmodernity are extremely serious, even life changing. Other cultural decisions that are routinely made today, however, have much more to do with taste or style than necessity. British historian Eric Hobsbawm has nicely described the difference. He says that relative to many others around the world, middle-class Westerners when planning what food to include in their meals now 'only need to decide whether they want a sandwich with French bread or *focaccia*, with cooked or smoked ham, and with fresh or dried tomatoes' (Hobsbawm 2000: 85–6).

The price of cultural freedom?

Individualism as it materializes in the hyper-commercialized context of global middle-class lifestyles sometimes reaches the point of absurdity, unconscionable luxury, or dangerous selfishness. Instant personal gratification and self-fulfillment through consumer activity are especially characteristic of contemporary US culture.

The range of personal cultural options is extraordinary. From beds that feature compartmentalized firmness and individually controlled temperature zones to 'personalized watercraft' (noisy jet skis), personalized ring tones for mobile phones and toolbars for personal computers, individual viewing screens on the back of airplane seats, the 'Army of One', 'My MTV', and 'Windows ME', in many ways the USA has become above all else an over-amped, over-hyped, over-stimulated world of 'It's all about me' and 'I want it all now!' The link between cultural individualism and capitalist economics that makes all this happen was succinctly captured in a line from the script of a 2003 television commercial sponsored by the US investment firm, Brown and Company: 'I believe in the market. I believe in me.'

Critical observers from the left and the right agree that although people generally have more cultural freedom today than ever before, that freedom exacts a heavy social price. Contemporary cultural activity widens disparities between social classes, the general argument goes, and threatens the stability of cultural communities. People rely upon and become identified with their roles as indi-vidual consumers of material and symbolic goods and services; the fascination with buying logos rather than sustainable goods is a prime example. The social

consequences of this mindset can be daunting. As the late Herbert Schiller specu-
lated in his last book:

> If present trends continue, all human interactions will be on a pay-for basis.
> This denies the social nature of human existence and elevates self and selfish-
> ness as the primary motivators of people. In such an order, common or
> national endeavors have little chance of acceptance, and agreeable human
> associations disappear.
>
> (Schiller 2000: 197)

As the mass media, information technology industries, and culture industries
assume ever greater presence and significance in everyday life, trends toward
increased individualism, autonomy, freedom, and mobility become more acute.
Proliferating cable and satellite TV channels, satellite radio, internet sales, market
segmentation, and niche media advertising – including 'addressable advertising'
techniques that target individual homes, rooms in homes, and cell phone numbers
– all reinforce and intensify individualism. Individualized reception of news and
entertainment from contemporary mega-channel media leaves people 'utterly
alone', according to the US sociologist Robert Putnam, and relieves individual
persons from the necessity to co-ordinate timing of their cultural experiences
with others. Putnam uses the analogy of 'parallel play' in child development to
warn of the potential dangers of individualization. It's normal for young children
to play in a sandbox, Putnam explains, with each child focused on his or her own
toy or territory, completely ignoring the other children. Healthy children eventually outgrow parallel play. Putnam argues that emersion in television (not to
mention GameBoys, PlayStations, personal computers, mp3 players, and mobile
phones) leaves adults at an 'arrested stage of development, rarely moving beyond
parallel attentiveness' (Putnam 2000: 244). Adult parallel play increases as media
content becomes more abundant and diverse, appealing to individuals according
to their own linguistic and cultural frameworks and biases, a development he
believes undermines the quality of civil society (Putnam 2000: 217, 216).

Individualization: 'a life of one's own'

Literally at the heart of the pull side of contemporary cultural experience is the
individual person. Despite the negative consequences of individualism, the individual person is not simply a 'product' of culture and not just a naïve follower of
traditions or trends, but an active, reflexive, imaginative subject who is motivated
to act in his or her perceived best interests that should not be understood to mean
only selfish concerns. The expansive transformation and mediation of time and
space underway today, changes in the most common routines of everyday life,

improvement in modes of transportation, and the unprecedented availability of symbolic forms and cultural resources brought on by modernization and globalization all significantly sharpen and accelerate the potential for individuals to act independently and creatively. Of course their actions never materialize under conditions of free will or complete range of motion. The rise of individualism itself can be understood in part as a structured process; each person is slotted by society's institutions into roles and responsibilities that carry heavy demands that individuals themselves increasingly face alone (Beck and Beck-Gernsheim 2002).

Does greater cultural autonomy imprison or liberate individual persons and societies? Some observers fear that the demands placed on individuals in contemporary Western societies, and more frequently throughout the world, have become overwhelming and clearly detrimental. In the Western-style 'individualized, privatized version of modernity', according to Zygmunt Bauman, 'the burden of pattern weaving and the responsibility for failure falls primarily on the individual's shoulders' (Bauman 2000: 8). In contrast with the communitarian mentality of socialistic, theocratic, and autocratic social systems, modern Western subjects in liberal democratic societies are 'expected to use, individually, their own wits, resources, and industry to lift themselves to a more satisfactory condition and leave behind whatever aspect of their present condition they may resent' (Bauman 2000: 135). Bauman finds this expectation of self-reliance, especially in today's uncertain and threatening world, to be morally unacceptable and impractical. Vulnerability of individual persons to the structures that surround them has long been a primary concern of leftist politicians, labor unions, civil rights advocates, and Marxist sociologists like Bauman. Indeed, sociology's 'credo states over and over again that ... individuals ... are denied insight into the social conditions and conditionality of their lives' (Beck and Beck-Gernsheim 2002: 15). Particularly because the economic exploitation of individuals has been so widespread throughout history, some critical scholars even consider the fundamental sociological category of the 'individual' to be a 'taboo construct'.

Zygmunt Bauman's gloomy contention that people are fundamentally ill-equipped to assume major personal responsibility for the challenges that face them in modern life, or that they shouldn't have to do so in the first place, seems oddly out of place today. The individual now is 'making a surprising return' in social theory and in practice, 'not simply as consumer or audience member, but as an active creator of his or her own life' (Sreberny 2002: 294). Most contemporary observers certainly would agree, however, that the increasingly individualized 'ways of being in the world' brought about by modern global standards of living and sweeping technological change continue to pose great risks and heavy challenges (Chaney 2002: 140, 23). In any encounter with twenty-first-century modernity, people must display 'initiative, flexibility, and tolerance of frustration' in the sociocultural 'evolution that has been unleashed by the ongoing individualization' that is so clearly on the upswing (Beck and Beck-Gernsheim 2002: 4, 31).

The phrase 'creating a life of one's own' nicely captures the essence of the trend toward greater individualization. Intensive individualization is encouraged by Western modernity and the institutional structures that accompany it, even on a global scale. Western societies routinely sort citizens into singular social categories in economic and civil terms ('chief executive officer', 'head of household', 'valedictorian', 'group leader', 'person responsible', etc.) in a process Talcott Parsons labeled 'institutionalized individualism' (Parsons 1978: 321). Such structured distribution of behavior and identity does not determine the consequences of the sorting, however, nor does it come close to explaining the whole of individualization. Individualizing tendencies long predate the modern evolutionary form of *Homo sapiens* as biological beings, and an entire discipline – psychology – thrives in part as a science of individual difference. Imagination, expressiveness, and creativity are all at work. These organic human properties are not simply derived or determined. As Paul Willis points out, individualization not only descends from ideological frameworks and institutional processes, but also develops actively and upwardly from personal engagements with cultural forms and from the 'symbolic work' of identity formation that often conflicts with dominant institutional roles and expectations (Willis 2000).

New cultural theorizations

The recent terrorist attacks have brought the significance of culture, identity, and community violently to the surface on a global scale and profoundly express the push side of culture in a globalizing world that is replete with pull tendencies. Although the fears and fetishes brougt on by terrorism have tended to unify (and divide) cultural groups in certain ways, cultural experience in practice always distributes differentially across individual persons and contexts – more so now than ever before. People sample, fuse, style, pierce, and feel their way through the complex matrices of external cultural forms available to them and through their inner states of well-being, pleasure and sensation. Associated trends toward increased individualization, personalization, and cultural entrepreneurship are all encouraged by a general loosening up of structural constraints in modern societies.

The interests and activities of the sociocultural individual do not develop independent of, nor are they necessarily positioned against, the interests and activities of the sociocultural collectivity. Individual persons engage the world with individual motivations and interests but they function within frameworks that are offered by and sometimes demanded by their Cultures. The dominant values of Culture never fully determine the consciousness of the individual, but individual agency does not function with any complete 'autonomy of spirit' either

(Eagleton: 2000: 4). People need both collective *and* individualized cultural experience. The push and pull of culture therefore refers to the undetermined, yet structured and inter-articulating spectrum of social and cultural activities in which collectivities (which themselves sub-divide into multiple social groups) and individuals (who never act completely alone) engage with varying degrees of awareness, motivation, and consent.

Any theoretical formulation that positions structure against agency in an all-embracing way is untenable on sociological and cultural grounds in any historical context but is completely unreasonable in today's effusive information and communication environment. The deeply resonating synergy between structure and agency has become more dynamic than ever now that structural constraints in most contemporary societies have become less predominant, in many respects, while ordinary people have become more culturally active and independent. The fundamental explanatory power of structuration theory – the idea that society's structural influences and the individualizing power of human agency should not be thought of only as opposing forces – clearly applies to matters of contemporary culture as much as it does to traditional sociological issues and concerns (Giddens 1984; Lull 2000).

The push and the pull of culture therefore does not describe a bipolar category *system* of cultural direction or influence; it refers to an ongoing, interactive, undetermined, mutually constitutive *process*. Even from a psychological point of view, it couldn't be any other way. Push and pull tendencies do not become manifest in individual human consciousness as cognitive opposites, and the discomforts people may experience moving between them need not be considered counterproductive or harmful. To the contrary, a robust array of collective affiliations and more individualized identities contributes to cognitive balance and stability. Culture frames, limits, and empowers all at the same time. The complexity, heterogeneity, and hybridity that routinely appear in the material and symbolic world of cultural representation also exist in the nuanced templates of individual human cognition and in routine patterns of situated social interaction.

How might we characterize the distinctive social connections and cultural communities that are now emerging? And what are the moral implications of the new cultural alignments and activities? Ulrich Beck has coined the term 'reciprocal individualization' to describe the social and cultural transitions now underway in many parts of the world: 'human mutuality and community rest no longer on solidly established traditions, but, rather on a paradoxical collectivity of reciprocal individualization' (Beck and Beck-Gernsheim 2002: xxi). David Mateo describes the emerging cultural relations within the framework of Chilean youth culture as 'collective individualism' (Mateo 2004). Barry Wellman and Howard Rheingold talk about 'personal communities' that are facilitated principally through the use of new communications technologies (Wellman 2001,

Rheingold 2002: 57). I have described the processes of 'personal cultural programming' and the creation of 'personal supercultures' (Lull 2000, 2001). These formulations help bridge the gap between what Terry Eagleton calls the 'empty universalism' of Culture and the 'narrow particularism' of culture. They render any sharp distinction between Culture and culture redundant by emphasizing how imagination, connectivity, communication, signification, and identification commute between the two.

Conclusion

The dramatic cultural transformations that are underway today promise unprecedented fulfillment of the human potential in many ways, yet individual accomplishment and satisfaction alone cannot provide an adequate moral or pragmatic base in the long run for cultivation of healthy and well-functioning societies or for the development of healthy, well-functioning individuals. Individualized cultural activity includes the freedom to choose from an expanded range of cultural resources that usually leads to reduced dependence on traditional, more proximate social attachments. All this does not simply pose problems. Developments in mass media, the culture industries, and personal communications technologies in some respects offer new and often better ways to connect, communicate, and form meaningful social relationships and communities. But as Anthony Giddens and William Hutton rightly put it, as a general principle

> individual choice alone ... cannot supply the social bonds necessary to sustain a stable and meaningful life. If individual freedom is to be extended then it must be accompanied by the construction of new cosmopolitan communities – otherwise the result is a generalized personal insecurity.
>
> (Giddens and Hutton 2000: 217)

What might those new cosmopolitan communities look like? Routine cultural experience today does not always embody respect or commitment to other people who share the same physical space. New communications technologies contribute to the decline of civility in key respects. One need only think of the loud-talking mobile-phone user stumbling and bumbling through a crowded public area or negotiating a turn in a vehicle without bothering to extend the courtesy of signaling. We are indeed creating new ways to ignore and inconvenience each other. Furthermore, many common contemporary cultural involvements appear 'abstract and cold blooded' and lack the traditional 'degree of emotional involvement we have with the family, the nation, or the little brown church in the wildwood' [not to mention the little mosque or synagogue down the street] (Boulding 1969: 348; insert mine). Recent developments in media transmission and reception appear to have diminished the sense of communal space generally and the sense of 'hearth' for families (Silverstone 1994). Although global terriorism has complicated the trend, for many people traditional strong ties to civil institutions have weakened overall (Bauman 2001: 22). Even the well-intentioned, popular celebration of cultural diversity and the creation of government policies to support multiculturalism – acting together with the vicis-situdes of market segmentation and media saturation – in some ways disrupt national solidarity and distract citizens from solving the social problems they face in common (Gitlin 2001). Modernity and globalization therefore can fuel a double withdrawal: individual persons frequently become more isolated in key respects from their particular micro-social environments while they also become more distant from their dominant cultural frameworks.

Overall, however, the global cultural scene need not be considered to be so bleak. All the instances of cultural erosion mentioned here are accompanied by positive, constructive engagements with the material and symbolic resources inherent in today's explosive cultural and technological environment. Although the new electronic networks have partially replaced the relatively stable and enduring traditional communities with which we are accustomed, they also facili-tate countless highly specialized social and cultural connections that otherwise would not take place. Millions of people all over the world are taking advantage.

Moreover, the same technological capabilities that put distance between people in some ways also help establish and deepen the ties people have with existing institutions and traditions in their own physical communities. In contrast to Robert Putnam's claim that immoderate television viewing in America has led to social and civic malaise, for instance, regular internet users are much more likely than people who are not connected to become involved with community organizations and connect with people of different ages, economic backgrounds, and ethnicities (Pew Internet and American Life 2002). This is particularly true for young people who typically are not attracted very much by traditional, hierar-chical avenues of civic or cultural involvement. Furthermore, the convenience of modern personal communications technology makes it possible to actually increase the amount of contact with family and friends. As technological and cultural landscapes evolve, the sense of belonging and community does not disap-pear; it changes shape.

The networks and communities presently being formed are generally less governed by the kinds of explicit moral codes to which individuals have tradition-ally been held accountable by their Cultures. They require an unprecedented commitment to personal and shared responsibility. Two extreme tendencies that are apparent today – autistic individualism and reactionary collectivism – threaten the kind of progress that can be made. To build viable individual communities and a world-wide civil society in the push and pull of global culture, diverse persons must dedicate themselves to 'a new balance between individual and collective responsibilities' (Giddens 1998: 37). That commitment will be realized, however, only when people everywhere believe they have a meaningful stake in its development and its consequences, and give the same consideration to others.

Notes

1 I will follow Terry Eagleton's (2000) useful stylistic device of capitalizing Culture when referring to the concept in the familiar, macro sense of dominant, traditional, or national culture.

2 In Silicon Valley parlance, 'true push' means that websites and other sources immediately send data to the user's home computer whenever an 'event' occurs – a change in market prices, for instance, or sports results. 'Managed push' refers to sender initiatives that are based on known or estimated user profiles and preferences – the so-called 'Tivo model'.

References

Agre, P. (2001) *Institutions and the Entrepreneurial Self*, http://dlis.gseis.ucla.edu.pagre/.

Bauman, Z. (2000) *Liquid Modernity*, Cambridge, UK: Polity Press.

—— (2001) In P. Beilharz (ed) *The Bauman Reader*, London: Blackwell.

Beck, U. (2000) 'Living your own life in a runaway world: individualisation, globalisation, and politics', in W. Hutton and A. Giddens (eds) *Global Capitalism*, New York: The New Press.

Beck, U. and Beck-Gernsheim, E. (2002) *Individualization*, London: Sage.

Boulding, K.E. (1969) 'The interplay of technology and values', in K. Baier and N. Rescher (eds) *Values and the Future*, New York: The Free Press.

Chaney, D. (2002) *Cultural Change and Everyday Life*, Hampshire: Palgrove.

Cowen, T. (2002) *Creative Destruction*, Princeton, NJ: Princeton University Press.

Eagleton, T. (2000) *The Idea of Culture*, Oxford: Blackwell.

Giddens, A. (1998) *The Third Way*, Cambridge, UK: Polity Press.

—— (1984) *The Constitution of Society*, Cambridge, UK: Polity Press.

Giddens, A. and Hutton, W. (eds) (2000) *Global Capitalism*, New York: The New Press.

Gitlin, T. (2001) *Media Unlimited*, New York: Henry Holt.

Hobsbawm, E. (2000) *On the Edge of the New Century*, New York: The New Press.

Huntington, S.P. (1996) *The Clash of Civilizations and the Remaking of World Order*, New York: Simon & Schuster.

Kopomaa, T. (2000) *Birth of the Mobile Information Society*, Helsinki: Gaudeamus.

Lull, J. (2000) *Media, Communication, Culture*, Cambridge, UK: Polity Press.

—— (2001). *Culture in the Communication Age*. London: Routledge.

Maslow, A.H. (ed.) (2001) *Culture in the Communication Age*, London: Routledge.

—— (1943) 'A theory of human motivation', *Psychological Review* 50: 370–96.

Mateo, D. (2004) 'Una mirada supercultural a la labor de los ravers en Chile', master's thesis, Universidad Diego Portales, Chile.

Parsons, T. (1978) *Religion in Postindustrial Society. In Action, Theory, and the Human Condition*, New York: Free Press.

Pew Internet and American Life (2002) www.pewinternet.org

Putnam, R.D. (2000) *Bowling Alone*, New York: Simon & Schuster.

Rheingold, H. (2002) *Smart Mobs*, Cambridge, MA: Perseus.

Schiller, H. (2000) *Living in the Number One Country*, New York: Seven Stories Press.

Silverstone, R. (1994) *Television and Everyday Life*. London: Routledge.

Soros, G. (2002) *George Soros on Globalization*, Oxford: Public Affairs, Ltd.

Sowell, T. (1994) *Race and Culture*, New York: Basic Books.

Sreberny, A. (2002) 'Globalization and me', in J.M. Chan and B. McIntyre (eds) *In Search of Boundaries*, Westport, CT: Ablex.

Turner, J.H. (2000) *On the Origins of Human Emotions*, Stanford: Stanford University Press.

Wellman, B. (2001). 'Physical place and cyberplace: The rise of personalized networking', *International Journal of Urban and Regional Research*, 25: 2 (227-252).

Willis, P. (2000) *The Ethnographic Imagination*, Cambridge, UK: Polity Press.

Zachary, G.P. (2000) *The Global Me*, New York: Public Affairs.

Chapter 4

Post-feminism and popular culture

Bridget Jones and the new gender regime

Angela McRobbie

Introduction: complexification or backlash?

This article presents a series of possible conceptual frames for engaging with what has come to be known as post-feminism. It understands post-feminism to refer to an active process by which feminist gains of the 1970s and 1980s come to be undermined. It proposes that, through an array of machinations, elements of contemporary popular culture are perniciously effective in regard to this undoing of feminism, while simultaneously appearing to be engaging in a well-informed and even well-intended response to 'feminism'. It then proposes that this 'undoing', which can be perceived in the broad cultural field, is compounded by some dynamics in sociological theory (including the work of Giddens and Beck) that appear to be most relevant to aspects of gender and social change. Finally it suggests that by means of the tropes of freedom and choice that are now inextricably connected with the category of 'young women', feminism is decisively 'aged' and made to seem redundant. Feminism is cast into the shadows, where at best it can expect to have some afterlife, where it might be regarded ambivalently by those young women who must in more public venues stake a distance from it, for the sake of social and sexual recognition. I propose a complexification then of the backlash thesis that gained currency within forms of journalism associated with popular feminism (Faludi 1992).

The backlash for Faludi was a concerted, conservative response to the achievements of feminism. My argument is that post-feminism positively draws on and invokes feminism as that which can be taken into account, to suggest that equality is achieved, in order to install a whole repertoire of new meanings which emphasise that it is no longer needed, it is a spent force. This was most vivid in the (UK) *Independent* newspaper column *Bridget Jones's Diary*, then in the enormously successful books and films that followed.[1] For my purposes here, post-feminism permits the close examination of a number of intersecting but also conflicting currents. It allows us to examine shifts of direction in the feminist academy, while also taking into account the seeming repudiation of feminism within this very same academic context by those young women who are its unruly (student) subjects. Broadly I am arguing that for feminism to be 'taken into account' it has to be understood as having already passed away. This is a movement detectable across popular culture, a site where 'power … is remade at various junctures within everyday life, (constituting) our tenuous sense of common sense' (Butler et al. 2000: 14). Some fleeting comments in Judith Butler's short book *Antigone's Claim* suggest to me that post-feminism can be explored through what I would describes as a 'double entanglement' (Butler 2000). This comprises the co-existence of neo-conservative values in relation to gender, sexuality and family life (for example George Bush supporting the campaign to encourage chastity among young people, and in March 2004 declaring that civilisation itself depends on traditional marriage), with processes of liberalisation in regard to choice and diversity in domestic, sexual and kinship relations (for example gay couples now able to adopt, foster or have their own children by whatever means, and, in the UK at least, full rights to 'civil partnerships'). It also encompasses the existence of feminism as at some level transformed into a form of Gramscian common sense, while also fiercely repudiated, indeed almost hated (McRobbie 2003). The 'taken into accountness' permits all the more thorough dismantling of feminist politics and the discrediting of the occasionally voiced need for its renewal.

Feminism dismantling itself

The impact of this 'double entanglement', which is manifest in popular and political culture, coincides, however, with feminism in the academy finding it necessary to dismantle itself. For the sake of periodisation we could say that 1990 (or thereabouts) marks a turning point, the moment of definitive self-critique in feminist theory. At this time the representational claims of second-wave feminism come to be fully interrogated by postcolonialist feminists like Spivak, Trinh and Mohanty among others, and by feminist theorists like Butler and Haraway who inaugurate the radical de-naturalising of the post-feminist body (Spivak 1988; Trinh 1989; Mohanty 1995; Butler 1990; Haraway 1991). Under the prevailing influence of Foucault, there is a shift away from feminist interest in centralised power blocks, e.g. the state, patriarchy, law, to more dispersed sites, events and instances of power conceptualised as flows and specific convergences and consolidations of talk, discourse and attentions. The body and also the subject come to represent a focal point for feminist interest, nowhere more so than in the work of Butler. The concept of subjectivity and the means by which cultural forms and interpellations (or dominant social processes) call women into being, produce them as subjects whilst ostensibly merely describing them as such, inevitably means that it is a problematic 'she', rather than an unproblematic 'we', which is indicative of a turn to what we might describe as the emerging politics of post-feminist inquiry (Butler 1990, 1993).

In feminist cultural studies the early 1990s also marks a moment of feminist reflexivity. In her article 'Pedagogies of the feminine' Brunsdon queried the (hitherto assumed) use value to feminist media scholarship of the binary opposition between femininity and feminism, or as she put it the extent to which the 'housewife' or 'ordinary woman' was conceived of as the assumed subject of attention for feminism (Brunsdon 1991, reprinted 1997). Looking back we can see how heavily utilised this dualism was, and also how particular it was to gender arrangements for largely white and relatively affluent (i.e. housewifely) women. The year 1990 also marked the moment at which the concept of popular feminism found expression. Andrea Stuart considered the wider circulation of feminist values across the landscape of popular culture, in particular magazines where quite suddenly issues that had been central to the formation of the women's movement, like domestic violence, equal pay, workplace harassment, were now addressed to a vast readership (Stuart 1990). The wider dissemination of feminist issues was also a key concern in my own writing at this time, in particular the intersection of these new representations with the daily lives of young women who, as subjects ('called into being') of popular feminism, might then be expected to embody more emboldened (though also of course 'failed') identities. This gave rise to the idea of feminist success. Of course no sooner is the word 'success' written than it is queried. How could this be gauged? What might be the criteria for judging degrees of feminist success?

Female success

Admittedly there is some extravagance in my claim for feminist success. It might be more accurate to remark on the keen interest across the quality and popular media (themselves wishing to increase their female readers and audiences) in ideas of female success. As feminist values are indeed taken on board within a range of institutions, including law, education, to an extent medicine, likewise employment and the media, high-profile or newsworthy achievement of women and girls in these sectors shows the institutions to be modern and abreast with social change. This is the context then within which feminism is acknowledged and this is what I mean by feminism taken into account. Feminist success has, so far, only been described sporadically (for accounts of girls' achievement in education see Arnot et al. 1999 and also Harris 2003). Within media and cultural studies both Brunsdon and myself have each considered how with feminism as part of the academic curriculum (i.e. 'canonised'), it is not surprising that it might also be countered, that is feminism must face up to the consequences of its own claims to representation and power, and not be so surprised when young women students decline the invitation to identify as a 'we' with their feminist teachers and scholars (Brunsdon 1997; McRobbie 1999a). This interface between the feminist academy and the student body has also been discussed in US feminist journals particularly in regard to the decline of women's studies

(Brown 1997). Back in the early 1990s (and following Butler) I saw this sense of contestation on the part of young women, and what I would call their 'distance from feminism', as one of potential, where a lively dialogue about how feminism might develop would commence (Butler 1992; McRobbie 1994). Indeed it seemed in the very nature of feminism that it gave rise to dis-identification as a kind of requirement for its existence. But still, it seems now, over a decade later, that this space of 'distance from feminism' and those utterances of forceful non-identity with feminism have consolidated into something closer to repudiation rather than ambivalence, and it is this vehemently denunciatory stance that is manifest across the field of popular gender debate. This is the cultural space of post-feminism.

In this context it requires both imagination and hopefulness to argue that the active, sustained and repetitive repudiation or repression of 'feminism' also marks its (still fearful) presence or even longevity (as afterlife). What I mean by this is that there are different kinds of repudiation and different investments in such a stance. The more gentle denunciations of feminism (as in the film *Bridget Jones's Diary*) co-exists however with the shrill championing of young women as a 'metaphor for social change' on the pages of the right-wing press in the UK, in particular the *Daily Mail* [2]. This anti-feminist endorsement of female individualisation is embodied in the figure of the ambitious 'TV blonde' (McRobbie 1999b). These so-called 'A1' girls are glamorous high achievers destined for Oxford or Cambridge and are usually pictured clutching A level examination certificates. We might say these are ideal girls, subjects *par excellence,* and also subjects of excellence. Nor are these notions of female success exclusive to the changing representations of young women in the countries of the affluent West. As Spivak has argued, in the impoverished zones of the world, governments and NGOs also look to the minds and bodies of young women for whom education comes to promise enormous economic and demographic rewards (Spivak 1999). Young women are a good investment, they can be trusted with micro-credit, they are the privileged subjects of social change. But the terms of these great expectations on the part of governments are that young women must do without more autonomous feminist politics. What is consistent is the displacement of feminism as a political movement. It is this displacement that is reflected in Butler's sorrowful account of Antigone's life after death. Her shadowy, lonely existence suggests a modality of feminist effectivity as spectral; she has to be cast out, indeed entombed, for social organisation to once again become intelligible.

Unpopular feminism

The media have become the key site for defining codes of sexual conduct. They cast judgement and establish the rules of play. Across these many channels of communication feminism is routinely disparaged. Why is feminism so hated? Why do young women recoil in horror at the very idea of the feminist? To count as a girl today appears to require this kind of ritualistic denunciation, which in turn suggests that one strategy in the disempowering of feminism includes it being historicised and generationalised, and thus easily rendered out of date. It would be far too simplistic to trace a pattern in media from popular feminism (or 'prime-time feminism' including TV programmes like *LA Law*), in the early 1990s, to niche feminism (BBC Radio 4's *Woman's Hour*, and the Women's Page of the *Guardian* newspaper), in the mid 1990s, and then to overtly unpopular feminism (new century), as though these charted a chronological 'great moving right show' as Stuart Hall once put it in another context (Hall 1989). We would need a more developed conceptual schema to account for the simultaneous feminisation of popular media with this accumulation of ambivalent, fearful responses. We would certainly need to signal the full enfranchisement of women in the West, of all ages as audiences, active consumers of media and the many products they promote, and, by virtue of education, earning power and consumer identity a sizeable block of target market. We would also need to be able to theorise female achievement predicated not on feminism, but on 'female individualism', on success that seems to be based on the invitation to young women by various governments that they might now consider themselves free to compete in education and in work as privileged subjects of the 'new meritocracy'. Is this then the New Deal for New Labour's 'modern' young women: female individualisation and the new meritocracy at the expense of feminist politics?

There are various sites within popular culture where this work of undoing feminism with some subtlety becomes visible (see also Brunsdon 2005). The Wonderbra advert, showing the model Eva Herzigova looking down admiringly at her substantial cleavage enhanced by the lacy pyrotechnics of the Wonderbra, was through the mid-1990s positioned in major high street locations in the UK on full-size billboards. The composition of the image had such a textbook 'sexist ad' dimension that one could be forgiven for supposing some ironic familiarity with both cultural studies and with feminist critiques of advertising (Williamson 1987). It was, in a sense, taking feminism into account by showing it to be a thing of the past, by provocatively 'enacting sexism' while at the same time playing with those debates in film theory about women as the object of the gaze (Mulvey 1975) and even with female desire (De Lauretis 1988; Coward 1984). The picture is in noirish black and white, and refers explicitly through its captions (from 'Hello Boys' to 'Or Are You Just Pleased To See Me?') to Hollywood and the famous lines of the actress Mae West. Here is an advertisement that plays back to its viewers well-known aspects of feminist media studies, film theory and semiotics. Indeed, it almost offers (albeit crudely) the viewer or passing driver Laura Mulvey's theory of women as object of the gaze projected as cityscape within the frame of the billboard. Also mobilised in this ad is the familiarity of the term political correctness, the efficacy of which resides in its warranting and unleashing such energetic reactions against the seemingly tyrannical regime of feminist puritanism. Everyone and especially young people can give a sigh of relief. Thank goodness, the advert seems to suggest, it is permissible, once again, to enjoy looking at the bodies of beautiful women. At the same time, the advertisement also hopes to provoke feminist condemnation as a means of generating publicity. Thus generational differences are also produced, the younger female viewer, along with her male counterparts, educated in irony and visually literate, is not made angry by such a repertoire. She appreciates its layers of meaning; she 'gets the joke'.

When in a TV advertisement (1998/9) another supermodel, Claudia Schiffer, takes off her clothes as she descends a flight of stairs in a luxury mansion on her way out of the door towards her new Citroën car, a similar rhetoric is at work. This advert appears to suggest that, yes, this is a self-consciously 'sexist ad'. Feminist critiques of it are deliberately evoked. Feminism is 'taken into account', but only to be shown to be no longer necessary. Why? Because it now seems that there is no exploitation here, there is nothing remotely naive about this striptease. She seems to be doing it out of choice, and for her own enjoyment. The advert works on the basis of its audience knowing Claudia to be one of the world's most famous and highly paid supermodels. Once again the shadow of disapproval is evoked (the striptease as site of female exploitation), only instantly to be dismissed as belonging to the past, to a time when feminists used to object to such imagery. To make such an objection nowadays would run the risk of ridicule. Objection is pre-empted with irony. In each of these cases a spectre of feminism is invoked so that it might be undone. For male viewers tradition is restored or as Beck puts it there is 'constructed certitude', while for the girls what is proposed is a movement beyond feminism, to a more comfortable zone where women are now free to choose for themselves (Beck 1992).

Feminism undone?

If we turn attention to some of the participatory dynamics in leisure and everyday life that see young women endorse (or else refuse to condemn) the ironic normalisation of pornography, where they indicate their approval of and desire to be 'pin-up girls' for the centrefolds of the soft-porn 'lad mags', where it is not at all unusual to pass young women in the street wearing T-shirts bearing phrases such as 'Porn Queen' or 'Pay To Touch' across the breasts, and where in the UK at least young women quite happily attend lap-dancing clubs (perhaps as a test of their sophistication and 'cool'), we are witness to a hyper-culture of commercial sexuality, one aspect of which is the repudiation of a feminism invoked only to be summarily dismissed (see also Gill 2003). As a mark of a post-feminist identity, young women journalists refuse to condemn the enormous growth of lap-dancing clubs. They know of the existence of the feminist critiques and debates (or at least this is my claim) through their education; as Shelley Budgeon has described the girls in her study, they are gender aware (Budgeon 2001). Thus the new female subject is, despite her freedom, called upon to be silent, to withhold critique in order to count as a modern sophisticated girl. Indeed this withholding of critique is a condition of her freedom. There is quietude and complicity in the manners of generationally specific notions of cool, and, more precisely, an uncritical relation to dominant commercially produced sexual representations that actively invoke hostility to assumed feminist positions from the past, in order to endorse a new regime of sexual meanings based on female consent, equality, participation and pleasure, free of politics.[3]

Female individualisation

By using the term female individualisation I am explicitly drawing on the concept of individualisation that is discussed at length by sociologists including Giddens (1991), Beck and Beck-Gernsheim (2002) as well as Zygmunt Bauman (2000, 2001). This work is to be distinguished from the more directly Foucauldian version found in the work of Nikolas Rose (2000). Although there is some shared ground between these authors, in so far as they all reflect on the expectations that individuals now avidly 'self-monitor' and that there appears to be greater capacity on the part of individuals to plan 'a life of one's own', there are also divergences. Beck and Giddens are less concerned with the effectivity of power in this new friendly guise as 'personal adviser', and instead emphasise the enlargement of freedom and choice, while in contrast Rose sees these modes of self-government as marking out 'the shaping of being', and thus the 'inculcation of a form of life' (Rose 2000). Bauman bewails the sheer unviability of naked individualisation as the resources of sociality (and welfare) are stripped away, leaving the individual to self-blame when success eludes him or her. (It is also possible to draw a political line between these authors, with Bauman and Rose to the left, and Giddens and Beck 'beyond left and right'.)[4] My emphasis here is on the work of Giddens and Beck, for the very reason that it appears to speak directly to the post-feminist generation. In their writing there are only distant echoes (if that) of the feminist struggles that were required to produce the newfound freedoms of young women in the West. There is little trace of the battles fought, of the power struggles embarked upon, or of the enduring inequities that still mark out the relations between men and women. All of this is airbrushed out of existence on the basis that, as they claim, 'emancipatory politics' has given way instead to life politics (or in Beck's terms the sub-politics of single-interest groups).

Both of these authors provide a sociological account of the dynamics of social change understood as 'reflexive modernisation'. The earlier period of modernisation ('first modernity') created a Welfare State and institutions, such as the education system, that allowed people in the 'second modernity' to become more independent and able for example to earn their own living. Young women are as a result now 'disembedded' from communities where gender roles were fixed. And, as the old structures of social class fade away, and lose their grip in the context of 'late' or 'second modernity', individuals are increasingly called upon to invent their own structures. They must do this internally and individualistically, so that self-monitoring practices (the diary, the life plan, the career pathway) replace reliance on set ways and structured pathways. Self-help guides, personal advisers, lifestyle coaches and gurus, and all sorts of self-improvement TV programmes provide the cultural means by which individualisation operates as a social process. As the overwhelming force of structure fades, so also, it is claimed, does the capacity for agency increase.

Individuals must now choose the kind of life they want to live. Girls must have a life plan. They must become more reflexive in regard to every aspect of their lives, from making the right choice in marriage, to taking responsibility for their own working lives and not being dependent on a job for life or on the stable and reliable operations of a large-scale bureaucracy, which in the past would have allocated its employees specific, and possibly unchanging, roles. Beck and Giddens each place a different inflection on their accounts of reflexive modernisation, and these arguments appear to fit very directly with the kinds of scenarios and dilemmas facing the young women characters in the narratives of contemporary popular culture (especially so-called chick lit). There is also a real evasion in this writing of the ongoing existence of deep and pernicious gender inequities (most manifest for older women of all social backgrounds but also for young black or Asian women, and also for young working-class women). Beck and Giddens are quite inattentive to the regulative dimensions of the popular discourses of personal choice and self-improvement. Choice is surely, within lifestyle culture, a modality of constraint. The individual is compelled to be the kind of subject who can make the right choices. By these means new lines and demarcations are drawn between those subjects who are judged responsive to the regime of personal responsibility, and those who fail miserably. Neither Giddens nor Beck mount a substantial critique of these power relations that work so effectively at the level of embodiment. They have no grasp that these are productive of new realms of injury and injustice.

Bridget Jones

The film *Bridget Jones's Diary* (an international box office success) draws together so many of these sociological themes it could almost have been scripted by Anthony Giddens himself. Aged thirty, living and working in London, Bridget is a free agent, single and childless, and able to enjoy herself in pubs, bars and restaurants. She is the product of modernity in that she has benefited from those institutions that have loosened the ties of tradition and community for women, making it possible for them to be 'disembedded' and to relocate to the city to earn an independent living without shame or danger. However, this also gives rise to new anxieties. There is the fear of loneliness for example, the stigma of remaining single and the risks and uncertainties of not finding the right partner to be a father to children, as well as a husband. In the film, the opening sequence shows Bridget in her pyjamas worrying about being alone and on the shelf. The soundtrack is 'All by Myself' by Jamie O'Neal and the audience laughs along with her, in this moment of self-doubt. We immediately know that what she is thinking is 'What will it be like if I never find the right man, if I never get married?' Bridget portrays the whole spectrum of attributes associated with the self-monitoring subject: she confides in her friends, she keeps a diary, she endlessly reflects on her fluctuating weight noting her calorie intake she plans, plots and has projects. She is also deeply uncertain as to what the future holds for her. Despite the choices she has, there are also any number of risks of which she is regularly reminded; the risk that she might let the right man slip from under her nose (hence she must always be on the lookout), the risk that not catching a man at the right time might mean she misses the chance of having children (her biological clock is ticking), there is also the risk that, partnerless, she will be isolated, marginalised from the world of happy couples. Now there is only the self to blame if the right partner is not found.

With the burden of self-management so apparent, Bridget fantasies about very traditional forms of happiness and fulfilment. After a flirtatious encounter with her boss (played by Hugh Grant) she imagines herself in a white wedding dress surrounded by bridesmaids, and the audience laughs loudly because they, like Bridget, know that this is not how young women these days are meant to think. Feminism has intervened to constrain these kinds of conventional desires. It is, then, a relief to escape this censorious politics and freely enjoy that which has been disapproved of. Thus feminism is only invoked in order to be relegated to the past. But this is not simply a return to the past; there are, of course, quite dramatic differences between the various female characters of current popular culture from Bridget Jones to the 'girls' in Sex and the City and to Ally McBeal, and those found in girls' and women's magazines from a pre-feminist era. The new young women are confident enough to declare their anxieties about possible failure in regard to finding a husband, they avoid any aggressive or overtly traditional men, and they brazenly enjoy their sexuality, without fear of the sexual double standard. In addition they are more than capable of earning their own living, and the degree of suffering or shame they anticipate in the absence of finding a husband is countered by sexual self-confidence. Being without a husband does not mean they will go without men.

With such light entertainment as this, suffused with irony and dedicated to reinventing highly successful women's genres of film and TV, an argument about feminism being so repudiated might seem heavy handed. These are hardly rabid antifeminist tracts. But relations of power are indeed made and remade within texts of enjoyment and rituals of relaxation and abandonment. These young women's genres are vital to the construction of a new 'gender regime', based on the double entanglement that I have described. They endorse wholeheartedly what Rose calls 'this ethic of freedom', and young women have come to the fore as the pre-eminent subjects of this new ethic. These popular texts normalise post-feminist gender anxieties so as to re-regulate young women by means of the language of personal choice. But even 'well-regulated liberty' can backfire (the source of comic effect), and this in turn gives rise to demarcated pathologies (leaving it too late to have a baby, failing to find a good catch, etc.) that carefully define the parameters of what constitutes liveable lives for young women without the occasion of reinvented feminism.

Notes

1   Bridget Jones's Diary appeared first as a weekly column in the UK *Independent* newspaper in 1996; its author Helen Fielding then published the diaries in book form, and the film *Bridget Jones's Diary*, directed by Sharon McGuire, opened in 2001. The sequel *Bridget Jones: The Edge of Reason*, directed by Beeban Kidron, opened in November 2004.

2   The *Daily Mail* has the highest volume of female readers of all daily newspapers in the UK. Its most frequent efforts in regard to promoting a post-feminist sensibility involve commissioning well-known former feminists to recant, and blame feminism for contemporary ills among women. For example Saturday 23 August 2003 had Fay Weldon on 'Look What We've Done'. The caption then reads, 'For years feminists campaigned for sexual liberation. But here, one of their leaders admits all they have created is a new generation of women for whom sex is utterly joyless and hollow', pp 12–13.

3   By the normalisation of porn, or 'ironic pornography', I am referring to the new popular mainstreaming of what in the past would have been soft-core pornography out of reach of the young on the 'top shelf'. In a post AIDS era, with sexual frankness as an imperative for prevention, the commercial UK youth media now produce vast quantities of explicit sexual material for the teenage audience; in recent years and as a strategy for being ahead of the competition this has been incorporated into the language of 'cool'. With irony as a trademark of knowingness sexual cool entails 'being up for it' without revealing any misgivings, never mind criticism, on the basis of the distance entailed in the ironic experience.

4   Anthony Giddens is the architect of the Third Way politics that were embraced by New Labour in its first term of office, and this writing in turn drew on his earlier work titled *Beyond Left and Right* (Giddens 1995, 1998). Likewise Ulrich Beck was connected with the *Neue Mitte* in Germany, though the German 'Third Way' had rather less success than its UK counterpart.

References

Arnot, M., David, M. and Weiner, G. (1999) *Closing the Gender Gap*, Cambridge: Polity Press.

Bauman, Z. (2000) *Liquid Modernity*, Cambridge: Polity Press.

—— (2001) *The Individualised Society*, Cambridge: Polity Press.

Beck, U. (1992) *Risk Society*, London: Sage.

Beck, U. and Beck-Gernsheim, E. (2001) *Individualisation*, Cambridge: Polity Press.

Beck, U., Giddens A. and Lash S. (1994) *Reflexive Modernization*, Cambridge: Polity Press.

Brown, W. (1997) 'The impossibility of women's studies', *Differences: A Journal of Feminist Cultural Studies* 9: 79–102.

Brunsdon, C. (1997) *Screen Tastes: Soap Opera to Satellite Dishes*, London: Routledge.

—— (2005) 'Feminism, post-feminism: Martha, Martha, and Nigella', *Cinema Journal* 44(2): 110–116.

Budgeon, S. (2001) 'Emergent feminist identities', *European Journal of Women's Studies* 8(1): 7–28.

Butler, J. (1990) *Gender Trouble*, New York: Routledge.

—— (1992) 'Contingent foundations: feminism and the question of postmodernism', in J. Butler and J.W. Scott (eds) *Feminists Theorise the Political*, New York: Routledge.

—— (1993) *Bodies That Matter*, New York: Routledge.

—— (2000) *Antigone's Claim: Kinship between Life and Death*, New York: Columbia University Press.

Butler, J., Laclau, E. and Zizek, S. (2000) *Contingency, Hegemony and Universality*, London: Verso.

Coward, R. (1984) *Female Desire*, London: Paladin.

De Lauretis, T. (1988) *Technologies of Gender: Essays on Theory, Film and Fiction*, Indianapolis: Indiana University Press.

Faludi, S. (1992) *Backlash: The Undeclared War against Women*, London: Vintage.

Giddens, A. (1991) *Modernity and Self Identity*, Cambridge: Polity Press.

—— (1995) *Beyond Left and Right*, Cambridge: Polity Press.

—— (1998) *The Third Way*, Cambridge: Polity Press.

Gill, R. (2003) 'From sexual objectification to sexual subjectification: the resexualisation of women's bodies in the media', *Feminist Media Studies* 3(1): 100–6.

Hall, S. (1989) *The Hard Road to Renewal*, London: Verso.

Haraway, D. (1991) *Simians, Cyborgs and Women*, London: Free Association Books.

Harris, A. (2003) *Future Girl*, New York and London: Routledge.

McRobbie, A. (1994) *Postmodernism and Popular Culture*, London: Routledge.

—— (1999a) *In the Culture Society*, London: Routledge.

—— (1999b) 'Feminism v the TV blondes', inaugural lecture, Goldsmiths College, University of London.

—— (2003) 'Mothers and fathers. Who needs them? A review essay of Butler's *Antigone*', *Feminist Review* 73, autumn: 129–36.

Mohanty, C.T. (1995) 'Under Western eyes', in B. Ashcroft, G. Griffiths and H. Tiffin (eds) *The Post-Colonial Studies Reader*, London: Routledge.

Mulvey, L. (1975) 'Visual pleasure and narrative cinema', *Screen* 16(3): 6–18.

Rose, N. (2000) *Powers of Freedom*, Cambridge: Cambridge University Press.

Spivak, G. (1999) *A Critique of Postcolonial Reason*, Cambridge, MA: Harvard University Press.

Stuart, A. (1990) 'Feminism: dead or alive?' in J. Rutherford (ed.) *Identity*, London: Lawrence & Wishart.

Trinh, T.M. (1989) *Women Native Other*, Bloomington: Indiana University Press.

Williamson, J. (1987) *Decoding Advertisements*, London: Marion Boyars.

Section II

Media, community and dialogue

In his chapter, Arvind Rajagopal addresses the transformations of questions of community, boundary and identity wrought within the USA by the events of 11 September 2001 in New York and the role of the media (and especially channels such as Fox News) in that process. Here we see the necessity, globalisation notwithstanding, for a continuing consideration of the role of national media and their articulation with questions of international politics and communications. If euphoric arguments were dominant only until recently, in which we were assured that peace and prosperity would result from globalisation, today terrorism and the spectre of Islamic fundamentalism signal a new era of US foreign policy unilateralism. This also portends diminished domestic civil liberties, which we see reflected in demands for a 'strong state', and suspicion, not affirmation, of cosmopolitanism. Rajagopal argues that if world-wide communication was never more intensive, the gulfs in understanding have seldom appeared so deep. He further argues that our understanding of the links between culture, politics and technology remain too limited – not least in assuming that free and easy social interchange will emerge spontaneously from new communication networks across a borderless world. The September 11 attacks, staged as a media spectacle, place a question mark against all such utopias, and their troubling aftermath thus provides for Rajagopal an opportunity to re-examine these optimistic preconceptions. The chapter focuses particularly on how the USA's internal Others become central to such an inquiry, as racial or national 'outsiders' whose presence (and status) within the borders of the USA now comes, increasingly, to be seen as problematic by the guardians of Homeland Security. Here, like Phil Cole (1998) in the UK, Rajagopal rightly insists on the linkages between foreign and domestic policies, and on their complex ramifications for questions of citizenship, race relations and immigration policy – matters that are highlighted by his account of the racist forms of abuse and harassment that he and many non-white Others have experienced in the period following the attacks on New York.

Kevin Robins's and Asu Aksoy's chapter looks at the development of transnational media systems and argues that these recent developments constitute a fundamental challenge to an imagination of culture and community predicated on the existence of a set of juxtaposed national spaces and media cultures. The new media space of transnational cultures is now a far more complex matter, with all kinds of new media networks layered across the old space of the national. Robins and Aksoy are concerned with exactly what kind of difference the presence of transnational broadcasting makes to the lives of migrants. In this respect they are critical of the established theoretical framework of diasporic media studies which, they claim, is still mainly caught up in a 'national mentality' in its focus on questions of displacement, belonging and nostalgia for a lost homeland. Centrally, they argue, such perspectives reduce migrants to the status of mere ciphers of the ethnicity to which they are supposed to 'belong' (cf. Harindrath's (2003) critique of Liebes and Katz (1991) for 'reducing' their respondents to their ethnicity). Robins and Aksoy attempt to explore what they call a 'new dynamics' of the management of both geographical and cultural distance in the lives of the Turkish migrants in London whom they have studied. For them, it is important to build a new theoretical framework capable of transcending the old boundaries of ethnic and racial identities – and, in this respect, they argue that we have much to learn by paying attention to the way in which his respondents discuss their own ambivalences about such matters.

Again, the concerns of these authors are closely linked, while different in focus and emphasis. If for Rajagopal the power of ascribed identities (especially in matters of race and ethnicity) is to the fore, Robins's and Aksoy's focus is on the internal dynamics and ambivalences of self-identity construction. While they are concerned with the need to transcend a merely national imagination, Rajagopal focuses on the dynamics of a situation where some who might previously have aspired to just such a form of recognition and 'national belonging' are suddenly excluded from its remit.

Gareth Stanton is also concerned with questions of identity and community. His approach is broadly anthropological and addresses questions of culture, globalisation and transnationalism – and their relation to issues of locality and belonging – not as abstract processes, but in their concrete particularity, as they are articulated at given moments and in particular geographies. Influenced not only by contemporary debates in transnational anthropology – such as those instigated by Arjun Appadurai's (1996) discussion of the flows of 'mediascapes' and 'ethnoscapes' – but also by the older traditions of the Mass Observation movement in the UK, with its commitment to the detailed scrutiny of patterns of everyday life, his chapter offers a detailed ethnographic study of urban complexity and community dynamics at 'ground level' in a particular (and increasingly multicultural) area. Like Rajagopal and Robins, he too is concerned with questions of 'community talk' (and with its complexities and dangers) with considerations of the 'value of place' and of the 'longing for community'. His perspective is, as he puts it, on 'the world seen through the prism of South London'. He offers a multidimensional portrait of the area he studies that attends not only to the forms of its media representation (notably in the BBC's long-running comedy series *Only Fools and Horses*, which was set in the area Stanton analyses) but also to the institutional history of community-building initiatives in the area, and to the prosaic patterns of local memory. As he addresses the modalities in which global flows are now transforming not only the buildings and the food markets, but also the churches of his chosen area, he demonstrates the necessity to move 'beyond the binding terms of collective identity' to address questions of community in all its multiple (and multiplying) senses. The question for Stanton is how to define a place not by its fixed and 'originary' constituent elements, but, rather, in terms of the flows of people, goods and cultures that pass through and meet in it.

John Durham Peters takes as his starting point the striking conundrum that in both contemporary social theory and media studies, where so little is agreed upon, almost everyone loves conversation. Indeed, one could argue that in recent debates, both academic and popular, about citizenship and the democratic role of the media, it is hard to avoid the notion. Thinkers at all wavelengths of the political and intellectual spectrum find something to value in conversation – if only in horror at its absence. The normative ideal of communication has, in fact, become that of participatory, interactive, and authentic conversation. His chapter examines various visions of the relationship of media and conversation – media as conversation, media without conversation and conversation as media – in hopes of dislodging the reigning vague consensus on conversation as an essential Good. His analysis ties these visions back to their theoretical roots and attempts to give a synoptic vision of the key issues surrounding this central concept. Thus, he points out that dialogic forms of interaction, contra the presumptions of much media theory (from Brecht (1932) and Enzensberger (1976) to the proselytisers of the 'new'/interactive media) are not necessarily the best form of communication for all purposes (a point that also resonates with Des Freedman's later critique of the contemporary forms of 'new'/interactive media hype). In yet another of his trenchant critiques of current intellectual fashions, Peters also questions the assumptions of the populist defenders of media 'talk shows' that the forms of 'personalisation' of issues that generally accompany their 'conversationalisation' are necessarily to be always preferred to more formal discourses. Here, again, like a number of other authors in the book (see the chapters by Schwarz and Robins) Peters also maps his position in relation to that advocated so influentially by Paddy Scannell (1996) while nonetheless also critiquing the limits of Scannell's tribute to the conversationalisation of British broadcasting.

References

Appadurai, A. (1996) *Modernity at Large*, Minneapolis: University of Minnesota Press.
Brecht, B. (1932) 'Theory of radio', in *Gesammelte Werke* Band VIII.
Cole, P. (1998) 'The limits of inclusion', *Soundings* 10.

Enzensberger, H.M. (1976) 'Constituents of a theory of the media', in *Raids and Reconstructions*, London: Pluto Press.

Harindrath, R. (2003) 'Reviving cultural imperialism', in L. Parks and S. Kumar (eds) *Planet TV*, New York: New York University Press.

Liebes, T. and Katz, E. (1991) *The Export of Meaning: Cross-Cultural Readings of Dallas*, Oxford: Oxford University Press.

Scannell, P. (1996) *Radio, Television and Modern Life*, Oxford: Blackwell.

Chapter 5

A nation and its immigration
The USA after September 11[1]

Arvind Rajagopal

Frank Roque, when arrested after killing a Sikh gas station attendant in Phoenix, Arizona: 'I'm an American! I'm a damn American all the way! Arrest me! Let those terrorists run wild!'

(Kaur 2002)

As Amrik Singh Chawla fled the collapsing towers on September 11 along with thousands of others, some men began to chase him, shouting. 'Take off that turban, you Arab.' [Chawla is a Manhattan financial consultant who grew up in Brooklyn, is Sikh and wears a turban.]

(ibid.)

When asked if he had decided if anyone of the detainees should be subject to a military tribunal, Bush replied, 'I excluded any Americans.' The questioner pointed out that he meant to ask about the captives in Guantanamo Bay, but Bush revealed he was thinking about people like John Walker Lindh.

(Monbiot 2002)

Media studies and invisible nationalism in the USA

The historian Isaac Deutscher once pointed out that a nation's foreign policy must always be seen as continuous with its domestic policy, and not as a separate entity as often assumed. Such a view has not in the past found favor in the USA, perhaps with reason. Those who are conservative on social and economic issues at home may oppose intervention abroad (e.g. former presidential candidate Patrick Buchanan), while self-described liberals may be more ambivalent. Labor support for US intervention abroad and the question of Palestine are other issues that divide liberals and the left in matters of US policy abroad.

The combination of a war on terror abroad and at home, however, has dramatized the fact that domestic and foreign affairs are nevertheless closely linked. In its immigration policy and in cultural attitudes to foreigners, the two domains of US politics telescope into each other. In this paper I will point to some of the effects of September 11 on immigrants to help illuminate the cultural form of US nationalism, and the effects it has. The character of US nationalism is something that for historical reasons appears difficult to examine dispassionately; it tends either to be endorsed, condemned, or, most often, excluded altogether from consideration (Rajagopal 2004).

Discussions of US media coverage can be clarified, however, by bringing in the issue of nationalism, since it is the over-arching frame within which news stories relating to national security are shaped. Unfortunately analysis of media coverage has been state-centric for the most part, focusing on war and terrorism, on violence by and against the US state in short. That is, the events have been treated along the lines of foreign news, where the media invariably follow the lead of the State Department and the Pentagon (see, for example, Gans 1979; Hallin 1989; on post-September 11 media coverage see Zelizer and Allan 2002).

Accordingly, critical commentary on the work of the news media has tended to focus on the sources of support for US policy, e.g. on channels like Fox News. Fox News is only the most prominent instance of a new kind of candor dawning on the news media, proving that the avowal of neutrality in the news is not a constraint. To the contrary, abandoning it for national chauvinism helps increase audiences. The extent of the effect of such reporting is becoming clear.

Polls suggest that over 60 percent of Americans held at least one of three mistaken impressions about the recent war in Iraq, contributing to much of the popular support for the war. These impressions were as follows: they believed that US forces found weapons of mass destruction in Iraq; that Saddam Hussein helped in the attacks on September 11; and, finally, that other nations either backed the US-led war or were evenly split between supporting and opposing it. In fact, no weapons of mass destruction were found in Iraq; there is no clear evidence that Saddam was involved in the September 11 attack of 2001; and large majorities opposed the war in most countries (as seen for instance in Gallup polls). Eighty percent of those who relied on Fox News had such misperceptions, compared to 71 percent of those who said they relied on CBS News; the comparable figures were 47 percent for those who said they relied most on newspapers and magazines, and 23 percent for those who said they relied on PBS or National Public Radio.[2]

This is not simply a problem of biased media. If there were not a prior receptivity, such reports could not proliferate. Indeed, Fox News congratulates itself on discovering an immense audience for 'patriotism' that it has now brought to the attention of other news media. I suggest that it is not useful simply to condemn the resulting news coverage. Even if Fox News is aberrant, it may reflect aspects of national culture that call for dispassionate inquiry, e.g. as to why such treatment finds such wide support. Even critical scholarship on news coverage after September 11, however, has tended to respect certain tacit boundaries of interrogation, as a result of which nationalist sentiment within the USA has not come properly into focus as a subject requiring understanding.

Cokie Roberts, a well-known commentator on National Public Radio, was asked on air whether there had been domestic reaction against the bombing in Afghanistan. She replied, 'None that mattered' (cited in McChesney 2002). Critics of pro-US media coverage have frequently described such coverage as 'patriotic' or at times 'jingoistic'. This represents an interesting choice of term, and a tacit avoidance of the issue of nationalism. For instance, James Carey admiringly cites 'a courageous essay' by Joan Konner that regretted the curtain of prescribed patriotism that descended over the media at this time (Carey 2002: 88).

Eric Hobsbawm has pointed out that the two terms, patriotism and nationalism, are distinct and not to be confused with each other. Patriotism refers to the sentiment subjects have for king and country, which may carry over to the modern state; *nationalism refers to people's relationship with each other,* one that may or may not be emblematized in a party or state (Hobsbawm 1993). It is not simply the presence or absence of pro-state sentiment, then, that is the issue, but a matter of how individuals perceive and accommodate their differences with each other. Nationalism arises in the age of democracy, and is a republican political formation, characterized by horizontal ties of citizenship rather than the more vertical links of traditional hierarchy. Routinely, however, this issue was obscured by assertions or denunciations of the need for 'loyalty'. Debates on the news following the attacks centered on the eclipse of irony and the re-emergence of a positive, committed journalism, one that even critical scholars welcomed (see for example Rosen 2002; Schudson 2002). In the mean time, thousands of foreigners and/or immigrants were being arrested and detained without charges. Many of them were denied legal representation and deported summarily. There was widespread criticism of such abuses of civil liberties, but such events fell into the category of local or domestic news, and, except in marginal commentary, could not be seen as tied to the nationalist politics being pursued abroad. In fact, nationalism was seen as exclusive to foreign affairs; within the USA, there were only decent people and bigots.

It was instructive to witness reactions to the events of September 11 when they occurred. I live in New York, and watched the World Trade Center towers fall down that morning, in a crowd on the corner of Franklin Street and West Broadway not far from what is now called Ground Zero. The scene of destruction was a riveting one. People were jumping to their deaths from above as the buildings were aflame and, when the towers came down, the clouds of smoke were barreling through the canyon-like streets. None of us could have felt entirely secure. One man was sobbing into his cell phone, 'I was supposed to be on that @#$%ing building!' Several people were weeping, and they became a magnet for attention, perhaps expressing what others could not, or reflecting what others had not experienced. Two gentlemen in suits were talking, speculating on what road they could use to exit Manhattan. I tried to join the conversation, asking about the viability of another route. But with my entry, the topic changed. 'It must have been bin Laden who did it,' one of them said, looking at me to see if I would confirm or deny this idea. I was caught off-guard and had no idea what to say. I was not clear why he thought I would have any information on the subject.

Here was a delicate reflection of a response to the disaster. My foreignness became the pivot of the interaction, and a familiar enemy was being sought. I had posed one question, and the man had, effectively, responded with another, reflecting his own deeper concerns. When I shared this story with some friends, they thought I was reading too much into it, and perhaps I was. But in the days that followed, the search for foreigners to blame began to be carried on at all levels of society.[3]

The War on Terror at home after September 11

As mentioned above, the civil rights of hundreds of immigrants held after September 11 were violated; there was 'a pattern of physical and verbal abuse' at a federal prison where 84 of them were held, according to a report issued by the Office of the Inspector General in the Justice Department. Citizens of more than 20 countries were among the 762 detainees surveyed. The inquiry focused on two detention facilities that housed the majority of the detainees. In each case, immigration laws had been violated in some way, the report found. No bail was allowed for 'terrorism suspects', who remained in jail for an average of three months. In addition, detainees faced overwhelming difficulties and weeks of delay before they were allowed to make phone calls and find lawyers. Some were kept for months in cells where the light was kept on 24 hours a day, and were escorted in handcuffs, leg irons, and waist chains. Some detainees in one Brooklyn detention facility reported that they were slammed against walls and taunted by guards, reports that inspectors found plausible (Fainaru 2002). The Justice Department issued a public notice asking undocumented immigrants to register without fear of being deported, and proceeded to use that information to find people to deport. More than 80,000 were registered, and more than 13,000 of them subsequently faced deportation proceedings. In addition, many thousands of people of 'Arab' origin were summoned by the US Attorney General for investigation (Swains 2003). South Asians for their part discovered that the boundary between the Middle East and South Asia, which during centuries past had been porous, once again became an open border, at least in the USA. Hundreds of physical and verbal attacks against South Asians were reported in the following months, according to the Asian American Legal Defense and Education Fund (2003). Pakistanis in fact comprised more than twice the number of federal detainees from any other country, and scores of them were deported, causing them to leave their families behind. It was difficult to avoid the conclusion that race, religion, and nationality were all involved in the targeting of foreigners, however erratic the assault.

This suggests that, however important each of these categories may be individually, none of them is by itself sufficient to understand how boundaries are redrawn between Americans and others in the domestic context. Taken together, however, these terms comprise a general sense of foreignness that marks each of the encounters noted above.

Foreigners and the open society

Although there is an extensive scholarly literature on immigration, the problem addressed is typically that of assimilation, using the figure of a melting-pot society as both description and norm. US race relations have dominated the discussions, with the black–white polarity structuring the patterns of assimilation. Over the past two centuries, new immigrants, especially those from outside Northern and Western Europe, when they entered the USA, have been positioned closer to blacks than to whites. Their struggle for acceptance over the years has been, in effect, a matter of winning the right to be treated as white. African Americans have not had this privilege, of course, and their battles to make room for racial difference is one of the more important challenges to pre-existing forms of US national identity. In the wake of September 11, however, we are reminded that the foreigner is in fact an empty category within which race, religion, and national difference may figure singly or together, and points to a strange ambivalence in a nation that prides itself as being built by immigrants. What aspects of US history and culture might illuminate this ambivalence?

The USA considers itself to represent the future of the world. Such a self-image is no mere flight of fancy. Enlightenment thinkers saw the USA as a new world where society could be imagined anew without impediments inherited from the *ancien régime*. Part of the USA's identity is that it is an open society, exemplified by its embrace of immigrants as the makers of the USA.

The root of nation is *natio*, to be born; even where nationality is technically open, the word imputes a common birth to its claimants. But in the USA this meant something like a political birth, accepting a set of values about citizenship and government. It is worth recalling that the USA is the first post-revolutionary nation. (The American Revolution occurred before the French one, and, what's more, the USA did not lapse into monarchy thereafter.) As such, there is a widespread consciousness about the politically formed character of the society. In few other nations is the Constitution so widely invoked, or constitutional rights so broadly asserted, with the idea of politics at the center of its normative structure. This points to its vulnerability to the kind of centralized power and despotism that Alexis de Tocqueville warned of. But it also illuminates the rapidity with which some previously central aspects have changed, stimulated by a combination of social movements and legislation. Thus, for instance, civil rights effected a sea change in race relations over a remarkably short period of time. My purpose is neither to idealize what was achieved, nor to diminish the magnitude of the problems that remain. It is rather to underline the unusual rapidity with which habitual race discrimination was diminished, in many cases quite sharply. This indicates, I suggest, the political character of US society. This should be recalled when we are tempted to make assertions about US society as having fixed tendencies of one kind or another.

There are other countries equally or more reliant on immigrants. Bonnie Honig points out, in her important book, *Democracy and the Foreigner* (2001), that the way in which the USA has tackled the question of the immigrant-foreigner is deeply revealing of its own enduring forms of nationalism. Canada, for instance, is as much of a new nation, as dependent on inflows of people from the old world, with immigrant quotas as large or larger. Immigrants and the idea of open borders or a melting pot do not form a significant part of Canadian national self-fashioning, however, although it is arguably a liberal polity. To take another example, about 20 percent of people living in France have at least one parent or grandparent of immigrant origin. If great-grandparents and foreign-born are included, the total is nearly one-third of the population of France. But certainly in relation to the USA, immigration plays little part in French national identity, quite the contrary. To take one example, while Ellis Island has become a national monument, the place where immigrants in the nineteenth century used to arrive in France has been razed (Noiriel 1995). (French openness to immigrants, to the extent it exists, perhaps works more through more cultural registers of Frenchness, e.g. language acquisition and use.)

In the USA today, census estimates of foreign-born residents as a fraction of the US population show that from a high of 14.7 percent in 1910, the figure declined steadily over the century, reaching 4.8 percent by 1970. Since then, the figure has climbed steeply, and is now 32.5 million as of March 2002, or 11.5 percent of the population. Over half of these are Latin American; Europe accounts for 14 percent and 'Asia' for 25.5 percent (United States Bureau of Census 1994, 2002). For the bulk of the twentieth century, therefore, first-generation immigrants have actually been relatively scarce, as a result of anti-immigrant legislation.[4] I suggest that in fact it is not the objective presence of immigrants that leads the USA to include them so prominently in its national mythology. Rather it reflects a specific way in which national identity is expressed in the USA. The centrality of the immigrant mirrors the extent to which the normative view of US society is one that emphasizes voluntarism and rational consent, rather than the historical events it has experienced. More precisely, rational consent itself is seen to be the dominant historical force, although of course there are other aspects of national history, including slavery, territorial expansion, wars of conquest, and, lately, superpower status, which complicate an emphasis on the acceptance of immigrants as exemplary of US values.[5]

The Puritan founding of the USA is often described as an act of immigrants, but their Puritanism was arguably more important than their immigrant identity at that time; their sense of religious mission, and their divinely sanctioned purpose of founding a new Israel, defined their actions to a much greater extent. These original European immigrants, moreover, assumed privileges before they were granted rights, and this unauthorized act informed the political philosophy underpinning the founding of the USA: the Puritans did not seek the permission of the Crown before settling in the New World; that came a few decades later, with Sir Walter Ralegh's charter to settle in Virginia.

Honig argues that there are three ways in which the 'foreigner as immigrant' functions in the USA as mechanisms for restoring vitality to the nation, and returning it to its founding principles, as it were. Immigrants may be seen as hard-working, frugal, still unspoiled by US affluence, and bringing a kind of yeoman spirit to an age when self-sacrifice has become rare – this might be seen as a kind of neo-Protestant ethic, rejuvenating the tired spirit of US capitalism. Second, the foreigner may be seen as a bulwark against the dissolution of family and community relationships, bringing, as he or she tends to, relatively large kin networks and older ideas about solidarity and belonging – and thus reduce the alienating impact of mobile capital, with its tendency to take jobs away from localities, and destroy existing communities. The more patriarchal character of immigrant cultures is seen to provide anchorage for a more wholesome and conservative value system.

Finally, liberal theorists see the consent proffered by immigrants as renewing the meaning of their own consent to US democracy. Here we have a vision of the polity at work that is informed by a republican view of politics, where, unless the willed consent and participation of citizens is rendered meaningful, democracy turns into an empty ritual, and at worst into despotism. Since in a large institutionalized polity, this is not possible, immigrant participation in society becomes the compensation for what otherwise cannot happen – we can say that the problem of consent is displaced onto foreigners and their mode of acceptance of/assimilation into the USA. Rendering foreigners into exemplary Americans puts a burden on them that they never bargained for, of course. They are required to enact the proof of civic responsibility from which ordinary Americans tend to be exonerated. This, at any rate, is the risk faced by such a model of national identity, which requires the immigrant foreigner to confirm the truth of national myths. In effect, when immigrants are good, they're very good, but when they're bad, they're better – better, that is, as a way of affirming the boundaries of US culture. The condition of the dominant society's interaction with immigrants is that the latter are a magic mirror, turning the image of the USA into a flattering picture. Should such a reflection fail to appear, it is not reality but the reflecting surface itself, the immigrant, who is deemed to be at fault.

Immigrants are expected to work hard and mind their own business, and show themselves to be models of civic and communitarian virtue in this way. But when things go wrong, and they reveal themselves to be out of touch with US sensibilities during a moment of crisis, they tend to be criticized for their failure to assimilate, for disregarding their public duties, and ignoring their responsibility to the larger community. This is a criticism being made about Muslim communities, for instance, often both from within and without these communities. Immigrants thus tend to get caught in a catch-22. It is precisely by virtue of being insulated from the larger, often fragmented and anomic society that they are able to survive, and to display their exemplary immigrant virtues. They are not necessarily able to slide into the larger established community, nor are they always invited to do so. They often constitute a material basis for mainstream society's ideals of civic virtue, but they achieve this at the price of *de facto* exclusion from mainstream society.

Ali Behdad has argued that, in fact, the way in which immigrants are identified is constitutively ambivalent in the USA, and that this ambivalence structures the performative space of US nationality, providing a set of strategies for disciplining and domesticating alien bodies in an uncertain process of naturalization (Behdad 1997). This ambivalence reflects the simultaneous xenophobia and xenophilia, as Behdad argues, of US attitudes to immigrants. Seen in a larger frame, the distinction between insiders and outsiders is based on a shifting set of registers, whether race, religion, nationality, or some combination of these terms, owing to circumstances that are external as well as internal and domestic. Here we return to the issue of empire (interestingly, a word that, together with imperialism, is not discussed in Honig's book).

A new kind of empire

The term 'empire' is increasingly applied to the USA, either as description, critique, or prescription (see for example Ferguson 2003; O'Brien and Clesse 2002). The invocation of this term has increased, citing a new post-Cold War geopolitical dispensation, one that has replaced the contest of superpowers with a single hyperpower. Empire was by no means a theme of political power in any consistent sense from the time of Puritan settlement; isolationism and republicanism were themes of early US debate alongside the assertion of US power. But democratic ideals of self-determination were repeatedly used as justification for asserting US hegemony, as for instance with the Monroe Doctrine, or with manifest destiny.[6] The obsolescence of the Monroe Doctrine after the First World War corresponded to the USA seeing a global rather than a merely hemispheric role for itself. Today, with the increase in media and migration, and with new political artifacts such as dual citizenship and hyphenated nationalities growing, empire is both more public and more contested than those that preceded it. The extent to which its operations tend to be subsumed under the general term 'globalization' indicates a blurring of the question.

To raise the topic of empire underlines that we cannot retain the fiction of a single national community attempting to negotiate its internal conflicts. Simultaneously, what is at issue is the terms of accommodation between the USA and foreign nations, and the attitudes of citizens to the maintenance of a different set of political standards, under a new and revised 'rule of colonial difference'.

The assertion of empire should not lead us to assume, however, that this is a unified or uninterrupted regime at work, or that it exists on a formal continuum with predecessors such as the British Empire. Empire has mutated. It is no longer quite the white man's burden. Civilizing 'lesser breeds without the law', in Kipling's bracing words, may remain desirable, but the interest in maintaining order, interpreted as the orderly maintenance of self-interest, is paramount. Self-interest itself is perceived variously, however, and offers no consistent guide to action.

Unlike earlier empires, US hegemony is uncontested, although not without its challenges. Its debt-driven growth, drawing on the savings of the rest of the world, vividly illustrates a striking new characteristic of geopolitical power, namely its ability to displace the location of accumulation from the direct extraction of wealth to the neutral operation of financial markets. As the world's political anchor, the USA presents more or less the safest risk for investors, at least for the present (the euro is obviously somewhat stronger at the moment, but only in strictly monetary terms). That is, the military and economic might of the USA can be treated as unrelated to each other, and this in part constitutes the cultural form of its national power. We would therefore be mistaken in seeking an imperial center at which the operations of US power can be located and described, an equivalent of a Rome from which Pax Americana issues forth. We can more usefully examine the everyday surfaces of US society, where for example self-professed real Americans encounter those whom they perceive as threats.

I will conclude with an extraordinary report by Somini Sengupta in the *New York Times*, 24 October 2001. Haider Rizvi, a freelance journalist and native of Pakistan, stepped out of a Pakistani-owned grocery store on Fifth Avenue on the morning of Sunday 21 October, when three men approached him. 'You look like Osama bin Laden,' he recalled one of them asking 'are you from Pakistan?' This was of course a *non sequitur,* since Osama is from Saudi Arabia. Ignoring the leap in logic, Rizvi replied to their question. 'Originally, yes,' he said. But this was mere hairsplitting. Rizvi says he remembers being kicked and punched, falling to the sidewalk and waking up at New York Methodist Hospital. His assailants had knocked out one of his front teeth and beaten him unconscious. Ironically, when in college in Pakistan, he had been beaten by members of the Jamaat-e-Islami; harassment by the Jamaat was one of the reasons he eventually left his country.

Some days before his attack, the editor of an Indian newsmagazine had sought an essay from him on being a Muslim in the USA. In reply, he asked her if she would consider a submission on what it is like to be an atheist living in the USA (Sengupta 2001).

Haider Rizvi's question, which he might have posed to his attackers if they allowed him, is worth considering. His attackers registered his race and, from this, fixed his religion, rejecting the possibility that he might not have one. The question they asked however was about his national identity. Even on this question, they did not draw a sharp distinction between Saudi Arabia and Pakistan, both, incidentally, staunch US allies. What Rizvi's attackers picked out was a certain kind of person, certainly non-white, and a relatively recent immigrant generationally speaking. That was enough for them.

Notes

1   I would like to thank Aswn Punathambekar for his help with research for this paper, and my thanks also to Raphael Rajendra for his helpful comments on a previous draft.
2   The poll, conducted by the Program on International Policy Attitudes, based at the University of Maryland in College Park, and the polling firm, Knowledge Networks, based in Menlo Park, California, included 9,611 respondents polled between January and September 2003, and had a margin of error from 2 to 3.5 percent; see Davies (2003). On Fox News, see Ackerman (2001).
3   For a theoretical discussion of affective ties materialised in new media contexts, see Rajagopal (2001).
4   Part of this section is in slightly revised form, drawn from a previous essay (Rajagopal 2002).
5   In fact, a 1790 statute that limited citizenship to free white men was invoked well into the twentieth century to deny non-white applicants for immigration. Only with the 1965 Immigration Act was this statute formally rescinded.
6   My discussion in this section and what follows draws on Honig (2001: 73–106).
7   Proclaimed in 1823, the Monroe Doctrine demarcated the Americas as a zone of non-intervention for European powers, as nations such as Argentina, Chile, and Venezuela became independent after the break-up of the Spanish Empire in the years following the Napoleonic Wars. Those nations expected the USA to come to their aid against European powers seeking to reassert control. The Monroe Doctrine asserted that the USA forbade European intervention, but went onto become the dominant political influence in Latin America. See for example May (1975).

References

Ackerman, Seth (2001) 'The most biased name in news: Fox News Channel's extraordinary right-wing tilt', *Extra!, A Special FAIR Report*, August.
Asian American Legal Defense and Education Fund (2003) www.aaldef.org, accessed July 23.
Behdad, Ali (1997) 'Nationalism and immigration to the United States', *Diaspora* 6(2): 155–78.

Carey, James (2002) 'American journalism on, before and after September 11', in Barbie Zelizer and Stuart Allan (eds) (2002) *Journalism after September 11*, London and New York: Routledge.

Davies, Frank (2003) 'Wrong impressions helped support Iraq war', *Philadelphia Inquirer* at Philly.com, 2 October.

Fainaru, Steve (2002) '9/11 detainees abused: Justice Dept review outlines immigrant rights violations', *Washington Post*, 3 June.

Ferguson, Niall (2003) *Empire: The Rise and Demise of the British World Order and the Lessons for Global Power*, New York: Basic Books.

Gans, Herbert J. (1979) *Deciding What's News: A Study of CBS Evening News, NBC Nightly News, Newsweek, and Time*, New York: Pantheon Books.

Hallin, Daniel C. (1989) *The Uncensored War. The Media and Vietnam*, Berkeley: University of California Press.

Hobsbawm, E.J. (1993) *Nations and Nationalism since 1780: Programme, Myth, Reality*, second rev. edn, Cambridge: Cambridge University Press.

Honig, Bonnie (2001) *Democracy and the Foreigner*, Princeton: Princeton University Press.

Kaur, Valarie (2002) 'Turbans and tenor: racism after September 11', *SikhSpectrum.com Monthly*, 5 October.

McChesney, Robert W. (2002) 'The structural limits of US journalism', in Barbie Zelizer and Stuart Allan (eds) (2002) *Journalism after September 11*, London and New York: Routledge.

May, Ernest R. (1975) *The Making of the Monroe Doctrine*, Cambridge, MA: Harvard University Press.

Monbiot, George (2002) 'War on the third world', *Guardian*, 5 March.

Noiriel, Gerard (1995) 'Immigration: amnesia and memory', *French Historical Studies* 19(2): 368–71.

O'Brien, Patrick Karl and Clesse, Annand (eds) (2002) *Two Hegemonies: Britain 1846–1941 and the United States, 1941–2001*, London: Ashgate.

Rajagopal, Arvind (2001) *Politics After Television: Hindu Nationalism and the Reshaping of the Public in India*, Cambridge: Cambridge University Press.

—— (2002) 'Living in a "time of emergency"', *Television and New Media*, spring: 44–7.

—— (2004) 'America and its others: Cosmopolitan terror as globalisation?', *Interventions* 6(3), pp. 317–329.

Rosen, Jay (2002) 'September 11 in the mind of American journalism', in Barbie Zelizer and Stuart Allan (eds) (2002) *Journalism after September 11*, London and New York: Routledge.

Schudson, Michael (2002) 'What's unusual about covering politics as usual', in Barbie Zelizer and Stuart Allan (eds) (2002) *Journalism after September 11*, London and New York: Routledge.

Sengupta, Somini (2001) 'Beaten in Pakistan, Battered in Brooklyn', *New York Times*, 24 October.

Solomon, Norman and Erlich, Reese (2003) *Target Iraq: What the News Media Didn't Tell You*, New York: Context Books.

Swains, Rachel L. (2003) 'Arab-Americans gather to build their civil rights activism', *New York Times*, 14 June.

United States Bureau of Census (1994) 'Foreign-born population in the US', Report pp. 20–4 86.

—— (2002) 'Foreign-born population in the US', Report P20–539.

Zelizer, Barbie and Allan, Stuart (eds) (2002) *Journalism after September 11*, London and New York: Routledge.

Chapter 6

Thinking experiences

Transnational media and migrants' minds

Kevin Robins and Asu Aksoy

As it was originally conceived, in a longer version (Aksoy and Robins 2003a), this chapter intended to make a contribution to the understanding of migratory and transnational cultures. It can also be read, however, as a contribution to media studies and, particularly, audience reception studies. And that is how we now present it. What it does is to take up the agenda developed by Paddy Scannell (1996, 2000), an agenda that was very much centred on the viewing experiences of national audiences – particularly, the British national audience – and to reflect on this agenda in the context of new transnational media experiences. Our argument focuses on transnational television viewing, then, and does so through the specific example of migrants of Turkish origin who are now living, and reflecting on their living, in Britain.

All across the European space now, Turkish-speaking populations are tuning in to the numerous satellite channels that are broadcasting programmes from Ankara and Istanbul. Just like other migrant groups – Maghrebis, Arabs, Chinese, Indians, and many more – they are now able to make use of transnational communications to gain access to media services from the country or region of origin. This has been an entirely new phenomenon, a development of the last decade, which has very significant implications for how migrants experience their lives, and for how they think and feel about their experiences. What, then, is this significance? What precisely is the difference that television makes for those who live in migrant contexts? What is the nature of their engagement with the new transnational media? These are key questions that we want to pose in the following discussion, with particular reference to Turks living in Europe (for further discussion, see also Aksoy and Robins 2000, 2003b; Robins and Aksoy 2001, 2004).

The difference that television makes

There is by now a growing body of work on transnational communications within the framework of what might be termed diasporic cultural studies. Here it is being argued that new media technologies are making it possible to transcend the distances that have separated 'diasporic communities' around the world from their 'communities of origin'. So-called diasporic media are said to be providing new means to promote transnational bonding, and thereby sustain (ethnic, national or religious) identities and cultures at-a-distance. They are being thought about in terms of the possibilities they offer for dislocated belonging among migrant communities anxious to maintain their identification with the 'homeland' (and the basic premise is that this kind of belonging must be the primary aspiration of any and every such 'community').

Now, of course we can recognise a certain kind of truth in this argument. From our own work on Turkish migrants in London, it is clear that access to Turkish-language media can, indeed, be important for overcoming the migrant's experience of cultural separation. But if there is some kind of truth here, we would say that it is only a partial truth. The problem with diasporic media studies is that its interests and concern generally come to an end at this point. The inquiry is brought to a premature halt, with the ready acceptance that transnational broadcasting does in fact, and quite unproblematically, support the long-distance cohesion of transnational 'imagined communities' – without ever confronting what it is that might be new and different about the experience of transnational broadcasting. Because it has been principally concerned with acts of bonding and belonging, the diasporic agenda has generally been blind to what else might be happening when migrants are, supposedly, connecting in to their 'homeland' culture.

The problem is that the theoretical categories available to diasporic media and cultural studies make it difficult to see anything other than diasporic forms of behaviour. Individuals are derived from the social orders to which they 'belong'; they amount to little more than their membership of, and participation in, an 'imagined community'. This is a clearly an example of the kind of social theory that is powerfully criticised by Anthony Cohen, an approach that treats society as an ontology that 'somehow becomes independent of its own members, and assumes that the self is required continuously to adjust to it' (Cohen 1994: 21). In this kind of approach there is no place for self-awareness and self-consciousness – and, as Cohen argues, by neglecting self-consciousness, we inevitably perpetrate fictions in our descriptions of other people' (Cohen 1994: 191). To see anything more than diasporic behaviour in migrant audiences, it is necessary to introduce the category of the self-conscious individual, who is 'someone who can reflect on her or his experience of and position in society, of "being oneself"' (Cohen 1994: 65). As Cohen says, the imperative should be 'to elicit and describe the thoughts and sentiments of individuals which we otherwise gloss over in the generalisations we derive from collective social categories' (Cohen 1994: 4). The crucial point is that individuals are endowed with the capacity for both emotion (feelings, moods) and thought (reflecting, comparing, interpreting, judging, and so on). We should be concerned, then, with their minds and sensibilities, and not their cultures or identities – concerned with how they think, rather than how they belong.

It is in such terms as these that we now want to think about the experiences of Turkish migrants living in London. What do they think and feel about Turkish channels and programming? What is the difference that transnational television has made for London Turks? We will start from the crucial question of distance – from the idea that the new media systems can now work to bridge global distances. And we will do so by reflecting on what this seemingly straightforward idea might actually mean. In the frame of the diasporic cultural studies, it is largely about the maintenance of at-a-distance ties – about the supposed capacity of transnational media to connect migrant communities back to the cultural space of their distant 'homeland'. On the basis of our own research, we would charac- terise what is happening somewhat differently: in terms of how – in the case of our informants – transnational media can now bring Turkish cultural products and services to them in London, and of how 'Turkey' is consequently brought closer to them. As one focus group participant puts it,

> [I]t gives you more freedom, because you don't feel so far away, because it's only six foot away from you, you don't feel so far away from it. Cyprus is like one switch of a button away, or Turkey even, mainland Turkey, you are there, aren't you?
>
> (Focus group, Enfield, 21 April 2000)

Television makes a difference because it is in its nature – in the nature of televi- sion as a medium – to bring things closer to its viewers.

In one of our group discussions, two women tell us of how satellite television now allows them to be synchronised with Turkish realities. 'Most certainly [Turkish] television is useful for us,' says one. 'It's almost as if we're living in Turkey, as if nothing has really changed for us.' The other confirmed this, saying that 'When you're home, you feel as if you are in Turkey. Our homes are already decorated Turkish style, everything about me is Turkish, and when I'm watching television too' (focus group, Hackney, London, 7 December 1999). The key issue here is to do with the meaning of this experience of 'as if nothing has really changed for us'. In the context of the diasporic agenda, this feeling of synchroni- sation would be thought of in terms of long-distance bonding with the 'homeland', the maintenance of at-a-distance links with a faraway 'somewhere else'. For us, in contrast, it is simply about the availability in London of imported things from Turkey – where we might regard the availability of television programmes as being on a continuum with the (equally common) availability of food, clothes or furnishings from Turkey. 'Nothing has really changed' does not refer, then, to ethnocultural reconnection to some imagined 'homeland', but simply to the possibility of having access in London now to Turkish consumer goods and the world of Turkish consumer culture. It is 'almost as if we're living in Turkey' in that sense, being Turkish in London, that is to say, and not at all in the sense of 'being taken back home'.

Television brings the ordinary, banal reality of Turkish life to the migrants living in London. The key to understanding transnational Turkish television is actually in its relation to banality. Vladimir Jankélévitch (1974: 346) notes how people who are in exile can imagine they are living double lives, carrying around within them 'inner voices … the voices of the past and of the distant city', whilst at the same time submitting to 'the banal and turbulent life of everyday action'. This is the mechanism of splitting, whereby the banality of the 'here and now' provides the stimulus for nostalgic dreams and fantasies about the 'there and then'. Now, what we regard as significant about transnational television is that, as a consequence of bringing the mundane, everyday reality of Turkey 'closer', it is undermining this false polarising logic. The 'here and now' reality of Turkish media culture disturbs the imagination of a 'there and then' Turkey – thereby working against the romance of diaspora-as-exile, against the tendency to false idealisation of the 'homeland'. We might say, then, that transnational Turkish television is an agent of cultural de-mythologisation.

This process of de-mythologisation can work in different ways. Here we will give just two examples of how television can be used as a kind of reality-testing device. The first comes from an interview with an active member of London's Turkish-Cypriot population, a man in his forties who has been settled in Britain for many years. We find ourselves discussing the question of young people, relationships and the family, and he expresses quite critical opinions about what he clearly regards as the out-of-date morality of the Turkish-Cypriot community in Britain. 'In many ways,' he says,

> you become almost frozen in your understanding of where your community is. The longer you are here the more you are likely to have views and attitudes that are more conservative and out of date. I've seen people my age and even younger expecting things of their children that they have rebelled against.

He then moves on to suggest that transnational television could actually play a positive role in countering this migrant conservatism. 'In many ways,' he comments,

> I wish they would watch more Turkish television. Some of their attitudes are far behind what the messages are. You turn on the Turkish television, and some of it is refreshingly modern. It's quite normal to watch people having

affairs, or who are having relationships, who aren't married, on Turkish television. You would never have had that twenty years ago. But some of the mind set is relating to that. The first time a girl is having a relationship is when they get married – you see that with second-generation people. They don't get that from satellite. They get it from their parents.

(Interview, Camden, London, 20 April 2000)

What he is arguing is that television programmes and images that show how life and morals are in Turkey now can serve as a valuable corrective to migrant attitudes that, he believes, have become stuck in some ideal and timeless image of Turkish-Cypriotness.

Our second example comes from a young woman of 18, we shall call her Hülya, who migrated to Britain from eastern Turkey when she was seven years old. At one point, towards the end of our discussion, she tells us how much she likes watching old Turkish movies on television, 'especially the love films', which she likes to watch 'to see the old Turkey. ... It gives you a very sweet sense.' But earlier she had spoken about a very different experience of watching Turkish television:

We have one TV set, and this is why we have arguments, because I'm irritated by the news. I find it bad for my health. You might find it funny but, really, you sit in front of the television, you are going to watch the news, you are relaxed, everybody is curious about what's happening in Turkey; and then it says, 'Good evening viewers, today four cars crashed into each other.' God bless them. They show these things, people covered in blood. People who know nothing about rescuing, trying to drag these people out, they pull them, and in front of your eyes people die. I am a very sensitive person. Somebody dies in front of you, and they show this, and they don't do anything. For me, this is like torture. For them maybe it is not like torture, but for me it is. Two or three years ago, I was very upset, when this guy was killed because he had a tattoo saying 'Allah' on his back. Then, I don't know this person, but I was so touched that I cried. And I called Ahmet Taner Kışlalı [a famous journalist based in Turkey]. These kinds of events make me very sad, because I'm delicate, and they wear me out, so for that reason I don't watch.

(Focus group, Hackney, London, 3 November 1999)

What is made apparent here is television's great capacity for conveying harsh and cruel aspects of the Turkish reality – Turkish news programmes are far more explicit than British ones in showing scenes of violence and bloodshed. For a great many Turkish viewers, news programmes are very disturbing – the often intense discomfort of watching the news was an issue that ran through practically all of our focus groups. In some parts of their schedules, then, television channels may nourish warm and nostalgic feelings. But at news time, especially, the principle of reality will always return, through images of Turkey that frequently provoke and shock. The news can be profoundly unsettling for migrant viewers. As Hülya says of her own experience, it 'creates a psychological disorder'.

What is particularly important is the evidential nature of television (which may be constructive, as in our first example, but also disturbing, as our second example makes clear). What we want to emphasise here is the capacity of the reality dimension of television to undercut the abstract nostalgia of the diasporic imagination. Turkish viewers come to participate in the mundane and banal world of everyday television. It is this aspect of television culture that goes against the idea that the proliferation of Turkish transnational media is now associated with an ethnicisation of media cultures and markets in Western Europe (for such an argument, see Becker 2001). In our own work, we have not found this to be the case. We are inclined to agree with Marisca Milikowski when she argues that it is, on the contrary, associated with a process of *de-ethnicisation*. As she says, Turkish satellite television 'helps Turkish migrants, and in particular their children, to liberate themselves from certain outdated and culturally imprisoning notions of Turkishness, which had survived in the isolation of migration' (Milikowski 2000: 444). The world of Turkish television is an ordinary world, and its significance resides, we suggest, in its ordinary, banal and everyday qualities – which qualities it has in common with countless other TV worlds.

Turkish audiences look to the ordinariness of Turkish television. Like any other viewers of broadcast television, they want 'the familiar – familiar sights, familiar faces, familiar voices', as Thomas Elsaesser (1994: 7) puts it, 'television that respects and knows who they are, where they are, and what time it is'. And, to a large extent, we may say that they are able to find what they are looking for. And yet, at the same time, there is still something that is wrong, something that does not quite work properly with transnational Turkish television. At the same time as they can enjoy them, migrants can also find Turkish channels disturbing, unsettling, frustrating. This is apparent in a very dramatic fashion in Hülya's abrupt shift from feeling relaxed in front of the television to feeling worn out by what she saw on it. Many, many other people expressed these kinds of affronted and disgruntled feelings about the programmes they were watching. In one group, a woman objects to the production standards of Turkish television. 'We perceive Turkish television as being of poor quality,' she says, 'and rather sensationalist, and unedited, so it's a bit crude. … I mean, it will show you things in an unedited way, whether it's blood and guts, or violence or whatever' (focus group, Haringey, London, 22 November 1999). There is something about Turkish television that presents itself as in some way inadequate, deficient, unacceptable. The experience of watching transnational television is ordinary, but never straightforward.

When Turkish people talk about what frustrates them, they point variously to the images, the programmes, the scheduling, or the nature of particular channels. But, somehow, it seems to us, this doesn't really get at what is 'wrong' with watching television from Turkey. There is something more that is disconcerting about watching transnational television, an elusive something else. We can perhaps get at what this something might be from a passing observation that was made by Hülya. We were talking about Muslim festivals, and about the sense that she and her friends had that the significance of religious holidays was diminishing in the London context. We asked whether Turkish television helps to remind people of the traditional holidays, and to create the festival atmosphere that seemed to have been lost. 'How could that help?' says one young woman sceptically. And then Hülya adds, 'It's coming from a distance. ... It's coming from too far. It loses its significance. I mean, it could have significance, but it's coming from too far.' Later, when asked whether the availability of satellite television had implications for her identity and her relation to Turkish culture, she picks up on the same idea. 'No,' she says, 'it can't, because it's too distant. Imagine that you were talking to me from I don't know how many thousand miles away. How much would this affect me?' (focus group, Hackney, London, 3 November 1999). Perhaps we can make sense of this by referring back to Thomas Elsaesser's observation that the audiences of broadcast television want television programmes that know who they are, where they are, and what time it is. Is it that television from Turkey doesn't seem to know its transnational audiences in this way? Is Hülya pointing to something that is new or different about the working of transnational television? Is she signalling something that might actually make transnational cultural interactions distinctive?

Migrant experience and television theory

Turkish migrants clearly have quite complex thoughts and sentiments about the television channels and programmes that they are watching. What is also clear is that they have a *critical* engagement with the new transnational television culture.

What they say demonstrates considerable awareness and thoughtfulness about different aspects of this culture, from the aesthetic and production values of particular programmes, through to the overall impact of the new services on the quality of their lives in Britain. What we now want to do is to go on and reflect on these complex attitudes and relations of Turkish migrants towards transnational television. We want to try to make sense of what Turkish people are telling us in the context of more general ideas about the role and significance of broadcasting in modern life (which Turks are, of course, as much a part of as any other group).

For the most part, as we have suggested above, transnational media of the kind we are concerned with here have been considered in the special context of 'diasporic culture' and identity politics. Migrant audiences have been seen as, in some way, different; and the study of their supposedly different dispositions and preoccupations has seemed to belong to the specialised domain of ethnic and migration research. We ourselves believe that their media activities should be looked at with the very same media theories that have been applied to 'ordinary' (i.e. national, sedentary) audiences. Marisca Milikowski (2000: 460) is quite right to insist that we should look at migrant viewing from the point of view of 'ordinary uses and gratifications' – for, as she observes, 'non-ideological and non-political gratifications usually go a long way to explain a certain popular interest'. This we regard as an important principle of methodological democracy and justice. We should reflect on what is happening through transnationalisation of Turkish media culture in the light of media theory concerned with ordinary uses of, and gratifications from, everyday television.

Here, we think that the work of Paddy Scannell can serve as a particularly useful and productive point of reference. We have reservations, we must say, about certain aspects of Scannell's overall project – it is very national in its orientation, and often seems to be treating British broadcasting as an ideal-type model (for critical observations on the politics of Scannell's agenda, see Morley 2000, ch. 5). But we do think that there is a great deal to be learned from his detailed analysis of the emergence of distinctive modes of address in broadcasting culture – how broadcasters learned to address listeners and viewers in appropriate ways (ways in which they would wish to be addressed). Scannell's work alerts us to the significance of the particular rhetorical structures that have come to mediate the relation of producers and consumers of broadcasting services. What he provides us with is a sustained account of the communicative structures and ethos that have made broadcasting culture work for its audiences. It is, moreover, a historically situated account, showing how the specific communicative forms of radio and television developed and functioned in the particular context of national broadcasting systems. Scannell's concern is with how, at a particular historical moment, broadcasting media came to develop communicative forms that functioned as, arguably, the primary mediation between the private domain of everyday life and the public life of the nation state.

It seems to us that these communicative and rhetorical aspects of programming and scheduling are absolutely crucial for our own exploration of transnational Turkish television and its audiences. Of course, the codes that have evolved in the Turkish context differ somewhat from those of Scannell's British case – the state broadcaster, TRT, has always had an 'official' tone, and it was only in the 1990s, through the development of private channels, that more informal modes of address came to be elaborated (Aksoy and Robins 1997). But we may say that they have functioned in the integrative way, working to mediate the relation between private and public spheres of life in Turkey. And what seems to us to be a key issue, in the context of our own present concern with Turkish satellite broadcasting in the European space, is what happens to these communicative structures in the changed circumstances of transnationalisation. The point about Scannell's analysis is that it is essentially a phenomenology of national broadcasting. It assumes that there is something universal and timeless about the way in which national broadcasting cultures have worked. What we would suggest is that there will be difficulties when communicative structures that have worked more or less well in a national context are then made to do service in new transnational contexts. We are concerned, then, with the communicative limits of structures that have served to mediate between the private and public lives of the nation.

There are two closely related arguments that we want to make here. The first is relatively straightforward, emerging directly from our previous discussion, and can be made quite briefly. Scannell is concerned with what he calls the 'care structures' of radio and television, by which he means the practices that 'produce and deliver an all-day everyday service that is ready-to-hand and available always anytime at the turn of a switch or the press of a button' (Scannell 1996: 145–6). What this involves, he says, is 'making programmes so that they "work" every time', and in such a way that viewers or listeners come to regard them as 'a natural, ordinary, unremarkable, everyday entitlement' (Scannell 1996: 145–6). In considering these care structures, Scannell has put particular emphasis on the temporality of broadcasting, on what he calls its 'dailiness'. 'This dailiness yields,' he says, 'the sense we all have of the ordinariness, the familiarity and obviousness of radio and television. It establishes their taken for granted, "seen but unnoticed" character' (Scannell 2000: 19). And what Scannell wants us to recognise and acknowledge is the immense pleasure that this mundane quality of broadcasting has for viewers – the pleasure that comes from the combination of familiarity, confirmation, entitlement and effortlessness.

Turkish broadcasting culture also exists as an ordinary and mundane culture. And the appeal of Turkish television, as with other broadcasting cultures, is equally the appeal of its ordinariness. Through it, Turks living in Europe have access to, or can extend their access to, what Jostein Gripsrud (1999) calls the domain of 'common knowledge'. They can be part of the great domain of 'anonymous discourse' that broadcasting has brought into existence, the great banal domain of 'inattentive attention' (Brune 1993: 37). What we are arguing, then, is that migrant viewers are looking to find what the national television culture has always provided. Like any other viewers, Turkish-speaking viewers in Europe are also in search of broadcast television that is meaningfully and effortlessly available. They are also wanting – and to a quite a large extent finding – the pleasures of familiarity and confirmation. And our point is that the desire for such an engagement with Turkish television is entirely *social*, and not at all ethnocultural or 'diasporic', in its motivation. Migrant viewers are in search of ordinary social gratifications, precisely the kinds of gratification that Scannell is concerned with.

Our second argument is a little more complex, and takes us back to what Hülya said about Turkish television seeming to come from a distance and, consequently, losing its significance. What we want to get at is the particular feeling of *ambivalence* that very many Turkish people have about transnational television (which is more than the routine ambivalence that we all seem to have). They enjoy and appreciate the programmes they see; and yet, at the same time, watching them can frequently cause frustration and provoke resentment. Sometimes, it seems, transnational engagement with Turkish television culture doesn't 'work'. In Scannell's terms, we may say that the care structures of television break down. And what we want to suggest, as an explanation for this, is that, whilst considerable gratification may be got from everyday television, there are particular difficulties with its 'sociable dimension', which Scannell regards as 'the most fundamental characteristic of broadcasting's communicative ethos' (Scannell 1996: 23). Put simply, Turkish television often seems to its transnational viewers to be failing or lacking in its sociable aspect.

Scannell draws our attention to the remarkable capacity of broadcasting to generate a sense of 'we-ness', through the creation of 'a public, shared and sociable world-in common between human beings' (Scannell 2000: 12). What Scannell means when he talks about the creation of a 'world in common' is, of course, a national world in common; what is at issue is the contribution of broadcasting to the institution of the 'imagined' community. His account is quite idealistic, but what we think Scannell usefully brings out is the way in which television and radio have worked to create a public world with 'an ordered, orderly, familiar, knowable appearance' (Scannell 1996: 153). It is a world in which television and radio contribute to the 'shaping of our sense of days' (Scannell 1996: 149). The dailiness of broadcast media gives rise to the sense of '*our* time – generational time – the time of *our* being with one another in the world' (Scannell 1996: 174). The broadcasting calendar 'creates a horizon of expectations, a mood of anticipation, a directedness towards that which is to come, thereby giving substance and structure (a 'texture of relevances') to everyday life' (Scannell 1996: 155). According to this ideal-type scenario, broadcasting produces a 'common world – a shareable, accessible, available public world'; what it does is 'to create and to allow ways of being-in-public for absent listeners and viewers' (Scannell 1996: 166, 168). It connects 'everyone's my-world' to the 'great world', which is 'a world in common, a world we share' (Scannell 1996: 172, 174).

And what we are arguing here is that it is this sociable functioning of broadcasting that doesn't 'work' properly for migrants watching Turkish television in Europe. Transnational viewers are often disconcerted because, on very many occasions, they cannot relate to Turkish programmes as a natural, ordinary, unremarkable, everyday entitlement. In the case of news this is particularly apparent. If, as Scannell argues, 'the care structures of news are designed to routinise eventfulness'

(Scannell 1996: 160), then we may say that in our Turkish case, at least, these care structures do not function well across distance. In the transnational context, there is a problem with the mode of address. Broadcasting works on the basis of what Scannell calls a 'for-anyone-as-someone' structure of address: it is addressing a mass audience, and yet appears to be addressing the members of that audience personally, as individuals. 'The for-anyone-as-someone structure expresses and embodies that which is between the impersonal third person and the personal first person, namely the second person (the me-and-you),' says Scannell (2000: 9). 'The for-anyone-as-someone structure expresses "we-ness". It articulates human social sociable life.' In the Turkish case, it seems that viewers may often be made to feel like no one in particular. The conditions no longer exist for feeling at home in the 'we-ness' of Turkish broadcasting culture.

Why does the 'my world' of Turkish migrants no longer resonate properly with a Turkish world in common? Why are there problems with the mode of address in the case of transnational broadcasting? Why are the care structures of broadcasting disrupted? The reasons are to do with the context of consumption. As we have said, transnational broadcasting is not about magically transporting migrant viewers back to a distant homeland. It is about broadcasting services being delivered to them in their new locations – in the case of the Turks we have been discussing, it is in London. What this means is that the world of broadcasting is not seamlessly connected to the world of the street outside, as it would be for viewers watching in Turkey. Migrant viewers cannot move routinely between the media space and the 'outside' space of everyday Turkish reality. And since so much of what broadcasting is about has to do with connecting viewers to the life and rhythms of the real world of the nation, there are bound to be difficulties with the dislocated kind of viewing that migrancy enforces. Turkish migrants will often protest that Turkish television exaggerates. 'When you see these things you naturally believe them,' one man said to us.

> But I've been back from Turkey for two weeks, and it's nothing like that really. It's nothing like how it's shown. Turkey is the same Turkey. Of course, there are scandals, and there are people who live through them. But television doesn't reflect things as they are.
>
> (Focus group, Hackney, London, 16 December 1999)

Migrants tend to forget that exaggeration is an integral part of television rhetoric in Turkey, and it is only when they go back for a visit that they recognise the discrepancy between screen reality and street reality (whereas viewers in Turkey are checking out this discrepancy on a continuous basis). We may say that the decontextualisation of the migrant viewing situation often results in a kind of interference in the reception of cultural signals from Turkey.

A further consequence of the dislocated context of consumption is that migrant viewers can never be in a position to watch Turkish television naively or innocently. We must be aware that they actually operate in and across two cultural registers (at least) – Turkish and British. As well as watching Turkish channels, most of them are very familiar with British television. And they will often make comparisons between the two broadcasting cultures (concerning, for example, programme quality, scheduling, bias, censorship). We may say that there is a constant implicit comparison going on, and very often the comparisons are explicit – Turkish programmes are always watched and thought about with an awareness of British television in mind. As one man put it to us, 'We have the opportunity to compare things we see with what happens here. Before, we didn't know what it was like here' (focus group, Hackney, London, 16 December 1999). When we say that Turkish migrants cannot watch Turkish television innocently, we mean that they can no longer watch it from the inside, as it were. They cannot recover the narrow perspective of monocultural (national) vision. They are compelled to think about Turkish culture in the light of other cultural experiences and possibilities.

We have said that watching transnational Turkish television can be a frustrating and often disillusioning experience. What we want to add in conclusion is that this disillusionment can also be a productive experience. Through their engagement with Turkish (alongside British) media culture, Turkish migrants develop a comparative and critical attitude, and may become more reflexively aware of the arbitrariness and provisionality of cultural orders. In the present argument, we have been principally concerned with how the ordinary world of broadcast television can work to undermine the diasporic imagination. What should also have become apparent in the course of our argument, however, is the potential that exists, too, for working against the grain of the national imagination, against the confining mentality of imagined community.

Conclusion: the minds of migrants

> It all depends on the rifts and leaps in a person, on the distance from the one to the other *within himself*.
>
> (Elias Canetti 1991: 20)

In this discussion of transnational broadcasting from Turkey, we have been actively working against the diasporic imagination. We have tried to show how the rhetorical structures of Turkish television – the structures that have been mobilised to organise the experience of the national audience – are disrupted in the transnational context. In the migrant context, we think, where the ideal rhetorical situation of Turkish national television is significantly undermined, there may be possibilities for a more reflexive and critical engagement with television from the 'homeland'. What we have tried to suggest is that, in the Turkish case at least, transnational television might actually be working to subvert the diasporic imagination and its imperatives of identification and belonging. But our critique goes further than this. We have also been arguing that it is necessary to jettison the basic concepts of 'identity', 'imagined community' and 'diaspora'. Like Anthony Cohen, we have felt it necessary to go against the grain of the prevailing culturalism, and to take greater account of human consciousness and self-consciousness – to recognise that the minds of Turkish migrants may provide a more significant and interesting research focus than their identities. This means moving our agenda away from the 'problem' of migrant culture and identity, to consider how it is that migrants experience migration, and how they think and talk about and make sense of their experiences.

The point about identities is that they require simplicity. In the case of minds and consciousness, what is important is always their complexity. And it seems to us that transnational developments might open up new possibilities for the way we think about mental space – putting a new value on the rifts and leaps inside a person, and provoking those who are open to experience to travel the distance from the one to the other within themselves.

References

Aksoy, Asu and Robins, Kevin (1997) 'Peripheral vision: cultural industries and cultural identities in Turkey', *Paragraph* 20(1): 75–99.

—— (2000) 'Thinking across spaces: transnational television from Turkey', *European Journal of Cultural Studies* 3(3): 345–67.

—— (2003a) 'Banal transnationalism: the difference that television makes', in Karim H. Karim (ed.) *The Media of Diaspora*, London: Routledge, pp. 89–104.

—— (2003b) 'The enlargement of meaning: social demand in a transnational context', *Gazette: The International Journal for Communication Studies* 65(4–5): 365–88.

Becker, Jörg (2001) 'Zwischen Abgrenzung und Integration: Anmerkungen zur Ethnisierung der türkischen Medienkultur', in Jörg Becker and Reinhard Behnisch (eds) *Zwischen Abgrenzung und Integration: Türkische Medienkultur in Deutschland*, Rehburg-Loccum: Evangelische Akademie: 9–24.

Brune, François (1993) *'Les médias pensent comme moi!': fragments du discours anonyme*, Paris: L'Harmattan.

Canetti, Elias (1991) *The Secret Heart of the Clock*, London: André Deutsch.

Cohen, Anthony P. (1994) *Self Consciousness: An Alternative Anthropology of Identity*, London: Routledge.

Elsaesser, Thomas (1994) 'European television and national identity, or "What's there to touch when the dust has settled"', paper presented to the conference on Turbulent Europe: Conflict, Identity and Culture, London, July.

Gripsrud, Jostein (ed.) (1999) *Television and Common Knowledge*, London: Routledge.

Jankélévitch, Vladimir (1974) *L'Irréversible et la nostalgie*, Paris: Flammarion.

Milikowski, Marisca (2000) 'Exploring a model of de-ethnicisation: the case of Turkish television in the Netherlands', *European Journal of Communication* 15(4): 443–68.

Morley, David (2000) *Home Territories: Media, Mobility and Identity*, London: Routledge.

Robins, Kevin and Aksoy, Asu (2001) 'From spaces of identity to mental spaces: lessons from Turkish-Cypriot cultural experience in Britain', *Journal of Ethnic and Migration Studies* 27(4): 685–711.

—— (2004) 'Parting from phantoms: what is at issue in the development of transnational television from Turkey', in Jonathan Friedman and Shalini Randeria (eds) *Worlds on the Move: Globalization, Migration and Cultural Security*, London: IB Tauris, pp. 179–206.

Scannell, Paddy (1996) *Radio, Television and Modern Life*, Oxford: Blackwell.

—— (2000) 'For-anyone-as-someone structures', *Media, Culture and Society* 22(1): 5–24.

Chapter 7

Peckham tales

Mass Observation and the modalities of community

Gareth Stanton

> The theory of community has for too long been associated with geographical definitions of belonging and traditional understandings of the bonds that hold people together.
>
> (Little 2002: 95–6)

> For it is still the case that no one lives in the world in general. Everybody, even the exiled, the drifting, the diasporic, or the perpetually moving, lives in some confined and limited stretch of it – 'the world around here'.
>
> (Geertz 1996: 262)

> Geographically, I know very little of England.
>
> (Gorer 1955: 2)

Henri Lefebvre (1996) suggests that all methods are germane to the study of what he often calls the 'urban', from semiology to the psychogeography of the situationists[1] and the related surrealist practice of the *dérive* (drift), although for him the latter are too individualistic and theatrical. This short chapter sets as its ambition to produce a fusion between several different concerns and will also adopt an eclectic approach. As a starting point, I want to insist on a conception of studying social life that begins from an empirical perspective rooted in conceptions of Geertzian 'thick description' and detailed ethnographic study, but that links up with contemporary trends in disciplines such as human geography and urban sociology. It follows in the footsteps of many recent authorities who are keen to interrogate the fashion in which sociological constructs such as locality, neighbourhood, identity, nationality and, of course, community have become ruptured under conditions of what Zygmunt Bauman calls 'liquid modernity' (Bauman 2001).[2] It is an attempt to face the challenge proposed by Kevin Robins, also borrowing from Bauman, and search for the positive aspects of the workings of urban complexity 'at ground level'. The aim, then, is to start to delineate the acts that people thrown together are capable of performing, 'rather than the binding traits of collective identity' (Robins 2001: 90). This seems a hopeful stance to begin with, but we must be careful not to slip back into the discourses of collective identity and community as immutable and bound to geography. In the British context, Robins invites us to see the nation through the prism of London. Part of what I hope to do here is to extend Robins's proposition and see the world through the prism of London. More particularly, I want to see the world through the prism of a district of south London: Peckham. One starting point for me in this work is the sociologically and anthropologically inspired phenomenon dating from the late 1930s that came to be called the Mass Observation (M-O) movement. I do not want to reassess the work done in its heyday (see Jeffrey 1978 for a survey), but rather to draw inspiration from the attention that the founders of the movement paid to the detail of social life. One of them, Tom Harrisson,[3] took particular inspiration from the world of bird-watching. In the contemporary humanities this might seem at best dubious, but what, I think, he sought to emphasize was the value of intense, in-depth and protracted looking and listening. This is what I would wish to emulate: the sense in the work of the movement that in the ordinary details of everyday life there are worlds of meaning that have not yet revealed themselves. Surreal portents of future existences lurk on the shelves of shops, in the design of labels, in the juxta-position of contents. We have to look long and hard for such matters to become apparent and they reveal themselves only fleetingly – hidden by the veil of custom, they are often incomprehensible to the ordinary gaze. Only from shifting, liminal vantage points do they reveal themselves. The M-O movement grasped this and, if anything, they set out to take community in a multiple sense and allow other worlds the freedom to speak. 'Community', however, is a slippery word and like 'culture' has to be served up with a variety of health warnings. In order to set this in some context we need a brief review of research into community in Britain.

Community, what community? Social life in Britain

Social-science work on Britain is remarkably poor in good ethnography.
(Armstrong 1993: 6)

For Fred Inglis, the 1960s saw a brief flowering of sociological inquiry into domestic life in Britain. Mainly the impetus was the work of the Manchester School of Anthropology, notably Frankenburg's 1966 *Communities in Britain*.[4] More recent studies have also grappled with an ethnographic approach to community. One work that has appeared since Armstrong made his observation is Gerd Baumann's *Contesting Culture*. He talks of the problems of ethnic reduc-tionism in studies of immigrants in Britain. However, he does not wish to dispense with the concept of community, 'community was a concept to be used and redefined contextually, but certainly it could not be written off as an irrele-vancy.' (Baumann 1996: 4) His dissatisfaction with earlier 'community studies' comes at the conceptual beginning, the moment at which such studies start by defining community: 'In Southall there seemed to be communities within communities, as well as cultures across communities' (Baumann 1996: 10). Baumann quotes Raymond Williams from *Keywords*: 'It was when I suddenly realised that no-one ever used "community" in a hostile sense that I saw how dangerous it was' (quoted, Baumann 1996: 15). Here I want to examine how some of the impetus behind the movement of M-O could be seen as a search for the roots of community in modern industrial society. 'Community talk' flourishes when its sociological reality has long passed, Zygmunt Bauman observes, borrowing from Eric Hobsbawm (Bauman 2001: 15). In its place we have talk of 'identity'. In all the talk of flows and connections some factors are simply accidental (even if it is possible to explain them). Baumann reflects on why Sikhs should make up the 'majority community' in Southall, London. As he states, rural Sikhs started to arrive in Britain in the 1950s, most being the sons of farmers in the Doab region of the Punjab:

> That it was Southall that should prove such a magnet for Sikhs was a matter of chance. ... A local manufacturing plant, specialising in motor accessories, was run by a managing director who had commanded a Sikh unit in the British Indian army. Now battling with labour shortages, he resorted to active recruitment among his former servicemen's networks.
>
> (Baumann 1996: 74)

Observing community

Mine does not seek to be a formal study, but shares some of the ambitions of the research conducted by Baumann in the area of Southall where he lived. Certainly, the living and looking component, which he advocated, the wandering and soaking up, are part of what informs this piece. It would be far too weighty here to talk of the 'biography of the research', as Solomos and Back do in their 1995 study of politics and race in Birmingham. If anything, I am seeking to explore the difficulties of approaching the study of the city from the perspective of the ethnographic. As I have noted, Kevin Robins suggests using the city as a cognitive tool for rethinking or rather thinking outside the confines of the national. Taylor *et al.* in their study of Sheffield and Manchester suggest that they are investigating the 'local structure of feeling' of the two cities, trying to account for certain similarities and differences. Cities, they suggest, can be seen, as Rafael Samuels has argued, as 'theatres of memory'. Part of their work comprises an attempt to construct a 'realist sociology of everyday life in the north', but it can hardly be described as ethnography. Much information is garnered from focus groups, but it is a useful exercise and serves to frame important social transformations. Changes in mental maps indicate elemental shifts in life. The transformation from modern to postmodern stands out in the fact that Sheffield's Meadowhall shopping complex is built on the site of a major local steelwork (Hadfield's).

Max Farrar attempts to reassert the usefulness of the term community in his study of the Chapletown district of Leeds. He sees it as a concept best left in the world of dreams or the imagination. His book, however, 'tracks the real social and political consequences of human efforts to pursue their dreams of "community"' (Farrar 2001: 3). In this context 'community' has often been a simple 'flag of convenience' adopted by different local actors (including agents of government and the local council) for a variety of reasons (some of which might be dubious). It has functioned, he suggests, to project 'a unified set of people with unified aims' (Farrar 2001: 5). However, this is an increasingly hard trick to pull off because difference and complexity are increasingly dominant; 'Heterogeneity is the new norm' (Farrar 2001: 6). I want to begin my exploration of Peckham with its media representation, that is to say, the Peckham that will be most familiar to British readers. I shall then continue by looking at two buildings that in themselves embody important aspects of the district's development and which represent two different epochs, two different ways of imagining Peckham and its place in the world. The first of these takes us into a realm of memory that has been mobilised in the present, as contemporary organisations review histories and personal memories to refashion the past. The second takes us to a vision of the future, which seeks to refashion the present almost by an act of will. The utopian heart of that project will be counterposed with an excavation of the present in relation to the cultural practice of shopping, looking in particular at the role of food as an indicator of the very complexity of the contemporary landscape. If there is ethnography in this paper it will be found here.

Media tales of Peckham

> One of the unintended consequences of modern capitalism is that it has strengthened the value of place, aroused a longing for community.
> (Richard Sennett, quoted by Little 2002: 122)

Few outside the area will be aware of the historic importance of Peckham for any history of British national identity and its nurturance through different forms of media. It was from a small church in Peckham that the first nationally broadcast service took place in 1923. That church is still there, but now it is only a short walk to the almost completed Peckham mosque. More recently, Peckham has become a presence on the imaginative map of the nation due to its representation in the hugely popular comedy series *Only Fools and Horses* (*OFAH*). Southwark council is keen to distance itself from the image of dodgy deals and tower blocks portrayed in the programme and points out that the bulk of the filming was in fact done in Bristol. The first series, broadcast in 1981, featured an episode called 'Slow Bus to Chingford' in which Del Boy sets up as a tour guide for 'Trotter's Ethnic Tours'. This gives us a crude indicator as to contemporary perceptions of Peckham. The name of the council block in which the Trotters live itself evokes a certain perception of local government pieties from a different era – Nelson Mandela House. The show's popularity can be seen in the websites dedicated to the programme.[5]

Peckham resident, Steven Bourne, has written extensively on the representation of black people in British entertainment media:

> My fascination with the performing arts, especially film and television stems from my school days. I was born in south London and grew up in a multicultural environment, on a council estate in Peckham in the 1960s and 1970s. I never did any homework. I spent most of my time watching films at my local cinema (Peckham Odeon), or in front of the television.
>
> (Bourne 1998: viii)

Bourne's particular interests and locality merge in the shape of *Desmond's*, the pioneering black sit-com set in a Peckham hairdresser's. The show was written by Trix Worrell and went on to four series that were transmitted between 1989 and 1994 on Channel 4. The sight of camera crews in Rye Lane was not uncommon during this period. There is still a hairdresser's in Peckham commemorating the show and it can be found a short walk from the building in Bellenden Road that was used as Michael Caine's butcher's shop in the film of Graham Swift's novel *Last Orders*. Bellenden Road gives its name to the regeneration scheme that has targeted the Bellenden Ward since the late 1990s as one of the most impoverished in the whole borough of Southwark and huge sums of money have been spent by the council to re-engineer the area (the same ethos that lies behind the construction of the new Peckham library). The streets now have specially commissioned bollards designed by Anthony Gormley who, along with fellow artist Tom Phillips, has studios in Bellenden Road. Elsewhere there are bollards modelled on sketches by fashion designer Zandra Rhodes. Phillips himself has chipped in with some natty street lights. This is the world of expensive designer T-shirts with the momentarily trendy logo 'I love Peckham'. I shall attempt to explore the relations such developments have to the world of *Desmond's*, which does have some sort of referent in the contemporary, and to the impulse behind *OFAH*, which belongs rightly in the realm of memories excavated by the Peckham Society and prominent local amateur historians such as John Beasley. By that, I mean the world of 'poor but happy' (and funny in this version) where you could leave your door open and, in Peckham at least, relax under a benevolent medical gaze at the Pioneer Centre, a pioneering Peckham institution from the time of the M-O movement. This latter world still has its vestiges. One is the last remaining pie and mash shop, Manzies.

Such shops and their other speciality, jellied eels, take us back to the days of Victorian social commentator Henry Mayhew and his sellers of 'pea soup and hot eels'. In those Victorian days, the Dutch eeling ships were moored off Billingsgate waiting to discharge their precious load. By the early 1990s, there were only two such shops in Peckham, but one closed at this time and is currently a Cote D'Ivoire social centre. This hints at a relatively unknown history, that of Africa in Peckham. Dr Moody, a prominent Peckham GP and founder of the League of Coloured Peoples in 1931, was a Jamaican and can be seen as a precursor of the world of Caribbean immigration that gives us the imaginative backdrop for *Desmond's*. The African student in that sit-com (very serious, only funny because he isn't funny) can perhaps also be seen as representing the world of the Nigerian schoolboy, Damilola Taylor, murdered on his way home in Peckham, his last fleeting images captured on CCTV outside the new Peckham library where he had been attending an after-school computer class. In these senses, the factual and the fictional begin to merge as they are reworked by the forces of memory. Food is important here and it can also help us think about culture. Later in this chapter, I shall use it as a guide to the current state of Rye Lane, Peckham's main shopping artery. Mayhew, it should be noted, gives us a clue to the derivation of the family name 'Trotter' in the sit-com *OFAH*. After describing the street trade in baked potatoes he moves on to discuss the matter of "'trotting" or "hawking" butchers' (Mayhew in Quennell: 124). First, however, I want to look at some buildings.

Peckham experiments: building one and building two

Building one: the Pioneer Health Centre[6]

> It was like a big white palace, it was absolutely beautiful.
> (Interviewee on BBC's *One Foot in the Past*)

> A second assumption I made about the English character, is that most English people are shy and afraid of strangers, and consequently very lonely. This assumption was developed less from literature than from observation. I had also been much impressed by my visits to the Pioneer Health Centre and the reports issued on the work of this pioneer institute. The Peckham Health Centre was established in one of the residential areas of South London as a means of studying the incidences of health, rather than sickness in the community.
> (Gorer 1955: 18)

Geoffrey Gorer, patrician anthropological chronicler of British life[7] and author of *Exploring English Character,* continues:

> All the members came from the same small neighborhood, in which many of them had lived for several years. Nonetheless it was altogether exceptional if a new member family, on joining, had any acquaintances or friends in the Centre. Most of them had no friends, unconnected by kinship ties, in London.
>
> (Gorer 1955: 18)

If 'community' is sometimes an idealised version of the past, an embellished memory we might say, then Gorer is out to disrupt this version of the past. Peckham in this period was not, in fact, always a jolly world of open doors and *bonhomie.* People were isolated, lonely. They needed to be brought together by outside forces. Community was imposed by the Centre. What was this Centre? Known also as the Peckham Experiment, it opened in 1935. Membership was a shilling a week and for that local families could use the leisure facilities of the Centre if they were agreeable to a general system of health checks and monitoring. The radical building employs various techniques, such as extensive use of concrete, which mark it out as part of the modernist movement in British architecture.[8]

In 1950 the Centre closed, much to the distress of its members, who certainly express, in the BBC programme *One Foot in the Past,* some sense that here was 'community' in the positive sense the term has come to have (the interviews were conducted in the 1990s). The Centre is now converted into luxury flats (open to the public on National Garden Day), which might serve as a starting point to rethink the actual forms of community in Peckham for the modern period. It is now necessary to look for new models of approaching the multidimensional aspects of the neighbourhood in post-colonial times. The Peckham Experiment itself is now memorialised in the name of a trendy café that has opened in the Bellenden Regeneration Zone of Peckham.

Building two: Peckham library

> [L]ike a giant insect, somehow trapped in south London.
> (Open University course notes, *From Here to Modernity*)[9]

The Peckham Library and Media Centre, built in 1999, and designed by the experimental architect Will Alsop, like the Pioneer Health Centre, figures in Open University courses. The striking building is located at the site of the canal head. Now dry, the canal traces an older geography when wood was carried up from the Thames for the building boom of the late Victorian period. Whitten's, the timber merchant, is visible from the library's externally located glass lifts. Next to it is the new Peckham Pulse (itself supposedly inspired by the Pioneer Centre). The building is not, the course notes suggest, another example of 'irreverent post-modern architecture'; it is, rather, 'a very serious building with a strong social mission' (ibid.). It is part of a regeneration project; the library is designed with its own plaza to form part of a hub, generating, the council allege, a sense of community.

Surveillance tales: lag-time places

> In the heart of Europe we have shanty towns of the mind.
>
> (Danziger 1996: 8)

> In the late twentieth century, unknown and threatening territories lie inside the boundaries of the metropolis, where there are many lag-times, temporal breaks in the imaginary matrix, and areas of forced delay put on hold in the process of postmodernization. ... Disavowed, overlooked, marginalized, left out of our accounts. These are the centre's truly invisible places.
>
> (Boyer 1996: 20)

In their book on the rise of CCTV in Britain, *The Maximum Surveillance Society* (1999), Norris and Armstrong conduct one of their case studies in a run-down district they call 'Inner City'. The location is Peckham and its main shopping artery Rye Lane. A description of one of the CCTV operators, Robert, alerts us to the situation: 'Although a "local", Robert rarely recognised anyone on the streets' (Norris and Armstrong 1999: 104). Another operative, who lives in a nearby council estate, takes an elaborate roundabout route to work in order not to have neighbours realise the nature of his work. In comparison with other areas that they studied, responses to behaviour in public places is muted: 'In the poor and rundown Inner City, street trading, *Big Issue* sellers, low levels of disorder, bill posting and littering were not seen as threats to the commercial attractiveness of an area already abandoned by large-scale retailers' (Norris and Armstrong 1999: 176).

After the Taylor killing a CCTV shot of the boy leaving his after-school computer class in the modernist Alsop-designed Peckham library was released – the last sighting of the boy before he died. Perhaps, more surveillance might have made a difference, but not if the authors are to be believed. A serious wounding takes place on camera but no action results: 'the reluctance of operators in Inner City to alert police is a reaction to the lack of police interest, even when alerted to serious incidents of violence and disorder' (Norris and Armstrong 1999: 178). Is the contemporary so unrelentingly gloomy, forcing people to comfort themselves with memories of Peckham, shards of nostalgia, or have the fictional and the factual become impossible to separate even in the present? To address this question I shall turn to the theme of food, in an effort to explore Rye Lane in close-up, dodging the gaze of CCTV.

Peckham meat tales: John Dell of Head's Butchers

John is well known to his customers. For many he is the last remaining vestige of something that makes them think of their past, the glorious past of Rye Lane when it was a shopping hub for southeast London and shoppers came from miles around. Now that is all gone some say, with the exception of John. No doubt this is a rose-tinted version of the past, but it is easy to see how this happens. John, simply, fails to abide by the normally accepted rules of the contemporary commercial game. He knows many of his customers by name and is prepared to spend considerable amounts of time in conversation. For a certain segment of his clientele he is the focus of the community. People waiting in the often lengthy queue will greet each other and exchange pleasantries in a way that they ordinarily would not do on the street. Whether you desire an expensive leg of lamb or simply a rasher of bacon it is all the same to John, he is equally interested in you. John could have expanded his trade hugely over recent decades but he chooses not to. He likes his enterprise to be small-scale, caring even, in the sense that that word once had, back in the mists of time. He makes his own sausages and chipolatas, grinds the cuts of beef for his own burgers, the antithesis of Schlosser's *Fast Food Nation*. Recent events, however, have threatened to destabilise his choices. To understand this it is necessary to be aware that John is a figure from a different era in more ways than one. If the huge *halal* butchers that dominate Rye Lane in its most recent incarnation bring a new style of meat preparation to the world of southeast London, then another trend of long standing has been the increasing decline of the family butcher, first in the face of the chain butchers, but now in the shape of the butcher's counters at the big supermarkets, where the rationalisation and profit maximisation motives have resulted in forms of deskilling that reach their apogee in Schlosser's world of the Big Mac. The truth of the matter is that John Dell is a qualified master butcher, a craftsman of his trade.[10] There is no other shop selling meat on Rye Lane that doesn't have it all displayed in its full bloody finery, wrapped in cling film, or simply in unrefrigerated stacks, exuding an odour that many passing on the street find repellent. With John you have to ask what's good or if he has the cut you want. If he does, he goes out to the cold store and brings the meat to the counter to cut off the required quantity. The meat is then trimmed and the rest returned to cold storage, out of sight of customers. Some of them, then, were surprised by the article in the *Evening Standard* on 28 December 2002, entitled 'Meaty role for butcher', accompanied by John's photo. As they must have been by the appearance around the same time of a Sky outside-broadcast van outside the shop. Until this point, Peckham's most famous butcher had been southeast London boy Michael Caine in the film adaptation of Graham Swift's *Last Orders*. While that fictional shop was set in Bermondsey, the filming, as stated previously, took place in Bellenden Road in Peckham. Scorsese's *Gangs of New York* spent several years under wraps before getting a general release. For this period of time John had been guarding a secret. His clientele range from frail old-age pensioners living in council accommodation to those living in the magnificent Georgian houses that line the Rye itself. A film producer living in one of these houses had recognised John's exceptional qualities behind his modest demeanour and had recommended John to be the man to train Daniel Day Lewis in the necessary butchering skills needed for his role in the film. Duly, during the course of filming, he had been flown out to Rome on successive weekends, put up in a five-star hotel and chauffeured to the set for the training sessions. John had not felt able to spend longer periods in Italy because he felt that this would have meant letting down his customers back in Peckham. John enjoyed his time working on the film and on parting gave Day Lewis the old and worn filleting knife that he had first acquired in the days when he too was learning his trade.

Many of John's regulars are members of the Peckham Society and he represents a contemporary manifestation of the nostalgic projection into the past represented by the Society in its battle for the integrity of Peckham, past and present (see Conn 2000). He is the hub of a complex network of Peckhamites who find questions of history interesting and who invest issues of local history with cultural capital. One day he will be gone and writers to the Peckham Society will talk of the days of real butchers on Rye Lane. This work of nostalgic memory can be seen in this context as a defence against change. It acts like a chemical fixative, generating a single image out of a molecular chaos. Is that fleeting image what we call community?

Rye Lane/bush meat

The shops in Rye Lane are in a constant state of flux. The many nations involved in their workings are invoked in the names, in the profusion of goods, the 'exotic' products.[11] Many strangers who venture here for the first time are astounded by the variety of edible goods on sale, not that they would be eating them. Those of a suspicious frame of mind suggest the sale of bush meat. It is the possible presence of such a commodity that marks out the slow transition of many of the shops on Rye Lane from one of predominantly Caribbean influence to something with a less mediated African quality. Africa is, of course, a mere spectre (see Mudimbe 1994) and individual shops stock more regional choices, something to be seen from the displays of videos available, which give some pointer to any national or ethnic affiliations. The reality is rather more difficult to pin down; the number of nationalities is stupefying. The increasing retail presence of many African-run shops, however, raises the ire of less recent arrivals who comment on the smell (which, in fact, comes mostly from dried stock fish).

Meat and practices surrounding meat are great symbolic markers and strictly policed in the West (see Fiddes 1992). For many in the West bush meat is the antithesis of food and this is why streets such as Rye Lane (and other London markets such as Brixton or Ridley Road) sometimes disturb.[12] In October 2002, the magazine *Environmental Health News* carried a piece entitled 'Human flesh tip-off triggers raid'. In a raid on a shop in Tottenham in north London two tonnes of unfit meat had been seized (including a crocodile head). Police suspect that places selling bush meat might also be sources of human meat to be used in witchcraft. As the author notes, 'Rumours have been circulating for some time that human flesh may be in some north London boroughs for ritual purposes.'[13] Those arrested for bush meat offences in Ridley Road market the year before resided in East Dulwich, close to Rye Lane.

Shopping tales/consumption worlds

How can we characterise the shopping experience in Rye Lane? I have tried to use meat as a starting point for a description of cultural elements of consumption, but this is no ethnography of shopping.[14] For all the confusion of the stalls in Chomert market and on Rye Lane itself, they present a sense of symbolic and cultural order that is familiar to those who shop here, even if they are a source of frustration for trading standards officers who have difficulty monitoring weights and measures, and tracking down owners.

For many of those old inhabitants who have recorded their memories in the pages of the Peckham Society journal, the story of shopping in Rye Lane is one of decline. Old reputable firms have gone, over time, replaced by unknown shops, new forms of merchandise, until suddenly, one day, nothing is recognisable any more. In the 'lag-time place' the remnants of the past stand in for the absence of evidence of today's modernity. John Dell, the butcher, becomes both salvation and redemption. He represents past and future simultaneously, both preserved in a warm bath of aspic. The expression 'lag-time places' is taken originally from the work of post-colonial scholar Homi Bhabha. As he observes, modernity is felt differently by different people at different times. Perhaps what Peckham library signifies is a regathering of the forces of modernity, the return of a dream of the future and of modernity. Past efforts to inject modernity back into the commercial life of the area resulted in the Aylesham Centre, a somewhat soulless place occupied chiefly by a branch of the supermarket chain, Safeway. It was here that artist Gillian Wearing chose to act out her strange mute dancing pieces.

Many of Rye Lane's shops now sell a variety of consumables, from vegetables through to large sacks of rice and a wealth of hair products. The range of goods and the price is why shoppers come from afar to stock up on basic staples such as rice. For such people there is no decline here.

The stores are always busy. If the goods on sale in these markets mirror those on sale in shops across Europe, then the customers themselves represent a particular sample of Peckham's rich and varied population. Other specialised shops hint at Peckham serving as a hub for wider areas. The Persian Emporium attracts Iranians from throughout Kent and the southeast. Pastries are flown in from Tehran on a weekly basis. Wing Thai provides products from the entire Indo-China region and serves as a magnet for Peckham's large Vietnamese population. Local foodies know it in particular for its Thai sweet basil, itself flown in from Bangkok. On Sundays the whole commercial ecology undergoes a massive transformation when the Canal Head, the area in front of the library, houses a farmer's market and the well-heeled venture forth to buy organic meat and vegetables, and Fair Trade coffee. The world is then truly turned on its head and the utopian planners' vision of regeneration is realised. The religious tone adopted here, however, is deliberate, as we shall see.

Peckham religious tales (now)

While the godless select their comestibles from the Peckham farmer's market there are other stirrings. A number of large retail spaces have been adopted by more usual forms of religious observance. On a Sunday these are thronged by worshippers and their parked cars line the street. Here it is Nietzsche who is dead, not God. At 117–25 Rye Lane is the South London Temple and the Temple College where Dr Shadrach Ofosuware ministers to his flock. Here community is at the centre of endeavours. At 181–3 Rye Lane is the Beneficial Veracious Christ Church and its miracle centre. Just along from the Southwark Credit Union and V and T Las Vegas Fashion Nails at 176 Rye Lane is the Universal Church of the Kingdom of God, with its emphasis on 'true-life testimony' (but not true life in the sense of the Peckham Society correspondents) and accounts of addicts and bankrupts saved for God. Advertised in the window is a fundraising 'Hair and Beauty Day' travelling between Birmingham, Peckham, Croydon, Brixton and Finsbury Park. The church has a 24-hour helpline. Friday is spiritual release day and features 'strong prayer to destroy witchcraft, demon-possession, nightmares, curses, envy, bad luck and all spiritual problems'. At 135 Rye Lane we find *Ijo Kerubu titun lati oke wa oko 1gbala Ikehin* (the New Congregation of Cherubim Last Vessel of Salvation). There are many others. This sounds close to the Harlem of Chester Himes and his 'holy rollers', and their giant limos and appetites. Such churches represent religious globalisation, and their cries for an end of ethnic suffering through redemptive love of Christ say much for histories that remain hidden and untold. Many of these churches really are global, but there is not a great deal of easily available research. Roy Kerridge's sensitive survey of black churches in Britain, *The Storm is Passing Over,* is a useful introduction, but there is little of a systematic nature. Kerridge describes the Brotherhood of the Cross and Star that, although it has no branch in Rye Lane, might be taken as representative. The church was founded in the late 1950s in the Calabar region of southeastern Nigeria by Olumba Olumba Olu (sometimes referred to as OOO or triple O). It now claims over a million adherents throughout the world. The church is open to all, but it comes as a surprise to find that the triple O's representative in Europe should be a white man, Jeremy Goring, one-time lecturer in history.[15] This is a curious version of the 'Empire writing back' – Nigerian forms of Christianity thriving in the godless metropolis of London, led by white men.

Conclusion

After an exploration such as this there can be no real conclusion. As ever, there are only beginnings. Lefebvre talks of the urban being more or less the *œuvre* of its citizens (*pace* Robins). For him, 'Critical analysis dissipates the privilege of the lived in urban situations' (Lefebvre 1996: 117). M-O privileges the lived and therefore can help us make a start in coming to grips with the complexity of an urban environment such as that presented by Peckham, but we do need to use a whole range of techniques and proceed with caution. In his own pioneering work on African markets in New York, Paul Stoller (2002) argues for a 'theoretically flexible orientation'. This, coupled with the voracious eye for detail of an observer such a Tom Harrisson, enables us to come at least a little way to getting to grips with what Marshall Berman calls the 'stuff and flow of everyday life' (Berman 1999: 168) in places such as Peckham. The streets of contemporary London call out for a new generation of Mayhews to document the lives they sustain.

Notes

1   Cf. Andrew Hussey's fine biography of Guy Debord in this respect.
2   See Morley (2000) for a recent exploration along these lines.
3   On Harrisson, see Stanton (1997).
4   Although the best work in this genre, for Inglis, remains Hoggart's *Uses of Literacy*.
5   One in particular, www.trotters-independent-traders.co.uk/info/info.htm, talks of the *OFAH* 'community': 'Join for free the biggest community in the world and chat to other *OFAH* fans'. The same site contains a glossary of lead character Del Boy's distinctive patter. As it suggests, he has a complete lingo of his own. The show's writer, John Sullivan, suggests that Del picks many of the phrases off sauce bottles and clothes labels (so the impulses of M-O are correct).
6   An archive of materials relating to the Centre and its founders can be found at the Wellcome Library, reference code GB 0120 SA/PHC.

7 See Stanton (2000) for an account of Gorer.

8 Film footage of the Centre was on view at the Design Museum's 1999 Modern Britain 1929–39 exhibition.

9 This can be found at:
http://students.open.ac.uk/open2netnet/modernity/3–18htm (accessed August 2003).

10 In the language of committees, I have here to declare a personal interest. The first time I entered John's shop after the birth of my second daughter, he gave me ten pounds to buy her a present. Exegesis escapes me at this point.

11 The development of the market for products such as yams in the London area can be traced by performing varieties of media archaeology. For an illustration of this, see Bill Schwarz's excellent 'Claudia Jones and the West Indian Gazette'.

12 This is a theme for North African migrants in France. The role of an illegal butcher's in a Lyon *bidonville* is evoked in Azouz Begag's semi-autobiographical novel, *Le Gone de Chaaba*.

13 Consulted at www.ehnonline.com/cgibin/news/news1/EpFVuylVpkXb1PQsRK.html (accessed August 2003). Cannibalism has long been the act of the 'other'; see Arens (1979).

14 It is interesting to note that, in his work on shopping based on research in north London, Daniel Miller (1998) suggests his ethnography was no more than 'attempted', because of 'the absence of community' (Miller 1998: 9). One could interpret this as meaning that ethnography cannot grasp contemporary complexity. I would prefer to think that it means rather that forms of ethnographic practice need to become more intensive.

15 See Goring's own account of the church and his role in it, 'Brotherhood of the Cross and Star: a brief introduction' on the web at http://freespace.virgin.net/dolly.daniels/ARTICLES/briefintr.htm (accessed 12 September 2003). Goring actually taught at Goldsmiths College in New Cross, an area near to Peckham.

References

Arens, W. (1979) *The Man-Eating Myth*, New York: Oxford University Press.

Armstrong, Gary (1993) 'Like that Desmond Morris', in Dick Hobbs and Tim May (eds) *Interpreting the Field: Accounts of Ethnography*, Oxford: Clarendon Press.

Bauman, Zygmunt (2001) *Community: Seeking Safety in an Insecure World*, Cambridge: Polity Press.

Baumann, Gerd (1996) *Contesting Culture: Discourses of Identity in a Multi-Ethnic London*, Cambridge: Cambridge University Press.

Berman, Marshall (1999) *Adventures in Marxism*, London: Verso.

Bhabha, Homi K (1994) *The Location of Culture*, London: Routledge.

Bourne, Stephen (1998) *Black in the British Frame: Black People in British Film and Television*, London: Cassell.

Boyer, M. Christine (1996) *Cybercities*, New York: Princeton Architectural Press.

Conn, Eileen (2000) 'The Peckham Society', in John Beasley (ed.) *Peckham and Nunhead Remembered*, Stroud: Tempus.

Danziger, Nick (1996) *Danziger's Britain: A Journey to the Edge*, London: HarperCollins.

Farrar, Max (2001) *The Struggle for Community in a British Multi-Ethnic Inner-City Area: Paradise in the Making*, Lampeter: The Edwin Mullin Press.

Fiddes, N. (1992) *Meat: A Natural Symbol*, London: Routledge.

Frankenburg, R. (1966) *Communities in Britain*, Harmondsworth: Penguin.

Geertz, Clifford (1996) 'Afterword', in Steven Feld and Keith Basso (eds) *Senses of Place*, Santa Fe: School of American Research Press.

Gorer, Geoffrey (1955) *Exploring English Character*, London: Cresset Press.

Hussey, Andrew (2001) *The Game of War: The life and death of Guy Debord*, London: Jonathan Cape.

Inglis, Fred (2002) *Clifford Geertz: Culture, Custom and Ethics*, Cambridge: Polity Press.

Jeffrey, Tom (1978) *Mass Observation – A Short History*, Centre for Contemporary Cultural Studies, General Series: no. 55.

Kerridge, Roy (1995) *The Storm is Passing Over*, London: Thames & Hudson.

Lefebvre, Henri (1996) *Writing on Cities*, Oxford: Blackwell.

Little, Adrian (2002) *The Politics of Community*, Edinburgh: University of Edinburgh Press.

Miller, Daniel (1998) *A Theory of Shopping*, Oxford: Polity.

Morley, David (2000) *Home Territories*, London: Routledge.

Mudimbe, V.Y. (1994) *The Invention of Africa*, Bloomington: Indiana.

Norris, Clive and Armstrong, Gary (1999) *The Maximum Surveillance Society*, Oxford: Berg.

Quennell, Peter (ed.) (1984) *Mayhew's London*, London: Bracken.

Robins, Kevin (2001) 'Becoming anybody: thinking against the nation and through the city', *City* 5(1): 77–90.

Sebald, W.G. (1996) *The Emigrants*, New York: New Directions.

Schlosser, Eric (2001) *Fast Food Nation*, London: Penguin.

Schwarz, Bill (2003) 'Claudia Jones and the West Indian Gazette: reflections on the emergence of post-colonial Britain', *Twentieth Century British History* 14(3): 264–85.

Solomos, John and Back, Les (1995) *Race, Politics and Social Change*, London: Routledge.

Stanton, Gareth (1997) 'In praise of savage civilisation', in Steve Nugent and Cris Shore (eds) *Anthropology and Cultural Studies*, London: Pluto Books.

—— (2000) *'Gorer's Gaze'*, London: Goldsmiths Anthropology Research Papers, No. 1.

Stoller, Paul, (2002) *Money Has No Smell: The Africanization of New York*, Chicago: University of Chicago Press.

Taylor, Ian, Evans, Karen and Fraser, Penny. (1996) *A Tale of Two Cities: Global Change, Local Feeling and Everyday Life in the North of England*, London: Routledge.

Chapter 8

Media as conversation, conversation as media[1]

John Durham Peters

The hegemony of conversation

It is an instructive fact that all of the political positions represented in contemporary cultural theory and media studies agree on the value of 'conversation'. The Marxist tradition calls for authentic modes of interaction, from Adorno's complaint that the one-way communication of the culture industry resembles the Führer in its ubiquitous, inescapable commands, or the dream, shared by Brecht and Raymond Williams among many others, of using the mass media as means of interactive public access. Leading sociologists such as Bourdieu, Giddens, and Habermas all favor versions of what Giddens calls dialogical democracy. So do social democrats, such as John Dewey and James Carey, who regard communities without conversation as little better than animal gatherings of intellectually passive creatures. John Stuart Mill and Elihu Katz, yet further toward the liberal mainstream, believe that conversation is a key step in the formation of public opinion in the space between press and parliament. Feminists and postcolonial theorists have long called for encounter and dialogue as contrasts to sexist and racist oppression. Even conservatives sign on: the fallen cyber-prophet George Gilder (1992) bluntly called broadcast television 'totalitarian' in its one-way flow of programming and lack of interactivity, celebrating digital television for allowing dialogic creation of content. One could multiply examples denouncing monologue and praising conversation from diverse political and intellectual points on the spectrum; even the Archbishop of Canterbury is not only a fan of *The Simpsons* but also of conversation as a theological ideal (Williams 1999). We live in the age of conversation. It is one of the unquestioned goods of the moment and a normative ideal of how the media are expected to work in a democracy.

If conversation is a good thing, then its absence is a bad one. The notion that media have usurped our powers of conversation is one of the stock images of how the twentieth century went bad. Perhaps the most explicit critique of modern media as destroyers of conversation was given by Harold Adams Innis in 1948.

> The quantitative pressure of modern knowledge has been responsible for the decay of oral dialectic and conversation. The passive reading of newspapers and newspaper placards and the small number of significant magazines and books point to the dominance of conversation by the newspaper and to the pervasive influence of discontinuity, which is, of course, the characteristic of the newspaper, as it is of the dictionary.
>
> (Innis 1991: 191–2)

Oral talk, he asserts, is distinct from 'the cruelty of mechanized communication' that marks the modern world. Note that arguments later directed to television here aim at the newspaper. More recently, the Italian sociologist Franco Ferrarotti has written a book 'on the social impact of the mass media' called *The End of Conversation*. Many others could be summoned to bear witness of the modern silences between people: existentialists, mass-society theorists, or popular songwriters from Joni Mitchell to Thom Yorke.

The pathos of media-without-conversation seems here to stay; even if largely false empirically, it is a metaphor that's too convenient to disappear any time soon. The cognitivists tell us that watching TV is an extremely complex attentive process; the ethnographers have found a variety of talkative behaviors, some outlandish, some mundane, which audiences perform in front of their sets. As a negative picture of an ideal, however, the nightmare of the aphasic audience raises the legitimate concern that the lifeworld can become spiritually or humanly hollow in an age of consumption and home entertainment. It is also the mirror image of the normative account of media and conversation. Here media stimulate conversation. Mill thought that parliament was a receiver of mass communication, and that the press would stir up and focus discussion throughout the land. In a similar spirit, the notion of the two-step flow, associated with Lazarsfeld and his disciples at Columbia, suggests that media do not ruin or distort conversation; they supplement and inform it. The media serve to stand as part for the whole in mediations on modernity. The fear of muteness is a variant on the defining twentieth-century worry about alienation.

Both the lament and the hope for media and conversation point to a curious consensus. How to understand this agreement? Why do thinkers normally so contentious about everything else agree on conversation? When everyone agrees it is usually a sign of a hegemony of some sort. Conversation's definition is elastic and can range from descriptive to normative, from chatter to soulful communion, from the artful dodging of courtly conversation, the bourgeois authenticity of intimacy, to the soul-flights of Platonic or Buberian dialogue and micro-analyses of conversation analysis. The stakes in arguments about this protean concept are always bigger than what is falsely called mere talk, and in what follows I hope to nuance the argument by placing it in the context of two long-term historical trends regarding media and conversation.

Media as conversation

Over the twentieth century the media became increasingly conversational. They learned to mimic speech styles and genres from ordinary life and to stage a variety of forms of talk. Interactive styles in media talk and format address viewers-listeners as conversation partners. In advertisements, political oratory, or newsprint the world is full of personae who bid to talk with us. Such discourse can have conversational markers such as 'turn-taking, turn-packaging, indications of mutual knowledge, and paralinguistic features' (Myers 1994: 113). What Malinowski called 'phatic communion' – the rituals of staying in touch – is certainly found in radio, TV, and advertising voices: 'and now this'; 'don't touch that dial!'; 'you pay only $15.99'; etc. The discourse formats of broadcasting are rarely elevated oratory delivered to whom it may concern, but eyeball-to-eyeball attempts at personal relationships.

A lingering question is the legitimacy of such conversation. Is there something pathological about conversations in which the participants cannot hear each other talk or even know of each other's existence? Or is this the essence of capitalist ideology, pretending to call out an individual subject via a manufactured form of mass address? Or are there potentials for genuine social communion at a distance?

One vote for the authenticity of broadcast conversation comes from Paddy Scannell, who offers the arresting thesis that mass communication historically ends rather than begins with radio broadcasting. He is not referring to size of audiences but to style of address. Broadcast programmers, facing an audience listening in the privacy of their homes, had to invent styles and formats that compensated for the alienation implicit in large-scale address and that fit the more intimate context of the household. 'Involvement-structures of talk' were developed that allowed a sense of intimacy. Even though radio listeners might imagine themselves part of a nationwide community, they experienced radio as individuals or small groups, not as faces in a vast throng. Old styles of public oratory were duds over the airwaves. Scannell shows how the BBC, for instance with its first Director of Talks, Hilda Matheson, experimented with colloquial and dialogic modes of speech. The same is clearly true in US radio in the 1930s and 1940s, from crooner Rudy Vallee's vaunted ability to sing as if he were singing to each member of his audience alone, through a rich history of radio comics, journalists, and dramatists (McCracken 2000). Today, in talk shows and call-in shows, news shows and political campaigns, infomercials and Internet pop-ups, conversationalism rules, although the home audience is rarely anything but a virtual (imaginary) participant in the flow of talk.

We also get a qualified 'yes' from Livingstone and Lunt on the legitimacy of media conversation: 'If not political participation, public forums such as access and participation programmes can be thought of as social events and so involve formal, social participation' (Livingstone and Lunt 1994: 29). Chat shows are not just Adornoesque delusions, but sites in which some sort of social action is possible. Scannell (1996) argues that the long-term effect of public broadcasting has been to enlarge the public realm in a serious way, such that there is a genuine connection with the larger world for audience members. Dayan and Katz (1992) argue that the role of the audience as a passive spectator dwelling at one remove from the media can intermittently – not routinely – transfigure audiences into participants at a distance, or, better yet, that distance itself can dissolve into a kind of festive presence. On the right occasion, the public coalesces and fantasies step off the screen into the realities of daily life. Media events are not collective delusions; they are conjurings of social substance. Here media conversationalism is seen neither as pathology nor ideology but ritual accomplishment.

The most famous conception of media as conversation is that of parasocial interaction. Analyzing such late 1940s programs as 'the Lonesome Gal' in which a sultry voiced actress carried on a sexy monologue addressed to a radio audience of fellow lonely hearts (she actually got married secretly during the series), Donald Horton and Richard Wohl (1956) explored the way that broadcasters stage scenarios in which audiences are invited to feel a personal connection with characters, actors, or announcers. Parasocial interaction involves a suspension of disbelief about one's air friends. It borders on a delusional fantasy that fails to distinguish fact ('real people') and fiction (media figures). The 'para' in 'parasocial' is reminiscent of 'paranoia': one imagines there are enemies out there, the other thinks there are friends. The essence of parasocial interaction is its 'simulacrum of give and take'. Horton and Wohl invite us to see more in media than one-way edicts. Television discourse, like radio discourse before (at least in the USA and UK), sought to establish cosy relations with its audiences- 'up close and personal' in the phrase of ABC guru Roone Arledge.

Historians of newspapers and political oratory also point to a similar process. Before broadcasting, the history of advertising language (copywriting in particular) was one of increasing mimicry of everyday talk (even if the oh-so-ordinary chatter in ads was often horribly stilted). Where ads in early nineteenth-century newspapers were sober and informative, prose stuffed into tight, visually uninviting patches of print, later in the century advertisers explored visually appealing glimpses into everyday lives, with snatches of overheard conversation providing us with clues about what medicines to buy or what biscuits to eat (Leech 1966: ch. 19). As Leonard (1999) argues, one of the chief motors in the history of US journalism is what he calls democratic marketing – the use of a variety of gimmicks (coupons, beauty and recipe contests, giveaways) to conjure into being a public of newspaper readers (and subscribers). The long-term shift from sober, syntactically complex styles to jazzier, vernacular, visual – sometimes crass – expression accompanies (or makes possible) the expansion of US newspaper circulation from an elite few in the early nineteenth century to millions at the turn of the twentieth. Other countries have similar paths.

Something similar happens, argues Kathleen Jamieson (1988), in the history of political oratory in the USA. In the early twentieth century political speech-making was largely masculinist and martial, confrontational and aggressive, represented by Teddy Roosevelt's pulpit-banging. By the end of the century, the dominant style, represented for her by Ronald Reagan (though Bill Clinton or Tony Blair makes the point just as well), is marked by sincerity and self-disclosure, human-interest stories and personal vignettes of a sort that classical rhetorical theorists would have disparaged as hopelessly feminine. In a capitalist society where the persuasion of audiences is essential for profits or a promotional society that considers image essential for votes, it is no surprise that communicative styles have evolved from sender-oriented to audience-oriented. The simulation of conversation is one of the major features of public discourse today. This observation allows one preliminary conclusion: perhaps the world does not have too little conversation in it; it has too much. Or at least of the wrong kind. The call for more conversation ignores the ways that media have already expropriated its styles and strategies.

The conversationalization of public discourse has its critics. To some, media-simulated conversation is simply another name for media without conversation. Adorno provides such a critique in his notion of pseudoindividualization, that is, of false intimacy, a fake personal address based on statistical guesswork. Adorno attacks not only the loudspeaker blasting away at stupefied publics, but also, more subtly, how being let in on the trick is often the trick itself. By being clued into the deception, audiences are flattered into thinking they can see through the phony spell of the commodity, whereas all the others are duped. If everybody's somebody, nobody's anybody (as Gilbert and Sullivan put it), and if everyone is privy to the trick, the exposé of mass deception is the vehicle of mass deception itself. Parasocial clues, for Adorno, are a sly gesture of fraternization that ultimately excludes the audience, as it were, by its inclusion. The trick lies in fancying oneself favored by the media gods instead of consigned to common stupidity.

Others are skeptical of the democratic claims to inclusiveness in conversationalized media. Norman Fairclough defines conversationalization as 'the colonization of public orders of discourse by the conversational practices of the order of discourse of everyday life' (in a nifty reversal of Habermas's usual direction for colonization, as the lifeworld here overpowers the official system world). Ordinary voices 'are "ventriloquized" rather than directly heard' (Fairclough 1998: 145, 148, 160). He doesn't quite say what 'direct hearing' would mean, but presumably he means speaking without being subject to someone else's editing. (There is no reason to think that face-to-face settings are any more free of framing than mediated ones.)

> The fact that conversationalization is so widely appropriated ideologically gives an aura of insincerity to even the most innocent and exemplary instances of it. Conversely, even where it is most clearly ideologically appropriated, the implicit claims it makes about common experience and equality put these issues on the public agenda.
>
> (Fairclough 1995: 14)

Conversationalization steals the prestige of democratic discussion while doing little to make alternative voices heard, but since it does expose other voices, its political meaning is ambivalent (a Gramscian point). By recoding the lifeworld, media conversationalism may invent a dream of pure conversation that we never before experienced face-to-face. (Great conversation may be a media fantasy-projection.)

Media discourse invites a rethinking of what counts of conversation. For my part, I find the chaotic conversational coupling of media and audience as suggestive for all kinds of talk, mediated or not (in a larger sense, as Goffman showed, all talk is mediated anyway). Theorists who lament the decline of conversation are often too strictly normative in what they accept. Parasocial interaction, for instance, should be relieved of its stigma as a psychic disturbance, however mild, which afflicts fans and immature people. Why is it a sign of mental illness to converse with entities that cannot quite reply – walls, books, oneself, or TV sets – when one-sided conversations are actually fitting for all kinds of settings, such as writing, prayer, reading, reverencing the dead and communing with babies, pets, or plants? To speak in settings where no response is guaranteed is not unusual. Monological forms are not necessarily corrupt. We practice them when we publish, lecture, or even (sometimes) when we converse with each other face-to-face. The concept of parasocial interaction, in showing that people simulate conversation in imagined relationships, reveals something relevant for all social relationships, not just mediated ones (ask any teenager in love for the first time). Parasocial interaction is only the tip of the iceberg – the ways in which we live amid exploded conversations, turns that never quite connect.

Conversation as media

If media discourse has become increasingly conversationalized over the past century, conversation has become increasingly mediated. Not only is the twentieth century the age of dialogue as salvation, but of dialogue as mishap and breakdown. All around us, we find disturbances of conversation. In Kafka's stories, derailed turn-taking systems are either cosmically unsettling or absurdly funny; in the Marx Brothers' films, communication breakdown is a constant theme enacted in *non-sequiturs*. Asks Groucho: 'Have you received the answer to my wire?' Answers Chico: 'No, I haven't sent it yet.' Groucho: 'In that case don't send it.' There is a deep skepticism about the 'naturalness' of conversation that extends from Woody Allen's movies to the sociological studies of Goffman, Garfinkel, and Sacks. Goffman named the experience of 'alienation from interaction' and thought the dyad too simple a category, analyzing each speaker into animator, author, and principal. In the plays of Sartre, Beckett, Ionesco, or Havel, the novels of Woolf or Camus, Murakami or Kundera, the films of Bergman or Antonioni, people only rarely connect. Twentieth-century culture is full of dialogue-follies. Demonstrating how our conversational habits might have changed historically is an extremely difficult task, but, intellectually, conversation-skepticism is a feature of our life just as the *representation* of conversation has been enormously complicated in drama, philosophy, literature, film, and, yes, linguistics. (One of the most obvious things about any transcript of a conversation, even with a simple transcription system, is just how much messier conversation is than it usually seems to us.)

The widespread nervousness about conversation likely has many sources, ranging from classic sociological analyses of privacy and anomie, to newer ones about gender roles and sociability, but one source I want to draw attention to is modern speech-machines that reorder interaction. Telephones cut conversations in two, the phonograph stores them for later playback, microphones selectively amplify voices, radio disembodies voices as film re-embodies them. By conversation as media, I mean not only the fact that media fare can become a topic in everyday talk, but also that everyday talk takes on the communicative characteristics of media, such as uncertainties of address, delays of response, and dubious delivery. In richer societies, much of our interaction is enabled by interpersonal media such as email and telephone, sites in which the broadcast and the interactive are hard to tell apart. In what we might call the 'great communications shift' face-to-face communication has taken on features once associated with mass communication at the same time that broadcast discourse has assumed dialogic features. Mass and interpersonal communication have switched places, rather like the 'Negroponte switch' in which the air now carries telephony and wires now carry broadcast programs. In private life, many of us talk like Beckett characters; in public discourse, celebrities present themselves as if they are our friends.

The new forms of writing light, sound, and text in the nineteenth century such as film, gramophone, and typewriter reordered the nature of discourse (Kittler 1999). By the late nineteenth century, observers were noting already that strange things were happening to conversation. Mark Twain's 1880 story (1917: 204–8), 'A telephonic conversation', is ironically titled, as the joke is that we can only hear one half of the conversation:

> Then followed that queerest of all the queer things in this world – a conversation with only one end to it. You hear questions asked; you don't hear the

answer. You hear invitations given; you hear no thanks in return. You have listening pauses of dead silence, followed by irrelevant or unjustifiable exclamations of glad surprise or sorrow or dismay. You can't make head or tail of the talk, because you never hear anything that the person at the other end of the wire says.

Twain then offers an account of one such 'conversation', a premise to indulge in a series of droll *non-sequiturs*, such as:

Pause.
It's forty-ninth Deuteronomy, sixty-fourth to ninety-seventh inclusive. I think we ought all to read it often.
Pause.
Perhaps so; I generally use a hair-pin.

Twain is facing a brave new fact: mediated conversation. The schizophrenic splitting of telephonic speech has become ordinary for us today.

Thomas Edison (1888) noted something similar eight years later.

But the phonograph receives, and then transmits to our ears again, every least thing that was said – exactly *as* it was said – with the faultless fidelity of the instantaneous photograph. We shall know for the first time what conversation really is; just as we have learned, only within a few years, through the instantaneous photograph, what attitudes are taken by the horse in motion.

Edison thus predicts conversation analysis, something not realized until the 1960s and the portable tape recorder. Machines such as the telephone and phonograph, and their long progeny, probably had much to do with the creation of the very notion of conversation.

They at least contributed much to modern comedy. In his movie *Rock a Bye Baby* (1958) Jerry Lewis stands behind a tubeless television set and acts out a series of routines for his girlfriend's drunken father, who thinks he is watching TV. The humor lies not only in Lewis's antic mimicry, but also the violation of the boundary between broadcast discourse on the tube and interactive presence of the body. There is something unholy, even idolatrous, about conversing with media, as we confuse machines and people, the animate and the inanimate, the near and the far. We face micro–macro confusions. In Bruce Springsteen's song, '57 Channels and Nothin' On', he shoots his TV after his girlfriend leaves; Carol Burnett, playing a lonely drunkard in the silly film *Little Orphan Annie*, takes a parasocial relationship to an absurdly literal extreme by snuggling and smooching her radio set in bed. Synecdochic mix-ups occur in webs of mass communication whose reach is intimate. Springsteen and Burnett perform part for whole interactions with media that, in each case, mirror or substitute for the disordered interactions they have with 'real-life' lovers.

One of the great analysts of mediated conversation was Sigmund Freud (1960); again, the issue is jokes. Over and over, he reveals turn-taking gone haywire as one of the fundamental resources of humor. Many of his jokes involve conversations whose logic has run away from the inept attempts of the participants. The prospective groom thus goes with the marriage-broker to a young woman's house and while awaiting her appearance is invited to admire the family's impressive collection of silver items. Ever skeptical, the prospective groom points out that they could have been borrowed for the occasion. The broker replies, 'Who'd lend these people anything anyway!' The marriage-broker's answer is a seemingly natural response (a turn in an adjacency-pair, as Harvey Sacks would call it) in the conversation, a reply designed to refute the groom's skepticism. But, instead, it radically undermines his own position and reinforces what it was meant to dispel. Or take another *Schadchen* joke: The broker brings along a companion to reinforce his testimony of the prospective bride's excellence. What eyes she has, you must see for yourself, says the broker. What eyes she has, says the sidekick. What posture, says the broker. And what posture, says the sidekick. What an education, says the broker. And what an education, says the sidekick. Oh, and she also has a hunchback, says the broker. And what a hunchback, comes the echo. The humor, as Freud remarks, turns on the automatism of the conversational logic, the helplessness of the broker to deceive, and his unwitting self-betrayal. The conversational motion somehow escapes the control of its participants, only to reveal his scheming in spite of himself. Freud believes that the truth will always out – slips of the tongue, jokes, dreams; you can't hide your love away. There is something deeply humane in these jokes, a kind of empathy for foolishness, but it all rests on turns of conversation that turn faster than their speakers can reckon with.

Isn't there something similar to conversing with a television set? The pathos and humor for Freud lie in the automatism of talk: the relentless flow of the conversation, its immunity to our intentions of control. (The phonograph gives us writing without a subject.) That conversation eludes us is something we have all experienced; the acuteness of this sense may be particularly modern. The misfires that Freud noted are institutionalized in the conversational efforts of promotional discourse generally: when I watched television in Athens, people spoke rapid Greek at me, asking me to buy cigarettes and tampons. I can neither understand them very well nor tell them that I have no use for their goods, but they just keep flowing relentlessly along. The breakdowns of communication and conversation are registered in everyday speech, but happen all around us. We live increasingly among *non-sequiturs*. This is the fate of the bazaar of public life. As the great nineteenth-century physicist James Clerk Maxwell asked, what if the book of nature were a magazine? His question reflects a long-term trend, as Raymond Williams pointed out, the increasing miscellaneity of public discourse.

Conversation, in our common experience and representation of it at least, has often come to approach something like mass communication, in its miscellaneity, juxtaposition, automatism, and jumbled editing. Conversation has taken on properties first seen clearly in media discourse. The publicity of scattered talk – the chatter of the agora – has penetrated the lifeworld, much to the lament of Innis and his colleagues. The notion of mediated conversation resembles the lament of media without conversation in its historical analysis, but not its implications. I disagree with the lament that conversation has died; rather, the yearning for perfect conversation was likely invented, or amplified, in the shadow of media. The problem with what Michael Schudson over two decades ago called the conversational ideal in media studies is not only that it misconstrues media, but also conversation as well! It's always been messy and mediated; our machines have simply helped us see to what degree.

Some conclusions

It is an irony that conversation should be held up as answer when it has long been diagnosed as diseased. Forms alone of communication matter less than what is done with them. Conversation is not the only format suited for democracy. We need both dissemination and dialogue. Anyone who has dealt with second- or third-world bureaucracy knows that a world in which only interpersonal communication existed could be a hell: no general announcements of rules or procedures, only the luck of getting someone's eye or exploiting personal connections. There is a place for a degree of formality in democratic discourse. Starch can be as valuable as sweatshirts. There is a need for presentational modes as well: dialogue is not the only way to carry culture. Anyone learning a new language knows that conversation is scarier than newspapers or television, since failure to understand is annoying to others and it is potentially embarrassing if you pretend to understand; the stakes in dialogue are always intensified. Dissemination offers the relief of tuning out or going at one's own speed. There is a dignity in mass communication, and a proper place and time for an aesthetics of awe, a decorum of hushed audiences. Listening to others is a profound democratic act. Perhaps public service media will always be somewhat stiffer than commercial ones; but they also have certain advantages, such as the chimes of Big Ben. Much of culture is non-reciprocal in form.

Like all media, conversation creates monopolies of knowledge; it can be tiring, impractical, and exclusive. Conversation, for instance, rarely allows for an extended performance (a lecture, a concert). 'Passive listening' is one of the worst ideas ever to infest cultural criticism – as if listening were not one of the most difficult things people ever do. Dialogue presupposes silence, indeed it demands it. Dialogue is not always active and participatory (Socrates' dialectic is one-way: it is a rare event indeed when he himself is transformed by dialogue). Dialogue only lets one voice speak at once. If we are serious about finding democratic forms of communication, we should appreciate formats that allow many to take part at once: singing, voting, dancing, striking, worshipping, protesting, cheering, petitioning. Watching and listening can be intensely active practices – as audience researchers tell us – and they are collective forms. Dialogue is valuable, but it is a strict and jealous god. It is not necessarily the most vernacular form of political talk, but the most demanding and difficult; dialogues' law is not self-expressive pleasure but rather self-denying listening. Conversation is no more free of history, power, and control than any other form of communication. It is a practice that can be demotic and playful, invigorating and demanding, but certainly not exhaustive of the communicative forms native to either our species or to democratic life. There is a necessity, even occasional nobility, in non-conversational forms.

Compare Greek tragedy and comedy in norms of audience decorum. In comedy, the audience is invited to participate; in tragedy a hushed tone prevails. Comedy's beginnings and endings are less crucial for understanding the plot, since the playwright knows the audience may be too busy talking to listen; Aristophanes regularly has a long warm-up dialogue while the audience settles down before he launches the plot. Tragedy starts at once. Applause may interrupt the State of the Union address, but not a symphony. Forms of communication, happily, are heterogeneous. We would be impoverished if all learning were via conversation, and if we had to discover everything afresh (Socrates thought so, but he could also be awfully tedious). It would also be bleak and alien if we only had presentational modes. Genres of deliberation and presentation, participation and passivity, are both key. Conversation is a very valuable genre, but certainly not the only one. In as much as life can sometimes be tragic as well as comic, we need more than conversation to anchor our theories of media and democratic life.

Notes

1   This chapter is a brief overview of what I hope to make into a book-length project. Much of its writing was supported by a generous grant from the Leverhulme Trust and generous colleagues at Goldsmiths College.

References

Dayan, D. and E. Katz (1992) *Media Events*, Cambridge: Harvard.
Edison, T. (1888) 'The perfected phonograph', *North American Review* 146. 648–9.
Fairclough, N. (1995) *Media Discourse,* London: Edward Arnold.

—— 1998. 'Political discourse in the media: an analytical framework', in A. Bell and P. Garrett (ed.) *Approaches to Media Discourse*, Oxford: Blackwell.

Ferrarotti, Franco (1988) The End of Conversation: The Impact of Mass Media on Modern Society, New York: Greenwood.

Freud, S. (1960 [1905]) *Jokes and Their Relation to the Unconscious*, New York: Norton.

Gilder, G. (1992) *Life after Television*, New York: Norton.

Horton, R. and Wohl, R. (1956) 'Mass communication and parasocial interaction', *Psychiatry* 19: 215–29.

Innis, H.A. (1991 [1948]) 'A critical review', in *The Bias of Communication*, Toronto: University of Toronto Press.

Jamieson, K. (1988) *Eloquence in an Electronic Age*, New York: Oxford University Press.

Kittler, F.A. (1999) *Gramophone, Film, Typewriter*, Stanford: Stanford.

Leech, G.N. (1966) *English in Advertising: A Linguistic Study of Advertising in Great Britain*, London: Longman.

Leonard, T. (1999) 'Making readers into citizens – the old-fashioned way', in T. Glasser (ed.) *The Idea of Public Journalism*, New York: Guilford, pp. 85–96.

Livingstone, S. and Lunt, P. (1994) *Talk on Television: Audience Participation and Public Debate*, London: Routledge.

McCracken, A. (2000) 'Real men don't sing: crooning and American culture, 1928–1933', doctoral dissertation, University of Iowa.

Myers, G. (1994) *Words in Ads*, London: Edward Arnold.

Scannell, P. (1996) *Radio, Television, & Modern Life*, Oxford: Blackwell.

Schudson, M. (1978) 'The ideal of conversation in the study of mass media', *Communication Research* 12: 320–9.

Twain, M. (1917 [1880]) 'A telephonic conversation', in *The $30,000 Bequest and Other Stories*, New York: Harpers, pp. 204–8.

Williams, R. (1999) *On Christian Theology*, Cambridge, MA: Blackwell.

Section III

Media power, ideology and markets

The essays in this section either offer general critiques of the field (Curran and Couldry) or focus on what we would regard as under-developed areas within it (Davis and Magder). James Curran offers a historical account of the development of media and cultural theory in Britain. His central argument is that this development needs to be understood in relation to wider social and political change, rather than exclusively as a set of 'internally' evolving ideas. This approach encourages a greater distance of perspective, which registers losses as well as gains in the evolution of the field. The ascendancy of neo-liberal thought during the last two decades has contributed, in his view, to an increasing reluctance to examine critically the distorting role of media markets, to engage with issues of class inequality, or to adequately acknowledge the negative aspects of globalisation.

Aeron Davis turns the spotlight on an over-theorised and under-researched area: the promotional industries (advertising, marketing and public relations). There are, he argues, four contending positions. Enthusiasts see promotion as a neutral mechanism that harmonises supply and demand, and facilitates communication and reciprocity. Critics see promotion as a tool used mainly by the powerful to increase their control, as a source of media corruption, and as an integral part of a consumerist culture that thrives on unfulfillable dreams and leads ultimately to personal dissatisfaction. Sceptics question whether promotion has the power and influence attributed to it by enthusiasts and critics alike, and stress the ability of both media staff and audiences to withstand promotional pressures. A fourth position (overlapping with the first) sees promotion as a constitutive part of postmodernity, and in some cases argues that it is part of a process that empowers citizen-consumers. Davis concludes by attempting a critical synthesis of these different perspectives.

Ted Magder takes us on a guided tour of an important and neglected area. While debates about public service broadcasting, media subsidies and the free market in a national setting are familiar to most media students (in Europe, at least), surprisingly little attention has been given to the principles and practice of international regulation of the media. Yet international regulation of communications dates back to the nineteenth century. It is becoming increasingly important as a consequence of intensified globalisation, and the pressure exerted by the world's sole superpower in favour of unrestricted cross-border flows of communication, and against national media subsidies. Magder provides a clear account of the competing principles and concerns - from technical standardisation to security, freedom of expression to diversity - which inform international regulation, and describes new demands that are currently being pressed. He also explains a Byzantine universe in which some international regulations are binding and others are not, and some are irrevocable and others are negotiable.

Nick Couldry argues that we should stand outside the conventional framework of media studies. The standard approach in our field, he argues, tends to focus on large-scale media, on the unargued assumption that these matter most. This assumption is sustained, according to Couldry, by three 'road-blocks': fashionable theorising about media spectacle, a pervasive and largely unacknowledged functionalism that relates the media to an imagined 'whole', and, above all, an involuntary 'media-centrism' that is manifested in a focus on television rather than the press, and on national rather than local, and on mainstream rather than alternative media. What is needed, he argues, is a new orientation in which what is important is investigated from the perspective of people's lives, in terms of what makes for a good or bad life, what opens up or closes down options, what contributes to knowledge and how this is used. This perspective, he hopes, will be better able to generate a new mapping of the role of a variety of media in our lives - a mapping informed by research rather than habitual assumption.

Chapter 9

Media and cultural theory in the age of market liberalism

James Curran

Introduction

Media and cultural studies has developed a distinctive rhetoric. It is proclaimed periodically that a new 'turn' is taking place. Authoritative figures are then cited to assure readers that if they join this 'turn', they will be travelling in good company to the latest intellectual fashion resort. There is, we are told, a new awareness of a central weakness in the field, or a general awakening to a new insight. Not to join this new 'turn' implies that one prefers to remain mired in error or to cut oneself off from the very latest in new thinking.

This rhetoric is usually an exercise in propaganda. Its central defect is that it presents the development of the field as being determined solely by an intellectual progression of thought, and ignores the wider context in which that thought has taken place. Instead, it advances a simple fable of intellectual improvement in which error or misunderstanding is regularly rectified. What, then, is the missing context that helps us to make sense of the way in which media and cultural studies has developed during the last quarter of a century, with particular reference to Britain (with an occasional sideways glance elsewhere)? A short, necessarily selective answer is that it was strongly influenced by four key developments. These shaped its concerns, terms of reference and research agendas.

Four key influences

One key influence was the historic victory of capitalist democracy. In 1989, the Berlin Wall came down. This symbolised the popular rejection of communism in East Germany – and implicitly in the Soviet bloc – by the people it was intended to benefit. In 1991, the Soviet Union disintegrated, and its communist regime was replaced by an authoritarian market democracy. China, the only remaining major communist power, enthusiastically embraced market reforms from the

1980s onwards because, in the words of its reforming leader, Deng Xiaoping, 'poverty is not socialism: to be rich is glorious' (Anon. 2004). China ceased to be, in an economic sense, a communist society.

These developments consolidated the neo-liberal hegemony of the right. The 1980s were dominated by right-wing governments – Reagan in the USA, Thatcher in Britain, and their equivalents in many other parts of the developed world. The fall of communism was presented as the end of history, the final arrival to a permanent terminus (Fukuyama 1993). It showed allegedly that the free market was the only viable, productive and efficient way of organising society. Regimes based on publicly owned economies had failed, while their capitalist rivals had triumphed. The market was the anchor of freedom and choice: the foundation of the morally superior system of liberal democracy. Part of the seductive power of this rhetoric stemmed from the spurious way in which deregulated capitalism and democracy were presented as joined-at-the-hip twins.

Yet, social democracy failed – in the view of some – to provide an alternative rallying point, despite its greater electoral successes in the 1990s and 2000s. The starting point of social democracy is that the state should redistribute resources from the rich to the poor, and from the fortunate to the unfortunate, in order to create a fairer, more fulfilled society. But in the post-Cold War period, social democratic governments were beset by numerous difficulties: tax revolts, a contraction of their working-class base, the ascendancy of neo-liberal thought, and above all the diminished ability of national governments to manage their economies in an era of deregulated global capitalism. Even showcase social democracies – most notably the Nordic and Rhineland models – downplayed redistribution and made increasing accommodations to the logic of the market by the early 2000s.

The post-Cold War era was thus a period of disorientation and disempowerment for the left. This was reinforced in Europe – though much less so in the USA – by the left's complex, subjective reactions to the historic defeat of communism. In the 1980s, relatively few radical intellectuals in Western Europe had illusions about the Soviet Union, in contrast to their counterparts in the 1930s. Most welcomed the fall of communism as a victory for democracy. But communism's eclipse also represented the end of a historic experiment based on a desire to build a more equal society. Its pathetic ending seemed, especially among an older, radical generation, to signify the closing down of possibilities, the limiting of what it was realistic to hope for. This is well expressed by the British playwright, David Edgar (born in 1948). 'I had never been,' he said, 'a communist and I had never felt that the Soviet Union was my team.' Yet, 'when the [Berlin] Wall came down, I did feel that it was the death of ideals that I had a relationship with' (O'Mahony 2004: 23).

Another key development that influenced the evolution of media and cultural studies had taken place earlier. Many of its pioneers in Britain had entered adulthood in the 1960s, and were profoundly influenced by the cultural revolt of that period. At the heart of this revolt was an assertion of individualism. This was widely interpreted at the time to be progressive since it took the form of an outspoken rejection of nationalism, racism, social hierarchy, bureaucracy, conformism and sexual repression. But it also registered at the same time a repudiation of the collectivism represented by traditional social democracy. Its political ambiguity became more apparent during the 1980s and 1990s when individualism became one of the forces harnessed by the right to sustain a new ideological hegemony (Hall 1988).

The ambiguities of the 1960s cultural revolt – its progressive rhetoric, its individualism, its anti-statism, its disconnection from parliamentary politics, its idealism – contributed to the ambiguities of British cultural studies as it developed over time. While this tradition clearly came from the left and continued to identify with the left, it travelled during the 1980s and 1990s a considerable political distance from where it started.

The third key development was the rise of women. Structural changes in the economy increased female participation in the paid workforce, at a growing trend rate in the period after 1970. New legislation in 1970 and 1975 outlawed sex discrimination over a wide area in Britain. Above all, the feminist movement mounted from the late 1960s onwards a sustained attack on traditionalist gender norms. While sharp gender disparities persisted in terms of power, responsibilities, income and life chances, they were lessened.

Gradual improvements in the position of women penetrated the academic world. Out of over thirty full-time, permanent academic staff employed in the pioneer media/cultural studies centres at Birmingham, Leeds and Leicester Universities, and the Polytechnic of Central London media department in 1976, there were just two women. This grotesque gender imbalance in academic staff was modified over time. In addition, the large majority of students studying media and cultural studies in Britain were, almost from the outset, women. Media and cultural studies – like English literature – was primarily a female option. These interrelated changes in society and in the academy transformed media and cultural studies. Gender became a central concern of the field, in marked contrast to the situation before 1980.

The fourth key influence was the intensification of globalisation. This contributed to a rewriting of media history in which the nation was portrayed as culturally constructed rather than 'given' (Curran 2002). It also resulted in globalisation becoming a salient concern in a field previously characterised by a high degree of parochialism.

Four key influences thus shaped the development of media and cultural studies in Britain during the last twenty-five years – the political ascendancy of market liberalism, the social dynamic of increasing individualism, the rise of women and intensified globalisation.[1] It is the first of these influences that we will mainly focus on in this chapter.

Exit strategies

Media and cultural studies in Britain developed in the margins of academic life. Its 'second-wave' pioneers in the 1970s tended to be non-conformist in both educational and political terms.[2] Indeed, many of them consciously sought to develop a new subject in Britain in a form that was different from its definition elsewhere, most notably in the USA.

The version of this new subject that took hold in Britain by the mid-1970s was a magpie tradition that stole from different disciplines and intellectual traditions, among them Marxism. However, this 'Marxisant' legacy was discreetly repudiated by many media and cultural studies academics in the 1980s and early 1990s. This was accomplished (sometimes, one suspects, unconsciously) by championing, emasculating and then discarding the work of two maverick Marxist theorists.

Stuart Hall introduced the work of the Italian Marxist theorist, Antonio Gramsci – mostly written in the 1920s and 1930s – in a celebrated essay (Hall 1977) with significant subsequent reinterpretations (Hall 1982 and 1985). Gramsci, and those who took up his work, emphasised that the social order is maintained not just through coercion but also through active consent. In hegemonic societies, this consent is secured through the cultural leadership of the dominant social grouping. This results in most people involuntarily making sense of society within its horizon of thought. However, this hegemonic ascendancy can be broken through the creation of a 'popular front' of the mind: through different groups coming together in opposition, and developing a coherent alternative understanding of society that connects to people's social experiences and identities, and is expressed through different symbolic forms.

This set of arguments provided a way of reconceiving the media as a battleground. It offered a new conceptual map of the sources of conflict and opposition in society. It also resulted in popular culture, from music to fashion, being viewed as an important arena of contest. During the 1980s, a Gramscian perspective became almost a new orthodoxy in British cultural studies research. However, in the process of becoming established and actively reinterpreted, certain themes were demoted and others were introduced. The original emphasis on contested *ascendancy* gave way to a stress just on contest, and the media were re-presented increasingly as open fora (with close similarities to a liberal pluralist conception of the media). Gender and ethnic groups were foregrounded, while social classes receded from view. Above all – and this represented the decisive break with the original analysis – the link between cultural struggle and a collective strategy for winning political control of the state, stressed by Gramsci himself, virtually disappeared. By 1990, Gramsci had been reinterpreted in a way that bore little resemblance to his work,[3] and by 2000 he had largely ceased to be cited. One moment Gramsci was a much admired guru; the next he was, like yesterday's pop star, rarely mentioned.

Something comparable – though occurring in a less extreme form – happened in relation to the German philosopher and social theorist, Jürgen Habermas. Nicholas Garnham (1986, revised 1990) introduced his work to the British media studies community, though it had been trailed earlier. Habermas (1989 [1962]) argued that there developed in the eighteenth century a 'public sphere' of rational-critical debate, sustained through the press, coffee-houses and salons of privileged society. This gave rise to independent, reasoned 'public opinion' that influenced government. However, this public sphere was allegedly colonised in the subsequent period by an expanded state and powerful corporate interests. Modern media fell, in Habermas's view, under the influence of public relations, advertising and big business, and offered shallow consumerism, empty political spectacle and pre-packaged convenience thought.

This analysis is a curious hybrid. Its description of the eighteenth-century public sphere owed much to traditional liberal history, whereas its pessimistic account of modern media drew heavily on the work of the Marxist Frankfurt School. Garnham drew selectively on this analysis, projecting Habermas's conception of the eighteenth-century public sphere forward in time, while playing down his Frankfurt pessimism. There is, argued Garnham, a contemporary public sphere that is best conceived as the space between the economy and the state. It should stage a rational, universalistic and inclusive form of public debate – an objective furthered by public service broadcasting.

Garnham's selective extrapolation from Habermas was extended by others who followed in his wake. While Garnham had portrayed the public sphere as an ideal-typification, it came to be discussed as a reality. Whereas Garnham had rightly viewed political parties as central components of the public sphere, the conception that took hold was that of an aggregation of individuals gathered together as a public. What people increasingly took from Habermas was a view of broadcasting as an institution that brought people together in reasoned and reciprocal debate (e.g. Scannell 1989) – almost the exact obverse of what Habermas had argued in his seminal work (Habermas 1989: 171).

References to Habermas, once almost a religious act of observance in some circles, became relatively infrequent by the late 1990s. Surprisingly few people in British media studies even noticed, still less discussed, Habermas's important (radical democratic) reconception of the nature and role of the public sphere in a contemporary context (Habermas 1996). The intellectual fashion – and the intellectual fashion-conscious – had moved on.

This strange taking up, and putting down, of two untypical Marxists, accompanied by very free reinterpretations of their work, was a way of settling past debts. For two different but overlapping groups – one centred in cultural studies (Gramsci) and the other in media studies (Habermas) – it represented a way of responding to the fading light of Marxism in the wider environment of the British left.

Postmodernism

A positive feature of the pioneering radical tradition in Britain was that it sought to relate the mass media and popular culture to the power dynamics of society. For example, a study of a moral panic about 'mugging' was situated in a synoptic analysis of the British state, politics, economy, culture and social relations over a period of almost two decades (Hall *et al.* 1978). Although this celebrated study was unusually intellectually confident even by the standards of the late 1970s, it came out of a 'holistic' tradition that attempted to think in broad terms about the media's relationship to society.

A growing number of media and cultural studies researchers abandoned this totalising approach during the climacteric period of the late 1980s and early 1990s. This was because they found it increasingly difficult to make sense of the rapidly changing world in which they lived. Some turned their perplexity into an intellectual virtue by trumpeting the merits of postmodernist work (some of which had been published over a decade earlier). Especially influential was the French philosopher, Jean-François Lyotard, who emphasised the fragmented nature of the social world, the impossibility of advancing claims to any universal truth, and the limitations of all foundational social theories and general interpretations of history (apart from postmodernism) (Lyotard 1984). Another revered postmodernist, Jean Baudrillard, proclaimed that the mass circulation of media images had transformed the world into a hall of mirrors, and led to an implosion of meaning. 'The medium and the real,' Baudrillard wrote, 'now form a single inscrutable nebula' resulting in 'the defusing of polarities, the short-circuiting of the poles of every differential system of meaning, the obliteration of distinctions and oppositions between terms, including the distinction between the medium and the real' (Baudrillard 1980:142).

This swirling mist of postmodernist language was accompanied by 'deconstructive' assaults on radical positions. It left some researchers disorientated and confused. It was hard to make critical sense of society, lamented one Baudrillard apostle, 'when no one is dominating, nothing is being dominated and no ground exists for a principle of liberation from domination' (Poster 1988: 6)

If one response was de-radicalised bafflement, another was circumspection. It was reasoned that since 'old' thinking, from Marxism to traditional socialist feminism, provided unreliable compass bearings for steering a ship in open seas, it was better to hug the shoreline. 'The dangers of easy categorisation and generalisation,' warned one influential essay, 'so characteristic of mainstream traditions in the social sciences (including mass communication theory and research), are greater than the benefits of a consistent particularism' in a context where post-modernism has highlighted 'the irreducible complexity and relentless heterogeneity of social life' (Ang and Hermes 1991: 323). In confusing times, cautious specification seemed safer than incautious generalisation.

A key figure in this postmodernist moment was an outstanding historian and social philosopher, Michel Foucault (who vehemently denied being a postmodernist). His powerful influence on media and cultural studies during the 1990s further undermined a totalising approach. Foucault's eclectic historical research into institutions as different as hospitals and prisons suggested that power is constituted by a multiplicity of specific relationships, and the discursive contexts in which these operate. The interaction between authority and discourse, he also argued, is both multilayered and dynamic. 'There is no power-relation,' wrote Foucault, 'without the correlative constitution of a field of knowledge, nor any knowledge that does not presuppose and constitute at the same time power-relations' (Foucault 1979: 27). Researchers in the Foucauldian tradition who sought to uncover this complexity were increasingly drawn towards narrowly focused micro-research.

The postmodernist moment occurred in the early 1990s, the High Noon of radical cultural studies when researchers sought refuge in the shadows of scepticism and particularism. It registered not just an erosion of radical certainty but also a growing sense of powerlessness during a period of right-wing ascendancy. Radical cultural studies research, coming out of Birmingham University in the 1970s, had communicated a sense of urgency and commitment. Baudrillard's postmodernism, by contrast, implied that all human endeavour was inspired by illusion, while Foucault's work seemed to suggest that simply unmasking the epistemic foundations of power would lead to human emancipation. The rise of postmodernism in cultural studies represented a significant shift. It is best summed up as a movement from the vanguard to the avant-garde, from collectivist to aesthetic politics.

Loving the market

If one route led towards postmodernism, another led to heart-warming populism. This latter transition is exemplified by a weathervane book written by Paul Willis (1990), a Birmingham cultural studies pioneer and the author of a classic study of working-class youth (Willis 1977). His 1990 volume, *Common Culture*, came out of a Gulbenkian research project in which many of the great and the good in radical cultural studies were involved. It is worth looking at briefly since it expresses in characteristic language the central themes of cultural populism.

Its starting point is a celebration of the resourcefulness and autonomy of the people, rooted in their rich inherited cultural resources and the social practices of their everyday life. 'There is now,' writes Paul Willis, 'a whole social and cultural medium of interwebbing common meaning and identity-making which blunts, deflects, minces up or transforms outside or top-down communication. In particular, elite or "official" culture has lost its dominance' (Willis 1990: 128).

Against this background, the market is viewed as liberating. It provides the raw material that audiences work on, and transfigure, as 'active producers of meaning'. Furthermore, 'the anarchic market' opens up new vistas. It is unconstrained by official culture, and subverts previous certainties and conventions (Willis 1990: 129–30 and 138). It offers 'better and freer materials for building security and coherence' in the search for self-actualisation (Willis 1990: 158).

This positive view of the market is contrasted with a more critical view of public provision. 'In general, the public sector cannot do better than the commercial sector in supplying attractive and usable symbolic resources' (Willis 1990: 131). Indeed, the market surpasses all alternatives in terms of facilitating self-realisation. 'The coming together of coherence and identity,' according to Paul Willis, takes place 'in leisure not work, through commodities not political parties, privately not collectively' (Willis 1990: 159).

Willis originated from a far-left tradition, contemptuous of social democracy. He was still committed, he assures us, to 'socialism', though in an 'unprefigured' form to be determined by the people in the future. So, what prompted his Damascene conversion to the virtues of the free market? One clue is provided by his anti-statist orientation and focus on individual self-realisation – a strand of 1960s radical culture that proved to be politically mobile in the 1980s. Another is his reference to 'the now-tumbling walls, towers, and ideas of the East', an allusion to the fall of the Berlin Wall in the previous year. Yet, in some ways still more revealing is his dismissal of 'many' radical alternatives as elitist and socially irrelevant, and his acknowledgement of the 'inevitability of some of the Thatcherite "reforms" of the last decade' (Willis 1990: 158–60).

Cultural populism

The cultural populist tradition usually took a tacitly favourable view of the market, rather than enthusing explicitly about its virtues in the style of Paul Willis. Its more mainstream exponent in the transitional, dying days of the Cold War period was perhaps John Fiske. The people, Fiske assured us, use 'the products of capitalism while rejecting the ideology they more normally bear' (Fiske 1987: 261–2). Audiences routinely redirect the meanings of the media in progressive or recalcitrant ways (Fiske 1987 and 1991). Audience power is, in this view, like an immune system protecting people from unwanted ideological bacteria.

Audiences are able to impose their own meaning, it was explained, partly because media content is often accessible to divergent interpretation. Market pressures compel the media to connect to the social experiences and concerns of the people, irrespective of the values of media owners or the dominant discourses of society. This can give rise to contradictions and tensions in 'media texts' that facilitate independent audience interpretation. Above all, audiences respond selectively to the media by drawing upon the social discourses of their everyday world.

This thesis gained a new lease of life in the 1990s by being redeployed in a debate about 'cultural imperialism'. A sophisticated orchestration of it appeared in John Tomlinson's synthesis of existing research (Tomlinson 1999). Global capitalism is not promoting a capitalist mono-culture, he argued, because the symbolic meaning of globally distributed cultural goods is transformed through local cultural appropriations. While radical critics view Coca-Cola as a symbol of US capitalism, many consumers think that it is a local product. Indeed, people in different countries attribute different magical properties to it (such as anti-wrinkling in Russia, raising the dead in Haiti). Similarly, the same television programmes are understood in divergent ways in different parts of the globe.

This celebration of popular cultural power, rooted in the divergent traditions of different peoples around the world, was linked to another theme: the dynamism of the global media economy. The notion that the 'media are American' fails to grasp, it is argued, that Hollywood's global domination of television has been challenged successfully by new centres of television production around the world, catering for different language markets (Sinclair et al. 1996). Global conglomerates have also been forced to adapt to the demands of local consumers. For example, MTV-Europe abandoned its attempt to impose a single service on Western Europe, and sub-divided into four regional services in order to cater for differences of language and musical taste (Roe and Meyer 2000). The global media market is portrayed, with occasional caveats, as dynamic, competitive and responsive to difference.

The central conclusion of this recycled cultural populism is that globalisation is an overwhelmingly positive development. It is a 'decentred' process that has no *necessary* affinity with the interests of the West (Tomlinson 1999: 94). Its most important consequence is to weaken nationalist prejudice, and foster a new openness to other ideas and peoples, a 'cosmopolitan disposition'. The implication of this analysis – although Tomlinson himself is rather circumspect – is that old-fashioned 1970s concerns about the USA's imperial power or about increasing indoctrination into consumer values, expressed for example by Schiller (1976), can now be given a decent funeral.

Happy days

The affirmative tenor of revisionist media and cultural theory was reinforced by the view that the world is changing for the better in two other, important respects. First, improvements in the position, status and economic power of women influenced media representations of gender. In the 1970s, radical feminist research tended to argue that the media portrayed women almost entirely negatively, and encouraged identification with 'hearth and home' (e.g. Tuchman 1978). In the 1980s and early 1990s, feminists tended to draw attention to ambiguities in media representations of women, arguing that these sometimes afforded vicarious identification with powerful, 'bad' women (Modleski 1982), or implicitly 'call[ed] into question women's anomalous position' or dramatised the 'tension between the conventional positioning of women and the entertainment of opposites' (Landy 1991: 17 and 485). Women's media could be quietly subversive on the side.

In the more recent period, this 'progress through stealth' argument has given way to the claim that media representations of women have improved (though in a context where representations of women still tend to be negative). Thus, a case study of a popular British magazine reported that it offered empowering understandings of what it was to be a contemporary woman (McRobbie 1996); an analysis of a leading US daily concluded that, between 1980 and 1996, most of its coverage of feminist politics had been 'overwhelmingly positive' (Costain and Fraizer 2000: 173); a wide-ranging overview judged that media portrayals of women were becoming, on balance, more emancipated (MacDonald 1995); while Jane Shattuc claimed that day-time, issue-oriented TV talk shows gave working-class women a new voice, and provided 'some of the most radical populist moments' in the history of US television between 1967 and 1993 (Shattuc 1997: 2). A sub-theme of much of this work is that the market encouraged the media to respond to changing – and more liberated – subjectivities among women.

Second, the advent of the Internet, Web and digital revolution was hailed as emancipatory. New media are expanding the diversity of the media (Compaine and Gomery 2000). They are promoting a user-driven, 'pull' culture in which people will no longer accept what is pushed at them by media conglomerates (Negroponte 1995). The Web is transferring power to the people, and facilitating the construction of emancipated subjectivities (Poster 2001). It is fostering global activism and a new form of progressive politics (Donk et al. 2004). The Internet has facilitated exciting new experiments in 'electronic democracy' (Tsagarousianou et al. 1998). It has brought into being a 'gay global village', a haven of emotional and practical support for sexual minorities who are persecuted or shunned around the world (Gross 2003). It is facilitating the emergence of a networked world and a dynamic 'new economy' (Castells 2000). Not all these accounts are unequivocal – the last cited text, for example, is especially eloquent about unequal global access to the benefits of new communications technology. But the general thrust of this literature leaves no room for doubt that our media system has been wonderfully enriched by the addition of new media.

The field thus shifted from its radical moorings in the 1970s, through free adaptations of Gramsci and Habermas, and the rise of postmodernism. New themes – audience power, improved gender representation, the benefits of global-isation and new media – entered centre stage. Even allowing for the debates that have been passed over for the sake of brevity, the general tenor of media and cultural studies in Britain (as in many other countries) became more affirmative, more approving of the world in which we live.

Gains and losses

Were these shifts part of an unfolding story of intellectual progress in which researchers responded to the new issues and concerns of a changed world? Or did the field become less critical because it was influenced by the assumptions of a more conservative era? Instead of answering directly these questions (and eliciting predictable polarised responses), perhaps it would be more useful to draw up a brief balance sheet of what was gained and lost in the evolution of British media and cultural research.

On the credit side, the rise of feminism addressed a major blind spot in radical media studies. The emphasis on conflict and audience autonomy (however over-drawn) in 1980s media research usefully undermined the simplifications of radical functionalism. The increased attention given to globalisation in the 1990s, and more recently the emergence of comparative media research, chipped away at the parochialism of much media and cultural theory. The booming literature on new communications technology illuminated as well as mythologised. To this shortlist could be added other gains, most notably major advances in film studies and in ways of analysing meaning.

However, there are also entries on the debit side. These need to be set out at greater length to offset numerous celebratory accounts of the field. The case has already been made that the received wisdom both overstates popular power over the media, and understates media influence on the public (Curran 2002). This does not need to be repeated here. Instead, we will focus on the way in which the neo-liberal ascendancy has promoted favourable impressions of the market.

The main body of work that subjects the market to critical scrutiny is radical media political economy.[4] It is widely attacked in Britain on the grounds that it is 'reductionist' (meaning that it reduces complex phenomena to simplistic economic explanation). This frequently issued health warning has helped to marginalise this work, and discourages researchers from even addressing the central question it raises: has critical economics anything to contribute to the study of the media and popular culture? The answer given in most of the British cultural studies literature is implicitly 'no'. However, it should really be 'don't know', since most cultural studies researchers in Britain, with occasional illuminating exceptions like Hesmondhalgh (2002), lack an economic dimension to their work.

Partial relief is coming from the USA, in an ironic reversal of history. British media studies originally defined itself in opposition to the uncritical nature of US media research (e.g. Curran *et al.* 1977). Yet, the USA is now the main home of critical, economically informed studies of the media. The growing travails of the 'Hutchins Commission' reform tradition, which sought to implant a public interest culture in the US media industries, has generated a rising volume of academic protest literature. Its main themes are that 'hypercommercialism' is undermining the decision-making power and autonomy of US journalists; weakening professional standards; undermining editorial quality through cost-cutting; and leading to increasingly inadequate journalism that is failing US society.[5]

Just one illustrative theme from this now extensive literature must suffice. Increasing pressure to realise 'market earnings expectations', in the context of deregulation and increased competition, contributed to a sharp increase of US television coverage of crime during the 1990s because it was both cheap and popular (Hamilton 2004; Bennett 2003b; Seib 2002). In 1992–3 there was a three-fold increase in crime coverage on US national television networks (Patterson 2003a: 89). By the mid-1990s, violent crime accounted for two-thirds of all local TV news in fifty-six US cities (Klite *et al.* 1997). This increased daily dosage of crime contributed to a spectacular rise in the proportion of Americans who said that crime was the most serious problem facing the nation, even though crime levels were actually falling (Patterson 2003b; Lowry *et al.* 2003). Local TV news tended also to focus on decontextualised acts of violent crime by black perpetrators in ways that strengthened racial hostility, and fuelled demands for punitive retribution (Iyengar 2000). While various factors (both cultural and political) were involved in the rise of TV crime, economics played a significant part.

An unwillingness to confront market issues also accounts for the one-sided understanding of globalisation that dominates media and cultural research. The prevailing orthodoxy adopts a broad, anthropological understanding of 'culture' as a way of life. Yet, it seldom gives more than passing consideration to the inequitable nature of the global market, even though this profoundly affects peoples' lives. While global market integration has generated additional wealth, its gains have been distributed very unequally. By the late 1990s, the richest fifth of the world's population possessed 86 per cent of the world's GDP, whereas the poorest fifth had just 1 per cent (United Nations Development Programme (UNDP) 2003 [1999]: 425). The gap between the world's rich and poor grew sharply in the 1990s. Whether this was the culmination of a long-term trend towards the polarisation of wealth within the world, fostered by globalisation, is a hotly contested and complex issue.[6] But what is not seriously disputed is that those living in dire poverty grew in absolute terms during the 1990s despite the sustained growth of the global economy (Stiglitz 2002; UNDP 2003; Wade and Wolf 2003, among others). The institutions of global governance failed to address adequately global inequality because they were dominated by wealthy nations, adhered to rules and assumptions that favoured these nations, were strongly influenced by Western financial elites, and were not democratically accountable (Stiglitz 2002; Sklair 2002; Hutton 2003).

But is not globalisation releasing new political forces operating on a global basis that are alert to a new politics (environmentalism, human rights, peace and world poverty), connected by new communications technology, transcending the limitations of nationalism, bridging the local and global, and forging new bases of common action and social purpose? This is the constantly repeated argument within the field. It is an important argument for which there is some evidence. But this affirmative view needs also to take account of counter-arguments. First, the rise of deregulated, global financial markets has weakened the economic effectiveness of national governments, and by implication the democratic power of the people (Leys 2001; Panitch and Leys 1999; Strange 1996). Second, global civil society is currently under-developed, sub-divided, unrepresentative, with only limited influence on structures of military and economic power (Keane 2003; Sklair 2002). Indeed, it would seem that we are passing through a transitional phase whose outcome is uncertain rather than the assured, positive future foretold by some cultural theorists. One form of democratic power, national government, and one progressive tradition, social democracy, are weakening. Yet new forms of democratic power and a new, progressive politics remain buds that have not yet fully flowered, in the context of greatly strengthened global corporate and financial influence, and the rise of the 'informal' US empire. It may be that an evolving, complex system of governance will be rendered more subject to democratic control, and will contribute to the welfare of humanity (Held 2004). But this is something that needs to be made concrete, and fought for. It is not an automatic corollary of globalisation.

In other words, globalisation has negative features – an inequitable global market and the weakening of democracy – to be set beside its positive features identified in 'cultural globalisation' analysis. In passing, it should be added that a similar one-sidedness prevails in the new media literature, much of which is given over to celebrating technological possibilities. This approach tends to play down societal cnostraints; and take for granted the architecture and conventions of the Internet and Web, which were shaped historically by the values of academic science, US counter-culture and European public service. However, this pre-market legacy is now being challenged by the colonising activities of established media conglomerates and the chequered rise of Internet commerce, supported by new technological developments, national legislation and global regulation (Schiller 2000; McChesney 1999; Lessig 1999 and 2001; and Curran and Seaton

2003). The historic nature of this contest, and its central implications for the future development of cyberspace, could not be more important. Yet, it has tended to be ignored because even the idea that the virtual world has a political economy is alien to most new media studies.

Negotiating hegemony

The ideological ascendancy of market liberalism also penetrated media and cultural research by influencing the way in which society was understood. Market liberalism sees society primarily as an aggregation of individuals rather than in the abstract terms of social groups. People now live, it is stressed, in open societies free of the rigidities associated with class because the market is an egalitarian force that promotes equality of opportunity in the interests of efficiency. Hard work, talent and enterprise are rewarded within market societies as a way of fostering wealth-creation, in the interests of all.

Some of these themes chimed with a reappraisal that took place in media and cultural research. A traditional Marxist view of conflict between social classes defined by their relationship to the system of production was increasingly rejected, mainly on the grounds that it failed to take account of the more complexly stratified and differentiated nature of contemporary society. Class and the world of work, it was also argued, had become less significant as sources of social identity. This reappraisal often led to a stress on social flux and change: the increasing fragmentation of society, the strengthening of multiple social identities, the reconfiguration of space and mental horizons as a consequence of globalisation, the erosion of tradition. The self-defining individual loomed large within this reconception, as did gender, ethnicity and sexuality that increasingly replaced class as a way of conceptualising disadvantage. This way of looking at the world echoed neo-liberal themes in stressing individual agency, social fluidity and the increasing redundancy of a class perspective. However, it also incorporated critical themes, derived from feminism and gay theory, which were not part of the liberal market tradition. It thus 'negotiated' rather than reproduced a neo-liberal vision of society.

This reorientation ignored a large accumulation of empirical evidence showing that class still strongly influences the distribution of life chances, experiences and rewards in contemporary advanced societies. OECD countries, including both Britain and the USA, are not in fact fluid, open societies. Social mobility – whether defined between generations or within a generation, between social classes or 'income groups' (the definition usually employed by economists) – is restricted (Devine and Waters 2004; Aldridge 2004; Heath and Payne 2000; Savage and Egerton 1997, among others). Movement is greater in the middle of society, less so at the bottom and top. Movement upwards has increased in absolute terms because the working class has contracted and the middle class expanded. But relative social mobility – the chances of a person in one social group making it to another social group – has been much more stable. In Britain, the chances of a middle-class child staying middle class are about four times greater than those of a working-class child becoming middle class (Roberts 2001: 194), with some data projecting even higher odds.

The reasons for restricted social mobility are complex. Social class is associated with multiple factors – self-esteem, confidence, expectation, sense of control over one's destiny, use of 'educated' language, cognitive development (reflected in differential test scores), educational attainment, social skills, social networks, access to information, and access to money and credit. These influences tend to be mutually reinforcing, creating a dynamic that is discernible very early in a person's life.

The moral rhetoric of 'hard work, talent and enterprise' is thus enormously misleading because it masks the pivotal structuring influence of class. Yet, it is invoked to provide spurious justification for large disparities in the distribution of income and wealth. For example, in the USA, the richest 20 per cent earn nine times more than the poorest 20 per cent (Hutton 2003: 187). Class difference also generates other forms of inequality. In Britain, people in unskilled and semi-skilled jobs are more likely than those in managerial and professional grades to die earlier; lose their job; be the victims of crime; and have children who become seriously ill (Aldridge 2004).

Inequalities also increased very rapidly, especially in countries where neo-liberal policies and attitudes became embedded (Castells 2000; Kelsey 1995). Thus, income disparities soared during the last quarter of the century in the United States, and even resulted in blue-collar workers earning on average less in *absolute* terms during the 1980s and part of the 1990s (Hutton 2003: 188). In Britain, incomes at the 90th percentile were 2.9 times those at the 10th percentile in 1976, but had risen to 4.1 by 2001. In the same period, the number of households with incomes below 40 per cent of the median rose 220 per cent (Aldridge 2004: 6).

In brief, media and cultural studies has been seduced by the discourse of market liberalism into bracketing out class. It has colluded in the perpetuation of myths that mask *inherited* privilege and legitimate inequality. It has also been distracted from investigating adequately the part played by the media in the growth of inequality in market liberal societies.

All market systems generate inequalities. These inequalities are alleviated by redistributions of money and resources authorised by the democratic state. The scale and nature of these 'social transfers' is determined by politics. What part did the media play in the politics of the last twenty years that sanctioned a sharp increase of class inequality? Despite occasional shafts of light (e.g. Hall 1988;

Deacon and Golding 1994), it is very difficult to answer this question in relation to Britain. This is because most media and cultural researchers, with notable exceptions like Murdock (2000) and Skeggs (1997), ceased to be interested in class inequality, and indeed displayed very limited interest in public policy of any kind. Concern with personal politics superseded interest in organised politics, while social recognition came to be viewed as more important than state redistribution.[7]

Retrospect

Numerous *ad hoc* narratives of the development of media and cultural studies proclaim a new insight, agenda or 'turn'. These narratives are usually self-serving. They tend also to be exclusively accounts of ideas that make no attempt to relate intellectual development to a wider context. Instead, they tell a simple story of progress in which error is confounded by enlightenment.

The contextualisation of media and cultural research offers a more complex picture. On the one hand, changes in society have promoted important new ideas and agendas in the field. Thus, the rise of feminism helped to establish gender as a central concern of media and cultural research. The more effective self-organisation of ethnic and sexual minority groups encouraged a revival of pluralist theory that stressed both the heterogeneity of society and also differences within these minority groups. Intensified globalisation caused Western, parochial definitions of cultural value and media theory to be questioned, and promoted a new interest in issues to do with transnationalism, deterritorialisation and the erosion of national identity.

On the other hand, wider changes in society have also given rise to blind spots in media and cultural research (a point emphasised in this chapter). During the last twenty-five years, neo-liberal ideas acquired a greater ascendancy in Britain than at any time since the later nineteenth century. This hegemony promoted within media and cultural research a tacitly positive view of the market as a *neutral* mechanism harmonising supply and demand that was simplistic and misleading. It also resulted in class being underestimated as an influence on contemporary society, and caused the relationship between deepening class inequality and the media and popular culture to be neglected. Neo-liberalism entered the bloodstream of media and cultural studies, almost without us noticing it.

In short, situating the development of research in relation to wider social and political change tends to undermine simple accounts of accumulated insight and wisdom. Instead, it encourages a greater distance of perspective that registers losses as well as gains. The second thing this historical review has highlighted is the fashion-driven nature of media and cultural studies. A field that prides itself on being innovatory and different emerges as rather conformist. If anything, this tendency to hunt as a pack is becoming even more entrenched. Perhaps the next time a collective 'turn' is proclaimed, fewer people should rush to join the caravanserai travelling to the new approved destination. It might be better if some people decided to journey in the opposite direction.

Notes

1 I have not followed numerous sociological accounts (for example Beck and Beck-Gernsheim 2002) in seeing the 'de-traditionalisation' of society as a key distinctive feature of the contemporary world. Tradition is questioned in almost every era. Indeed, tradition is probably less under attack now than it was, for example, in sixteenth-century Europe, when absolutely fundamental beliefs and social practices – which invested life with meaning – were challenged and, in some cases, overthrown.

2 Many of the 1960s pioneers in Britain, such as Tunstall, McQuail, Blumler, Himmelweit and Halloran, were strongly influenced by the US social science communications tradition, though they tended to write from a centre-left perspective. The 'second-wave' pioneers in the 1970s, many of whom were influenced by the Birmingham cultural studies tradition, tended to be more radical and humanities-based. The best (and implicitly historical) account of British cultural studies is provided by Turner (2002). For a historical portrait of a sub-group within British media studies, see Curran (2004).

3 In fact, Gramsci was assimilated in media and cultural studies, from the outset, in ways that were significantly different from the interpretation of his fragmentary work in radical political studies, typified by Forgacs (1989).

4 Good studies in the media political economy tradition include Garnham (1990), Gitlin (1994), Golding and Murdock (1997), McChesney (1999) and Leys (2001). Useful introductions to media economics are provided by Picard (2002), Doyle (2002) and Albarran (1996).

5 Recent, illuminating publications in this tradition include Hamilton (2004), Bennett (2003b), Shanor (2003), Kovach and Rosenstiel (1999 and 2003), Seib (2002), Croteau and Hoynes, (2001), Sabato et al. (2000), Glasser (1999), McChesney (1999) and, in a more theoretical mode, Baker (2002).

6 The rise of the Southeastern Asian economies, notably those of Taiwan and South Korea, followed by rapid growth in China and also India, goes against simplistic versions of the global 'polarisation' thesis. What view is taken depends on what categories are used, over what time span, and also crucially on what can be attributed to globalisation as distinct from other influences. For an illuminating debate see Wade and Wolf (2003), and the subsequent observations of Wolf (2004) and Held (2004).

7 For an attempt to connect these cast two concerns, see Curran, Gaber and Petley (2005).

References

Albarran, A. (1996) *Media Economics*, Ames, IO: Iowa University Press.

Aldridge, S. (2004) 'Life chances and social mobility: an overview of the evidence', Cabinet Office, Prime Minister's Strategy Unit (30 March), www.strategy.gov.uk/files/pdf/lifechances-socialmobility.pdf.

Ang, I. and Hermes, J. (1991) 'Gender and/in media consumption', in J. Curran and M. Gurevitch (eds) *Mass Media and Society*, London: Edward Arnold.

Anon. (2004) 'Deng Xiaoping quotes and quotations', www.brainyquote.com/quotes/authors/d/deng-xiaoping.html.

Baker, C. Edwin (2002) *Media, Markets, and Democracy*, New York: Cambridge University Press.

Baudrillard, J. (1980) 'The implosion of meaning in the media and the implosion of the social in the masses', in K. Woodward (ed.) *The Myths of Information*, London: Routledge & Kegan Paul.

Beck, U. and Beck-Gernsheim, E. (2002) *Individualization*, London: Sage.

Bennett, W. (2003a) 'New media power: the Internet and global activism', in N. Couldry and J. Curran (eds) *Contesting Media Power*, Lanham, MA: Rowman & Littlefield.

—— (2003b) *News*, 5th edn, New York: Longman.

Castells, M. (2000) *End of Millennium*, 2nd edn, Oxford: Blackwell.

Compaine, B. and Gomery, D. (2000) *Who Owns the Media?* 3rd edn, Mahwah, NJ: Lawrence Erlbaum.

Costain, A. and Fraizer, H. (2000) 'Media portrayal of "second wave" feminist groups', in S. Chambers and A. Costain (eds) *Deliberation, Democracy and the Media*, Lanham, MA: Rowman & Littlefield.

Croteau, D. and Hoynes, W. (2001) *The Business of Media*, Thousand Oaks, CA: Pine Forge.

Curran, J. (2002) *Media and Power*, London: Routledge.

—— (2004) 'The rise of the Westminster School', in A. Calabrese and C. Sparks (eds) *Toward a Political Economy of Culture*, Lanham, MA: Rowman & Littlefield.

Curran, J., Gurevitch, M. and Woollacott, J. (1977) *Mass Communication and Society*, London: Arnold.

Curran, J. and Seaton, J. (2003) *Power without Responsibility*, 6th edn, London: Routledge.

Curran, J., Gaber, I. and Petley, J. (2005) *Culture Wars: The Media and the British Left*, Edinburgh: Edinburgh University Press.

Deacon, D. and Golding, P. (1994) *Taxation and Representation*, London: John Libbey.

Devine, F. and Waters, M. (eds) (2004) *Social Inequalities in Comparative Perspective*, Oxford: Blackwell.

Donk, W. Van de, Loader, B., Nihon, P. and Rucht, D. (2004) *Cyberprotest*, London: Routledge.

Doyle, G. (2002) *Understanding Media Economics*, London: Sage.

Fiske, J. (1987) *Television Culture*, London: Routledge.

—— (1991) 'Postmodernism and television', in J. Curran and M. Gurevitch (eds) *Mass Media and Society*, London: Arnold.

Forgacs, D. (1989) 'Gramsci and Marxism in Britain', *New Left Review* 176.

Foucault, M. (1979) *Discipline and Punish*, Harmondsworth: Penguin.

Fukuyama, F. (1993) *The End of History and the Last Man*, Harmondsworth: Penguin.

Garnham, N. (1986) 'The media and the public sphere', in P. Golding, G. Murdock and P. Schlesinger (eds) *Communicating Politics*, Leicester: Leicester University Press.

—— (1990) *Capitalism and Communication*, London: Sage.

Gitlin, T. (1994) Inside Prime Time, rev. edn, London: Routledge.

Glasser, T. (1999) (ed.) *The Idea of Public Journalism*, New York: Guilford.

Golding, P. and Murdock, G. (1997) *Political Economy of the Media*, vols 1 and 2, Cheltenham: Elgar.

Gross, L. (2003) 'The gay global village in cyberspace', in N. Couldry and J. Curran (eds) *Contesting Media Power*, Lanham, MA: Rowman & Littlefield.

Habermas, J. (1989) *The Structural Transformation of the Public Sphere*, Cambridge: Polity [pub. in German in 1962].

—— (1996) *Between Facts and Norms*, Cambridge: Polity [pub. in German in 1992].

Hall, S. (1977) 'Culture, the media and the "ideological effect"', in J. Curran, M. Gurevitch and J. Wollacott (eds) *Mass Communication and Society*, London: Edward Arnold.

—— (1982) 'The rediscovery of "ideology": the return of the repressed in media studies', in M. Gurevitch, T. Bennett, J. Curran and J. Woollacott (eds) *Culture, Society and the Media*, London: Methuen.

—— (1985) 'Signification, representation, ideology: Althusser and the poststructuralist debates', *Critical Studies in Mass Communication 2*.

—— (1988) *The Hard Road to Renewal*, London: Verso.

Hall, S., Critcher, C., Jefferson, T., Clarke, J. and Roberts, B. (1978) *Policing the Crisis*, Basingstoke: Macmillan Education.

Hamilton, J. (2004) *All the News That's Fit to Sell*, Princeton, NJ: Princeton University Press.

Heath, A. and Payne, C. (2000) 'Social mobility', in A.H. Halsey with J. Webb (eds) *Twentieth-Century British Social Trends*, Basingstoke: Macmillan.

Held, D. (2004) *Global Covenant*, Cambridge: Polity.

Held, D., McGrew, A., Goldblatt, D. and Perraton, J. (1999) *Global Transformations*, Cambridge: Polity.

Hesmondhalgh, D. (2002) *The Cultural Industries*, London: Sage.

Hutton, W. (2003) *The World We're In*, rev. edn, London: Abacus.

Iyengar, S. (2000) 'Media effects: paradigms for the analysis of local television news', in S. Chambers and A. Costain (eds) *Deliberation, Democracy and the Media*, Lanham: MA, Rowman & Littlefield.

Keane, J. (2003) *Global Civil Society?*, Cambridge: Cambridge University Press.

Kelsey, J. (1995) *The New Zealand Experiment*, Auckland: Auckland University Press.

Klite, P., Bardwell, R. and Salzman, J. (1997) 'Local TV news: getting away with murder', *Press/Politics* 2(2).

Kovach, B. and Rosenstiel, T. (1999) *Warp Speed*, New York: Century Foundation.

—— (2003) *The Elements of Journalism*, London: Atlantic Books.

Landy, M. (1991) *British Genres*, Princeton: Princeton University Press.

Lessig, L. (1999) *Code and Other Laws of Cyberspace*, New York: Basic Books.

—— (2001) *The Future of Ideas*, New York: Random House.

Leys, C. (2001) *Market-Driven Politics*, London: Verso.

Lowry, D., Ching, T., Nio, J. and Leitner, D. (2003) 'Setting the public fear agenda: a longitudinal analysis of network TV crime reporting, public perceptions of crime, and FBI crime statistics', *Journal of Communication*, March.

Lyotard, J.-F. (1984) *The Postmodern Condition*, Manchester: Manchester University Press.

McChesney, R. (1999) *Rich Media, Poor Democracy*, Urbana, IL: Illinois.

MacDonald, M. (1995) *Representing Women*, London: Arnold.

McRobbie, A. (1996) '*More!*: new sexualities in girls' and women's magazines', in J. Curran, D. Morley and V. Walkerdine (eds) *Cultural Studies and Communications*, London: Routledge.

Manning, P. (2001) *News and News Sources*, London: Sage.

Modleski, T. (1982) *Loving With a Vengeance*, Hamden, CT: Arch Books.

Murdock, G. (2000) 'Reconstructing the ruined tower: contemporary communications and questions of class', in J. Curran and M. Gurevitch (eds) *Mass Media and Society*, 3rd edn, London: Arnold.

Negroponte, N. (1995), *Being Digital*, London: Hodder & Stoughton.

O'Mahony, J. (2004) 'David Edgar', *Guardian* (Review Section), 20 March 2004.

Panitch, L. and Leys, C. (eds) (1999) *Global Capitalism versus Democracy* [Socialist Register 1999], Rendlesham: Merlin.

Patterson, T. (2003a) *The Vanishing Voter*, New York: Vintage.

—— (2003 b) 'The search for a standard: markets and media', *Political Communication 20*.

Picard, R. (2002) *The Economics and Financing of Media Companies*, New York: Fordham University Press.

Poster, M. (1988) 'Introduction', in M. Poster (ed.) *Baudrillard: Selected Writings*, Stanford, CA: Stanford University Press.

—— (2001) *What's the Matter with the Internet?* Minneapolis: University of Minnesota Press.

Roberts, K. (2001) *Class in Modern Britain*, Basingstoke: Palgrave.

Roe, K. and Meyer, G. de (2000) 'Music television: MTV-Europe', in J. Wieten, G. Murdock and P. Dahlgren (eds) *Television across Europe*, London: Sage.

Sabato, L., Stencel, M. and Lichter, S. (2000) *Peep Show*, Lanham, MA: Rowman & Littlefield.

Savage, M. and Egerton, M. (1997) 'Social mobility, individual ability and the inheritance of class inequality', *Sociology 31*.

Scannell, P. (1989) 'Public service broadcasting and modern public life', *Media, Culture and Society* 11(2).

Schiller, D. (2000) *Digital Capitalism,* Cambridge, MA: MIT Press.

Schiller, H. (1976) *Communication and Cultural Domination*, White Plains, NY: Sharpe.

Seib, P. (2002) *Going Live*, Lanham, MA: Rowman & Littlefield.

Shanor, D. (2003) *News from Abroad*, New York: Columbia University Press.

Shattuc, J. (1997) *The Talking Cure*, New York: Routledge.

Sinclair, J., Jacka, E. and Cunnigham, S. (eds) (1996) *New Patterns in Global Television*, Oxford: Oxford University Press.

Sklair, L. (2002) *Globalization*, 3rd edn, Oxford: Oxford University Press.

Skeggs, B. (1997) *Formation of Class and Gender*, London: Sage.

Stiglitz, J. (2002) *Globalization and its Discontents*, London: Penguin.

Strange, S. (1996) *The Retreat of the State*, Cambridge: Cambridge University Press.

Tomlinson, J. (1999) *Globalization and Culture*, London: Routledge.

Tsagarousianou, R., Tambini, D. and Bryan, C. (eds) (1998) *Cyberdemocracy*, London: Routledge.

Tuchman, G. (1978) 'Introduction: the symbolic annihilation of women by the mass media', in G. Tuchman, A. Kaplan and J. Benet (eds) *Hearth and Home*, New York: Oxford University Press.

Turner, G. (2002) *British Cultural Studies*, 3rd edn, London: Routledge.

United Nations Development Programme (2003) 'Patterns of global inequality' [Human Development Report 1999] in D. Held and A. McGrew (eds) *The Global Transformations Reader*, 2nd edn, Cambridge: Polity.

Wade, R. and Wolf, M. (2003) 'Are global poverty and inequality getting worse?' in D. Held and A. McGrew (eds) *The Global Transformations Reader*, 2nd edn, Cambridge: Polity.

Willis, P. (1977) *Learning to Labour*, London: Saxon House.

—— (1990) *Common Culture*, Milton Keynes: Open University Press.

Wolf, M. (2004) *Why Globalization Works*, New Haven: Yale University Press.

Chapter 10

Placing promotional culture

Aeron Davis

Introduction

This chapter asks what is the significance of the rise of promotional culture in contemporary society? That the growth and development of promotional culture has been inseparable from that of much of media and popular culture is indisputable. However, accounts of the social and cultural impacts of promotion in media and cultural studies have varied considerably. Clarification of the part it plays in social change and power relations, in an increasingly mediated society, seems long overdue. This chapter thus attempts to offer an organising survey of some of the more common perspectives on promotion that have developed.

Historically, it is virtually impossible to separate the development of promotional culture from that of most forms of mass media and culture. Advertising has been an integral part of the evolution of mass communications (Curran 1986; see Leiss *et al.* 1990; Garnham 1990; Curran and Seaton 1999), in many cases providing a greater source of producer income than customer sales. Similarly, public relations techniques and 'information subsidy' supply have become a supportive mainstay, albeit a less measurable one, of the media (see Boorstin 1962; Gandy 1982; Tiffen 1990; Davis 2002). In recent decades, the budgets and numbers employed in the promotional professions themselves have risen quite considerably. In 2002, in the USA, where the promotional professions are most developed, $144.4 billion was spent on advertising (ZenithOptimedia), approximately 750,000 people were employed in marketing (AMA), and 200,000 in public relations (Cutlip *et al.* 2000). In the UK, second only to the USA in the development of its promotional industries, £16.5 billion was spent on advertising (AA), 60,000 people were members of the Chartered Institute of Marketing (CIM), and the PR industry was worth an estimated £1.2 billion and employed 30,000 people (IPR). Such numbers suggest that promotional intermediaries are frequently outnumbering journalists and artists in their respective fields, and that promotion does rather more than fund media and culture; it is a fundamental part of it.

Indeed, as many of the texts below observe, promotional intermediaries have come to play a key role in all aspects of the production and consumption of commodities and culture. They are now present at all stages: from influencing initial investment/policy decisions, to product/policy development, to shaping media and cultural formats, to the influence of fashions, trends and guidelines that affect the choices of consumer-citizens. In effect, promotional culture has become much more than the means by which sellers promote their products to buyers. The promotional professions have become involved, to a greater or lesser extent, in the creation of products, values, ideas, political and market trends, and even markets and democratic processes themselves. The extent of their influence and involvement will be discussed below. As will become apparent, opinions vary considerably over the extent to which promotional intermediaries and promotional culture contribute to society. So it is asked: What part, if any, does promotion play in social change? Is it generally beneficial to society or not? Does it privilege certain interests, such as producers or political leaders, over others?

First, some clarification of the terms 'promotional culture' and 'promotional intermediaries' is needed. When Andrew Wernick (1991) first used the term 'promotional culture', the phrase came to mean more than the professional activities of promotion. He concluded that 'culture' more generally had become 'saturated in the medium of promotion'. No object (image, product or form of communication) could be separated from the promotion of itself and all objects linked to it through communications. All objects are thus connected by 'an endless chain of mutual reference and implication'. Similarly, when Bourdieu (1984: 359) first used the term 'cultural intermediaries' he referred to the 'new petit bourgeoisie' that were employed 'in all the occupations involving presentation and representation', 'in all the institutions providing symbolic goods and services ... and in cultural production and organization'. In other words, a broad section of society employed in a wide range of activities. Both terms, with their open-ended descriptions, have thus come to be widely interpreted and used. For the purposes of this chapter (and with future empirically based research in mind) my definitions are more restricted. In referring to promotional culture I mean principally the activities and outputs of the industries of marketing, advertising and public relations. 'Promotional intermediaries', as opposed to cultural intermediaries, are those employed in these professions.

Such professions are themselves notoriously hard to map and define empirically. Despite this, one may attempt to frame them in terms of the evolution of 'professional' practices, institutions, norms and definitions. We might start by looking at how the industries define themselves. Although multiple interpretations exist in all three professions, there are also several identifiable points of convergence. Each profession is concerned to identify the following four elements for its clients: a saleable product (be it a commodity, message or idea), a potential audience (citizen or consumer), a communications medium (formal/information or informal/cultural) and a message. For industry historians (see, for example, Leiss *et al.* 1990; Norris 1990; Lears 1995; Cutlip *et al.* 2000), these occupations have established themselves as 'professions' via several social developments. These include: the rise of independent firms who only offer specific promotional services to clients; the emergence of professional bodies and associations; the development of professional qualifications and published research; the keeping of official industry records and the emergence of regulatory bodies. At the start of the twenty-first century, each of these occupations claimed to be established in terms of several of these developments. Although none might be accorded the same 'professional status' and accountability as say law, medicine or accountancy, they might be considered on a par with say journalism, plumbing or academia.

Enhancing markets and democracies

For industry historians and advocates (see above and also Grunig and Hunt 1984; Baker 1996; Wilmshurst and Mackay 1999) the promotional professions have been a key ingredient in the development of both market systems and democracies. The Industrial Revolution, with its need to match producers with consumers in ever more expanding and competitive markets, naturally necessitated the evolution of the promotional professions. Representative democracy, with universal suffrage, a competitive party system and government's information requirements, similarly encouraged the rise of promotional culture. Mass communications, essential to markets and democracies, could only expand by relying on the financial and information subsidies offered by promoters. As commercial markets have expanded, democracies matured, and new communications media evolved, so they have been accompanied by parallel expansions and developments in the promotional professions. Capitalist democracies could not function without the promotional professions and the promotional professions could not function without capitalist democracies.

And this is where positive accounts of the impact of the promotional professions begin. Starting with markets, although some question the value and potential distorting influences of advertising, the majority of industrialists, economists and promotional intermediaries (not surprisingly) offer a positive assessment. Market research identifies what new products, and improvements/variations on old products, that people want. It also identifies the consumers most likely to be interested in products and the best media outlets with which to communicate to them. Advertising and public relations then informs potential consumers about products in the most cost-efficient way and stimulate competition in the process. As such promotional culture is a key contributor to the economic ideal of perfect markets where multiple suppliers and multiple buyers are connected through efficient communications. Monopolies and other negative

market influences are avoided, prices are kept competitive and inefficient businesses and bad products are weeded out.

The same industry perspective on promotional culture is transferable to the
political sphere. Democracies are, in essence, political markets. Market research
makes political parties and governments more responsive to citizens by identifying support for new policies and leaders. Advertising and public relations
informs citizens in the most comprehendible ways about competing political
parties and policies. It is also used to communicate the interests of competing
groups and wider public opinion to government. Lastly, advertising and PR are
cost-effective means of government communication to citizens about national
developments and new legislation. While those looking at political communications tend to be more sceptical about the benefits of promotional culture to the
political process, several argue its merits. In comparison to less mediated times,
more people are informed about the business of government and a greater range
of interest groups are successfully using promotional culture to voice their
concerns to policy-makers (see Shoemaker 1989; Scammell 1995; Anderson
1997; Neuman 2001; McNair 2003).

Taken together there is a clear line of reasoning about the positive effects of
promotional culture on markets and capitalist democracies. Promotional culture
makes markets run efficiently, benefits the economy and creates jobs, ensures
freedom of choice for consumer-citizens, encourages commercially and politically
responsive societies, and supports the independent mass communications forms
necessary for the successful running of both markets and democracy. Thus, as
Wilmshurst and Mackay declare,

> There is in fact a strong case for arguing that advertising is an essential facility
> if there is to be freedom of choice for consumers. Such freedom implies the
> necessity for businesses to have efficient means of placing their products and
> services before the public ... [and] advertising makes it easier for a wide
> range of media to exist without government support (and hence control) ...
> advertising in all its forms has been an accepted part of the scene and plays an
> ever more prominent role. The 'market economy' way of running things has
> virtually no rival ... and is here to stay, virtually unquestioned, for the fore-
> seeable future.
>
> (Wilmshurst and Mackay 1999: 20)

Perpetuating producer interests and inequality

Critics of promotional culture are generally to be found in the work of (post-)
Marxist scholars across media studies, sociology and politics – but often find
support amongst despairing liberal sociologists and journalists. In many ways crit-

ical accounts of the rise and influence of promotional culture are very similar to those produced by industry advocates. They agree about the significance of the promotional professions to the evolution and sustenance of markets and capitalist democracy more generally. However, there are fundamental interpretive differences. Principally, industry advocates assume properly functioning markets, democracies and the mass media are neutral systems that ultimately benefit everyone. Promotional culture plays a vital role in oiling the cogs of 'the system' but does not influence that system.

Critics, however, go substantially further in their assessments. Promotional culture is not only essential for markets and capitalist democracy, but also it has shaped, and increasingly shapes, all components and individuals involved in markets. It also does so in a way that encourages the flaws and inequalities that are associated with market systems. In the first place, promotional culture aids (usually larger, established) producer-sellers rather more than consumers because, quite simply, promotional intermediaries are employed almost exclusively by producers. Historically (see Packard 1957; Ewen 1976, 1996; Marchand 1998) the promotional industries expanded at the expense of public, social and legal norms and traditions. Such intermediaries were employed to neutralise negative publicity, sell the benefits of new companies and services, and, of course, encourage mass demand and consumption. In recent years, it is still sellers (in politics and commerce) who employ the vast majority (over 90 per cent) of promotional intermediaries and account for the vast majority of promotional expenditure (see Jhally 1990; Miller and Dinan 2000; Davis 2002; Cutlip et al. 2000). Thus, those that claim that promotional culture simply provides a neutral information service between buyers and sellers are being disingenuous.

Producer interests have a continuing impact on all aspects of the production and consumption of goods, services and culture; and promotional culture plays a leading role in this impact. Starting with production, the Frankfurt School (see Adorno and Horkheimer 1979 [1947]; Adorno 1991) identify promotion as a necessary component of efficient mass production processes. While efficiency demands 'standardisation' and 'interchangeability' of parts during production of goods (cultural and industrial), goods must be presented as new by attributing a 'pseudo-individuality' to them in the sales process. Hence promotional culture is necessary to identify where standardisation is required and then to promote similar goods as different. In the long term, promotional intermediaries thus have an increasing influence on commercial decisions about what products to produce and how they are shaped for an identified audience; from the sphere of cultural production (Gitlin 1994; D'Acci 1994; Nixon 1996; du Gay 1997; Burston 2000) to that of industrial production (see, for example, Aglietta 1987; Harvey 1989; Wernick 1991) to the sphere of political policy-making (Franklin 1994; Scammell 1995; Bennett and Manheim 2001; Davis 2003). In effect, producers, managers and political leaders use promotional intermediaries to increase their control of production as they attempt to maximise profits/gains and reduce risks/losses. In the longer term this results in restrictions on creativity and innovation, and the homogenisation of cultural, social and political values and policies as promotion becomes central to production.

The negative impact of promotional culture is also apparent in its corruption of public information channels because of the political and economic influence of producer promotional activity. On the one hand, that has meant that many powerful advertisers and 'spin doctors' (see also Herman and Chomsky 1988; Franklin 1994; Jones 1995; Stauber and Rampton 1995) have repeatedly abused their positions to put pressure on journalists to alter information content. On the other, advertising and public relations have subtly shaped media markets, individual media products and media content more generally. Which media audiences are catered to, the evolution of 'pseudo-events' and 'soundbites', many media styles and formats, and the general commodification and 'tabloidisation' of media, are all the results of promotional culture (see also Boorstin 1962; Postman 1985; Nelson 1989; Hallin 1994; Fallows 1996; Franklin 1997). Such developments have had a variety of impacts on citizens and public debate. Promotional culture and the commodification of public information has been at the expense of citizens. It has encouraged unequal access, public exclusion and a reduction of reporting on public interest issues (ibid.; see also Schiller 1989; Herman and McChesney 1997; Golding and Murdock 2000; Bennett and Manheim 2001; Davis 2002). This has led to greater state management of public consent, a 'refeudalised' public sphere, and a crisis of public confidence and political participation (Packard 1957; Ewen 1976, 1996; Herman and Chomsky 1988; Deacon and Golding 1994; Blumler and Gurevitch 1995; Ansolabehere and Iyengar 1995).

In the commercial sphere, promotional culture creates a 'magic system' (Williams 1980) that fuels an endless cycle of dissatisfaction amongst consumers. Promotional practices create 'false needs', then imbue new products with 'false symbolism' to encourage consumption as a solution for sating needs (see Williamson 1978; Jhally 1990; Goldman 1992). Consequently, alienated individuals are condemned to be driven by the empty and ongoing cycle of 'commodity fetishism' – something that sustains producers and market systems but never conquers personal dissatisfaction. On the cultural level, fashions, tastes and, to a certain extent, identities are frequently influenced by elite producers employing forms of promotional culture. This is certainly suggested, in different ways, in work on the history of fashion (Roche 1994; Klein 2000) and 'the arts' (Adorno and Horkheimer 1979 [1947]; Berger 1972; Bourdieu 1984; Wernick 1991).

Ultimately, promotional culture, acting through markets, contributes to the sustenance of the flawed and contradictory system of capitalist democracy (in all its forms). For the authors cited (see also Lasch 1976; Jameson 1991) there are a number of social, political and cultural repercussions. These include: the decline of high culture and social values; the elevation of individual good over social goods; the commodification of non-commodities, such as individuals, welfare services and political policies; the elevation of exchange value over use value; the obfuscation of the true relations of, and extreme inequalities generated by, capitalist democracies; generally contributing to the producer-oriented dominant ideologies that keep consumer-citizens subdued.

The denial of promotional influence

In contrast to promotional culture's advocates and critics there also exists a substantial body of work which simply denies that promotional culture has any real significance at all. The case against is mostly to be found in cultural and audience studies, liberal media sociology and effects research. First, it is argued that promotional culture does not advantage producers because it simply does not work. The pseudo-scientific claims of promotional intermediaries, to be able to classify and target audiences, are no more than selling devices designed to gain contracts and reduce 'producer anxiety' (see Ang 1991; Nava 1992; Lury and Warde 1997). In terms of the production process, the signs are that promotional culture is rather less significant than critical theorists have assumed. For those looking at 'cultures of production' (du Gay 1997; Negus 1999; see also Fowles 1996), cultural production is a messy, fragmented business that allows for lots of creative autonomy. External 'genre cultures', as well as wider cultural factors, impact upon product development. Powerful decision-makers, when questioned (see also Negus 1992; Gitlin 1994), admit that they often prefer their 'gut-instinct', rather than the marketing research at their disposal, when making production decisions.

Additionally, there are several counters to critical concerns about information channels and the public sphere. It is argued that the 'earlier golden age' thesis of communications – be it applied to journalism, popular culture or the public sphere – was never a reality. In reference to journalism, it is stated that true objectivity and a fully functioning public sphere has always been an ideal to aim at rather than a reality (Schudson 1995; McNair 1998; Lichtenberg 2000). As long as there continues to be a large number of competing news outlets, and journalists adhere to professional codes and are responsive to their publics, public information channels will remain relatively untainted by promotional culture (see also Gans 1979; Harrison 1985; Tiffen 1989). In cultural studies several authors equate promotional culture with popular culture and, accordingly, link the defence of the two together (Nava 1992; Fowles 1996; Twitchell 1996; Myers 1999). Criticism of promotional culture can thus be dismissed as another form of elitist, golden-age harping. It is also argued that a public sphere with more popular and promotional elements encourages additional, rather than simply detrimental, forms of public communication and debate (Dahlgren 1995; Street 2001; Delli Carpini and Williams 2001).

Likewise, when the discussion reaches the consumer-citizen (or buyer or audience), there is a considerable amount of work which argues that the impact of promotional culture is negligible. Advertising only encourages people to change to competitor brands, not to change their patterns of consumption (Schudson 1984). As any study of the cultural industries will confirm (see, for instance, Garnham 1990; Gitlin 1994) the vast majority of cultural products are financial failures – in spite of their promotional budgets. Texts, even focused promotional ones, are polysemic (Nava 1992; Fowles 1996; Storey 1999) and therefore open to multiple interpretations. Individual readings of texts are influenced by a number of personal social circumstances and experiences; thus all communications contain a large degree of 'interpretive openness' (ibid.; de Certeau 1984; Hebdige 1988; Fiske 1989; Morley 1992). Finally, the consensus of several decades of effects research in social psychology and political communications (see summaries in, for example, Livingstone 1998; Norris 1999; McQuail 2000) suggests that promotional culture, like communications generally, has little impact on the thinking, behaviour or political participation of most people.

Brave new worlds

Just as many cultural theorists and psychologists have sought to dismiss promotional culture, an alternative grouping of sociologists and cultural thinkers have placed it at the heart of social change. Several accounts have attempted to identify a new form of society, driven by the changing dynamics of market systems, culture and communications. These diverse accounts of 'Postmodernism', 'Post-Industrialism', 'Post-Fordism', the 'Information Society' and the 'Consumer Society', while not focusing on promotional culture specifically, all involve it in social transformation.

At first sight postmodernity is the most obvious new world where promotional culture seems to play a key part. The mass media and promotional culture are central features of several thinkers associated with 'the postmodern condition' (Baudrillard 1988; Hebdige 1988; Fiske 1989; Wernick 1991; Featherstone 1991; Nava 1992). Implicit, especially in the writing of Wernick (1991) and in Baudrillard's earlier work (1988: chs 1, 2, 3), is a strong sense that advertising transformed capitalism and social relations. Advertising prioritised exchange value over use value but, in the process, subordinated both to symbolic value. Processes of production, exchange and consumption are now more involved with signs rather than material objects. In contemporary society what typifies the 'postmodern condition' more than advertising and promotion? Promotional culture is fragmented, endlessly derivative and referential, shallow, temporary and meaning-less. However, if the early work of Baudrillard and initial chapters of Wernick identify the significance of promotional culture for social change, as their thinking evolves (Baudrillard 1988: chs 7, 9) promotional culture appears instead to contribute to its own redundancy. Promotional culture has become indistinguish-able from a general condition where the endless circulation of signs and simulations has left society unable to distinguish the real from the hyper-real. At the same time, history and social change have, themselves, become irrelevant concepts. In the end one must conclude that postmodernists are better linked with those who deny that promotional culture has any contemporary significance at all.

Perhaps the 'new worlders' who are most positive about promotional culture are those who, in one way or another, focus on post-industrialism, post-Fordism and, ultimately, the consumer society. Here industrialists and economists join with sociologists and cultural theorists. Each sees promotional culture as being essential to bringing about a more consumer-citizen-oriented society.

Beginning with the industrial and economic spheres, there are those social theorists who describe a continuing transformation in society of a 'post-indus-trial' or 'post-Fordist' nature. At the heart of this literature (Bell 1973; Piore and Sabel 1984; Lash and Urry 1987, 1994) is the change in the organisation of capitalism, from Fordism-Taylorism, with its mass production, mass consump-tion-driven society, towards a more consumer-focused form of production. These flexible forms of management, production and distribution give greater autonomy and choice to workers and consumers. This general transition also gives rise to the expansion of the new 'service class' or 'new petit bourgeoisie' and results in the decline of the mass-organised manual worker. For much of this work, the prime determining factor in change is technology. However, promo-tional culture has also been fundamental in enabling markets to grow and spread globally, to become more flexible and diverse, and more adaptable and reflexive: at each stage keeping producers in harmony with consumers. Although not specif-ically explored in the industrial literature, the part played by promotional culture in the changing production–consumption dynamic is certainly a feature of work on cultural production (see Hall and Jacques 1989; Wasko 1994; Nixon 1996; du Gay 1997; Crane 2000).

Promotional intermediaries similarly provide the link when it comes to looking at current-day markets and democratic systems. In industry and political communications literature (Grunig and Hunt 1984; Scammell 1995; Wilmshurst and Mackay 1999; Lees-Marshment 2001), marketing, polling, focus groups, etc. all work to feed public opinion and demand back to producers. Policies, goods and services are produced in accordance with such opinion and demand. Better, promotionally enhanced communications, in terms of advertising and public rela-tions, ensure consumer-citizens are heard and that their rights and freedoms as individuals are upheld. Promotional culture enables consumers to have greater choice, makes producers more responsive to consumer needs, keeps prices down, and provides essential support for an independent and responsive entertainment and news media.

Ethnographic work on audiences and consumption goes further in its privileging of the consumer. Consumers are increasingly adept at decoding promotional culture and, far from being directed by producers, actively choose to use promotional culture as they wish (Nava 1992; Myers 1999). In the bricoleur tradition, consumers can pick, choose and interpret the elements they want – either to develop personal opinions and identities or, quite simply, for the pleasure of consumption itself (Barthes 1975; Ang 1985; Mort 1989; Fiske 1990). As in industrial and economic accounts, the emphasis has moved away from the top-down diffusion of culture via promotion, to the bottom-up influence of the 'collective taste' on cultural producers (Blumler 1969; Nava 1992; Fowles 1996; Crane 2000). Because for producers to survive in the consumer society they must continue to respond to consumer demand – something that has become fundamental to the development of promotional strategies.

Ultimately, brave new worlders, in conjunction with the deniers of promotional culture, unite in making the case that long-running critiques of promotional culture are no longer applicable to our contemporary society. Such critical positions, they argue, are based on: nineteenth-century Marxist accounts of industrialisation and class conflict, twentieth-century notions of Fordist mass production/consumption models, and the 'grand narratives' of modernism generally. Instead, fragmentation, hyper-segmentation, polycentrism, diversity, flexibility, pluralism, and active/reflexive consumption are more appropriate descriptions to apply to the processes of production and consumption of communications and culture. Promotional culture, thus, is either irrelevant, another form of pleasurable popular culture, or a force for positive social transformation that liberates economies, democratic systems and consumer-citizens.

Conclusions

To return to the questions asked in the introduction to this chapter: has promotional culture contributed to social change and has that change been generally beneficial or not? In terms of social change, most of the diverse accounts of market and democratic systems assume that promotional culture has played a central, if not clearly identifiable, part. For economists and political scientists society could not run without it and, if not a determining factor of change, it is certainly implicated in it. For critics and brave new worlders it has been a fundamental part of social change – for better or worse. In opposition stand a sizable group of audience and effects researchers in cultural studies and psychology. Arguably, this individual subject-centred work is too narrowly focused in its opposition. Even if individuals use promotional culture, rather than being duped by it, they still choose from culture that is either increasingly promotional in nature or influenced in construction/communication by promotional intermediaries. The promotional industries employ more people, have larger budgets, take up more of the production budget of all commodities, and are the subject of more news and cultural commentary. Even if promotion does not work, more people, organisations and governments act as if they do; and that is socially significant.

In terms of social benefit, left-wing critics and a few notable liberal thinkers argue that promotional culture has only benefited producers and political elites, and has had a generally detrimental effect on society. These objectors find themselves increasingly out of academic fashion. Their wholesale pessimism over promotional culture is also too narrow. Promotional culture has become fundamental to properly functioning democratic and market systems, and, in many ways, made governments and companies more receptive to their publics. Cries of human subjugation and cultural poverty have been over-amplified.

Despite this, many of their original concerns, as well as their more recent counter-criticisms, do seem significant. Industry advocates and post-Fordists conveniently forget the fact that promotional intermediaries are primarily employed by producers and political elites, and, therefore, promote producer interests over others – even if that means appearing to fulfil consumer-citizen expectations in the process. For many observers (e.g. Harvey 1989; Bauman 1997; Webster 2002) the consumer/post-Fordist society is a social reality for only a few. The problems associated with Fordist/capitalist democracies – such as corporate conglomeration, rising inequality, environmental degradation, over-production and economic crises – persist for a majority of people. Similarly, too many supporters of the active audience/consumer society blithely assume that consumption can be equated to political liberation or engaged citizenship (Curran 1990; Morris 1990; McGuigan 1992; Ferguson and Golding 1997), or that consumption has few political or economic consequences.

However, even in those wealthy post-something societies, there appear to be major imbalances that might be linked to over-promotion and 'the freedom to consume'. Taking the USA and UK, where both promotional culture and the cult of individual consumption/liberation are most advanced, these countries are also amongst the OECD market leaders in terms of levels of (see also Castells 1997, 1998; Schlosser 2001; Moore 2001): obesity and cardio-vascular disease, personal debt, inequality, per capita waste and environmental pollution, restrictive union legislation, long working hours and casualised employment, and political cynicism. They also have amongst the lowest levels of public spending on welfare and transport infrastructures, and lowest electoral turnouts. In other words, our greater rights to consume also involve our greater rights to work longer, destroy our personal health, pollute our environment, increase our debt, ruin our social support systems, and disconnect ourselves from politics altogether. It might thus be concluded that promotional culture has simply worked to replace estranged labour with estranged consumption.

References

AA (Advertising Association, UK) website: www.adassoc.org.uk.

AMA (American Marketing Association) website: www.marketingpower.com.

Adorno, T. (1991) *The Culture Industry: Selected Essays on Mass Culture*, ed. J. Bernstein, London: Routledge.

Adorno, T. and Horkheimer, M. (1979 [1947]) *Dialectic of Enlightenment*, London: Verso.

Aglietta, M. (1987) *A Theory of Capitalist Regulation: The US Experience*, London: Verso.

Anderson, A. (1997) *Media, Culture and the Environment*, London: UCL Press

Ang, I. (1985) *Watching Dallas*, London: Methuen.

—— (1991) *Desperately Seeking the Audience*, London: Routledge.

Ansolabehere, S. and Iyengar, S. (1995) *Going Negative: How Political Advertisements Shrink and Polarise the Electorate*, New York: Free Press.

Baker, M. (1996) *Marketing: An Introductory Text*, 6th edn, Basingstoke: Macmillan.

Barthes, R. (1975) *The Pleasure of the Text*, London: Paladin.

Baudrillard, J. (1988) *Jean Baudrillard: Selected Writings*, ed. M. Poster, Cambridge: Polity.

Bauman, Z. (1997) *Work, Consumerism and the New Poor*, Buckingham, Milton Keynes: Open University Press.

Bell, D. (1973) *The Coming of Post-Industrial Society: A Venture in Social Forecasting*, Harmondsworth: Penguin.

Bennett, W. Lance and Manheim, J.B. (2001) 'The big spin: strategic communication and the transformation of pluralist democracy', in W. Lance Bennett and R.M. Entman (eds) *Mediated Politics: Communication in the Future of Democracy*, Cambridge: Cambridge University Press.

Berger, J. (1972) *Ways of Seeing*, London: Penguin/BBC.

Blumler, H. (1969) 'Fashion: from class differentiation to collective selection', in *Sociological Quarterly* 10.

Blumler, J. and Gurevitch, M. (1995) *The Crisis of Public Communication*, London: Routledge.

Boorstin, D. (1962) *The Image*, London: Weidenfeld & Nicolson.

Bourdieu, P. (1984) *Distinction*, London: Routledge.

Burston, J. (2000) 'Spectacle, synergy and megamusicals: the global-industrialisation of the live-entertainment economy', in J Curran (ed.) *Media Organisations in Society*, London: Arnold.

CIM (Chartered Institute of Marketing, UK) website: www.cim.co.uk.

Campbell, C. (1989) *The Romantic Ethic and the Spirit of Modern Consumerism*, Oxford: Blackwell.

Castells, M. (1997) *The Power of Identity*, Oxford: Blackwell.

—— (1998) *End of Millennium*, Oxford: Blackwell.

Crane, D. (2000) *Fashion and its Social Agendas: Class, Gender and Identity in Clothing*, Chicago: Chicago University Press.

Curran, J. (1986) 'The impact of advertising on the British mass media', in R. Collins, J. Curran, N. Garnham, P. Scannell, P. Schlesinger and C. Sparks (eds) *Media, Culture and Society*, London: Sage.

—— (1990) 'The new revisionism in mass communications research: a reappraisal', *European Journal of Communication* 5.

Curran, J. and Seaton, J. (1999) *Power without Responsibility*, 5th edn, London: Routledge.

Cutlip, S., Centre, A. and Broom, G. (2000) *Effective Public Relations*, 8th edn, Englewood Cliffs, NJ: Prentice-Hall.

D'Acci, J. (1994) *Defining Women*, Chapel Hill: University of North Carolina.

Dahlgren, P. (1995) *Television and the Public Sphere*, London: Sage.

Davis, A. (2002) *Public Relations Democracy*, Manchester: Manchester University Press.

—— (2003) 'Whither mass media and power? Evidence for a critical elite theory alternative', *Media, Culture and Society* 25(5).

de Certeau, M. (1984) *The Practice of Everyday Life*, Berkeley and Los Angeles: University of California Press.

Deacon, D. and Golding, P. (1994) *Taxation and Representation*, London: John Libby Press.

Delli Carpini, M.X. and Williams, B. (2001) 'Let us infotain you: politics in the new media environment', in W. Lance Bennett and R.M. Entman (eds) *Mediated Politics: Communication in the Future of Democracy*, Cambridge: Cambridge University Press.

du Gay, P. (ed.) (1997) *Production of Culture / Cultures of Production*, London: Sage / Open University.

Ewen, S. (1976) *Captains of Consciousness: Advertising and the Social Roots of Consumer Culture*, New York: McGraw-Hill.

—— (1996) *PR! A Social History of Spin*, New York: Basic Books.

Fallows, J. (1996) *Breaking the News: How the Media Undermine American Democracy*, New York: Pantheon.

Featherstone, M. (1991) *Consumer Culture and Postmodernism*, London: Sage.

Ferguson, M. and Golding, P. (eds) (1997) *Cultural Studies in Question*, London: Sage.

Fiske, J. (1989) *Understanding Popular Culture*, London: Unwin Hyman.

—— (1990) *Reading the Popular,* London: Unwin Hyman.

Fowles, J. (1996) *Advertising and Popular Culture*, London: Sage.

Franklin, B. (1994) *Packaging Politics*, London: Arnold.

—— (1997) *Newszak and News Media*, London, Arnold.

Gandy, O. (1982) *Beyond Agenda Setting: Information Subsidies and Public Policy*, NJ: Ablex Publishing Corporation.

Gans, H.J. (1979) *Deciding What's News: A Study of CBS Evening News, NBC Nightly News, Newsweek and Time*, New York: Pantheon.

Garnham, N. (1990) *Capitalism and Communication: Global Culture and the Economics of Information,* London: Sage.

Gitlin, T. (1994) *Inside Prime Time*, London: Routledge.

Golding, P. and Murdock, G. (2000) 'Culture, communications and political economy', in J. Curran and M. Gurevitch (eds) *Mass Media and Society*, 3rd edn, London: Arnold.

Goldman, R. (1992) *Reading Ads Socially*, London: Routledge.

Grunig, J. and Hunt, T. (1984) *Managing Public Relations*, New York: Holt, Rinehart & Winston.

Habermas, J. (1989) *The Structural Transformation of the Public Sphere*, Cambridge: Polity.

Hall, S. and Jacques, M. (1989) *New Times*, London: Lawrence & Wishart.

Hallin, D. (1994) *We Keep America on Top of the World*, London: Routledge.

Harrison, M. (1985) *Television News: Whose Bias?* Hermitage: Policy Journals Publication.

Hebdige, D. (1988) *Hiding in the Light*, London: Comedia.

Herman, E. and Chomsky, N. (1988) *Manufacturing Consent: The Political Economy of the Mass Media*, New York: Pantheon Books.

Herman, E. and McChesney, R. (1997) *The Global Media: The New Missionaries of Global Capitalism,* London: Cassell.

IPR (Institute of Public Relations) website: www.ipr.org.uk.

Jameson, F. (1991) *Postmodernism or the Cultural Logic of Late Capitalism*, London: Verso.

Jhally, S. (1990) *The Codes of Advertising – Fetishism and the Political Economy of Meaning in Consumer Society*, London: Routledge.

Jones, N. (1995) *Soundbites and Spin Doctors – How Politicians Manipulate the Media and Vice Versa*, London: Cassell.

Klein, N. (2000) *No Logo*, London: Flamingo.

Lasch, C. (1976) *The Culture of Narcissism: American Life in an Age of Diminishing Expectations*, New York: Norton.

Lash, S. and Urry, J. (1987) *The End of Organised Capitalism*, Cambridge: Polity.

—— (1994) *Economies of Signs and Spaces*, London: Sage.

Lears, T. (1995) *Fables of Abundance: A Cultural History of Advertising in America*, New York: Basic Books.

Lees-Marshment, J. (2001) *Political Marketing and British Politics*, Manchester: Manchester University Press.

Leiss, W., Kline, S. and Jhally, S. (1990) *Social Communication in Advertising*, London: Routledge.

Lichtenberg, J. (2000) 'In defence of objectivity', in J. Curran and M. Gurevitch (eds) *Mass Media and Society*, 3rd edn, London: Arnold.

Livingstone, S. (1998) *Making Sense of Television: The Psychology of Audience Interpretation*, London: Routledge.

Lury, C. and Warde, A. (1997) 'Investments in the imaginary consumer', in M. Nava. A. Blake, I. MacRury and B. Richards (eds) *Buy This Book*, London: Routledge.

McGuigan, J. (1992) *Cultural Populism*, London: Routledge.

McNair, B. (1998) *The Sociology of Journalism*, London: Arnold.

—— (2003) *An Introduction to Political Communications*, 3rd edn, London: Routledge.

McQuail, D. (2000) *Mass Communications Theory*, 4th edn, London, Sage.

Marchand, R. (1998) *Creating the Corporate Soul*, Berkeley: University of California Press.

Miller, D. and Dinan, W. (2000) 'The rise of the PR industry in Britain, 1979–98', *European Journal of Communication* 15(1).

Moore, M. (2001) *Stupid White Men*, New York: Harper Collins.

Morley, D. (1992) *Television, Audiences and Cultural Studies*, London: Routledge.

Morris, M. (1990) 'Banality in cultural studies' in P. Mellencamp (ed.) *Logics of Television: Essays in Cultural Criticism*, Bloomington: Indiana University Press.

Mort, F. (1989) 'The politics of consumption', in S. Hall and M. Jacques (eds) *New Times*, London: Lawrence & Wishart.

Myers, G. (1999) *AdWorlds: Brands, Media, Audiences*, London: Arnold.

Nava, M. (1992) *Changing Cultures: Feminism, Youth and Consumerism*, London, Sage

Negus, K. (1992) *Producing Pop: Culture and Conflict in the Popular Music Industry*, London: Arnold.

—— (1999) *Music Genres and Corporate Cultures*, London: Routledge.

Nelson, J. (1989) *Sultans of Sleaze – Public Relations and the Media*, Toronto: Between the Lines.

Neuman, W. (2001) 'The impact of the new media', in W. Lance Bennett and R.M. Entman (eds) *Mediated Politics: Communication in the Future of Democracy*, Cambridge: Cambridge University Press.

Nixon, S. (1996) *Hard Looks*, London: UCL Press.

Norris, J. (1990) *Advertising and the Transformation of American Society, 1865–1920*, New York: Greenwood.

Norris, P., Curtice, J., Sanders, D., Scammell, M. and Semetko, H. (1990) *On Message: Communicating the Campaign*, London: Sage.

Packard, V. (1957) *The Hidden Persuaders*, London: Longman.

Piore, M. and Sabel, C. (1984) *The Second Industrial Divide*, New York: Basic Books.

Postman, N. (1985) *Amusing Ourselves to Death*, London: Methuen.

Roche, D. (1994) *The Culture of Clothing: Dress and Fashion in the 'Ancient Regime'*, Cambridge: Cambridge University Press.

Scammell, M. (1995) *Designer Politics: How Elections Are Won*, London: Macmillan.

Schiller, H. (1989) *Culture Inc. The Corporate Takeover of Public Expression*, New York: Oxford University Press.

Schlosser, E. (2001) *Fast Food Nation: What the All-American Meal is Doing to the World*, London: Allen Lane.

Schudson, M. (1984) *Advertising, The Uneasy Persuasion*, New York: Basic Books.

—— (1995) *The Power of News*, Cambridge, MA: Harvard University Press.

Shoemaker, P. (1989) 'Public relations versus journalism – comments on Turrow', *American Behavioural Scientist* 33(2).

Stauber, J. and Rampton, S. (1995) *Toxic Sludge is Good For You – Lies, Damn Lies and the Public Relations Industry*, Monroe, ME: Common Courage Press.

Storey, J. (1999) *Cultural Consumption and Everyday Life*, London: Arnold.

Street, J. (2001) 'The transformation of political modernity', in B. Axford and R. Huggins (eds) *New Media and Politics*, London: Sage.

Tiffen, R. (1989) *News and Power*, Sydney, Allen & Unwin.

Twitchell, J.B. (1996) *Adcult USA: The Triumph of Advertising in American Culture*, New York: Columbia University Press.

Wasko, J. (1994) *Hollywood in the Information Age*, Cambridge: Polity.

Webster, F. (2002) *Theories of the Information Society*, 2nd edn, London: Routledge.

Wernick, A. (1991) *Promotional Culture*, London: Sage.

Williams, R. (1980) *Problems in Materialism and Culture*, London: Verso.

Williamson, J. (1978) *Decoding Advertisements*, London: Marion Boyars.

Wilmshurst, J. and Mackay, A. (1999) *The Fundamentals of Advertising*, Oxford: Butterworth-Heinemann.

ZenithOptimedia (2003) *Advertising Expenditure Forecasts July 2003*, ZenithOptimedia.

Chapter 11

International agreements and the regulation of world communication

Ted Magder

Introduction

When the People's Republic of China joined the World Trade Organization (WTO) in 2001, its list of commitments included revisions to trade-related regulations for media goods and services. China agreed to raise its annual theatrical quota on foreign film imports from ten to 20 films in 2002, increasing to 50 films annually by 2005. In the interest of 'expanding foreign cultural exchange and economic cooperation', China also agreed to permit joint business ventures with foreign companies in the ownership and operation of movie theatres, entertainment complexes, advertising agencies, and audiovisual distributors (WTO 2002a, 2002b). Each of these commitments comes with some fine print. Audio and video distributors are obligated to 'disseminate the ideological, ethical, scientific, technological, and cultural knowledge conducive to economic development and social progress' (WTO 2002a); joint-venture movie theatres may not adopt the names of foreign theatres or TV stations; and box-office revenues from foreign films will still be shared with China Film Export and Import Corporation (a state-owned entity with the sole right to legally import theatrical films into China). Alongside these reforms, China also committed to liberalize its telecommunication market and to honour the international regime of intellectual property rights overseen by the WTO. Even as a package the measures are hardly revolutionary, especially given the Chinese government's tight control over the range of media and information sources available to its citizens (Hong 1998; Lee 2000). But they do serve to illustrate an emerging trend.

What sovereign states can do to regulate the flow of media across their borders and what they can do to regulate media activities within those borders is increasingly influenced by a web of international agreements. These agreements are far older and more numerous than those overseen by the WTO. They date back, at the very least, to the creation of the International Telegraph Union in 1865 and the Universal Postal Union in 1874, to name but two. Since then, the number of supranational and international agreements – including treaties, covenants, protocols, declarations, and charters – that affect the flow of communication across borders has multiplied many times over.[1]

The impact of international agreements on the flow of communication within and across borders is difficult to discern. There is nothing like a co-ordinated global regime for the governance of media and communication. No widely accepted hierarchy of principles exists and the administrative application of most agreements is characterized by inconsistency. Many of the agreements have no enforcement mechanisms; those that do, such as GATT, GATS and TRIPS, require some mastery in international law to decipher. Most important, the regulation of media is still, by and large, the prerogative of sovereign states, as the example of China attests. Rather than heralding the death of the nation state, these international agreements have become one more important factor in shaping the regulatory and legal environment influencing the production and circulation of the daily messages imparted and received, within and across frontiers.

Generally, the literature in media and communication studies has been less than scrupulous in taking account of this trend.[2] For a time, it was fashionable to declare that the age of media and communication governance was near an end: that the Internet, digitization, and convergence would make regulations designed to increase diversity or pluralism or to restrict the flow of messages either unnecessary or obsolete (de Sola Pool 1984; Negroponte 1996). That view has receded as governments and non-governmental bodies move to manage such issues as privacy, security, indecent and obscene content, domain names, and the protection of intellectual property (Marsden 2000; Kahin and Nesson 1997; Loader 1997).

A second scholarly approach acknowledges the emergence of international governance but is critical of its recent trajectory. The most forceful version of this argument depicts the current wave of international trade agreements as full-scale victories for transnational media and telecommunication firms, and their efforts to privatize and commodify the sphere of public expression (Herman and McChesney 1997; Venturelli 1998; McChesney 2000). Certainly, recent changes in intellectual property have aided and abetted the corporate giants in the business of media production (Vaidhyanathan 2001). Moreover, the link between corporate expansion and international agreements goes much further back: the telegraph conventions of the late nineteenth and early twentieth centuries made it easier for a few European (and later US) news agencies to dominate the daily flow of international news; the first GATT agreement aided the overseas expansion of Hollywood.

To claim that current international agreements serve the interests of transnational firms eager to profit from trade in media products and communication services is one thing. It is quite another to claim that this is all they do, or all they can do. Communication scholars have long understood the value of law and public policy to promote core values such as freedom of expression, pluralism, and diversity in public expression. Can these values be enshrined and advanced in international agreements that influence the flow of media and communication across frontiers? Not surprisingly, the answer does not come easily. For one thing, the long tradition of respecting the sovereignty of states in the conduct of their cultural and political affairs argues against a universal and binding legal code. While some states might see international agreements as another meddlesome manifestation of 'Western' values, others recoil at the prospect of losing the ability to promote a vibrant space for domestic public expression. Authoritarian governments close borders and limit internal freedoms in an effort to control what is said and heard in public; most liberal democratic governments use public money and intricate regulations – like ownership restrictions and content quotas – to counter the perceived tendency of liberalized media markets to reduce or eliminate local expression. No country is ready to cede all its policy prerogatives to an international body, even though some, such as the USA and Japan, would prefer greater liberalization of media and communication markets. The question of values, as well as questions of substance, brings to the foreground fundamental disagreements over the rights of states as international actors, the nature of public life, and the balance that should be struck both between individual and collective rights, and between politics and markets.

Sovereignty and international law: realism and liberal internationalism

International agreements have a peculiar status because they bring together sovereign states, entities with a long history of using law backed by the use of force (and sometimes the use of force alone) to establish and maintain their interests within, across, and in the making of, borders. Two approaches dominate the study of international relations. Realist theories (Morgenthau 1948; Gilpin 2002) view international relations as a struggle for power among sovereign states, characterized by periods of anarchy, periods of balance, and periods of imperialism and unilateralism. Nothing much matters but the actions of states, aggrandizing power and pursuing their self-interest. Powerful states matter most. They are likely to determine the nature of international agreements and the mechanisms of international governance. A competing approach to international politics is much more sanguine about the prospects for international agreements and international co-operation. Liberal internationalism maintains that international relations are increasingly characterized by enlightened self-interest, a desire to avoid conflict, and an emergent moral code emphasizing human rights, human dignity, justice, and the search for perpetual peace (Keohane 1984; Long 1996).

While liberal internationalism runs the risk of under-estimating the part played by power in international relations, it is a useful corrective to realist theories. The dramatic increase in international agreements over the past century, and the now dense networks of interaction and interdependence among states, suggest that hard-boiled realism has become less and less a feature of daily international relations. Moreover, in their classic formulations both versions of international relations have a tendency to focus attention almost exclusively on the role of states. Newer versions of each take account of the rise in importance of non-state actors, including intergovernmental organizations (such as the ITU), transnational organizations without formal government representation (such as ICANN), and non-governmental organizations (including business organizations, such as the Motion Picture Association, and non-profit or public interest organizations, such as Amnesty International) (Hamelink 1994). International agreements in the field of world communication can be understood, in part, as the playing out of the tensions between realist and internationalist tendencies, in theory and in practice.

Core principles of world communication

Nineteenth-century telegraph conventions were based on two principles that continue to frame the debate over world communication: the freedom of individuals to communicate across borders, and the right of states to regulate and police the flow of international communication (Codding 1952). Of the two, the sovereignty of the state was paramount. So, for example, while the International Telegraph Convention (1875) laid down the basic technical standards for cross-border communication and granted 'to all persons the right to correspond by means of all international telegraphs', it also granted governments 'the right to stop the transmission of any private telegram which may appear dangerous to the safety of the state, or which may be contrary to the laws of the country, to public order, or good morals'. And while states were obliged 'to take all the necessary measures to ensure the secrecy of the correspondence and its safe transmission', only the state itself could write and transmit messages 'in secret language'.

The proliferation of international agreements in the early twentieth century engendered new principles, part of the general trend toward the application of human rights in international law. The 1906 International Wireless Telegraph Convention (US 1907), for example, introduced the world-wide use of the SOS emergency signal for ships at sea, ensuring that telegraph operators made the preservation of human life their highest priority regardless of nationality. As the organization of radio broadcasting proceeded along the lines of existing states, and as some states began to experiment with radio's propaganda potential, twenty-eight members of the League of Nations signed the International Convention Concerning the Use of Broadcasting in the Cause of Peace in the 1930s. The Convention outlined rules to prohibit broadcasts that were 'incompatible with the internal order or security of contracting parties', and rules to ensure 'that any transmission likely to harm international understanding by incorrect statements shall be rectified at the earliest possible moment', sometimes referred to as the right of correction (Hamelink 1994: 19).

The SOS signal was a small triumph in the history of international relations. It saved lives. But the League's attempt to broaden the moral standards that underpin international communication came to naught. For one thing, fascist regimes, and countries outside the League, such as the USA, did not sign the Convention on Broadcasting and Peace. Even if they had, the Convention was flawed for a more substantial reason: as written, its right of correction would have created a burdensome, uncertain, and conflict-ridden process. By what means would 'incorrect' statements be determined and rectified? Even within a single country, such questions stretch the limits of dispute resolution. In the international arena, they seem sure to flounder. Good intentions aside, the Convention highlights the risk in extending the range of principles to be pursued through international agreements.

In the immediate post-war period, at the high point of liberal internationalist sentiment, the United Nations adopted the Universal Declaration of Human Rights, now the benchmark for the application of human rights in international affairs. The Declaration does not bind member states to its articles. Rather, it serves as a moral compass, an aspiring statement of the fundamental values that should guide world affairs. Two of its articles bear directly on world communication. Article 19 reads: 'Everyone has the right to freedom of opinion and expression; this right includes freedom to hold opinions without interference and to seek, receive and impart information and ideas through any media and regardless of frontiers' (UN 1948).

Article 19 is the result of an uneasy and incomplete compromise struck within the Sub-Commission on Freedom of Information and the Press, the legacy of the ill-fated attempt to draft a detailed Convention on Freedom of the Press (Kleinwachter 1989a, 1989b). The main points of contention concerned the addition of the right of correction for false and misleading reports (a legacy of the League's Convention on Broadcasting and Peace) and the right of governments to block the entry of war and racial propaganda, both in contradistinction to the emerging doctrine of a free flow of information across borders. Initially, delegates from Western countries, including the USA, were amenable to clauses that would permit governments to block certain messages and employ a modified right of correction. But as the Cold War intensified, the USA and the Soviet Union hardened their positions. Article 19 is all that remains. Even so, Article 19 stands as the single most important statement regarding the fundamental principles of world communication. It remains the best foundation for the legal and regulatory design of world communication.

The debate over the legal and moral tenets of world communication resurfaced with some fury within the United Nations Educational, Scientific and Cultural Organization (UNESCO) in the 1970s in discussions on the New World Information and Communication Order (NWICO) (Masmoudi 1979; Roach 1987, Hamelink 1994). Though the NWICO discussions are typically depicted as ending in stalemate or failure – culminating in the departure from UNESCO of the USA and the UK –

they did help to crystallize two new principles for the conduct and management of world communication: the first is most clearly formulated as 'the right to communicate'; the second pertains to cultural autonomy and the importance of maintaining and promoting cultural diversity, and is often referred to as 'the right of culture'.

Of the two, the principle of a right to culture has a longer history. It grows out of Article 27 of the Universal Declaration on Human Rights (UN 1948), which states: 'Everyone has the right freely to participate in the cultural life of the community, to enjoy the arts and to share in scientific advancement and benefits.'[3] The import of Article 27 lay dormant until a rich body of literature on cultural imperialism and cultural homogenization made the case that US-led, Western dominance over the media, together with the ever-deepening networks of globalization, posed a serious threat to indigenous cultures (Schiller 1976; Schiller and Nordenstreng 1979; Hamelink 1983). As a result of stark imbalances in the global exchange of media, the argument goes, national cultures face the prospect of marginalization, even annihilation. The prospects for a global dialogue were giving way to cultural homogenization and synchronization. The merits of this argument have been hotly debated, especially with respect to the more dire predictions regarding the decline and fall of indigenous cultures outside the imperial core (Tomlinson 1991, 1999; Curran and Park 2000). For our purposes, what matters most is the increasing attention paid to the idea of cultural diversity as a value in and of itself, and as a moral and legal principle of world communication. Governments adopted the right of culture as the basis for a host of policy practices designed to protect and promote indigenous forms of expression and to facilitate communicative diversity. For one, the Council of Europe (2000) has endorsed the principle and, in so doing, pulled away from the project of creating a pan-European citizen with a common cultural identity (Schlesinger 1997).

UNESCO has given the right of culture its imprimatur most recently in the Universal Declaration on Cultural Diversity. Article 1 reads:

> Culture takes diverse forms across time and space. This diversity is embodied in the uniqueness and plurality of the identities of the groups and societies making up humankind. As a source of exchange, innovation and creativity, cultural diversity is as necessary for humankind as biodiversity is for nature.
>
> (UNESCO 2001)

As appealing as they may seem, the right to culture and the movement to protect and promote cultural diversity have their drawbacks. Because cultures are inherently the embodiment – in symbols and practices – of collectivities, efforts to bolster cultural diversity may trump an individual's right to communicate within or across frontiers; this is especially likely in places where the state has an already poor record of protecting individual rights and where the state has declared itself to be the proper guardian or custodian of culture. Tellingly, the catalogue of human rights enunciated in UNESCO's Declaration makes no mention of Article 19. Without formal recognition of the primacy of an individual's freedom to communicate across borders, an international convention in support of cultural diversity would grant existing states considerable leverage in determining the boundaries of public expression. We should be wary of any legal code that gives governments the option of putting culture before citizenship as they go about the task of regulating the 'market for loyalties' (Price 1995, 2002). Put another way, the legitimacy of cultural rights depends, in the first instance, on the freedom of individuals to determine those customs and traditions and values that are worth preserving and promoting (Sen 2000: ch. 10; Benhabib 2002).

Of all the principles to emerge in the debates over world communication, the 'right to communicate' is the newest. In 1969, Jean D'Arcy made the case that Article 19 was premised on a linear and centralized model of communication in which large, bureaucratic media institutions, operated under the aegis of the state or capital, hold sway. Technological developments in mediated communication, D'Arcy argued, had made possible a model of communication that was far decentralized, interactive, and dialogical. Freedom to communicate is a negative right; it obliges governments not to interfere with an individual's efforts to impart and receive information across frontiers. The right to communicate is a positive right; it includes, as D'Arcy put it, 'both for individuals and societies, the concepts of access, participation, and two-way information flow, all of which are vital, as we now sense, for the harmonious development of man and mankind' (in Fisher 2002: 39). It enjoins governments to create the conditions and capabilities necessary – in the form of resources, access, and education – for broad-based participation in public communication (Sen 2000). Though it informed the work of UNESCO's McBride Commission, the right to communicate was not formally adopted, in part because of objections from the Soviet bloc. It has become the fundamental principle behind the work of various public interest groups intent on influencing the international regime of world communication (Hamelink 2002).

International trade agreements: *GATTing* the media and culture

Until the end of 1993, when France and the USA tangled over the inclusion of audiovisual products in the Uruguay Round of trade negotiations, less attention had been paid to how the GATT affects the movement of media across borders (Miller 1996). Signed in 1947 as an integral part of the post-war effort to stabilize the international monetary and trade regime, GATT set out to reduce 'tariffs and barriers to trade', and to eliminate 'discriminatory treatment in international commerce' (GATT 1947). Among other things, it lays down clear language on the cross-frontier movement of media and cultural artifacts.

Article IV of the GATT, 'Special Provisions relating to Cinematograph Films' is an effort to address the patchwork of bilateral agreements affecting the international trade in movies negotiated before and after the Second World War.[4] Article IV gives contracting parties the right to establish or maintain 'internal quantitative regulations relating to exposed cinematograph films' (GATT 1947). These regulations can only take the form of 'screen quotas' that require theatres to exhibit films of 'national origin' during a specified 'minimum proportion of total screen time' – like those in France. Import quotas are no longer permitted. Films cannot be stopped at the border, or limited by number, because of their nationality. For the USA, Article IV highlights the value of formalizing general and predictable rules of trade. Article IV also gives other countries some measure of protection against Hollywood's global ambitions. It is, in other words, a compromise.[5] It remains a feature of the international trade regime.

One other GATT article bears directly on the movement of media and cultural products across borders. Article XX permits states to take measures 'necessary to protect public morals', and 'for the protection of national treasures of artistic, historic or archaeological value', provided that such measures are not 'disguised restrictions on international trade' and not 'a means of arbitrary or unjustifiable discrimination between countries'. The protection of public morals has been a feature of international agreements since the telegraph conventions, but GATT's language is not a blanket license to close a border to offensive foreign content. For example, a law that banned the importation of publications containing indecent material would violate GATT if domestic publications with similar content were permitted. The 'protection of national treasures' has been given further elaboration in at least three other international agreements: the *UNESCO Convention on the Means of Prohibiting and Preventing the Illicit Import, Export and Transfer of Ownership of Cultural Property* (1970), the *UNESCO Convention concerning the Protection of World Cultural and Natural Heritage* (1972), and the *UNIDROIT Convention on Stolen and Illegally Exported Cultural Property* (1995). We cannot here examine the history and application of these agreements (see Merryman 2001; Doyal 2001). We can say this: first, the GATT acknowledges that certain cultural objects may be protected from the disciplines of open and freer trade; second, inclusion of an item in GATT – such as artistic national treasures – can also be subject to other, more elaborate and detailed, international instruments.

Curiously, given its formidable legal language, up until 1994, GATT represented a form of shallow integration (Ruggie 1994; Rodrik 2000; Howse 2002). Violations of GATT articles were not subject to a binding dispute resolution mechanism. So, for example, a member of GATT could ignore its provisions, as Italy did by maintaining an import quota on feature films (only 185 US films a year) until 1962. Back-room diplomacy was the preferred route for settlement of disputes.

GATT 1994 introduced a binding dispute resolution mechanism – in essence, a judicial process – under the auspices of the WTO (Dunhoff 2001). And though the language in GATT referring to media and culture was not changed, the dispute resolution mechanism made a difference. To date the most significant example involves a 1997 US complaint against policy measures adopted by Canada to protect and promote domestic magazines (Magder 1998). The US objected to Canada's efforts to restrict the sale in Canada of foreign split-run magazines, publications that combine recycled editorial content from a foreign edition with some original content and new advertising directed toward Canadian readers. The measures were not designed to prevent Canadians from reading US magazines, but to ensure that advertising expenditures by Canadian firms were directed, as much as possible, to Canadian publications.[6] After a protracted legal and diplomatic battle, the WTO sided with the USA, concluding that since Canadian magazines derive more revenue from the sale of readers to advertisers than the sale of magazines to readers, split-run magazines should be characterized as 'direct competitors'. The ruling forced Canada to redesign its magazine policy from the ground up.

The GATT now exists alongside the General Agreement on Trade in Services (GATS). The GATS contains language on audiovisual services, as well as advertising services. It too is a compromise. GATS signatories choose the level of their commitment to trade liberalization. At the outset, 13 countries made commitments in the audiovisual sector: the USA, Japan, New Zealand, Israel, Hong Kong, India, Kenya, Korea, Malaysia, Mexico, Nicaragua, Singapore, and Thailand. Since then, 13 other countries – including Albania, Jordan, Panama, and China – have activated commitments in the audiovisual sector. In most cases, the commitments are not absolute: even the USA, for example, reserves the right to restrict foreign investment in broadcasting. The European Union and 33 other countries have invoked the most favored nation (MFN) exemptions for audiovisual services (Pauwels and Loisen 2003). The premise of GATS is that over time more and more countries will make commitments to trade liberalization. Once they do, they cannot reverse course, as New Zealand discovered when it tried to reintroduce a national quota for broadcasting in 2001.

The USA has signaled its intention to reopen negotiations on audiovisual services in the current round of WTO negotiations, calling for 'an open and predictable environment that recognizes public concern for the preservation and promotion of cultural values and identity'. This framework would include 'an understanding on subsidies that will respect each nation's need to foster its cultural identity by creating an environment to nurture local culture' (WTO 2000). And there is some evidence that this is more than rhetoric. In the aftermath of the WTO's magazine ruling, the USA agreed to limits on the sale of new advertising space in split-run magazines and to public subsidies in Canada to promote Canadian magazines (Magder 1999; Acheson and Maule 2000). Still, the main thrust of the US position is a reduction in barriers to cross-border trade and limits to public subsidies. In a recently completed trade deal with the USA, Australia agreed to quantitative limits on domestic quotas for television programs and to limits on the amount of money that domestic cable and pay-TV broadcasters can be required to spend on local content (Smith 2004). We can expect the USA to insist on similar language in the over 20 bilateral trade agreements currently under negotiation.

Conclusion

In the aftermath of the WTO's ruling on magazines, Canada spearheaded the International Network on Cultural Policy (INCP). Consisting of sixteen countries, including France, Italy, Greece, Sweden, and Burkina Faso, the INCP has recently called for a legally binding convention on cultural diversity to be administered by UNESCO (Bristow 2003). The objectives seem simple enough: to reduce the importance of the GATT and GATS as instruments governing the flow of media and cultural content across borders, and to advance the idea of cultural diversity as a principle of world communication.[7] The WTO regime has been much vilified of late. In its current guise it favors the rich over the poor, commerce over citizenship, opacity over transparency. It is not the place to work through a comprehensive international agreement that guarantees the right to hold opinions without interference and to seek, receive, and impart information and ideas through any media and regardless of frontiers. But a convention on cultural diversity has risks of its own, not the least of which is that to date the INCP and UNESCO seem lukewarm in their commitment to Article 19. A binding international agreement on the principles of world communication is a long way off. The opposition to such an agreement comes in many guises: there are states that proclaim the sovereign right to control all aspects of their own media space, just as there are states and private actors that want to treat media and culture as little more than the objects of commercial exchange. A neat resolution is a long way off. That this is so should be no cause for panic or inaction. Fundamental rights and fundamental freedoms may be easy to proclaim, but they are hard to do. The debate is only a century old.

Notes

1   Ivan Bernier and H.R. Fabri (2002) list over sixty.
2   Notable exceptions include: Hamelink 1994; Baker 2002; O'Siochru and Girard 2002; Raboy 2002; Price 2002.
3   Article 27 has a second clause recognizing the importance of copyright protection.
4   In 1936, the USA and France signed the Marchandeau Accord, allowing the French government to limit the importation of dubbed foreign films to 188 per year, of which 150 could be US. One year after the war, France and the USA agreed to a screen quota for French films, initially set at four weeks per quarter (see Jeancolas 1998). On the UK, see Dickinson (1983) and Jarvie (1992). On Canada, see Magder (1993).
5   In 1961, the USA claimed that Article IV did not set a precedent for other cultural products and that television programming was a just another 'good' within the

meaning of GATT. In response, leading GATT signatories argued that Article IV should be extended to cover television programming, and second that television programming was a service, not a good, and therefore fell outside of GATT. The parties agreed to disagree (WTO 1990).

6   The case resembles an important European Union decision in 1988 overturning Dutch cable television regulations banning cross-border advertising directed at Dutch citizens (see Bond Van Adverteerders vs. The Netherlands [1988]. ECR 2085, Case 352/85).

7   Canada has notified the WTO that it will not make any new commitments that restrict its ability to achieve cultural policy objectives 'until a new international instrument, specifically designed to safeguard the right of countries to promote and preserve cultural diversity, can be established' (WTO 2001).

References

Acheson, K. and Maule, C. (2000) 'Rethinking Canadian magazine policy', *Gazette* 62(3–4).

Baker, C. Edwin (2002) *Media, Markets and Democracy*, Cambridge, UK: Cambridge University Press.

Benhabib, Seyla (2002) *The Claims of Culture: Equality and Diversity in the Global Era*, Princeton: Princeton University Press.

Bernier, Ivan and Fabri, H.R. (2002) *Evaluation of the Legal Feasibility of an International Instrument Governing Cultural Diversity*, Quebec: Groupe de Travail Franco-Québécois sur la Diversité Culturelle.

Bristow, Jason (2003) *Symbolic Tokenism in Canada–U.S. Cultural Sector Trade Relations*, Canadian–American Public Policy. No. 55, Orono: University of Maine

Codding, George A. (1952) *The International Telegraph Union: An Experiment in International Organization*, Leiden: E.J. Brill.

Council of Europe (2000) *Declaration on Cultural Diversity*, adopted by the Committee of Ministers, 7 December 2000.

Curran, James and Park, Myung-Jin (eds) (2000) *De-Westernizing Media Studies*, London: Routledge.

D'Arcy, Jean (1969) 'Direct broadcast satellites and the right to communicate', *EBU Review* 118.

de Sola Pool, Ithiel (1984) *Technologies of Freedom; On Free Speech in an Electronic Age*, Cambridge, MA: Belknap Press.

Dickinson, Margaret (1983) 'The state and the consolidation of monopoly', in J. Curran and V. Porter (eds) *British Cinema History*, London: Wiedenfeld & Nicolson.

Doyal, Stephanie (2001) 'Implementing the UNIDROIT Convention on Cultural Property into domestic law: the case of Italy,' *Columbia Journal of Transnational Law* 39.

Dunhoff, Jeffrey (2001) 'Global trade issues in the new millennium: the WTO in transition: of constituents, competence and coherence', *George Washington International Law Review* 33.

Fisher, Desmond (2002) 'A new beginning: the campaign for a right to communicate', *Intermedia* 30(5).

GATT (1947) *The General Agreement on Tariffs and Trade*, available at: www.wto.org/english/docs_e/legal_e/gatt47_e.pdf.

Gilpin, Robert (2002) 'A realist perspective on international governance', in D. Held and A. McGrew (eds) *Governing Globalization: Power, Authority and Global Governance*, London: Polity Press.

Hamelink, Cees (1983) *Cultural Autonomy in Global Communication*, New York: Longmans.

—— (1994) *The Politics of World Communication*, London: Sage.

—— (2002) 'The civil society challenge to global media policy', in Marc Raboy (ed.) *Global Media Policy in the New Millennium*, Luton: University of Luton Press.

Herman, Edward and McChesney, R. (1997) *The Global Media: The New Missionaries of Corporate Power*, London: Cassell.

Hong, Junhao (1998) *The Internationalization of Television in China: The Evolution of Ideology, Society, and Media since the Reform*, Westport, CT: Praeger.

Howse, Robert (2002) 'The boundaries of the WTO: from politics to technocracy – and back again: the fate of the multilateral trading regime', *The American Journal of International Law* 96(94), January.

International Telegraph Convention (1875) signed at St Petersburg, July 10/22, available at http://earlyradiohistory.us/1906conv.htm#articles.

Jarvie, Ian (1992) *Hollywood's Overseas Campaign: The North Atlantic Movie Trade 1920–1950*, Cambridge: Cambridge University Press.

Jeancolas, Jean Pierre (1998) 'From the Blum–Byrnes agreement to the GATT affair', in Geoffrey Nowell-Smith and Steven Ricci (eds) *Hollywood and Empire: Economics, Culture and Identity, 1945–95*, London: British Film Institute.

Kahin, Brian and C. Nesson (eds) (1997) *Borders in Cyberspace*, Cambridge, MA: MIT Press.

Keohane, Robert (1984) *After Hegemony: Cooperation and Discord in the World Political Economy*, New York: Addison-Wesley.

Kleinwachter, Wolfgang (1989a) 'Human rights, the right to communicate and international law', *Media Law and Practice*, March.

—— (1989b) 'The birth of Article 19 – a twin concept of the United Nations', in *Media, Law and Practice*, September.

Lee, Chin-Chuan (ed.) (2000) *Money, Power, and Media: Communications Patterns and Bureaucratic Control in Cultural China*, Evanston, IL: Northwestern University Press.

Loader, Brian (ed.) (1997) *The Governance of Cyberspace*, London: Routledge.

Long, D. (1996) *Towards a New Liberal Internationalism*, Cambridge: Cambridge University Press.

McChesney, Robert (2000) *Rich Media, Poor Democracy: Communication Policies in Dubious Times*, New York: The New Press.

Magder, Ted (1993) *Canada's Hollywood: Feature Films and the Canadian State*, Toronto: University of Toronto Press.

—— (1998) *Franchising the Candy Store: Split-Run Magazines and a New International Regime for Trade in Culture*, Canadian–American Public Policy. No. 34, Orono: University of Maine.

—— (1999) 'Going global', *The Canadian Forum*, August.

Marsden, Christoper (ed.) (2000) *Regulating the Global Information Society*, London: Routledge.

Masmoudi, M. (1979) 'The new world information order', *Journal of Communication* 29(2).

Merryman, John H. (2001) 'Cultural property, international law, and human rights', *Cardozo Arts and Entertainment Law Journal* 19.

Miller, Toby (1996) 'The crime of Monsieur Lang; GATT, the screen and the new international division of cultural labour', in A. Moran (ed.) *Film Policy: International, National and Regional Perspectives*, London: Routledge.

Morgenthau, Hans J. (1948) *Politics among Nations: The Struggle for Power and Peace*, New York: Knopf.

Negroponte, Nicholas (1996) *Being Digital*, New York: Vintage.

O'Siochru, Sean and Girard, B. (2002) *Global Media Governance: A Beginner's Guide*, Lanham, MA: Rowan & Littlefield.

Pauwels, Caroline and Loisen, Jan (2003) 'The WTO and the audiovisual sector: economic free trade vs. cultural horse-trading?' *European Journal of Communication* 18(3).

Price, Monroe (1995) *Television: The Public Sphere and National Identity*, Oxford: Clarendon.

—— (2002) *Media and Sovereignty: The Global Information Revolution and Its Challenge to State Power*, Cambridge, MA: MIT Press.

Raboy, Marc (ed.) (2002) *Global Media Policy in the New Millennium*, Luton: University of Luton Press.

Roach, C. (1987) 'The US position on the new world information and communication order', *Journal of Communication* 37(4).

Rodrik, Dani (2000) 'Governance of economic globalization', in Joseph Nye and John Donahue (eds) *Governance in a Globalizing World*, Washington, DC: Brookings Institution Press.

Ruggie, John (1994) 'Trade, protectionism, and the future of welfare capitalism', *Journal of International Affairs* 48(1), summer.

Schiller, Herbert (1969) *Mass Communication and American Empire*, New York: Augustus M. Kelly.

—— (1976) *Communication and Cultural Domination*, New York: M.E. Sharpe.

Schiller, H. and Nordenstreng, K. (eds) (1979) *National Sovereignty and International Communication*, New Jersey: Ablex.

Schlesinger, Phillip (1997) 'From cultural defence to political culture: media, politics and collective identity in the European Union', *Media, Culture and Society* 19(3).

Sen, Amartya (2000) *Development as Freedom*, New York: Anchor Books.

Smith, Bec (2004) 'Aussie production groups express issues with FTA', *Hollywood Reporter*, 5 March.

Tomlinson, John (1991) *Cultural Imperialism*, Baltimore: Johns Hopkins University Press.

—— (1999) *Globalization and Culture*, Cambridge: Polity.

UNESCO (1980) *Many Voices, One World, Final Report of the MacBride Commission*, Paris.

—— (2001) *Universal Declaration on Cultural Diversity*, adopted 31st General Conference, 2 November.

United Nations (1948) *Universal Declaration of Human Rights*, adopted and proclaimed by General Assembly resolution 217 A (III) of 10 December 1948, available at: www.un.org/Overview/rights.html.

United States (1907) *International Wireless Telegraph Convention*, Washington: Government Printing Office, signed Berlin, 3 November 1906.

Vaidhyanathan, Siva (2001) *Copyrights and Copywrongs: The Rise of Intellectual Property and How it Threatens Creativity*, New York: New York University Press.

Venturelli, Shalini (1998) *Liberalizing the European Media: Politics, Regulation and the Public Sphere*, London: Clarendon.

World Trade Organization (WTO) (1990) 'Matters related to trade in audiovisual services', Uruguay Round Working Group on Audiovisual Policy. MTN.GNS/AUD/W/1.

—— (1998) 'Audiovisual services: background note by the Secretariat', 15 June, S/C/W/40.

—— (2000) 'Council for Trade in Services – special session – communication from the US – audio-visual and related services', 18 December, S/CSS/W/21.

—— (2001) 'Council for Trade in Services, communication from Canada, initial Canadian negotiating proposals', 14 March, S/CSS/W/46.

—— (2002a) China. 'Notification pursuant to Article III: 3 of the General Agreement on Trade in Services', 24 December, S/C/N/219.

—— (2002b) China. 'Notification pursuant to Article III: 3 of the General Agreement on Trade in Services', 24 December, S/C/N/220.

Chapter 12

Transvaluing media studies

Or, beyond the myth of the mediated centre

Nick Couldry

Media studies has become too close to, and too distant from, media, its object of analysis: too close, in that media studies readily reproduces one picture of what media are, which only makes sense if you stand close up to the highly centralised media forms we have until recently taken for granted; too distant, in that this myopia prevents media studies from grasping the broader landscape of how media do, and do not, figure in people's lives.

In this chapter, I will, first, diagnose several forms of this problem that each contribute to a phenomenon stretching well beyond media studies: the social construction I call 'the myth of the mediated centre' (cf. Couldry 2003a). I will then describe how the landscape of media studies might look, if it were free of that myth, offering, if not a new paradigm for media studies, at least a new map of its possibilities for those tired of the old one.

Some background

Until recently, the history of modern media has been the history of the emergence of centralised mass systems of mediation, sometimes, although not always, from more scattered beginnings. That history belongs to a wider story of the expansion of the nation state and modern systems of government. Media studies, and equally the area of US communication studies focused on media rather than on communication in the broader sense, emerged as disciplines whose primary object was mass media and their social consequences. Although, in various ways, media studies has complicated earlier mass media models (most importantly through studying the diversity of audience interpretations), it is its original relation to centralised mass media that continues to shape its dominant interpretative frameworks and research priorities: textual analysis of media produced by large-scale media institutions, audience negotiations of those same media and the production cultures that lie behind those media. While those areas of research are noble enough in themselves, they become an empirical problem when they block from view other regions of media production; this becomes a theoretical problem when it justifies that narrow focus by mythical claims about what is 'really' 'central' in contemporary societies; which, in turn, becomes a political problem when such theoretical bias blinds us to media's contributions to social life (and politics) beyond, or indeed within, the centralising pressures of the nation state.

A research agenda focused almost exclusively on the production, circulation and reception of mainstream media risks forfeiting media studies' critical edge. Its underlying assumptions miss crucial dimensions of media change. It remains uncertain (and will be for a long time) whether expanding opportunities to make and circulate media beyond large-scale institutions (especially via the Internet), the steady globalisation of media flows of all types (institutional and non-institutional), and the erosion of authority affecting the institutional clusters comprising the late modern nation-state, will, taken together, produce in time an experience of media that is radically less centralised than the one we take for granted; there are, after all, significant commercial forces attempting to close down precisely that possibility. But there are *sufficient* centrifugal pressures in motion to require a vantage-point at some distance from what I call 'the mediated centre', if we want to grasp the wider landscape.

By the mediated centre, I mean the social construction of centralised media ('the media' in common parlance) as our central access-point to the 'central realities' of the social world, whatever they are. Built into this construction, I will argue, are outmoded, indeed conservative, theoretical biases that no longer explain what we need to explain, and which we must move beyond.

Removing the roadblocks

Elsewhere, I have analysed the myth of the mediated centre and its role in underpinning the media-oriented practices I call 'media rituals' (Couldry 2003a: 45–8). This chapter considers the forms that myth takes when built into the *theoretical* frameworks of mainstream media studies. There are three such mythical forms: functionalism, centrism and spectacularism.

Functionalism[1]

Functionalism, at least in any explicitly developed form, has long since died out in sociology and anthropology. Its heyday was in the 1940s and 1950s in the work of the US sociologist Talcott Parsons (1951) and the British anthropologist A. Radcliffe-Brown (1952); true, it has had a revival in Germany in the work of the sociologist Niklas Luhmann (1982), but neither Luhmann's general theory of 'autopoietic systems' nor his late work on media (1999) has yet been influential in media studies, so it is safe to consider functionalism in its traditional guise without a detailed consideration of Luhmann's more recent work. All the more striking then that, while the functionalist model is out-of-date, it lives on in media institutions' discourses about themselves (where it fulfils a direct institutional purpose: self-justification) and in academic analyses of media.

Functionalism is the idea (contentious, when stated directly) that large regions of human activity ('societies', 'cultures', and so on) can best be understood as if they were self-sufficient, complex, functioning systems. Depending on taste, the metaphor of functioning can be biological (the natural organism, such as the human body) or technological (the artificial system, such as the machine). Societies, or cultures, are conceived in functionalist accounts as complex 'wholes' formed of a series of 'parts', each of which 'functions' by contributing to the successful working of the 'whole'. Action at the level of society's or culture's 'parts' has no unanticipated effects, and, even if it does, it is quickly absorbed back into the wider functioning of the 'whole' through positive feedback loops.

There are many problems with functionalist attempts to model the multi-dimensionality of social and cultural practice. Looking back from the beginning of the twenty-first century, one obvious problem is the difficulty of conceiving *any* 'society' or 'culture' as a self-*sufficient* system, given the huge range of forces operating across societal and cultural borders (see Urry 2000, on 'society'). This might suggest that the problems of functionalism are recent, derived from the globalising pressures of late modernity; could functionalist models then still work, if applied cautiously and locally? It is certainly true that national media remain an important reference-point in many, if not most, people's media universes, whatever globalisation theorists say; why not then treat functionalism as a local truth? That would be a mistake, because the problems with function-alism are more fundamental and long-standing. The main problem lies with functionalism's underlying claim that there *are* such totalities as 'societies' and 'cultures' that 'function' as working systems. This, perhaps, seems too abstract to contest outright (but for a powerful attack on the notion of 'culture', see Hannerz 1992); the problems become clearer when this claim is applied in detail. We need go no further than Steven Lukes's (1975) classic deconstruction of functionalist accounts of political ritual, which analyse political rituals in terms of how they contribute to society's political 'stability' by affirming certain central beliefs and values. But even if there are such centrally held beliefs and values, which Lukes questions, this account begs deeper questions about 'whether, to what extent, and in what ways society *does* hold together' (Lukes 1975: 297). *Is there*, in other words, a functioning social 'whole' of which political rituals could be a 'part'?

A superficial attraction of functionalist arguments is that they tie up all the loose ends – until you realise the price paid in the assumptions that drive func-tionalism in the first place. Elsewhere I have analysed Dayan's and Katz's influential (1992) account of 'media events' as a functionalist model that revives the least convincing aspects of Emile Durkheim's model of how societies hold together through collective representations (Couldry 2003a: ch. 4).[2] Rather than repeat that argument, let us trace functionalist symptoms elsewhere in media studies. A clear attempt at revivalism is Jeffrey Alexander's and Ronald Jacobs's essay 'Mass communication, ritual and civil society' (Alexander and Jacobs 1998). As they realise, the idea that media perform a positive social function can no longer simply mean arguing that media reproduce certain shared sets of beliefs or ideologies: how could such a simple model account for the enormous diversification of mediated publics? Instead, Alexander and Jacobs build, first, on Dayan's and Katz's claim for the central explanatory importance of 'media events': 'the narrative elaboration of events and crises – understood as social dramas – is crucial for providing a sense of historical continuity in the crisis-bound, episodic constructions of universalistic solidarity that continually form and reform civil society' (Alexander and Jacobs 1998: 23). Note that the 'whole' here is 'civil society', which Alexander and Jacobs claim is continually 'formed and reformed' by media events, and so can contribute to the wider 'whole' of society (Alexander and Jacobs 1998: 25). Media events 'provide the cultural grounds for attachment to the social imaginary of society, and ... plot points for updating the ongoing public narratives of civil society and nation' (Alexander and Jacobs 1998: 28). But on what is this huge feedback loop involving media, civil society and nation based? It is based on seeing media as providing society's principal interpretative closures:

> '[Media operate] as a cultural space where actors and events become typified into more general codes (e.g. sacred/profane, pure/impure/ democratic/ antidemocratic, citizen/enemy) and more generic story forms which resonate with the society's culture. Expressive media – such as novels or movies – are fictional symbolic forms that weave the binary codes of civil society into broad narratives and popular genres. ... [as a result] the mass media ... provides the cultural environment from which common identities and solidarities can be constructed.'
>
> (Alexander and Jacobs 1998: 29–30)

This is a highly problematic account of media's social role, but we must be clear about where exactly the problem lies. It does not lie in the claim that there are *pressures towards* 'order' and 'closure' in the contemporary social world to which media are major contributors; the whole point of analysing 'media rituals', for example, is to *register* such pressures. The problem lies in the assumption, first, that such pressures, when combined with everything else, produce a clear, unambiguous causal outcome and, second, that this outcome is a relatively stable social 'order'. Put less abstractly, why believe 1) that civil society is based on certain 'binary' codes at all or 2) that those binary codes' stability causes something we might call 'social stability'? Why not social instability? Stability of what exactly? And, even if we could answer that, what could serve as evidence, for or against, Alexander's and Jacobs's thesis? All this remains unclear.

There is, then, plenty of indeterminacy in functionalist accounts of the media. It is this, perhaps, that allows Michael Schudson, having convincingly argued against over-playing the ideological impacts of news (Schudson 1995: 17), to endorse a socially integrationist role for media institutions, while simultaneously undercutting it:

> [The media's] capacity to publicly include is perhaps their most important feature. [The fact that we each read the same paper as elites] is empowering ... the impression it promotes of equality and commonality, *illusion though it is,* sustains a hope of democratic life.
>
> (Schudson 1995: 25, added emphasis)

This is a disarmingly honest, if inevitably therefore contradictory, statement of one of liberal democracy's working assumptions. We find traces of it in later versions of Habermas's public sphere thesis (Habermas 1996) that conceives media as a complex network of spaces for public discussion and identification; the saving grace in Habermas's case is that he intends his analysis normatively, not necessarily as the truth about how media work. It would be useful, however, to develop more complex ways for thinking about the media's social consequences: for example, Liebes's and Peri's (1998) account of how in Israel there is *both* the multiplication of mass media melodramas *and* new public 'sphericules' of localised community media. The total-ising tendency of functionalist explanations may miss the point entirely.

Yet functionalist explanations continue to crop up in surprising places. The standard positions in debates about stardom and celebrity culture assume, at root, that the industrial production of celebrity discourse 'must' contribute to some wider social 'function', whether we call it identity-formation or social integration or both. The classic functionalist account of stars is Alberoni (1972), but there are clear traces of such thinking in more recent accounts: Dyer (1986: 17), Reeves (1988), Lumby (1999), Turner *et al.* (2000).[3] Such approaches can also live with functionalism's indeterminacy, if in postmodern guise: 'contradictory and tainted with inauthenticity as they may be, it seems clear that celebrities perform a signif-icant social function for media consumers' (Turner *et al.* 2000: 13). McKenzie Wark is even bolder:

> we may not like the same celebrities, we may not like any of them at all, but it is the existence of a population of celebrities, about whom to disagree, that *makes it possible* to constitute a sense of belonging.
>
> (Wark, 1999: 33, my emphasis, quoted in Turner *et al.* 2000: 14)

The problem with such functionalism, whatever its 'postmodern' guise, is that it closes down massively our options for explaining what is actually going on, and in a way that fits far too neatly with the social 'functions' that relevant media institutions (film distributors, celebrity magazines, PR firms) might like to ascribe to themselves. Where is the evidence that people 'identify' with celebrities in any simple way, or even that they regard 'celebrity culture' as important, rather than a temporary distraction? The absence of *empirical* work in this area illustrates how functionalism can block off the routes to open-minded research.

There are still more places where we might find functionalism lurking in media studies,[4] but instead I want to turn to two other frameworks that shore up an automatic sense of the media as social centre.

Centrism

If functionalism, at least in its original form, is quite a distinct framework for interpreting the media, 'centrism' is more diffuse. I mean by this term the tendency in media studies (whether in accounts of media production, distribution or consumption) to assume that it is the largest media institutions and our relationships to them that are the overwhelming research priority, so that any media outside that institutional space are of marginal importance. Centrism closes down the field of media we analyse and (in so doing) reinforces its own validity in an endless self-fulfilling prophecy. Centrism is distinct from functionalism, since it need involve no assumption that society (as opposed to media) has a 'centre'. It is worth also distinguishing 'centrism' from another problematic idea, usually called *media*centrism: the automatic assumption that media are central to explaining the dynamics of contemporary societies. The latter is a difficulty inherent to all media analysis, which needs separate discussion (see below).

Centrism is so entrenched in the media studies landscape that it may seem impolite to name it *as such*. It takes many forms. First, it underlies a bias towards nationally distributed media and against locally distributed media. As an example, consider that, even in a country as large as the USA, it took until 1991 for an authoritative study of local media (that is non-national media, including media focused on catchment areas as large as Chicago) to be written (Kaniss 1991). Local media remains a little studied area, even though for many people it is local versions of media (especially of the press) that they consume. Second, we can detect centrism at work, among other things, in media studies' concentration on media assumed to have the largest (that is, the most centrally focused) audiences: television and film, as opposed to the press and radio. There are off-setting factors here, of course, such as the greater ease of creating and accessing archives of press versus television and radio. But the underlying presumption, when deciding research priorities, in favour of audience size remains significant, even though it cuts across a factor that should be equally, if not more, important: the significance that particular media outputs actually play in people's everyday practice (which may be greater, after all, for local media or highly specialised 'cult' media than for mass-distributed media).

This leads to a third point: the relative inattention to media made and received outside the dominant systems of circulation despite the important work already done on 'alternative media' (Downing 1984, 2001; Rodriguez 2001; Atton 2001, but note there is a large, if scattered, research tradition beyond these prominent books). A resurgence of interest in 'alternative media' may now be under way in the context of new, increasingly globalised, social activism. This only sharpens the paradox of why alternative media are not given greater prominence in media research agendas (Couldry 2002).

Inattention to alternative media is properly called centrist, rather than functionalist. An influential example is Nicholas Garnham's work. Garnham (2000: 68) has mocked the 'productivist romanticism' of visions of a less centralised system of media production such as Brecht's (1979–80) famous vision of an open space of radio producer/consumers; this position is rooted in a long-standing conviction that alternative media is of minimal political relevance (Garnham 1990). This marginalisation is inadequate to a world where alternative media production, such as the Independent Media Centre movement, is integral to activism (the protests against the Seattle World Trade Organisation meetings in 1999) that has influenced mainstream policy debates, and where the anti-centrist media strategy of organisations such as the Zapatistas has influenced mainstream news agendas. The global momentum of research into alternative media can no longer be ignored, if we are interested in a comparative understanding of media's potential contribution to social change (Couldry and Curran 2003).

Spectacularism

It is worth noting briefly a recent variant on functionalism and centrism, which also blocks our view of the contemporary media landscape: spectacularism. By this I mean the tendency, whether celebratory or critical, to treat the spectacular aspects of recent mainstream media as if they were permanent features of how mediated societies will from now on be organised.

Spectacularism too has a postmodernist version of which is anti-functionalist, since it is highly sceptical of any social 'centre' or 'essence' waiting to be 'expressed' through media spectacle. Yet such work offers a surprisingly romantic (not to say, implicitly centrist) account of the social solidarity apparently produced by media spectacle. Here is Nestor Garcia Canclini in a generally insightful argument identifying as one aspect of 'the new sociocultural scene':

> [T]he shift from the citizen as a representative of public opinion to the consumer interested in enjoying quality of life. One indication of this change is that argumentative and critical forms of participation cede their place to the pleasure taken in electronic media spectacles where narration or the simple accumulation of anecdotes prevails over reasoned solutions to problems.
>
> (Garcia Canclini 2001: 24)

Or here, less cautiously (and much closer to functionalism) is Michel Maffesoli:

> television permits participants to 'vibrate' together. One cries, laughs, or stamps one's feet in unison, and this, without actually being in the presence of each other, a kind of communion is created whose social effects are still to be measured.
>
> (Maffesoli 1996: 57)

As Maffesoli disarmingly notes, such effects *are* still to be measured! There is no unproblematic evidence for the changes Garcia Canclini and Maffesoli detect, and yet their intuition of a fundamental shift in media practice and consumption is here already reified into an upbeat rereading of Baudrillard's earlier pessimism about the age of 'simulation'.

There is no such romanticism in Douglas Kellner's important recent deconstruction of 'media spectacle' (Kellner 2003). There is a danger, even in Kellner's laudably critical account, of reproducing precisely the assumptions about the centralising power of media spectacle from which he wants to get critical distance. Thus Kellner writes that 'the celebrities of media culture are the icons of the present age, the deities of an entertainment society, in which money, looks, fame and success are the ideals and goals of the dreaming billions who inhabit Planet Earth' (Kellner 2003: viii) and, later on, that 'media spectacles are those phenomena of media culture that embody contemporary society's basic values' (Kellner 2003: 2) as media play 'an ever-escalating role in everyday life' (Kellner 2003: 2) with 'media culture ... *the stage* on which social conflicts unfold and *social reality is constructed*' (Kellner 2003: 89, added emphasis). Clearly Kellner does not endorse centrism or spectacularism as values – quite the opposite. My point, however, is that entangled with the apparently innocent notion of 'spectacle' is a theoretical framework that is basically structural-functionalist (cf. Shils 1975). If we use terms such as 'spectacle' in media sociology, it must be with caution, and with the empirical safety valve of asking: what in fact *do* people think about media spectacle? Is there as much disbelief as belief? If so, in what sense *are* they reproductions of 'shared values'? How 'central', and for whom, is the mediated 'centre' that contemporary media spectacle tries to project? It is just such questions that functionalism, centrism, and approaches derived from them, close off.

The view is clearing ...

Fortunately there are theoretical developments under way, which encourage a move in this direction. The 1960s and 1970s attacks on functionalism have been reinforced by post-structuralist arguments: for example, Foucault's (1980) attack on the idea that power operates through its concentration, like a substance, at particular central sites, rather than through the structured flow of practices across the whole of social space; Laclau's (1990) attack on 'society' as an impossible totality. More recently, the concept of 'society' as a container of social action has been dismantled within sociology, particular in work on globalisation. Crucial here has been Ulrich Beck's argument for a 'methodological cosmopolitanism' that analyses the social world from beyond the confines of the nation state, without however reducing the local and national to insignificance (Beck 2000; cf. Urry 2000). These theoretical shifts do not resolve all the issues; there is, perhaps, an implicit *media*-centrism in Urry's account of a 'sociology beyond societies' that ascribes automatic and drastic effects to global media flows, without enough evidence of *how* they take effect, on whom, and under what conditions. These difficulties aside, a crucial step is made when Beck challenges the social sciences' 'secret Hegelianism' (Beck 2000: 80), 'which sees society as derived from the state's claim to embody the principle of order'. We need an equivalent distance from media studies' 'Hegelianism' that installs national media concentrations as the only reference-point for explaining the media's social consequences. It is in this spirit that I want, shortly, to turn to a wider space of possibilities – theoretical, empirical and political – for understanding media.

Transvaluation?

First, however, I must justify this chapter's title. You might still baulk at its claim of transvaluing media studies. What exactly is involved in 'transvaluation'?

The philosopher Friedrich Nietzsche claimed to have 'transvalued' conventional morality by reducing it to prejudices that were anything but moral: morality, he argued, is based not in the grand 'values' of fairness or justice, but in 'rancour' (Nietzsche 1956 [1887]: 170). Nietzsche extended his attack to science and truth, arguing that beneath the 'will to truth' lay an 'impetuous demand for certainty', indeed the 'physiological demands for the preservation of a certain species of life' (Nietzsche 1974 [1887]: 288; 1973 [1886]: 35). For Nietzsche 'transvaluation' means reducing a framework of thought to forces directly at odds with its self-image and professed 'values'; through transvaluation, we can stand outside that framework and grasp a wider field of possibility (Nietzsche 1974 [1887]: 280). We don't have to agree with each one of Nietzsche's transvaluations to see the general value of this approach. It has had a lasting influence through

Michel Foucault's adoption of Nietzsche's genealogical method (Foucault 1977): Foucault's analysis of discourse not 'as groups of signs ... but as practices which systematically form the objects of which they speak' (Foucault 1972: 49) is an extended application of the principle of transvaluation.

I am not claiming, of course, to have offered anything so grand as a 'genealogy' of media studies: that would require a much longer historical argument. But, in offering a perspective *beyond* media studies' excessive focus on the centralised systems of media production that were originally its object, I want to signal the more open field of research that results when we distance ourselves from that love of the 'mediated centre'. 'Transvaluation' is a useful metaphor for this shift.[5]

Wittgenstein offers an alternative metaphor. In the course of unpicking the illusions into which language traps philosophy, Wittgenstein argues that it is the 'preconceived idea of the crystalline purity' of language that philosophy must transcend. What matters here is not (fortunately!) that enormous issue, but the way Wittgenstein argues we should proceed. The problem with the idea of language's transparency, he argues, is that it is merely the *effect* of how we use language when trying to explain its workings, not the explanation of those workings: 'we predicate of the thing what lies in the method of representing it. Impressed by the possibility of a comparison, we think we are perceiving a state of affairs of the highest generality' (Wittgenstein 1978 [1953]: 46). The situation is similar with the conventional framework of media studies. Because, having been formed within a highly centralised system of media production, we *can* make sense of media as necessarily centralised, we *do* make sense of media that way, ignoring everything beyond our usual focus. Instead we need, as Wittgenstein says, to 'turn ... our whole examination around' and to see the hidden connections between those old assumptions and the form of social organisation that gave rise to them – in the past, but not necessarily in the future.

This makes clear that, as well as avoiding functionalism, centrism and their recent variant, spectacularism, we must also avoid *media-centrism*, that is, giving undue prominence to media rather than other causal factors in explaining social phenomena (cf. Martin-Barbero 1993). If we want to understand what media do in the world, we must look beyond the standard lines of explanation that media discourses (above all, the myth of the mediated centre) encourage us to adopt.

A new map of media studies

How might the landscape of media studies (both its recent past and its future research priorities) look if we jettisoned the myth of the mediated centre and explored more openly how media are produced, circulated, received and (quite possibly) *ignored* in the contemporary social world?

To orientate ourselves, let's be clear where we start from. First, empirical research must start out from a question, not an assumption, regarding the existence of anything like a mediated centre. We need to know much more about the *relative* importance in people's lives of 1) mainstream media institutions, 2) other media productions, and 3) *non-media* influences, and to understand better the range of variation here among individuals and sociological types. Second, as the range of media themselves increases, and the complexity of their potential inter-actions increases exponentially, our research *can* take for granted a mediated environment (in certain parts of the world at least: I come back to issues of comparative research later) that is *super-saturated*. While important factors close down individuals' choice of media (so generating 'ideal types' of media consumer remains possible), the range of paths that individuals *might* choose across the media environment is huge, including a path along which media have minimal direct significance. Third, while it is beyond doubt that the flow of media has increased absolutely, this may not be an even distribution and the task is to under-stand how media density differs between my living space and yours, this work environment, or leisure context, and that one.

Along these three axes – engagement, selection, spatial distribution – we need to know more, much more, about the variation between individuals' and groups' orientations to media. If we trace out a map of the resulting landscape of media research (present and future), it has two crucial landmarks (knowledge, agency) that, assuming media research still wants a critical edge, imply a third (ethics).

Knowledge

By knowledge, I mean not our knowledge of media as researchers, but the rela-tionship between media and the social distribution of knowledge about the world. The primary question, then, is not the analysis of this or that media form, but the role, if any (and there could be huge variation here), of different media in people's acquisition and use of knowledge, including knowledge of the social world.

This is an area where much important empirical work has been done in recent years: for example, the Glasgow Media Group's work on media influence on audience understandings of public issues (see Kitzinger 1999 for useful summary), work on media and the economy (Gavin 1999), and on media's rela-tion to public opinion generally (Lewis 2001).[6] My point here is not to condense a literature review into a few lines, but to emphasise that public knowledge is surely *the* issue by which media research should orient itself (cf. Corner 1995); if we cannot say anything about media's possible contribution to the distribution of knowledge of the world in which we act, then something fundamental is missing (cf. Kitzinger 1999: 17).

Yet it is clear there are a number of issues on which further research is needed: first, about the uses towards which media-sourced knowledge is put (or indeed not put) by individuals and groups across a range of real-life contexts; second, about the status of media relative to other potential sources of knowledge or authoritative information, both when information is originally acquired and when it is later put back into circulation (in argument, in self-presentation, and so on). Third, developing from the second, we need to know much more about the less explicit, more embedded and naturalised, use of mediated 'knowledge' in everyday interaction and thought, again across of a range of contexts (including those of media production, which is where the causal loop turns back onto itself). There is value here, I suggest, in rethinking Durkheim's notion of the social 'category' to grasp the more systematic dimensions of the media's contribution to how the social world is constructed (cf. 2003b). Whether Durkheim or perhaps other models help us most is of course a matter for debate, a debate needed within media studies and with sociology more generally. For if most media sociologists' gut instincts are right – and media play a significant role in influencing the circulation of knowledge – then media studies has much to contribute to a renewed sociology of knowledge. This, however, requires media studies to be more open to the social sciences in general (cf. Tulloch 2000: 19–32).

Agency

If one key focus of media research is knowledge (what do media contribute to the knowledge agents have of the world in which they act?), another is agency itself. Nicholas Garnham has expressed this perhaps better than anyone, in his critical discussion of audience research: 'the point is not whether the audience is active or passive, but rather the fields of action which are opened up or closed down' (Garnham 1999: 118).[7] Accumulating evidence about how people read or engage with this or that text is not, by itself, enough unless it contributes to our understanding of how they act in the social and personal world, with *or without* reference to media.

Having said this, agency must be researched at many levels, which I can only begin to sketch here. We need more research on how (under what conditions and with what result) people exercise their agency in relation to media flows. There is the basic, but vital, question of how people *select* from what is potentially on offer or (more drastically) *screen out* media that are imposed upon them (in public or working spaces, or within the constraints of their home). There is the question also of how people allocate their *attention and emotional investments* among the media they happen to consume; there is a great difference between media that merely passes before us and media with which we sense a strong connection (whether public or private). Fan studies has done much to explore this difference,[8] but the difference arises in contexts other than fandom. Such questions only become more difficult as the media environment itself becomes more complex and multi-layered (see Everett 2003 on the meanings of online 'interactivity'). We need also to understand better how media contribute to people's agency across various institutional spheres outside media. Every sphere of life requires separate study (for example, consumption, personal relations, health, education, work, politics). While some work exists on the connections between media and these non-media spheres, it is around people's orientations, specifically, to media institutions that a significant literature has grown in the 1990s, as researchers have become curious about how people *think*, or in some cases find it difficult to think, about their own media consumption (Press 1991; Lembo 2000; Seiter 1999; Schroder 2000; Hoover 2003; BFI/OU 2003).

Related to agency is the more general question of how media connect to belief: people's belief about, or trust in, the authority of institutions (state, school, religious institutions). Indeed, once we drop the centrist framework criticised earlier in the chapter, the question of people's beliefs about, or even orientation towards, *media* institutions becomes particularly interesting (Couldry 2000); what, for example, of those who have only a minimal orientation to media? This, in turn, raises the question of how far different media territories, operating under specific historical trajectories, are characterised by different patterns of media belief (see, for example, Rajagopal's interesting (2001) account of the new significance of centralised media in nationalist Hindu politics in India).

Finally, there is the difficult question of how media might *diminish* people's sense of agency. The assumption has usually been that media are at worst neutral in this regard and at best add to people's possibilities for agency (for example, Scannell 1996). This, however, ignores another possibility, which is that the structured asymmetry of media communication works to limit at least some people's sense of agency, just as happens in the structured asymmetry of work and class relations (Couldry 2000: 22, cf. Sennett and Cobb 1972). This is one reason (but strong arguments can also be made in relation to knowledge and ethics) why alternative media must be studied: because their less asymmetrical patterns of production may generate alternative forms of agency and civic practice (Rodriguez 2001).

In these, and no doubt many other, ways, the study of media should aim to contribute to our broader understanding of agency in the contemporary world and, in so doing, connect with important debates in the social sciences (Touraine 1988; Dubet 1994).

Ethics

Knowledge and agency each raise ethical and political implications, but if media studies is to remain a critical, not purely administrative, tradition of research, it must consider what *explicit* ethical stance it should adopt to media.

Such discussion has normally been limited to the importance of media studies taking a stance on questions of power. Much less debated and much more contentious are explicit questions of media ethics. These come into view, once we abandon the assumption that today's centralised system of media production and distribution is the only possibility; what are the ethical implications of the media we currently have? Aspects of such a debate have, of course, been underway for some time, for example in relation to Habermas's concept of the public sphere, but that debate is largely about media's contribution to political deliberation. This is not the only, or even the most, important dimension of media ethics.

The subject of ethics is the type of life it is good to lead, so an ethics of media, at its simplest, would concern the contribution of media production/consumption, under prevailing conditions, to the good life of each person. Difficult ethical questions arise about the extent to which, in societies saturated by media, a good life should be a public, that is, to some degree mediated, one; difficult moral questions arise about the grounds on which it is right to impose media publicity on another without their full consent (cf. O'Neill, 1990). Even more difficult ethical and moral questions arise about the long-term consequences of how media tend to cover public matters, such as war or human disasters (Robins 1995; Boltanski 1999). What has been lacking so far, however, is any *theoretical framework* for debating such issues. From philosophy, Derrida and Stiegler (1996) have pointed in the direction of an ethics of audiovisual literacy, while Hubert Dreyfus (2001) has started debate on the ethical consequences of the Internet as a form of social interaction; from the direction of media studies, three recent books have begun to explore the implications of philosophical debates, past and present, for thinking about media and power (Garnham 1999; Peters 1999; Silverstone 1999). But, as yet, there has been no systematic engagement between the relevant branches of philosophy (ethics, political theory) and media sociology. This debate is much needed, and requires a cosmopolitan perspective that takes seriously the role of media discourses in *constructing* the (often merely national) contexts for particular types of politics and their hidden exclusions (Isin 2002).

It can only happen, I suggest, by building, from the side of media studies, on the questions of knowledge and agency discussed already. Here, in debates around narrative, agency and ethics (Ricoeur 1992), textual analysis of media has much to contribute: not for its own sake, but as part of an examination of how media narratives do, and should, help us imagine our place in the world.

Concluding note

It might seem strange to mention textual analysis only at the end of tracing a new map of media research; even stranger not to have mentioned political economy at all. But this is deliberate.

When media studies stood too close to a particular, centralised system of media production, distribution and consumption, the primary questions were, quite plausibly: what economics drive that system, how can we analyse its outputs and people's specific interpretations of them? But without that assumed central focus, the research questions for social science inquiry into media (literary-style analysis is another matter) are necessarily decentered, and more complex: how and on what terms do certain media, rather than others, contribute to the knowledge and agency of individuals and groups in a particular social environment? And (from an explicitly ethical perspective) how, if at all, should and could things be otherwise? Political economy and textual analysis, those two dominant traditions of earlier media studies, still play a vital role, of course, in helping us answer those larger questions, but they are not our required starting-points.

Admittedly, the map I have sketched invites media studies researchers to travel much more widely than in the past across the terrain of historical and social science inquiry. The opportunity, however, for media studies by so doing to establish itself more securely within that wider terrain will, I hope, make the journey worthwhile.

Notes

1 For a more detailed discussion of functionalist accounts of 'ritual' in media studies, see Couldry (2005).
2 As I make clear in Couldry (2003a), there are other non-functionalist ways of applying Durkheim.
3 A theoretically more complex approach is Marshall (1997), but even here note the unguarded comment at the beginning of the book: 'Celebrity status operates at the *very center of the culture* as it resonates with conceptions of individuality that are the ideological growth of Western culture' (1999: x, added emphasis). What centre?
4 See for example my earlier discussion of Paddy Scannell's work (Couldry 2000: 10–12).
5 Note however that I intend the term in a different sense from some recent interpreters of Nietzsche who argue that his transvaluation of values removes the possibility of, or need for, critical perspective on society's myths (Vattimo 1992: 24–5: chs 1–3; cf. Maffesoli 1996: 19). On the contrary, such relativising accounts of contemporary mediascapes are part of what I want to move beyond (see 'spectacularism' above). I cannot, however, avoid the ambiguities built into Nietzsche's metaphors, indeed his whole philosophical style.
6 Cf. the essays in Gripsrud (1999).
7 Larry Grossberg had, from a different perspective, already made a similar point: 'we need…not a theory of audiences, but a theory of the organization and possibilities of agency at specific sites in everyday life' (Grossberg 1997: 341).
8 See Barker and Brooks (1997), Harrington and Bielby (1995) for very open-minded empirical accounts.

References

Alberoni, Francesco (1972) 'The "powerless elite"', in D. MacQuail (ed.) *Sociology of Mass Communication*, Harmondsworth: Penguin.

Alexander, Jeffrey and Jacobs, Ronald (1998) 'Mass communication, ritual and civil society', in T. Liebes and J. Curran (eds) *Media Ritual and Identity*, London: Routledge.

Atton, Chris (2001) *Alternative Media*, London: Sage.

Barker, Martin and Brooks, Kate (1997) *Knowing Audiences*, Luton: University of Luton Press.

Beck, Ulrich (2000) 'The cosmopolitan perspective: sociology of the second age of modernity?' *British Journal of Sociology* 51(1): 79–105.

BFI/Open University (2003) 'After September 11: television news and transnational audiences', available from http://afterseptember11.tv.

Boltanski, Luc (1999) *Distant Suffering*, Cambridge: Cambridge University Press.

Brecht, Bertolt (1979–80 [1932]) 'Radio as a means of communication', *Screen*, 20(3–4): 24–8.

Corner, John (1995) *Television Form and Public Address*, London: Arnold.

Couldry, Nick (2000) *The Place of Media Power*, London: Routledge.

—— (2002) 'Mediation and alternative media, or relocating the centre of media and communication studies', *Media International Australia* 103: 24–41.

—— (2003a) *Media Rituals: A Critical Approach*, London: Routledge.

—— (2003b) 'Media-meta-capital: extending the range of Bourdieu's field theory', *Theory and Society*, 32(5–6), 653–377.

—— (2005) 'Media rituals: beyond functionalism', in E. Rothenbuhler and M. Coman (eds) *Media Anthropology*.

Couldry, Nick and Curran, James (2003) 'Introduction', in N. Couldry and J. Curran (eds) *Contesting Media Power*, Lanham, MD: Rowman & Littlefield.

Dayan, Daniel and Katz, Elihu (1992) *Media Events*, Cambridge, MA: Harvard University Press.

Derrida, Jacques and Stiegler, Bernard (1996) *Echnographies de la télévision*, Paris: Galilée/INA.

Downing, John (1984) *Radical Media*, Boston: South End Press.

—— (2001) *Radical Media*, 2nd edn, Thousand Oaks: Sage.

Dreyfus, Hubert (2001) *On the Internet*, London: Routledge.

Dubet, Francois (1994) 'The system, the actor and the social subject', *Thesis Eleven* 38: 16–35.

Dyer, Richard (1986) *Heavenly Bodies*, London: BFI.

Everett, Anna (2003) 'Digitextuality and click theory', in A. Everett and J. Caldwell (eds) *New Media: Theories and Practice of Digitextuality*, New York: Routledge.

Foucault, Michel (1972) *The Archaeology of Knowledge*, London: Routledge and Kegan Paul.

—— (1977) 'Nietzsche, genealogy, history', in *Language, Counter-Memory, Practice*, Ithaca, NJ: Cornell University Press.

—— (1980) *Discipline and Punish*, Harmondsworth: Penguin.

Garcia Canclini, Nestor (2001) *Citizens and Consumers*, Minneapolis: University of Minnesota Press.

Garnham, Nicholas (1990) *Capitalism and Communication*, London: Sage.

—— (2000) *Emancipation, the Media and Modernity*, Oxford: Oxford University Press.

Gavin, Neil (ed.) (1999) *The Economy, Media and Public Knowledge*, Leicester: University of Leicester Press.

Gripsrud, Jostein (ed.) (1999) *Television and Common Knowledge*, London: Routledge.

Grossberg, Lawrence (1997) *Bringing It All Back Home*, Durham, NC: Duke University Press.

Habermas, Jurgen (1996) *Between Facts and Norms*, Cambridge, MA: Harvard University Press.

Hannerz, Ulf (1992) *Cultural Complexity*, New York: Columbia University Press.

Harrington, Lee and Bielby, Denise (1995) *Soap Fans*, Philadelphia: Temple University Press.

Hoover, Stewart (2003) 'Media audiences and their narratives', paper presented to annual ICA conference, San Diego, 26 May.

Isin, Engin (2002) *Being Political*, Minneapolis: University of Minnesota Press.

Kaniss, Phyllis (1991) *Making Local News*, Chicago: Chicago University Press.

Kellner, Douglas (2003) *Media Spectacle*, London: Routledge.

Kitzinger, Jenny (1999) 'A sociology of media power: key issues in audience reception research', in G. Philo (ed.) *Message Received*, Harlow: Longman.

Laclau, Ernesto (1990) 'The impossibility of society', in *New Reflections on the Revolution of Our Time*, London: Verso.

Lembo, Ron (2000) *Thinking through Television*, Cambridge: Cambridge University Press.

Lewis, Justin (2001) *Constructing Public Opinion*, Chicago: University of Chicago Press.

Liebes, Tamar and Peri, Yoram (1998) 'Electronic journalism in segmented societies: lessons from the 1996 Elections', *Political Communication* 15: 27–43.

Luhmann, Niklas (1982) *The Differentiation of Society*, New York: Columbia University Press.

—— (1999) *The Reality of the Media*, Cambridge: Polity.

Lukes, Steven (1975) 'Political ritual and social integration', *Sociology* 29: 289–305.

Lumby, Catherine (1999) *Gotcha: Living in a Tabloid World*, Sydney: Allen & Unwin.

Maffesoli, Michel (1996) *The Contemplation of the World*, Minneapolis: University of Minnesota Press.

Marshall, David (1997) *Celebrity and Power*, Minneapolis: University of Minnesota Press.

Martin-Barbero, Jesus (1993) *Communication Culture and Hegemony*, London: Sage.

Nietzsche, Friedrich (1956 [1887]) *The Genealogy of Morals* [published with *The Birth of Tragedy*], New York: Anchor Books.

—— (1973 [1886]) *Beyond Good and Evil*, Harmondsworth: Penguin.

—— (1974 [1887]) *The Gay Science*, New York: Vintage.

O'Neill, Onora (1990) 'Practices of toleration', in J. Lichtenberg (ed.) *Democracy and the Mass Media*, Cambridge: Cambridge University Press.

Parsons, Talcott (1951) *The Social System*, New York: Free Press.

Peters, John Durham (1999) *Speaking into the Air*, Chicago: University of Chicago Press.

Press, Andrea (1991) *Women Watching Television*, Philadelphia: University of Pennsylvania Press.

Radcliffe-Brown, A.R. (1952) *Structure and Function in Primitive Society*, London: Cohen & West.

Rajagopal, Arvind (2001) *Politics after Television*, Cambridge: Cambridge University Press.

Reeves, Jimmy (1988) 'Television stardom: a ritual of social typification and individualization', in J. Carey (ed.) *Media Myths and Narratives*, Thousand Oaks: Sage.

Ricoeur, Paul (1992) *Oneself as Another*, Chicago: University of Chicago Press.

Robins, Kevin (1995) *Into the Image*, London: Routledge.

Rodriguez, Clemencia (2001) *Fissures in the Mediascape*, Cresskill, NJ: The Hampton Press.

Scannell, Paddy (1996) *Radio, Television and Modern Life*, Oxford: Blackwell.

Schudson, Michael (1995) *The Power of News*, Cambridge, MA: Harvard University Press.

Schroder, Kim (2000) 'Making sense of audience discourses', *European Journal of Cultural Studies* 3(2): 233–58.

Seiter, Ellen (1999) *New Media Audiences*, Oxford: Oxford University Press.

Sennett, R. and Cobb, J. (1972) The Hidden Injuries of Class, Cambridge: Cambridge University Press.

Shils, Edward (1975) *Center and Periphery*, Chicago: Chicago University Press.

Silverstone, Roger (1999) *Why Study the Media?* London: Sage.

Tulloch, John (2000) *Watching Television Audiences*, London: Arnold.

Touraine, Alain (1988) *Return of the Actor*, Minneapolis: University of Minnesota Press.

Turner, Graeme, Bonner, Frances and Marshall, David (2000) *Fame Games*, Cambridge: Cambridge University Press.

Urry, John (2000) *Sociology beyond Societies*, London: Routledge.

Vattimo, Giovanni (1992) *The Transparent Society*, Cambridge: Polity.

Wark, McKenzie (1999) *Celebrities, Culture and Cyberspace*, Sydney: Pluto.

Wittgenstein, Ludwig (1978 [1953]) *Philosophical Investigations*, Oxford: Blackwell.

Section IV

Cultural production, consumption and aesthetics

In this section, the opening essay surveys the literature on cultural production, and is followed by a wide screen view of media consumption and gender identities. The last essay addresses questions of cultural value and aesthetics by means of a detailed textual analysis of the low-status genre of soap opera

Keith Negus begins his literature survey by highlighting the steady movement in recent work in this field away from a critical, Frankfurt School-inspired 'cultural industry' approach to a more celebratory 'creative industries' perspective. For all its gains, this he suggests has involved conceptual losses along the way. However, the key point he emphasises is that all industry-centred perspectives, in whatever form, are flawed because they pay too little attention to wider external influences. The works of Becker and Bourdieu usefully illuminate this point in contrasting ways. Whereas Becker sees cultural work as being shaped cumulatively by co-operation and agreement between social networks and individuals, Bourdieu argues that cultural production (and consumption) are influenced by a struggle between groups and institutions over recognition, reputation and financial reward. Yet, despite their differences, both Becker and Bourdieu are at one in seeing cultural work as being strongly shaped by the wider environment. This conclusion underlines the need for the study of cultural production to draw on both industry-centred and wider sociological explanation.

Lisa Blackman examines media consumption in relation to the development of contemporary forms of femininity. She foregrounds in particular the 'fiction of autonomous selfhood' extolled in some women's media. From one perspective, this could almost be seen as a feminist version of the neo-liberal political project. It stresses the ethic of individual self-fulfilment and achievement in which women, whatever their social context, take control of their lives through embracing independence, self-reliance, and discriminating consumer lifestyle choices (health-oriented foods, keep fit regimes and so on). This process of autonomous self-invention and self-transformation implies moving away from more traditional understandings of womanhood, linked to security, monogamy, emotionality, warmth and closeness to others. This disjunction, Blackman argues, can set up a field of tension that is relieved in women's media through irony and self-depre-cating wit, but often in more troubled ways in real life. As indicated earlier, in this respect Blackman's essay resonates strongly with McRobbie's analysis of post-femi-nist discourses in contemporary British culture in Section I, while taking a rather different slant on the significance of the personalised and conversational discourses of media genres such as talk shows than does Peters in Section II.

Christine Geraghty offers a groundbreaking approach to questions of quality and aesthetics in television studies, taking as her object of study the genre of soap opera, which, as she notes, has more usually been studied in terms of its supposed effects on its audiences, rather than with reference to its own specific textual features and mechanisms. Her argument follows the approach of Richard Hoggart (1958) in the early cultural studies tradition, in arguing that low-status texts are no less worthy of serious textual and aesthetic analysis than are the products of High Culture. Taking as her object of study the specific modalities of presentation deployed in recent years by the BBC prime-time Soap *EastEnders,* Geraghty argues for recontextualising our approach to the programme within the broader theoret-ical frame of studies of melodrama, such as those proposed by Gledhill (1987) and by situating our analysis of the visual aspects of the text in relation to art historical questions – in this case, those such as the specific modalities of Victorian narrative painting. By so doing, she is also able to demonstrate precisely why melodrama might usefully be understood as supplying a set of valuable aesthetic resources for portraying the particular social dramas of a 'Risk Society'. Thus, in an almost Lukacsian (1962) manner, Geraghty demonstrates how melodrama is particularly well-suited to expressing the fears and anxieties of the now de-indus-trialised societies of the West, while linking her close textual analysis of the programme to the work of Bauman and Beck. The erosion of the Welfare State and the breakdown of old communities throws many people back into the desperate search for 'biographical solutions' to the social upheavals of our age – dramas that can then be seen to play themselves out in the highly personalised and melodramatic terms which are the forte of the genre Geraghty analyses.

References

Gledhill, C. (1987) *Home is Where the Heart Is*, London: British Film Institute.
Hoggart, R. (1958) *The Uses of Literacy*, Harmondsworth: Penguin.
Lukacs, G. (1962) *The Historical Novel*, London: Merlin Press.

Chapter 13

Rethinking creative production away from the cultural industries

Keith Negus

When questions about business and industry have featured in the field of media and cultural studies over recent years it has usually followed (implicitly or explicitly) Nicholas Garnham's call for 'an analysis of culture structured around the concept of the cultural industries' (Garnham 1990: 155). One characteristic that is particularly striking about the literature here is the shift in emphasis which occurred in this writing during the twentieth century. This is signalled by the movement from a notion of 'the culture industry' (singular) as a critical concept introduced in the writings of Theodor Adorno and Max Horkheimer, towards a concept of the cultural industries as a plural and a descriptive concept. This has been accompanied by another shift, from a concern with the plight of the creative artist to a concern with the character of a creative industry. The shift is from the concerns of how capitalism impacts upon creative work, to how capitalism manages, organises and provides the conditions within which creativity can be recognised and rewarded.

The aim of the first part of this chapter will be to provide a critical assessment of the value and limitations of such an industry-oriented approach to cultural production by highlighting the shift from Adorno's singular critical concept of 'culture industry' to the more recent descriptive category of 'culture industries' and the uncritical and even celebratory reasoning associated with notions of 'the creative industries'. In the second part of this chapter I will argue for a broader approach to cultural production, one that can draw insights from the surprisingly neglected work of Howard Becker and some of the less followed strands in the theories of cultural production elaborated by Pierre Bourdieu. My point will be that, rather than just making the industries as central to our study of aesthetics and culture, we should also be making the struggles over aesthetics and culture as more central to our study of industry.

From culture industry to creative industries

The concept of a 'culture industry' was first introduced in the work of Adorno and Horkheimer as part of a critique of the industrial, capitalist commodification of culture and society. As their work has been extensively discussed elsewhere, I will not rehearse in detail some familiar arguments, but highlight how a belief in the possibility for a critically reflexive, if not entirely autonomous, type of creativity informs this argument and is perhaps one of its enduring positive legacies for those of us thinking about cultural production today.

Adorno and Horkheimer were writing at a time when ideas about collective democracy had moved from being associated with emancipatory political movements and were incorporated into the vocabularies used to comprehend the new electronic media of communication and aesthetic reproduction. They coined the term 'culture industry' to distance themselves from the idea that 'mass culture' could be equated with people's culture as 'something like a culture that arises spontaneously from the masses themselves' (Adorno 1991: 85). This was a time when new cultural forms such as radio, television and cinema were being viewed as potentially liberating, and often seen as both of the people and for the people, encouraging democracy and continuing a process of greater public enlightenment. Adorno and Horkheimer were suspicious of such apparently democratic possibilities of communicating to numerous people and vehemently critical of the impact on individual creative work. Their point was that this was deceptive. The rhetoric of public democracy was being used commercially to generate profits for private corporations, and also politically for the purposes of propaganda. Adorno and Horkheimer sought to challenge those who were celebrating the possibilities provided by these new media and cultural technologies.

The culture industry essay was one part of their critique of the paradoxical character of enlightenment reason and written in a deliberately polemical and provocative style that was a challenge to the postures of positivistic social scientists. Hence, it is misleading to assume that their references to the 'assembly line' quality of the culture industry should be taken literally – as if it was intended as a description of an entity that was to be empirically described or statistically verified. Despite his continual emphasis on rational standardisation, Adorno also noted that 'producing hit songs still remains at the handicraft stage' (Adorno 1990: 306). In making this and other observations he suggested that the standardisation that occurs in cultural production is different from the 'standardisation of motor car and breakfast cereals' (Adorno 1990: 306). The song composer, novelist or filmmaker was not physically located on a rationally organised factory assembly line. Instead, the pressure to adhere to formulas was induced by the need to compete for attention in a commercial market where standard patterns were more easily distributed, promoted and recognised. Adorno and Horkheimer were seeking to highlight a *process* they observed occurring – the fusion of art forms as a result of commodification and due to the commercial use of new technologies of mass communication. Accordingly, they emphasised the overall standardised character of cultural production, and the way in which the culture industry seeks to incorporate producer and consumer, artist and audience, into this process.

Their argument can be interpreted as deliberately ironic in the way that it sought to retain rather than resolve the contradictions which arise when culture meets industry and the 'paradoxes of using market forces as a measure of cultural value' (Williams 2001: 9). The last sentence from the culture industry essay tells us that the 'triumph of advertising in the culture industry is that consumers feel compelled to buy and use its products even though they see through them' (Adorno and Horkheimer 1979: 167). As Jay Bernstein observes in his introduction to a collection of Adorno's essays, a recurring theme in Adorno's writings is that of the public 'simultaneously seeing through and obeying ... not believing and believing at the same time' (Bernstein in Adorno 1991: 11). This is a point Adorno elaborated on in his analysis of the astrology column of the *Los Angeles Times* (Adorno 1994). In their account of the culture industry, Adorno and Horkheimer were implying neither a passive consumer nor passivity on the part of the creative artist – both producers and audiences were equally capable of becoming aware of how the culture industry influenced their actions. Nevertheless, there was a certain compulsion and appeal in its products that was hard to resist – hence, the public sees through the scam but knowingly buys into it.

The paradoxes, tensions, the hope for an alternative and even the mystical human possibility that sometimes informs Adorno's more speculative and contentious remarks have been lost in the subsequent pluralised notion of the cultural industries that has been adopted by a number of writers. This still claims a debt to Adorno's critique but begins to adopt a more revisionist and descriptive stance towards the institutions of cultural production. Three texts signal this shift occurring at the end of the 1970s and beginning of the 1980s: a report by UNESCO (1982), a book by Bernard Miège (an English translation of writings originally published in French in the late 1970s and early 1980s) and an article initially written by Nicholas Garnham (1990) in 1984 as a briefing document for the Greater London Council. All three texts acknowledge Adorno's and Horkheimer's essay as their starting point and all seek to move beyond it – crucially, because they wish to establish an agenda for intervening institutionally in cultural production.

Between them Garnham, Miège and the UNESCO report reconstruct a notion of the many plural cultural industries as a subject of study and as an object of more formal institutional policy intervention. Garnham is quite explicit about the way he adopts the notion of the 'cultural industries ... as a descriptive term' to refer to 'industrial corporations' involved in 'producing and disseminating symbols in the form of cultural goods and services' (Garnham 1990: 156). Anxious about what he perceives as an excessive drift towards a concern with audiences and texts, Garnham called for the study of culture to be 'structured around' the notion of the cultural industries. Miège (1989) was critical of what he perceived as Adorno's emphasis on the individual creative artist. He argued for a shift away from the idea that an artist confronts the power of industry and capital (a common image and certainly one that informs a number of Adorno's writings). Miège argued that this type of approach can imply that creativity entails the individual in an ideal state of free creation (a notion that Adorno certainly didn't subscribe to anyway). Garnham made a similar point, when criticising what he saw as the guiding principles informing public intervention in the arts in Britain. This had been mainly based on subsidies for individuals. Like other writers, Garnham argued that it was misleading to assume that great individuals are the source of cultural value.

More recently, a similar approach has been adopted by David Hesmondhalgh (2002) who has argued against the idea of the term 'artists' in favour of the phrase 'symbol creators' to describe 'those who make up, interpret or rework stories, songs, images etc.' (Hesmondhalgh 2002: 4–5). Hesmondhalgh divides the cultural industries into categories of 'core' (more concerned with the production of 'social meaning') and 'peripheral' in order to argue that the study of cultural industries is about understanding the changing work of these generalised and undifferentiated 'symbol creators'. The key issue for Hesmondhalgh becomes how creativity is managed, and how we should understand this with a view to intervening or advocating some sort of modification to the industrial, institutional structure. Likewise, Tony Bennett has suggested that the study of culture should be a pragmatic 'reformer's science' engaging in 'cultural policy studies'. In his own words his proposal is 'for cultural studies to be developed in closer association with the policy concerns of government and industry' (Bennett 1998: 17).

There is a clear agenda here, one that seeks to define the parameters of what counts as creativity, the cultural industries and the study of culture. This has become pronounced in policy writings adopted by various governments, particularly the British Labour government that came to power in 1997. An insight into this reasoning can be gained by consulting Chris Smith's collection of speeches that is entitled *Creative Britain*. What writers such as Garnham were calling the cultural industries have here been relabelled as creative industries, and are listed in an appendix – 'A summary map of the creative industries': advertising, architecture, art and antiques, computer games, crafts, design, designer fashion, film, music, performing arts, publishing, software, television and radio. For the Labour government, in the process of reformulating a cultural policy, these were identified as significant due to their potential for increasing amounts of wealth creation, employment and the generation of income from exports (Smith 1997).

The arguments for the importance of these industries have an undoubted value and place within the unfolding history of theoretical attempts to understand media culture, and they are all part of a concerted attempt to move away from a short-term over-emphasis on audiences and the polysemantic interpretation of

texts during the 1980s and early 1990s. These are laudable aims, even if it's something of a sociological commonplace to de-emphasise the individual creator, the
isolated text, and seek to emphasise, if not valorise, the social and collective. But
one consequence of this type of shift entails a movement away from the creativity
of artists and towards the creativity of industries. One of the implications of such
a sociological critique entails an undialectical non-ironic reversal: from creative
artist to creative industries. The consequence is a move from Adorno's anxiety
about the impact of capitalist industry *on* the creative act and artist (or the constitution of their mediated art within a capitalist system) to the designation of a
vaguely defined category of capitalist industries *as* creative. By calling something a
'creative' industry, or even by saying that the cultural industries are the key site
for studying creativity, aesthetic value is being superimposed on market value,
leading in some cases to a celebration of capitalist industries *as* creative. Yet, we
don't have to look too far to know how misleading this can be. As Angela
McRobbie's (1998) research within the fashion trade has shown, the epithets of
creative or cultural that are applied to these industries conceal a less glamorous
world of hard work, long hours, insecurity, temporary contracts, gender inequalities and discrimination.

There are two deceptively simple questions that might be asked here: What is
creative about the creative industries? And why should the cultural industries be a
prime focus for any discussion of creativity? These questions clearly concern the
contribution of those personnel who derive their livelihood from an involvement
in the production of music, film, art works, theatre, poetry and novels, and who
claim a particular mediating role in 'the creative process'. There can be little
doubt that arts and entertainment corporations occupy a significant position
between artist and audience, and, as such, are a crucial site for studying and
understanding the mediations and modifications that connect the intentions of
artists with the interpretations of their listeners and viewers. Nonetheless, we
cannot assume that the work of these 'symbol creators' is necessarily any more
creative than other business, or that these should be privileged as 'core' cultural
industries – as if food, banking, tobacco, insurance, and other industries are not
creative and somehow less concerned with circulating meanings and influencing
cultural practices. Indeed, there is a long history of 'mass communication'
research which suggests that daily work in media- and culture-producing organisations is based on a limited number of known routines, formulas, repertoires and
untaxing administrative tasks (McQuail 2000).

In making this last point I do not mean to imply that staff in record labels, film
production companies or publishing houses and art galleries have no impact on
the creative process. However, I do think that the role of such commercial institutions needs formulating in a careful way. This, if only to avoid the twin tendency
of either portraying workers as commercially driven manipulators in a capitalist

bureaucracy, or viewing individual personnel through misty humanistic lenses as they make a voluntaristic contribution to popular art (in the 'creative' industry). It might be better to draw on all of the developments in sociology, management studies, economics, anthropology and business psychology in order to study the cultural *industries* as *industries* like other *industries*, rather than as a special place, bracketed from the rest due to the particular type of artistic value or creativity that is assumed to reside there. As the author of an account of (yet another) 'crisis' within the music industry remarked, the problem with the music business is not ultimately how it works with music and musicians (this is one of its skills) but how it works as a *business* (Sandall 2003). Rather than look to the cultural (or 'creative') industries to tell us something about creativity, we should look to them for more general insights into the workings of capitalist industry, big and small business, regulatory regimes and the institutions of production.

When thinking about the dynamics of creative production we should acknowledge that this does not take place simply within an industrial context structured according to the requirements of capitalist production or organisational formulas, but in relation to broader culture formations, economic practices and social divisions. Cultural production is not confined to the formal occupational tasks within a corporate world, but stretched across a range of activities that blur such conventional distinctions as public/private, professional judgement/personal preference and work/leisure time (see Negus 1999). To get an insight into the dynamics and struggles through which creative work is realised, recognised and rewarded then it is my contention that we have to take a broader perspective and think away, outwards, from the industries. Two writers who can provide important pointers to the direction this could take and who I wish to follow here are Howard Becker and Pierre Bourdieu.

In the footsteps of Becker and Bourdieu

Becker and Bourdieu both wish to think about cultural production in terms of a broader social space or arena. For Becker the key concept is that of the art world, while for Bourdieu it is the field of cultural production. Becker draws the term 'art world' from vernacular usage, but he uses it specifically: 'Art worlds consist of all the people whose activities are necessary to the production and characteristic works which that world, and perhaps others as well, define as art' (Becker 1984: 34). Art worlds are comprised of networks of people who co-operate and organise their artistic practices around a shared knowledge of conventions, and through co-operation and collaboration.

Becker cites examples of how cultural production depends upon collaboration, listing the numerous personnel who can be involved in filmmaking, for example – director, producer, camera operators, editors, effects people, props, stylists, dialogue coaches and so on through an often extensive and hierarchical division of labour. We can also think of the collaboration involved in music-making or television programming. Becker also wishes to stress the collective and co-operative activities that go into such apparently individual work as poetry or novel writing. Using the example of T.S. Eliot's *The Wasteland*, which was extensively edited, cut and added to by Ezra Pound and Eliot's wife Vivian Eliot, Becker points out that even the most apparently individual of works can be the result of collaboration (even if the poem is only attributed to one author). The artist is not alone but performs the 'core activity' at the 'centre of a network of co-operating people' (Becker 1984, 24–5). The general point is that a novel, the most 'individual' of creations, can be considered a 'collective' or 'collaborative' creation.

Becker highlights how a large part of the daily creative work within art worlds entails 'editing', and this editing involves choices. This does not just apply to novels or poetry, and might include the one photo chosen for public circulation after shooting ten rolls of film, and the one singing performance chosen for an album after recording ten vocal tracks. These choices help give the work its final shape and suggest future directions for creativity. As Barry Cryer observed when paying tribute to Bob Hope:

> Bob made no claim to be a writer but he was a brilliant editor. He had the ability to take a page of material written for him, within seconds singling out the ones he thought work for him and scrubbing out the rest.
>
> (Cryer 2003: 5)

Becker encourages us to think about how art emerges as a result of a huge number of choices, and an acute and perceptive sense of editing, rather than appearing spontaneously. In discussing these choices, Becker argues that artists orient themselves according to taken-for-granted, internalised conventions. These govern the use of materials, the choice of notes or rhythms, the use of notions of perspective, of the length of a performance, or the length of a novel. Conventions are enabling – they allow artistic work to occur, and creative communication to take place. Aesthetic conventions are seldom rigid and unchanging – every performance (music, play, dance) being subtly different, every art form continually being reinterpreted. Conventions *allow* for variations, improvisation and for communication to be realised. They cannot simply be reduced to industrial standardisation as Adorno implies.

Becker discusses two distinct stances towards conventions. One is adopted by 'integrated professionals', those who 'know, understand, and habitually use the conventions on which their world runs', and who 'fit easily into all its standard activities'. These will include composers whose music can be easily performed according to traditional notation and on available instruments, or painters who 'use available materials to produce works which, in size, form, design and colour, and content, fit into the available spaces and into people's ability to respond appropriately' (Becker 1984: 229).

In contrast, 'mavericks' are those who have been part of an art world and who decide to disrupt its conventions. They may receive a hostile reception, and have difficulty getting their work distributed or performed. They may be seen as innovators within art worlds despite their disruption of certain conventions, yet they still 'orient themselves to the world of canonical and conventional art. They change some of its conventions and more or less unwittingly accept the rest' (Becker 1984: 244).

It is the integrated professional who is more likely to get economic support and a relevant response, and gain resources and recognition. Mavericks may be considered odd. They may be dismissed for not doing things the right way, for writing notes that don't sound right, for not using paint or not operating a camera with the correct technique. When they are accorded some form of recognition, it may merely confirm their oddness, or it may entail a reassessment of the whole history of an art world, so hailing their creative extension of a relatively settled tradition.

Although Becker places considerable emphasis on agreed conventions, there have been numerous occasions when the conventions of art worlds have been challenged and this highlights just how fragile any artistic consensus can be. Here Becker's approach is somewhat partial in that it presupposes a sense of belonging to the art world and a willingness to co-operate in its conventions even as some of these are broken. The assumption that the art world is bounded and maintained according to co-operation and agreement tends towards the abstraction of certain characteristic features – detached from their living, changing context – and a process of theoretical reification whereby the bounded art world (rather than commerce or industry) seems to hover threateningly over the creative practices that are being studied.

The limitations of Becker's emphasis on collaboration and co-operation can be supplemented by turning to Bourdieu (1993, 1996), who provides an immediate contrast by emphasising the competitive arena within which *struggles* take place over resources and access to them. Like Becker, Bourdieu relativises artistic conventions, but he also relates them to how individuals and groups are positioned in relation to one another. He focuses on the power struggles that occur between individuals and groups as they compete within a 'space of position takings' that constitutes the field of cultural production. Like Becker, he conceives of creative practices as occurring within certain types of networks – but these are characterised by antagonism rather than co-operation.

Bourdieu's field is made up of a series of positions that are occupied by artists, whether they be poets, novelists, painters or musicians. These are positions adopted by individuals, but this approach emphasises the positions taken by particular genres, or sub-categories of art and literature. Bourdieu observes that different genres – of writing, of painting – are not simply defined according to their own internal conventions, codes and practices, but through their relationship to other categories.

Take, for example, the field of literature. The critical and commercial status of different types of literature is visibly articulated in bookshops, publishers' catalogues, the teaching programmes in universities and schools, or the organisation of literature suggested in the arts sections of newspapers and magazines. How much space is devoted to a new novel by Ian McEwan, Sarah Waters or Salman Rushdie, compared to a new crime novel? All this will give a tangible sense of how specific genres and writers are positioned in relation to one another.

So, the writer of spy stories occupies a particular location within the field of literary production, positioned in relation to genres such as romance, science fiction, and also in relation to modern novels and the selection of texts categorised as classics. When John Le Carré's *A Perfect Spy* was first published in 1986, Philip Roth reviewed it in the *Observer* and declared it to be the 'best English novel since the war'. There then followed a debate amongst various writers and critics within the literary field as to whether this was a novel or merely a piece of genre fiction. Was Le Carré now a modern novelist or still a writer of genre fiction (spy novels)? For some, Le Carré was using the spy form but with 'pretensions … towards writing literature' and adopting highly 'stylised' techniques, particularly in his opening chapters (Bradbury 1990: 130–6). Yet Le Carré's work has continually communicated beyond the spy genre, using the form critically as he 'reacts against the constraints imposed by playing with, even mocking, their conventions' (Hayes 1990: 119).

In certain respects this is a debate about literary style, but its consequences for reputations and careers can be profound. Whilst the novelist will still make money, there is far greater prestige to be gained from assuming the position of modern novelist than that of genre fiction writer. There will be different types of recognition, reputation and reward.

Hence, drawing from Bourdieu it can be argued that the meaning of an artistic work, and the conditions of its production, should not be approached in isolation and can only be understood in these relational contexts. The commercial and critical value of any play, painting or pop song arises in direct *relation* to other plays, pictures, performers and their producers – it is not intrinsic to the person or piece. To view genres and art forms relationally is not a particularly new observation, but Bourdieu's insight is to stress the sociological struggles over position, power and prestige that underpin the production of textual forms and reputations, and how the specific networks of power relations orient the strategies of artists. So, it follows from this that if you want to publish a novel, or get a record contract, or act in a movie, or display a sculpture, your chances may well be shaped by a specific talent and an acquired repertoire of skills. But this is only the beginning. You will also have to negotiate the conventions of art worlds and the various struggles that make up the field of cultural production. Only then can any creative possibilities be realised and recognised. As other people will be competing, the chance of realising such possibilities may be more to do with struggles over position than with any skill or talent. Artistic success may have more to do with professional manœuvrings, and wheeler-dealing, than sustained creative effort or artistic inspiration.

As these struggles occur, writers, musicians and artists compete to influence how their work is judged. Both Becker and Bourdieu are concerned with the production of beliefs and values that legitimate art. Since it is not an inherent quality of the art object, the question for Becker is how art comes to be labelled as art. A key issue concerns the dynamics of distribution and the systems in place that enable art works to be circulated. If art can't get distributed, how can we ever know about it? Becker gives the example of e.e. cummings's poetry, noting that printers were reluctant to set the poetry on the page as cummings had specified, and that this held up publication. He also refers to sculptures that are too large for an exhibition space. There may be a play that lasts too long to be performed within the conventional format of theatres. The lack of distribution channels, of a public arena or outlet for the work, does not halt the creative process, but it does impact on the way it might be recognised and valued.

A further issue that follows from this last point concerns the importance of those who are in a position to influence the attribution of value. Bourdieu observes that the production of critical discourse is one of the conditions for the production and legitimation of the work of art. So, within the field of cultural production, there is another struggle going on. This is a struggle for the monopoly of legitimate discourse about the work of art. It involves continual conflict over the values by which works of art will be judged. This can involve authors, critics, entrepreneurs and academics, as much as marketing staff, publicists and public relations people. All attempt to influence the ideas through which a work of art or literature is valued and appreciated. For example, the catalogue produced by art galleries to accompany exhibitions can be seen as providing instruction on how to appreciate the art on display. It is written by an authority. Similarly, critical reviews, literary guides and teaching texts tell us how to interpret and appreciate a novel or musical composition.

This results in what Bourdieu calls legitimation struggles – competitive battles to impose, and maintain as legitimate, definitions of what is artistic. Legitimation struggles are continually occurring in various artistic and cultural fields, and, as people are positioned differently according to their ability to influence the outcome of these aesthetic disputes, for Bourdieu they are ultimately power struggles, with dominant interests seeking to impose *their* values as legitimate.

In this way, Bourdieu links the field of cultural production to a more profound set of power struggles that connect the actions of participants in the aesthetic field to a field of power. In the contemporary world the field of power is primarily, but not exclusively shaped by the competition, collusion and tensions between government/state institutions and private capital/commercial interests. At certain moments the state may exert a decisive influence in the struggles to define aesthetic meaning, attributing explicitly ideological and political anchors to art, incorporating the aesthetic into patterns of propaganda and domination. An example might be the *Entartete Kunst* exhibition of 1937, a collection of 'degenerate art' that had been removed from German museums and staged by the Nazi Party. Many of these struggles have been more market oriented. In London during the late twentieth and early twenty-first century, there was a struggle to define the value of British art with the collector Charles Saatchi occupying a pivotal position in the legitimation struggles amongst artists, critics, gallery owners and private corporations (see Cook 2000; Hatton and Walker 2000).

As Bourdieu argues, it is ultimately a type of institutional power – political, economic, social – which not only impacts upon the production of artefacts but which informs the entire field of artistic production, influencing the establishment of reputations and struggles over economic, cultural and political resources. The art world, the field of cultural production and the cultural industry are continually implicated in the wielding of, resistance to, and struggle for, power.

Concluding remarks

I have drawn on Becker and Bourdieu to argue for a movement away from a narrow focus on the cultural industries and to challenge any simple assumption about the impact of an industry *upon* creative practice. I also wish to take issue with the idea that a cultural industry provides the main context within which cultural production takes place, managing how creativity is formally recognised and commercially rewarded. Instead, I am suggesting that the study of cultural production should draw insights from Becker's art world of co-operative interactions and Bourdieu's field of cultural production made up of position-takings and struggles for position. Becker's symbolic interactionism and Bourdieu's structural sociology provide significant insights into the visible interactions and the less tangible structural forces through which power is manifested and contested during cultural production. It is my belief that a more sophisticated understanding of cultural production can be developed if we pursue the issues opened up by these approaches along with a willingness to follow Adorno in interrogating (rather than attempting to resolve) the tensions, paradoxes and possibilities that are generated when culture meets industry. Such an approach can still retain the important aims proposed in the agendas of writers such as Garnham, Miège and

Hesmondhalgh – an emphasis on institutions and corporate power. But, it might place these within a broader context, allowing for an acknowledgement of the cultural, inter-personal and aesthetic struggles through which the work of a creative artist is realised, recognised and valued.

References

Adorno, T. (1990) 'On popular music', in S. Frith and A. Goodwin (eds) *On Record*, London: Routledge, pp. 301–14.

—— (1991) *The Culture Industry, Selected Essays on Mass Culture*, ed. J. Bernstein, London: Routledge.

—— (1994) *The Stars Down to Earth*, London: Routledge.

Adorno, T. and Horkheimer, M. (1979) *Dialectic of Enlightenment*, London: Verso.

Becker, H. (1984) *Art Worlds*, Berkeley and Los Angeles: University of California Press.

Bennett, T. (1998) *Culture, A Reformers Science,* London: Sage.

Bernstein, J. (1991) 'Introduction', in T. Adorno, *The Culture Industry, Selected Essays on Mass Culture*, ed. J. Bernstein, London: Routledge, pp. 1–25.

Bourdieu, P. (1993) *The Field of Cultural Production*, Cambridge: Polity Press.

—— (1996) *The Rules of Art*, Cambridge: Polity Press.

Bradbury, R. (1990) 'Reading John le Carré', in Clive Bloom (ed.) *Spy Thrillers, from Buchan to le Carré*, Basingstoke: Macmillan, pp. 130–9.

Cook, R (2000) 'The mediated manufacture of an 'avant garde': a Bourdieusian analysis of the field of contemporary art in London, 1997–9', in B. Fowler (ed.) *Reading Bourdieu on Society and Culture*, Oxford: Blackwell, pp. 164–85.

Cryer, B. (2003) 'Sheer hard graft made him a national monument', *Independent*, 29 July, p. 5.

Garnham, N. (1990) *Capitalism and Communication: Global Culture and the Economics of Information*, London: Sage.

Hatton, R. and Walker, J. (2000) *Supercollector, a Critique of Charles Saatchi*, London: Ellipsis.

Hayes, M (1990) 'Are you telling me lies David? The work of John le Carré', in C. Bloom (ed.) *Spy Thrillers, from Buchan to le Carré*, Basingstoke: Macmillan, pp. 113–29.

Hesmondhalgh, D. (2002) *The Cultural Industries*, London: Sage.

McQuail, D. (2000) *Mass Communication Theory*, London: Sage.

McRobbie, A. (1998) *British Fashion Design*, London: Routledge.

Miège, B. (1989) *The Capitalization of Cultural Production*, New York: International General.

Negus, Keith (1999) *Music Genres and Corporate Cultures*, London: Routledge.

Sandall, R. (2003) 'The day the music industry died', *Sunday Times Magazine*, 16 February, pp. 24–30.

Smith, C. (1997) *Creative Britain*, London: Faber & Faber.

UNESCO (1982) *Culture Industries: A Challenge for the Future of Culture*, Paris: UNESCO.

Williams, A. (2001) *Constructing Musicology*, Aldershot: Ashgate.

Chapter 14

'Inventing the psychological'

Lifestyle magazines and the fiction of autonomous self

Lisa Blackman

Neo-liberalism and subjectivity

In Ulrich Beck's and Elizabeth Beck-Gernsheim's (2001) recent book, *Individualization*, they chart a series of changing scenarios in the workplace, familial and personal relationships, health care, welfare and gender, within an argument that suggests there is an increasing trend towards individualisation within neo-liberalism. This trend, they argue, is evident in the way in which people articulate and understand their own success and failure, and take steps to maximise their success, happiness and fulfilment across a range of practices in which they are subjects. They term the narratives that have become increasingly central to how we understand our life trajectories 'reflexive biographies', and argue that it is how we rationalise the choices we have made in relation to our successes and failures that capture this trend. The psychological ramifications of this shift are related to the ways in which failure in the workplace, in our intimate lives, even in relation to our lived experience of health and illness, is tied to a particular economy of emotions, such as personal inadequacy, guilt, anxiety and neurosis, rather than a blow of fate, circumstance or part and parcel of what we might term the mundane psychopathology of life. This is a 'reflexive self' governed by an ethic of self-fulfilment and achievement that is matched by the production of a particular psychopathology that besets modern life.

What is interesting about the Becks' argument is the way in which general sociological trends are tied to the production of particular kinds of psychology and subjectivity. Critical sociologists such as Nikolas Rose (1990) have made similar arguments, tying the production of these new forms of selfhood more explicitly to the psychological sciences. Rather than simply describing selfhood, he argues, they are helping to align and orient subjects' own self-practice and understanding with forms of citizenship that underpin the political project of neo-liberalism. The fiction of autonomous selfhood is viewed as a distinctive regime of self-understanding and practice that forms the basis of how the 'self' is made intelligible in the world of work, health, education, welfare and consumer culture. It is seen to characterise a relationship we are encouraged to develop with ourselves, where we understand the key to success, happiness, satisfaction and so forth as being subject to our own efforts and capacity to constantly rein-vent and transform ourselves, increasingly framed by the discourses of counselling and therapy.

These kinds of general sociological arguments that focus upon the production of particular kinds of psychology look in particular at the ways in which institutional practices, and the discourses that support them, help to produce particular kinds of self-understanding and practice. These discourses tend to be ordered, regulated and systematised, and operate according to internal norms of truth and falsehood that govern what can be said and done (Blackman 2001). One aim of this chapter is to explore how the concepts that articulate the autonomous self shift and change in meaning (and therefore self-practice) when we examine their circulation within popular discourse across the category of gender. Popular discourse is inherently dilemmatic and is structured by ambiguity and contradiction (Billig *et al*. 1988). This chapter will argue that if one of the structuring principles of popular discourse is dilemma and contradiction, then this raises questions about how actual subjects inhabit and embody cultural categories in their everyday lives. This work also points to the lack of specificity and generality within many of the sociological arguments that posit race, class, gender and sexuality as structural positionings, enabling or constraining certain ways of understanding the world. This model, as Stuart Hall reminds us in his contestation of the 'problem of identity', (Hall 1996), relies upon a homogenisation of identity, at the expense of any discursive under-standing of the production of individual biographies and narratives. Hall suggests that the key issue is to find ways of analysing subjects' investment or subjective commitment to cultural categories and positionings; a problem that he cogently locates within the various psychoanalytic projects which have rethought agency through analysing the intertwining of the social and the psychic.

These thorny questions are those that 'critical psychology' has been engaging with over the past three decades (see Blackman and Walkerdine 2001; Henriques *et al*. 1984). There is however very little engagement with 'critical psychology' by media and cultural theorists, despite the call for cultural theorists to engage with the psychological dimensions of media and cultural forms through frameworks that reject essentialism (see McRobbie 1996). With a shift to ethnography and lived experience within culturalist perspectives, and a focus upon consumers rather than producers of texts, critical psychology, rather than orthodox psychology or psychoanalysis, is one arena that offers cultural theorists a range of methods for dealing with these pressing concerns (Billig 1997). This chapter will signal ways forward by analysing how popular discourse translates, transforms and reproduces the 'fiction of autonomous selfhood' across the designation of gender. This work at the intersection of media and cultural studies and critical psychology is central to understanding how the privatisation of risk, managed through the development of 'reflexive biographies' (Beck and Beck-Gernsheim 2001), presents subjects with decisions, which are 'sometimes un-decidable, or painfully ambiguous ones' (Elliot 2002: 18). These lead to further dilemmas, problems and questions. It is the dilemmas that popular discourses help to construct and mediate, which are crucial to understanding media consumption beyond reinstating a structural way of understanding social designations.

Magazine culture

In previous writing I have suggested that magazine culture is a good site for examining the kinds of cultural translations that occur when the 'autonomous self' is articulated across gendered, classed, raced and sexed designations (Blackman 2004). Magazine analysis is structured through arguments that both point to the cultural and psychological significance of magazines in our lives, and to their changing form and potential for reconfiguring what it means to be a subject within contemporary life (Beetham 1996; Ferguson 1983). Audiences are no longer viewed as being taken in hook, line and sinker by the kinds of fantasies contained within its pages, and are viewed as having a knowingness about the desires and aspirations they are being invited to inhabit. Nevertheless, there is no clear sense of the basis of readers' identifications, and the extent to which the kinds of fractured address open up the potential for unfixing femininity and remaking it beyond patriarchal concerns (McRobbie 1999).

Critical psychology in recent decades has been concerned with how to theorise the production of the 'psychological' in and through the social, without seeing subjects as either 'free to choose' from the cultural categories shaping their identities or constructed in such a way as there is no room for manoeuvre (Henriques et al. 1984; Blackman and Walkerdine 2001). This work draws on both Foucauldian conceptions of discourse (Foucault 1972), postcolonial work on the construction and mediation of the Other through fears, fetish and phobia (BhaBha 1994), as well as considering questions of subjective commitment through a focus upon iteration and the social production of psychic fears, desires and anxieties (Butler 1993; Hall 1996). This work suggests that there is no easy or straightforward inhabiting of any new cultural categories or identities, and that the unease, linguistic or otherwise, which is part of how categories function, creates hesitancies rather than any simple identification on the part of readers or subjects (cf. Riley 2000). These arguments about 'the psychological' will be explored through an interrogation of the kinds of concepts that articulate autonomy in relation to the post-feminist woman and her capacity and desire to achieve intimacy in her personal relationships. On the surface women are invited to stand alone, single, happy, working on self-confidence and their achievements in relationships and the workplace. Although these new fictions of femininity move away from traditional discourses that tie women to the realm of the domestic and do not privilege romantic relationships as a solution to misery, failure or psychological distress, the gaps, contradictions and silences in these representations can also tell us something significant about the dilemmas that face women in the twenty-first century. What will be explored are the different discourses and structures of inequality that produce different dilemmas for women, as opposed to men, when we look at how autonomy as a practice is translated in the area of intimate relations within women's lifestyle magazines.

The invention of the psychological

The study I will refer to[1] aimed to explore the extent to which the general address or injunction to understand psychological reinvention and transformation as central to success or satisfaction organised the ways in which intimate relationships, their problems and possible resolutions were made intelligible and translated across the markers of race, sexuality and gender. The study focused on magazines targeting black and Asian audiences, people with different sexualities and men and women. The focus in this chapter will be on the vexed question of femininity and its possible reproduction and transformation.

Intimacy and relationships

The arena of relationships as a focus of study may provide possible sites through which some of the dynamics, conflicts and struggles that are part and parcel of the 'fiction of autonomous selfhood' are played out. Sennett (1977) presents a general sociological treatise which suggests that the ways in which we experience our intimate relations with an Other are being transformed. He argues that our expectations for intimate relationships are such that they are the place where we reveal our innermost thoughts, feelings and emotions, expecting this sense of selfhood to be recognised, valued and reflected back to us. In this sense, he suggests that intimate relations are governed by a market place of self-confessions, through an ethic of self-fulfilment and achievement – the very kind of 'reflexive self' that the Becks characterise as capturing the new kind of subject brought into being under neo-liberalism. He argues that intimate relationships are inevitably destructive in this respect, because they become 'contests for personal legitimation' rather than an awareness and examination of the kinds of relational dynamic that two or more people create together.

> Openness to others in the hope of sharing feelings is the modern meaning of gemeinshaft. It operates on the principle that selfhood can be generated

through mutual confession and revelation, and under the illusion that experiences of power, inequity, or domination all have a meaning subsumed in psychological categories.

(Sennett 1977: 185).

Although interesting from both a social and psychological perspective, these are generalised arguments that do not examine the ways in which competing injunctions to understand one's life and intimate relations are lived and experienced by actual subjects. Emotions become de-gendered, de-sexualised and de-racialised, and exist as the expression of thwarted relationships conducted by subjects abstracted from their very real social and psychological locations. Sennett's work is important as it directs our attention to the importance of having recourse to a form of psychological theorising that can engage with the social and psychic or the social and psychological as interdependent processes. However, it glosses over the ways in which different subjects cope with the complexity of their social positionings, and particularly with the ways in which competing demands are made on subjects through the different injunctions that address them across a range of cultural and social practices (Walkerdine *et al.* 2001).

Rhetorical psychology

The issue of the kinds of dilemmas that regulate one's reflection on particular problems of existence and thus govern social and psychological life has been developed in rhetorical psychology (Billig *et al.* 1988). This qualitative method allows the dilemmas in speech and popular discourse to be examined in relation to a broader argumentative context. Relationship 'talk' and the different discourses that help to produce the conflicts and dilemmas facing individuals when reflecting on their desires for intimacy and their own autonomy is an interesting site for this kind of analysis.

Rhetorical psychology starts from the premise that popular discourse is dilemmatic. This work develops insights from the arguments of Bakhtin and Voloshinov concerned more with language use, the multi-accentuality of the sign and the 'dialogic unconscious' (Billig 1997). Popular discourse is structured through themes and contrary themes, which are contradictory and produce the kinds of 'thought space' that allow people to debate, disagree, argue and hold contradictory views. Popular discourse is not neatly systematised and the kinds of concepts and discourses that make people's self-understanding and practice intelligible are not necessarily easily available for analysis.

Rhetorical psychology pays equal attention to the unsaid and what is absent, as to those themes that can be read off from the surface of the magazine. The principles of rhetorical analysis pay attention to the often more implicit ways in which dilemmas are being articulated, constructed and resolved. Those that are implicit are conceptualised in such a way as to pay attention to the kinds of discourses and concepts they are implicitly refuting or refusing. Thus, the implicit, that is, what is absent or silent, if one remains at the surface level of the text, actually makes possible the particular form of articulation or argumentation. This is referred to as the contrary theme.[2] As Billig argues in relation to the project of media and cultural studies, 'the meaning of any utterance, or piece of logos, must be understood in terms of its dialogical context, and this means in terms of the anti-logos, which it seeks to counter' (Billig 1997: 225). Rather than view discourses as co-existing, opening up possibilities for more choice and agency, the focus is on the kinds of tensions and cultural anxieties that help to produce as much as deny particular cultural categories and discourses. This conception of discourse is more dialogic and looks at how discourses speak to each other, through their disavowal, such that they are affirmed at the moments they are also denied.[3] This is important to focus upon the kinds of anxieties and dilemmas that govern gender under neo-liberalism, and particularly produce the tensions and contradictions that surround the enactment of any new identity positioning.

This form of analysis was complemented by a focus upon the kinds of self-practices that readers were encouraged to engage in to resolve possible dilemmas and conflicts. This develops work in magazine analysis that has focused upon the psychosocial tensions created for women who are addressed by contradictory impulses, and the ways in which they are resolved through addressing the woman through self-help practices. Ferguson argues that self-help 'is the new doctrine of salvation for all areas of a woman's life from the most public to the most private' (Ferguson 1983: 185). The resolutions pro-offered to possible conflicts and dilemmas were investigated by focusing upon what Foucault (1990) termed the 'ethical substance' or ontology of practices of the self. This focuses upon what is marked out as in need of attention, and the discourses that make this intelligible. Nikolas Rose (1996) has used these kinds of methodological principles to analyse more regulated discourses, such as counselling and therapeutics. He has cogently argued that there is usually a privileging of the pathological over the normal in how subjects understand and act upon themselves. The important point is, therefore, how the arena of relationships is made intelligible and what concepts allow the distinctions between the normal and the pathological to be thought. What is sanctioned or valorised as that which must be avoided, regulated, sought after or worked upon in order to manage the dilemma between being, for example, a self-made woman and being in or wanting to be in a relationship with an intimate other? I will now give you a sense of some of the patterns of relating and the injunctions and relationships of self to self produced within women's magazine culture.

Happy go lucky!

Morgan

> Lifestyle: I've got an amazing group of friends and I'm never without some-
> thing to do. I'm out two to four nights a week, often straight from work, and
> go clubbing at weekends.
>
> Men: I don't like these New Age, feminine men. I like my man to be a
> man.
>
> Ideal Relationship: I don't have time for a serious relationship. I never go
> out on the pull and I'm often with guys, so I don't get approached. I'd just
> like someone to have fun with.
>
> *(Marie Claire, 2001)*

Morgan presents herself as adventurous and ambitious with a passionate
approach to love and life, always on the go and not constantly on the look out
for a man. There is a particular emphasis on her popularity and her claim that,
'I'm never without something to do'. This is of course a popular construction of
the self-made or post-feminist woman, who is single, forward looking, independent, standing alone and in control of her life. However, as mentioned
previously, rhetorical analysis attempts to uncover the unsaid, or implicit
themes, as well as the explicit. In this example, characteristic of many in
women's lifestyle magazines, we can also explore this warrant as a 'claim against'
or refutation of other possible kinds of behaviours, conduct, and ways of being
and doing. This would involve identifying the discourses or concepts that are
being repudiated in the defensive organisation of the post-feminist woman.
Wendy Hollway (1984) has identified a set of concepts that she argues are part
of a 'have–hold' discourse, whereby relationships are constructed through terms
such as commitment, interdependency, trust and emotional security and safety
(in the arms of another). However, they are read in more negative terms through
some of the other kinds of discourses that map out what it means to be in a relationship (what Billig (1996) would term the 'argumentative context'). These
include the 'permissive' and 'sexual drive' discourses, which have historically
been associated with masculine wants, desires and expectations, and which mark
out those signifiers that construct relationships within the 'have–hold' discourse
as signs of a person's emotional insecurity and weakness, i.e. as neediness or
desperation (see Stenner 1993).

In many of the examples analysed it was found that presentations of the female
self as a 'self-made woman' also function as refutations of the pejorative readings
of the 'have–hold' discourse, i.e. a statement that the woman is not needy or
dependent or sexually available (i.e. although it is taken for granted that women
have sexual agency, this is regulated and circumscribed through discourses that

re-embed women's sexual desire and practices within traditional fictions of femininity). This positioning and marking out of what is problematic and to be avoided, rejected and so on are those very concepts that articulate relationships through constructing the woman as waiting for a man to complete her. Although we might want to celebrate this move as one of increasing choice on offer to women, what rhetorical psychology focuses upon are the kinds of dilemmas that are managed through particular presentational strategies, and how these dilemmas are always 'in dialogue' with a particular argumentative context – one in this case where the injunction to understand self-invention as the key to success and happiness is articulated alongside competing injunctions that require women to also refute and distance themselves from discourses which have traditionally aligned women with a need for emotional closeness, intimacy and commitment in relationships. Female desire is viewed as circumscribed by the very signifiers of relationship that the self-made woman is required to refuse, commitment, security, monogamy, emotionality, closeness, warmth and safety (Hollway 1984). These concepts and the discourses they regulate appeared in the argumentative context as the unspeakable and yet affirmed categories.

The dilemmas, and indeed the potential psychopathology created for women by the ambivalence and contradiction produced through these tensions, are managed within the pages of women's magazines primarily by presenting women with the necessity of self-transformation and psychological reinvention as the means to improve satisfaction and success in intimate relationships. Women were primarily urged to work on relationships through an injunction that privileged their engagement in practices of self-monitoring, evaluation, scrutiny and bodily, emotional and/or psychological transformation in order to achieve certain desired ends. This project of self-transformation was also subsumed within a consumer discourse where diet programmes, fitness, cosmetics, health-oriented foods, cosmetic surgery and other body techniques were promoted and valorised through a vocabulary of choice that addressed the (female) reader as being able to achieve success and happiness through her choice amongst a range of options and preferences.

There have been many arguments to suggest that what characterises global cultures is an increasing blurring of the boundaries between consumer culture and popular culture (Franklin *et al.* 2000; Harbord 2002). These arguments suggest that by consuming particular media or cultural forms, we inhabit specific 'taste cultures' that simultaneously construct and make manifest our identity positionings as subjects. Consumer culture is accorded a central role in producing the kinds of 'tastes' and styles viewed as increasingly central to how people form their identities as subjects. Although, in the study I am recounting, magazine culture is a good example of a form where consumer culture and popular culture are thoroughly intertwined, rather than according this particular 'taste culture' a formative role, I want to examine how cultural forms work alongside or in conjunction with desires, fears and aspirations already present in the lives of many readers targeted by different publications. I also seek to bring the body back into these kinds of analyses and begin to think about the kinds of embodied experience that readers bring to their consumption of cultural forms. Although much work in media studies focuses upon language and the kinds of interpretive structures that readers bring to bear on texts, the neglect of the body and embodied experiences presumes a cognitivist subject who perceives primarily through the structures of language and discourse (Blackman and Walkerdine 2001). This reifies the mind and does not adequately conceive or explore readers as socially informed embodied subjects (Burkitt 1999).

Psychologies of survival

One of the key tropes through which suffering is expressed within cultural texts that have been celebrated as post-feminist is through the use of humour to recount and confess the woman's struggles, failings and inadequacies. From *Bridget Jones* and *Ally McBeal* to *Sex and the City*, stoic humour and irony are used to make visible the tensions and anxieties that exist in such close proximity. It would seem that one of the most culturally sanctioned ways of articulating suffering, particularly for women, is through the use of humorous sound bites (by being tough and witty) and comedic parody. This stands in sharp contrast to the kinds of painful disclosure of feelings of guilt, shame and humiliation, and feelings of powerlessness and persecution, expressed by educated working-class women who have entered typically middle-class professions. Valerie Walkerdine (1996) has explored how the women embody the kinds of ambivalences and contradictions that address them through practices of consumption, leisure and advertising, as well as cultural and scientific discourses that construct the working class as Other: stupid, animal, reactionary, dependent and pathological. Walkerdine develops Bhabha's (1994) concept of the 'colonial stereotype' to explore how class is feared and desired, denigrated and envied. These ambivalences exist alongside the more normative addresses of consumer culture where selfhood is produced as a project of self-transformation and development. The forms of psychopathology produced by the lived experience of these contradictions are those that are then read off within scientific discourses and practices as signs of working-class inadequacy, inferiority or even biological illness (Blackman 1996, 2001). As Walkerdine (1996) suggests, the women feel that they must never break down, get angry or even cry; an injunction that places the burden of inequality firmly in relation to their own efforts to continually re-enact their own self-transformation.

These kinds of strategies of survival are those that are reiterated across the pages of women's magazines. Particular problems of social existence such as losing one's job, health, beauty, relationships and friendships are constituted as stimuli for self-improvement. The autonomous woman who does not lean on or need others and who above all can 'believe in herself' stands as the regulatory ideal in these addresses (Blackman 1999). The self-made woman waits for nobody and through her own hard work, effort and positivity makes things happen. The 'modern woman' gets, does, improves and rationalises her emotions on her path of self-transformation. Jackie Stacey (1997), talking about the kinds of personal narratives that tend to structure 'cancer stories' similarly argues that self-help or 'self-health' constructs suffering in a particular kind of way. Failure in these practices is constituted as a temporary obstacle to overcome, and as we have seen these practices map onto the very kinds of embodied experience that 'make up' many women's subjectivities[4] I want to suggest that the dilemmatic quality of feminine discourses, and the regulative practices pro-offered as resolutions, condense a range of bodily sensations, anxieties, tensions and forms of psychopathology that are 'already constituted' lived realities for many of the readers engaging with these magazines. This work brings together much work in media studies analysing women's magazine culture, which emphasises both its fragmentary quality (McRobbie 1999), and also the more systematic and repeated ways in which women are encouraged to see and understand themselves as subjects (Ferguson 1983). It allows us to explore the cultural purchase and potency of particular practices (Franklin *et al.* 2000), as well as highlighting the need to reformulate studies of media consumption in relation to the embodied negotiation of the different kinds of cultural anxieties and personal tensions that readers bring to the text.

Conclusion

What this work points towards is the urgent need for cultural theorists to take seriously the psychological dimensions of cultural products in order to understand the possible ways in which actual subjects might engage with changing media representations. I would argue that the concepts of dilemma and dialogue give us a way of reconceptualising the question of subject commitment and investment through investigating the interdependence of the social and the psychological. This work also suggests the urgent need for cultural theorists to respond to some of the more general sociological arguments about new forms of subjectivity by examining and analysing the ways in which popular discourse translates these injunctions across the categories of gender, race, sexuality and class. The cultural logic of neo-liberalism is founded on the hope, longing and imagining of individuals that things could be different. This enables subjects to conceive of themselves as active, autonomous agents (Walkerdine *et al.* 2001). The examination of popular discourse through the intersection of critical psychology and media and cultural studies may provide a new framework for addressing the conditions under which this cultural logic might break down.

Notes

1 This study was funded by the Arts and Humanities Research Board (AN6596/APN 10894). My thanks to the research assistant, Dr Laura Miller.

2 To bring these implicit meanings to the surface, the analyst faces a greater interpretative or hermeneutic task, for a counter-theme needs to be interpreted within discourse that seems *prima facie* to be arguing straightforwardly for a particular point. If contrary counter-themes can be said to be concealed within discourse, they are not hidden in the way that Freudian theorists believe that certain inconsistent themes are hidden by repression from the conscious mind. The concealment is not a deliberate or even subconscious concealment, but may operate within layers of meaning of language. Discourse that seems to be arguing for one point may contain implicit meanings which could be made explicit to argue for the counter-point. Thus discourse can contain its own negation, and this is part of its implicit, rather than explicit, meaning (Billig *et al.* 1988: 22).

3 See an important development of this dialogic approach to discourse in the work of Jackie Stacey (1997) who analyses the unspeakable tropes of cancer and lesbian sexuality in her cultural study of cancer. She refers to them euphemistically as the 'C word' and the 'L word'.

4 'In contemporary western culture, we are encouraged to think of ourselves as coherent stories of success, progress and movement. Loss and failure have their place but only as part of a broader picture of ascendance' (Stacey 1997: 9).

References

Beck, U. and Beck-Gernsheim, E. (2001) *Individualization*, London and Thousand Oaks: Sage.

Beetham, M. (1996) A Magazine of Her Own? Domesticity and Desire in the Women's Magazine. 1800–1914, London: Routledge.

Bhabha, H. (1994) *The Location of Culture*, London and New York: Routledge.

Billig, M. (1997) 'Cultural studies, discourse and psychology: from codes to utterances', in P. Golding and M. Ferguson (eds) *Beyond Cultural Studies*, London: Sage.

Billig, M., Condor, S., Edwards, D. and Gane, M. (1988) *Ideological Dilemmas. A Social Psychology of Everyday Thinking*, London: Sage.

Blackman, L. (1996) 'The dangerous classes: re-telling the psychiatric story', *Feminism and Psychology* 6(3): 361–79.

—— (1999) 'An extraordinary life: the legacy of an ambivalence', *New Formations* 'Diana and Democracy' (special issue) 36; 111–24.

—— (2001) *Hearing Voices: Embodiment and Experience*, London and New York: Free Association Books.

—— (2004) 'Self-help, media cultures and the problem of female psychopathology', *European Journal of Cultural Studies* 7(2): 241–58.

Blackman, L. and Walkerdine, V. (2001) *Mass Hysteria: Critical Psychology and Media Studies*, Basingstoke and New York: Palgrave.

Burkitt, I. (1999) *Bodies of Thought. Embodiment, Identity and Modernity*, London: Sage.

Butler, J. (1993) *Bodies That Matter*, London and New York: Routledge.

Elliot, A. (2002) 'Identity politics and privatisation', in V. Walkerdine (ed.) *Challenging Subjects. Critical Psychology for a New Millennium*, Basingstoke and New York: Palgrave.

Ferguson, M. (1983) Forever Feminine. Women's Magazines and the Cult of Femininity, London: Heinemann.

Foucault, M. (1972) *The Archaeology of Knowledge*, London and New York: Routledge.

—— (1990) *The Care of the Self. The History of Sexuality*, Vol. 3, London: Penguin.

Franklin, S., Lury, C. and Stacey, J. (2000) *Global Nature, Global Culture*, London, Thousand Oaks and New Delhi: Sage.

Hall, S. (1996) 'Introduction', in S. Hall and P. Du Gay (eds) *Questions of Cultural Identity*, London: Sage.

Harbord, J. (2002) *Film Cultures*, London and New York: Routledge.

Henriques, J., Hollway, W., Urwin, C., Venn, C. and Walkerdine, V (1984) *Changing the Subject. Psychology, Social Regulation and Subjectivity*, London: Methuen.

Hollway, W. (1984) 'Gender difference and the production of subjectivity', in J. Henriques, W. Hollway, C. Urwin, C. Venn and V. Walderdine (1984) *Changing the Subject. Psychology, Social Regulation and Subjectivity*, London: Methuen.

McRobbie, A. (1996) '*More*!: new sexualities in girls' and women's magazines', in J. Curran, D. Morley and V. Walkerdine (eds) *Cultural Studies and Communications*, London: Routledge.

—— (1999) *In the Culture Society*, London and New York: Routledge.

Marie Claire (2001) 'Sex: which one would men sleep with? Who would they marry?' September.

Riley, D. (2000) *The Words of Selves: Identity, Solidarity, Irony*, Stanford, CA: Stanford University Press.

Rose, N. (1990) *Governing the Soul: The Shaping of the Private Self*, London and New York: Routledge.

—— (1996) *Inventing Ourselves. Psychology, Power and Personhood*, Cambridge, New York and Melbourne: Cambridge University Press.

Sennett, R (1977) 'Destructive gemeinshaft', in N. Birnbaum (ed.) *Beyond the Crisis*, Oxford and New York: Oxford University Press.

Stacey, J. (1997) *Teratologies. A Cultural Study of Cancer*, London and New York: Routledge.

Stenner, P (1993) 'Discoursing jealousy', in E. Burman and I. Parker (eds) *Discourse Analytic Research*, London and New York: Routledge.

Walkerdine, V. (1996) 'Psychological and social aspects of survival', in S. Wilkinson (ed.) *Feminist Social Psychologies*, Buckingham and Philadelphia: Open University Press.

Walkerdine, V., Lucey, H. and Melody, J. (2001) *Growing Up Girl. Psychosocial Explorations of Gender and Class*, Basingstoke and New York: Palgrave.

Chapter 15

Discussing quality

Critical vocabularies and popular television drama

Christine Geraghty

The terms 'quality' and 'soaps' are seldom linked in discussions of television. In a British context, whether set against single plays of the 1960s, classic serials of the 1980s or US HBO series in the 1990s, soaps generally represent the worst tendencies of formulaic, repetitive and aesthetically predictable television. For many, quality television fiction now comes in the shape of US series and sit-coms (see Jancovich and Lyons 2003) and Lez Cooke in a recent history of British television drama found no soaps to add to his list of contemporary British programmes that could challenge the best of US television. In media and cultural studies, soaps tend to be studied in terms of their audiences, their social significance and their narrative organisation. Arguments about quality involve attention to textual detail that is hard to maintain as yet another episode sweeps by.

This essay seeks to make a number of arguments about the aesthetic mode of a particular soap, BBC1's *EastEnders*. I will argue that *EastEnders*, a continuous serial that revolves around a number of families living in Albert Square, has in recent years developed a distinctive aesthetic based on a bold use of melodrama for its most effective and disturbing storylines; that this can be linked to a decline in the possibilities of community which have traditionally been the distinctive feature of British soaps; and that television criticism lacks the vocabulary to judge a soap like *EastEnders* as television drama. In the process of making the argument, I need to stop the flow of *EastEnders*' narrative and subject isolated episodes to the kind of textual analysis that might be given to other forms of television drama. This essay therefore focuses on a particular week (1–5 October 2001) when a special storyline, spread across four episodes, revealed the secrets of the Slaters. The Slater family, a relatively recent addition to the soap, consisted of a battle-axe of a grandmother, a widowed father, Charlie, and five daughters; an uncle, Harry, had followed them to the Square and become engaged to Peggy Mitchell, the soap's prime matriarch. During the week, it was revealed that Zoe, at 17 the youngest in the family, was in fact the daughter of one of her sisters, Kat. She had been conceived in an abusive relationship between Kat, then aged 13, and her uncle, Harry, though Charlie had not known that his brother was the father. The revelations occurred on the eve of the wedding of another of the sisters, Lynne, and caused a great deal of anguish. The week ended with father punching brother, the wedding abandoned, Kat attempting suicide and Zoe running away from her disrupted home.[1]

EastEnders and a shift to melodrama

In a British critical context, soap operas tend to be valued in so far as they operate in a realist mode. David Hare, for instance, praised *EastEnders* for creating television drama which recognises 'that the editing and organisation of reality is a genuine skill' (2002). Realism has also been a defence against the criticism that soaps are too violent and salacious; it was characteristic that the producer, John Yorke, defended the abuse storyline on the grounds that 'we try and reflect the world as it is' (quoted in the *Observer*, 7 October 2001). This links to a public service function of educating audiences about the modern world, a remit that could fit Kat's abuse alongside the stories of rape, domestic violence, drug use and AIDS which have featured since the programme began in 1985. Accuracy and social responsibility are watchwords here as Yorke demonstrated when he defended the story by using the realist concept of changing the world by exposing its flaws: 'before we plotted it, we talked to the Samaritans, to child psychiatrists and to the NSPCC. All said the same thing – "This story needs telling. Will you please let people know that this goes on"' (Yorke 2002). This education process involves showing how characters learn to understand and accept problematic situations in their community. British soap operas often focus on communities that provide moral and social support to characters in difficulties and which celebrate their own solidarity. While the representation of community is sometimes seen as excessively nostalgic, it is still presented as a microcosm of British society and an important resource for characters in trouble. Given all this, claims about *EastEnders'* status as drama tend to rest on its continuation of the valued traditions of representational realism with stories rooted in social obligations and communal relationships.

But the story of the Slater sisters had a rather different approach, one which foregrounded the aesthetic pleasures of its telling. The four episodes put a social problem into a familiar context – the characters and spaces of Albert Square, the expected narrative events of the stag night and the hen party, the doubts of the groom and the settled, rather unromantic convictions of the bride. But out of this familiar material was made a story that layered past on present, created precarious understandings between characters that were immediately challenged and used its *mise-en-scène* to present a world transformed. The episodes were formally balanced: the first and last worked with the traditional parallel stories of a soap, while episode two focused on Kat and Zoe, and episode three, though less intensely, on Charlie's response to the news that his brother had abused his child. There were rhythms within episodes: episode two was a long two-hander between Kat and Zoe in which they came together and parted, whispered and shouted, fought and were still. The camera work was more elaborate than usual: a moving camera around the table at the women's celebration matched the ebb and flow of the jokes and stories, weaving the women into intimacy while close-ups scrutinised individual reactions. Unusual devices – the voice-overs of the women, in the first episode, as the visuals showed their men, extreme close-ups of eyes at painful moments – drew attention to the *mise-en-scène* while, less overtly, the use of closed doors to separate characters and open doorways to frame them underpinned Kat's tale of how she, as a frightened girl, had overheard the adults deciding what should be done with her and her unborn baby. Stories and photographs, a common way of referring to the past in soaps, were reinforced in the final episode by highly unusual flashbacks of the catastrophic event. Acting was showcased: as Jessie Wallace recreated her character as a child, she lightened her voice and changed her facial expression so that the 13-year-old Kat could be seen struggling through. The writing could handle not only Kat's set-pieces but Garry's solemn ruminations on the nature of love, Charlie's fierce responses and Zoe's shift from a proud assertion of self-confidence at the hen night to mute incomprehension in the final episode.

Crucially, the motif of the moon bound this complex *mise-en-scène* together. The first episode begins with a shot of the moon shining over the square and the strains of 'Blue Moon' can be heard from the pub. In the 'truth or dare' game at the hen night, Dot tells of a stolen kiss and astonishingly finishes the story with a quotation from Dylan Thomas about the 'mile high moon'. The alternating party scenes are bathed in warm light and bright colours but other, more intimate scenes are lit by the cold, blue moonlight. Zoe, for instance, listens to the first part of Kat's account from behind the closed door of her bedroom, her face turned up to the moon. The motif of the moon is specifically alluded to, in a key scene in the third episode, when Kat reminds her father of the promise he had made her, when she was six years old, that the Man in the Moon would keep her safe when she was in bed. As the moon shines in on the grown-up Kat, she tells her father how the moon had shone down on her when Harry had entered her room to abuse her, making her realise that, despite her father's promise, she was no longer safe. Later, Kat looks up at the moon as she sits in the Square, planning suicide. And the final image of the week was of a full moon, dramatically filling the screen as Zoe left the Square and Kat looked up from her hospital bed.

Is it fanciful to link this to a Victorian narrative painting 'Past and Present' by August Egg, a work of rather different artistic prestige, which hangs in Tate Britain gallery? It is a triptych, telling the story of a fallen woman. The central, larger picture shows the adulterous wife, lying on the floor, having apparently been pushed away by her husband while her small daughters look uncomprehendingly on. The pictures on either side show the situation years later: in one, the rejected wife is destitute, sheltering at night under an arch looking over the Thames; in the other, her grown-up daughters are alone and sad in a bare room. In these two pictures, the implacable moon shines down, just as it had on Kat and Zoe, giving a temporal unity to the two scenes but emphasising the desolate isolation of the scattered family. 'Past and Present' is working within a strong tradition of melodrama and it is this term we need to use to understand what is going on in these episodes of *EastEnders*

Melodrama, a negative word for television critics, tends to be seen as a strong but undesirable element in British television, marked by stock characters, predictable narrative moments and over-wrought acting. But in its handling of the abuse storyline, *EastEnders* seemed to be drawing on something more dynamic that, in its theme and use of metaphors, was more akin to the definitions of melodrama developed outside television studies. In looking at cinema, Christine Gledhill (1987) drew specifically on Peter Brook's study, *The Melodramatic Imagination*, for her influential discussion of how the term might be used in film analysis. She identified a number of features of melodrama that included: the notion of melodrama as an aesthetic response to the social upheaval in society; the construction of a highly polarised world view in which good and evil are clearly delineated, and in which evil threatens to overwhelm good; the personification of good as an innocent woman and sexual seduction or rape as the vehicle of the threat; and the eventual assertion of good when the woman speaks in order to name and identify evil. The enactment of this struggle, Gledhill suggested, 'draws into a public arena desires, fears, values and identities which lie beneath the surface of the publicly acknowledged world' (Gledhill 1987: 33).[2]

Just as the parallels with 'Past and Present' help to position the aesthetic devices of these *EastEnders* episodes so this broader description of nineteenth-century melo-drama illuminates the story of the Slaters in which the rape of Kat and the secret of Zoe's birth are finally made public. Kat's strong maternal feelings, Zoe's confusion about her identity, Charlie's unacknowledged disgust at his own daughter's preg-nancy struggle up to the surface and have to be faced. The abuser is identified and Kat confronts Harry as evil, insisting on the fact of her innocence while despairing at the way the abuse had distorted her sexual feelings. Yorke later described the story as a morality play that involved 'helping others, exposing evil and giving voice to the voiceless' (Yorke 2002), a classic description of the melodramatic impulse.

Representing a 'society under siege'

Why then should *EastEnders* use melodramatic tropes to tell this story despite the undervaluing of this mode on British television? With their strong tradition of dealing progressively with social issues, British soaps claim to provide reassurance and support for women both in the storylines (women work to reclaim their own lives) and the helplines that are advertised at the end of each episode. So we could

see the Slater story as a reflection of contemporary issues with perhaps a sensationalist element generated by the story's connections to the 'name and shame'
approach of the popular press. But that does not seem to explain fully the story's
intensity and, in particular, the use of the moon not just as a striking image but as
an over-full signifier comparable to that of the Victorian painting. Such imagery
seemed to indicate a more overwhelming sense of loss and of fate being worked
out under the implacable moon.

Gledhill, following Brook, linked film melodrama to broader upheavals in society
and I would suggest that something similar is happening with British soaps at the
beginning of the twenty-first century. One of the key issues in the storyline is lack of
trust. Zoe is shattered to learn that the family relationships she had taken for granted
were based on lies. Kat's trust in the adults of her family, her father and mother as
well as her uncle, had been abused since one result of her uncle's abuse is that her
own father believes her to be sexually guilty. Questions of trust, risk and instability
have been much debated by contemporary philosophers and sociologists, including
Zygmunt Bauman. Drawing on a range of work on globalisation and the risk society,
Bauman, in *Society under Siege*, argues that we increasingly find ourselves in a position
in which we can trust in nothing except, rather despairingly, ourselves. Global business practices demand fluid and unstable modes of organisation that nation states are
proving powerless to control or ameliorate. Families, communities and relationships
all seem vulnerable, jobs are on short contracts, skills become obsolete. The nation
state, he argues, is becoming incapable of providing the economic and social support
we call society and individuals are thrown back on 'biographical solutions' (Bauman
2002: 36), individual attempts to deal with uncertainty by seeing life as a series of
new starts, of relationships that are never stable and of self-improvement plans that
are never achieved. 'What seems to be gone' he suggests 'is the image of society as
the "common property" of its members which at least in principle can be conceivably
tended to, run and managed in common' (Bauman 2002: 49). And if private life has
become something individuals try to manage rather than something that the state
organises, then outside ourselves we have 'a horrifying sense of a world that is neither
managed nor, as far as one can see, manageable' (Bauman 2002: 18).

Bauman himself uses television for some of his examples and his work can be
well applied to British soap opera. If we accept that the structures and stabilities
which sustained the idea of society are under siege, we can see that this might
pose specific problems for television programmes that have their basis in the
realist representation of a socially cohesive world. For a time, British soap operas
indeed seemed to be working against the notion that society was irrelevant, a
point the BBC's Head of Drama, Mal Young, specifically made when defending
them at a television conference: 'Mrs Thatcher used the 80s to dismantle the
community, encouraging us to become more self-obsessed, while all along we
clung to the hope and optimistic feeling that still existed in our soaps' (quoted in

the *Guardian*, 17 September 1999). The emphasis was on communal action at times of crisis, on people's day-to-day contacts with their neighbours and on clear roles for a variety of individuals who were connected in a common space. The characters and stories that came out of this nexus provided a vivid illustration of how society could, to repeat Bauman's phrase, be 'tended to, run and managed in common'. That this process was sometimes difficult and fractious, especially in *EastEnders*, is less important for this argument, than the example it offered of how society, in a local and national context, could be conceptualised.

It seems to me, however, that the Slater story is an example of how the increasing use of melodrama on British television can be seen not as a set of devices nor indeed a response to the production conditions necessary to produce the required number of episodes but as an expression of an aesthetic world view. The turn to melodrama can be understood as a way of trying to fill the vacuum created by the instabilities and lack of trust that Bauman describes and the consequent inadequacies of realism as an explanatory mode. And so gradually in *EastEnders* we can see a different aesthetic taking shape marked by the following shift:

Traditional realist modes	*Melodramatic modes*
relative moral values	extremes of good and evil
consistent, complex characters	characters reworked to personify good and evil in particular stories
characters in relationships, relationships to be worked through	isolated characters, relationships to be escaped from
strong women characters	women as victims
stories as ongoing	stories as special events
everyday stories with liberal lessons	extreme stories of death, violence
deferral of moral judgments	clear moral judgments
territorial, internal geography, space defined by community	symbolic spaces (gravesides, cliff edges) outside soap's territory
time in parallel with viewer	time organised dramatically
talk and discussion	visual rendering of emotional state
no music	music (but still diegetically sourced)
continuous stories	endings
significant objects embedded	symbolic objects highlighted
urban space, man-made setting	weather, countryside, nature as symbolic devices
melodramatic devices restrained by realism	melodramatic devices feed into sensationalism
stoicism, endurance, getting by	crying, fighting, going for broke
community as a resource	individuals outside society

The differences between the two modes indicate a shift that has several dimensions – a shift from the emphasis on individuals in a community to those who feel isolated and unsupported; a change in the deployment of time and space to emphasise that moral isolation; a change in aesthetics with a greater emphasis on symbols, settings, camera work and lighting that help to express inner emotion. And although traditional morality normally wins out and the bad characters suffer or disappear, the effect of this shift to the melodramatic mode is to present a world that is darker and more precarious than before, to represent indeed a society under siege.

Kat's and Zoe's story demonstrates a number of features associated with the melodramatic mode. This was a special story, trailed extensively as a special event. The usual organisation of time on a day-by-day basis was abandoned so that while the episodes ran through the week the events told occurred in a single night. Objects such as the moon, Zoe's teddy bear and a whisky bottle are given close-ups that emphasise their symbolic meaning rather than their function as realist props. The task of the story is to delineate clearly the evil action of abuse and to demand clarity of judgement; Charlie's muddled attempt to see more than one point of view is singled out as inappropriate. For this to happen, Kat has to be reinvented as innocent, hence the emphasis in the *mise-en-scène* on recreating the childhood scene of the moon shining into her bedroom; it is significant also that during these scenes Lynne's white wedding dress hung on the bedroom door, a reminder of Kat's loss and a visual reinforcement of the white light of the moon. Although other family members tried to help, Kat and Zoe were presented as isolated victims not only of specific events but also of fate itself; indeed, once Harry had been driven out, Peggy was also shown sitting alone and abandoned in the moonlight. All three women were, at this point, beyond the help that might be offered by the community's social structures. While the action was not particularly violent, it was characterised by the direct expression of extreme emotion, particularly in the second episode, a two-hander between Kat and Zoe. And finally the four episodes worked as a whole, with the story raised and resolved during this period, the resolution being given narrative form with Harry's expulsion and Kat's recovery from her suicide bid, and aesthetic closure achieved by the final image of the moon that referred back to the first shot.

EastEnders has not entirely abandoned the traditional forms of its origins. Indeed, it is possible to identify strong elements of its more usual stoical realism in these episodes, for instance in the communal way in which the drunken Garry and his friends celebrate his stag night. Other dramatic stories since 2000, including, I would argue, most of a storyline dealing with the domestic violence suffered by another Slater sister, Little Mo, continued to be handled in the more progressive realist manner of the community-orientated British soap. It is also true that *EastEnders* has since its inception called on melodramatic tropes for some of its stories and characters, in particular in its representation of the dastardly Nick Cotton who had the evil panache of a Victorian villain.

However, I would argue that, in the early 2000s, the programme has adopted melodramatic tropes more consistently and boldly for its big storylines and that the aesthetic is used not only for the clear delineation of morality but also to express a darker vision of the world than was previously the case. Other examples of such storylines, most of which were screened in ways that diverged from the normal schedule, would be the argument between Phil and Lisa about the disputed custody of their child, which took place on the edge of a cliff in a remote part of Portugal; the death of Jamie in which the motif of the moon, this time as a symbol of constancy, reappeared; the kidnapping and fire that brought to an end Trevor's reign of terror over his wife Little Mo in contrast to the legal system that had failed her; and, perhaps the most extraordinary story of all in this context, Dot Cotton's crisis of faith in which she was shown weeping in the empty church, abandoned by God.[3]

It is perhaps important to note that the programme presses its melodramatic stories not as postmodern pastiches to be watched ironically but as emotionally saturated expressions of loss. John Ellis suggested that television 'provides a relatively safe area in which uncertainty can be entertained, and be entertaining' (Ellis 2000: 82). Watching *EastEnders* is not in the great scheme of things 'unsafe' and yet it seems to me that the programme has been giving full rein to the perils of uncertainty in a way that is made the more poignant because of the previous notion of the positive resources of community and social progress. Melodrama is supposed to be an ameliorative and consoling form in which order is restored but, in this version of it, the capacity of melodrama to represent the fears beneath the surface challenges its capacity to assuage them.

Critical responses – judging melodrama

In isolating these episodes of *EastEnders* and reading them with the grain of melodrama, I am working against the usual way of looking at soaps. This was not a move the television critics of the day were willing to make. We can divide the critical press coverage of the programme into three – listings; recommendations to view; and post-viewing reviews.[4] Almost all papers carried a brief description of the programme in their television schedules. Nearly all of these were fairly standard accounts taken from publicity that give tantalising hooks to view. Sometimes they cannot resist making a dig, as the *Independent*'s comment on the second episode indicates: 'tension grows in the Slater household which is about as predictable as saying that Pauline looks a bit miserable or that there's something not quite right about Terry's hair'. Recommendations identify programmes for the viewers trying to construct an evening's viewing. Most broadsheet or 'quality' newspapers did not recommend *EastEnders* to their readers that week and, even when *EastEnders* is flagged up, generic boundaries are clearly maintained: the programmes should be viewed by soap viewers. Thus, the *Evening Standard* recommended the first episode as 'an absolute stormer' but saves its drama recommendation for a series, *Bob and Rose*, while the specialist *Radio Times* previewed the episodes in its 'Soap Flannel' column. The reviews of the programmes were even more limited. Ian Hyland of the *Sunday Mirror* reviewed it favourably and the specialist soap reviewer, Jaci Stephen, in the *Daily Mail*'s 'Soap Watch' column praised 'an extraordinary week in *EastEnders*' history'. The regular television reviewers of *The Times*, the *Independent*, *Daily Telegraph*, *Daily Mail* and their Sunday equivalents ignored it in favour of a variety of other programmes including single plays, documentaries, reality television programmes and the US series *Band of Brothers*. The *Guardian* was the exception: the regular reviewer Gareth McLean gave his whole column to the first episode while the veteran reviewer Nancy Banks-Smith later commented on the whole week more favourably.

These episodes of *EastEnders* failed therefore to break the tradition that serious television reviewing does not discuss long-running serials. What such critics might have made of it is hinted at by the *Telegraph*'s James Walton in a review of another drama that, he says, managed to avoid any 'soap opera shenanigans' by having its leading characters behave 'throughout with a level of restraint that Trevor Howard and Celia Johnson might have envied'. Despite the inevitable irony practised by television reviewers, it is possible to see here a valuing of emotional restraint, the lack of which is automatically associated with soap operas. This ironic approach is also apparent in some of the praise offered. The *Evening Standard*'s 'Soap Box', recommending the second episode, comments 'It's waterworks and mascara all over the place as Zoe struggles to cope with the news that Kat is now mummy dearest.' Here is the reverse of restraint, a knowing wallowing in emotion with a reminder of the grotesqueries of Joan Crawford for good measure. Hyland's enthusiastic review praised the 'best week of *EastEnders* this year – great acting, award-winning, etc. etc.' but confesses to inappropriate laughter at Kat's appearance despite the demand for tears. The vocabulary and tone of these comments have a similar pattern – an acknowledgment of emotional affect is immediately warded off by a joke aimed at the very character, Kat, with whom the audience is being asked to identify. Alison Graham in 'Soap Flannel' takes a similar tack with a different emphasis:

> Before long we have plunged deep into Chekhov territory (though it's not
> *The Cherry Orchard*, more like *The Allotment*).... There is much weeping and

wailing and possibly even rending of garments as the full import of the dark-
ness at the heart of this family becomes apparent.

Here the 'weeping and wailing' is warded off by what appears to be mockery of
the soap's artistic pretensions, with smart references to the Bible and Conrad as
well as the (wide of the mark) Chekhov allusion.

Gareth McLean's review is the most extensive and in some ways the most
extreme. It is headed 'Secrets and Lies' as if continuing the ironic referencing of
higher culture, in this case Mike Leigh's 1996 film. The review begins with two
columns of parody presenting 'an exclusive extract from ... Secret Diary of Kat
Slater'. This extraordinary outburst comments on her way of speaking, her television viewing, her appearance, her choice of clothes and her promiscuous sexuality
with references to specific shops (Argos, Pizza Hut, Mark One) and behaviour that
pin her down in terms of class and gender. This section finishes with Kat going for
a night out – 'Now where did I put me coil?' – and thus segues into the first
episode via an extended metaphor that compares the Slaters' troubles to shit
hitting the fan and thus besmirching various examples of pure whiteness ('an
immaculate room', 'white silk', 'newly laundered linen'). McLean then makes a
scatological (and allegedly ironic) connection between this shit and the Indian meal
the women eat at the hen night. The review is written in clotted prose but it seems
there are some things to praise: there are 'mercifully few embarrassing "artistic
touches"', it is 'bursting with tension'. McLean suggests that soap writing has got
better and the review ends with what might be a compliment about the handling of
narrative: 'if soaps' success relies upon their open-endedness and the delay of gratification that comes with closure, this week's *EastEnders* is positively tantric'.

McLean's ironic mode is handled savagely but its patronising approach to character and television audience gives him no position from which to actually deal with
Kat's story as television drama. It is hard to tell whether McLean is unaware of his
own hysterical determination to damn Kat when reviewing a storyline that works to
render her innocent or whether he is elaborately challenging the melodramatic
modes used to tell the story. Jaci Smith and Nancy Banks-Smith are mercifully free
from irony (and this seems to be deliberate since both can use humour effectively in
their columns). Smith describes 'exquisitely written episodes, finely acted, understated direction (although a bit heavy on that cardboard-style full moon effect)' while
Banks-Smith praises the episodes 'as exceptionally well written', points to Tony
Jordan's repeated use of a closed door as 'a symbol of estrangement' and gives a
sympathetic nod to particular moments including Dot's use of poetry. One could
disagree with these reviews but they are, at least, rooted in acute observation that
responds to the emotional pull of the storylines rather than using irony to ward it off.

The vocabulary of the critics with their emphasis on 'weeping and wailing'
largely failed to convey what *EastEnders* was doing that week. The *Radio Times*

later carried a number of readers' letter that praised the episodes and this may have prompted the editorial comment that also appeared. The editor, to praise the programme, had to put it once again into a realist framework, suggesting that it 'confounded those critics who say that soaps cannot handle social issues' and linking it to *Band of Brothers*, which had been given more respectful attention: 'in having the courage to tackle painful truths, both programmes have struck a similar chord'. By contrast, I would argue that it is only when the programme's melodramatic resonances are taken seriously that its aesthetic and dramatic qualities can be best understood and critically judged.

Notes

1 A DVD about the Slaters was issued by the BBC in November 2003 and this episode is one of a number featured on the BBC's *EastEnders* classic clips website at www.bbc.co.uk/eastenders/classicclips/classic_kat_zoe.shtm.

2 It has been more common to discuss US programmes in terms of this broader approach to melodrama. See in particular Feuer and Gripsrud for discussions of US prime-time soaps.

3 Bauman himself, comparing Little Mo to Antigone, commented that 'one can hardly hear the residents of Albert Square mentioning God (the few who do, quickly disappear from the soap saga, as blatantly out of place)' (Bauman 2003: 27). Dot's existential drama proved the dangers of being too categoric about what might happen in soap opera. This shift to melodrama is also taking place in another British soap, *Coronation Street*, though I would argue that it was much less well handled in the 2002/3 story of Richard, the husband as serial killer.

4 The story was heavily promoted by the BBC and featured in the tabloids and magazine articles. The *Sunday Mirror*'s TV Week of 30 September featured Zoe on the cover with a byline that gave away the story.

References

Bauman, Z. (2002) *Society under Siege*, Cambridge: Polity.

—— (2003) *Liquid Love*, Cambridge: Polity.

Cooke, L. (2003) *British Television Drama*, London: BFI.

Ellis, J. (2000) *Seeing Things Television in the Age of Uncertainty*, London: I.B. Taurus.

Feuer, J. (1995) *Seeing through the Eighties: Television and Reaganism*, Durham, NC: Duke University Press.

Gledhill, C. (1987) 'The melodramatic field: an investigation', in *Home is Where the Heart Is*, London: BFI.

Gripsrud, J. (1995) *The Dynasty Years: Hollywood, Television and Critical Media Studies*, London: Routledge.

Hare, D. (2002) 'Why fabulate?' *Guardian*, Saturday Review, 2 February.

Jancovich, M. and Lyons, J. (eds) (2003) *Quality British Television*, London: BFI.

Yorke, J. (2002) 'Our modern morality plays', *Guardian*, 4 September.

Newspaper material on the Slater episodes

Daily Telegraph, James Walton, 4 October 2001, p. 32.

Daily Mail Weekend, 'Soap Watch', Jaci Smith, p. 35.

Evening Standard, 'Previews', 1 October 2001, p. 45; 'Soap Box', 2 October 2001, p. 45.

Guardian G2, 'Secrets and Lies', Gareth McLean, 2 October 2001, p. 22; Nancy Banks-Smith, p. 18.

Independent, Listings, 2 October 2001, p. 16.

Radio Times, 'Soap Flannel', Alison Graham, 29 September–5 October 2001, p. 32.

Radio Times, Editorial, 20–6 October 2001, p. 7.

Sunday Mirror, 'TV Week', Ian Hyland, 7 October 2001.

Section V

New technologies and cultural forms

The industry–society debate foregrounded by Keith Negus in Section IV has a counterpart in the technological determinist–social constructionist debate in new media studies. Sarah Kember implicitly argues for a synthesis, but in a form that attributes more influence to technology than is the current convention. In particular, developing Haraway's work on the cyborg, Kember offers an important challenge to the presumed centrality of humanism in much of media and cultural studies. Here Kember also offers a commentary on the important debates instigated by Lister *et al.* (2003) among others, surrounding the critical question of whether Raymond Williams's (1974) long canonical dismissal of McLuhan's (1964) crude technological determinism has perhaps had the unfortunate effect of removing the materiality of technology from any serious consideration, to a point where technology is now often accredited no agency at all. Kember urges that, in the context of the rebirth of Darwinism, the recent development of sociobiology and the surrounding 'science wars', these matters are now overdue for critical review. She argues that an understanding of biotechnology and the debates around it – which remains, on the whole, outside the conventional terms of reference of media research – is central to making sense of the dynamics, form and influence of new media – including the 'intelligent media' that are now a real possibility.

In his discussion of the increasing importance of computer graphics techniques in the new film industries of 'Siliwood' in which many of today's film stars are digital rather than human characters – 'Synthespians' in his terms – Jonathan Burston offers an argument that might perhaps be seen as a concrete instantiation of the very issues that Kember addresses in more abstract and theoretical terms. In a world where we see a whole new cinematic grammar of technological production rapidly developing, in which 'digital actors' replace those who are now sometimes disparagingly referred to as 'meat puppets' or 'blood actors', Kember's critique of the humanist foundations of the conventional cultural studies approach to these issues has a striking and obvious relevance. As Burston notes, the development of 'synthespianism' has now gone far beyond the marginal realm of 'special effects', and is now an increasingly integral part of film production Among other things, these new 'working cyborgs' who now populate the world of entertainment labour have profound consequences for something that is very rarely considered in studies of media production – the welfare of media workers. The increasing deployment of digital characters in mainstream films (such as *The Lord of the Rings*) may be creating new animation work but, according to Burston, it is likely to affect very adversely the livelihoods and prospects of jobbing actors in an already insecure industry.

Both Janet Harbord and Des Freedman take issue with the view that new technology is transforming the media. In the case of the cinema, argues Harbord, digitisation is contributing an incremental cultural shift. It is facilitating the development of cinema cultures as being different from one another by enabling distinctive production innovations, from storytelling in 4/4 time in 'independent' films to spectacular special effects in Hollywood epics. It is also contributing to an expansion of cinema sites (including improved home viewing) as well as viewing practices. In short, it is advancing a gradual process of pluralisation rather than inaugurating an apocalyptic transformation (whether for good or bad).

Similarly Des Freedman argues that, although the Internet offers much that is valuable and has had a significant impact on traditional media (most notably on recorded music and publishing), it has not been the transformative force that many analysts anticipated. The Internet has been held back by its inability to generate a large income, as well as by technical and access problems. People also tend to visit a narrow range of websites rather than take full advantage of the net's diversity. Old media still command mass audiences, while television remains the main source of news. Indeed, the Internet has come to supplement rather than replace traditional media and thus cannot be argued to adequately offset the continuing shortcomings of established and still-powerful systems of the 'old' media.

References

Lister, M., Dovey, J., Giddings, S., Grant, I. and Kelly, K. (2003) *New Media: A Critical Introduction*, London: Routledge.

McLuhan, M. (1964) *Understanding Media*, London: Routledge & Kegan Paul.

Williams, R. (1974) *Television, Technology and Cultural Form*, London: Fontana.

Chapter 16

Doing technoscience as ('new') media

Sarah Kember

This chapter is concerned with the questions and challenges posed by doing technoscience as 'new' media. The term 'technoscience' refers to the irre- ducibility (connectedness) of science and technology, and I am concerned with the irreducibility (which is not the same as indistinguishability) of science, tech- nology and media. The questions and challenges are both conceptual and methodological, and these are explored below. More implicit in what follows is the *reason* for doing technoscience as 'new' media. The short response is precisely that science, technology and media are becoming – more manifestly, more complexly – connected.

A number of assumptions are being made here: namely that connections between technoscience and new media studies are currently undeveloped (even given the presence, in the messy disciplinary mix, of something called cybercul- ture studies); that it is not possible or desirable to clearly separate (any more than completely collapse) notions of media and technology (and science) or form and content; and that new media forms are (not newly but) increasingly informed by biology. Even if we stop short of accepting the universalism (and fatalism) of Marshall McLuhan's vision of all media technologies as extensions of the human body (1964), it is clear that, in different ways and at different times, we engage with the media on a physical as well as intellectual or imaginative level. It is not necessary to strike an anti-Cartesian philosophical pose in order to assert this, and indeed Roland Barthes put it succinctly and rather poignantly in his last work *Camera Lucida* (1980). Declaring his 'ultimate dissatisfaction' with critical language (Barthes 1980: 8) he resolves to make himself 'the measure of photographic "knowledge"', asking 'what does my body know of Photography?' (Barthes 1980: 9). With the widespread development of biotechnology since that time – I refer here not just to the technologisation of biology from mechanical metaphors of the heart as pump to the genetic informationalisation of life itself, but also to the biologisation of technology from cybernetics to artificial intelligence to artificial life – it was arguably only a matter of time until biotechnology became more than simply 'content', or the subject of documentaries, science fiction films and so on.

It has long been my contention that over at least the past decade there has been and continues to be a widespread cultural evolutionism (Kember 2001, 2002, 2003) – a resurgence of 'Darwin among the machines' (Dyson 1997). The source for this cultural evolutionism is partly the hegemonic associated fields of evolutionary psychology, artificial life and genomics, and its rationale is predominantly conservative, an attempt at the 'conceptual containment' as Lynne Segal puts it of 'potentially unlimited shifts in gender beliefs and practices' (1999) and also of the core categories by which Western societies make sense of the world: nature/culture, human/machine for instance. The 'return to Darwin' (Segal 1999) tidies up those categories and kinds that biotechnology messes up, and it does so by underscoring the concept of nature (versus culture). It is a means to renaturalise that which is in the process of being denaturalised.

Evolutionism as a discourse needs to be recognised and responded to not least because of its political efficacy. But evolutionism is more than a discourse, it is a praxis, a means of developing (as well as selling) media and/as technologies. Computer programming techniques that simulate genetic, biological and evolutionary processes, and which have been part of the quest for artificial intelligence and artificial life, are becoming part of the story of convergence. In as far as electronic agents and evolutionary computer games already exist, the prospect of intelligent media, the latest chapter in the story of convergence, may not be so futuristic. Intelligent media might include any medium from television and film to fabrics, software and toys that can display biologically based 'behaviours' such as the ability to adapt to the environment, learn and communicate. Apart from the existing well-documented difficulties experienced, for example at MIT, in getting biologically based technologies to 'scale-up' to anything remotely resembling intelligent behaviour (Kember 2003), the only truly ridiculous thing about this would be to ignore it. The quest for intelligent media may well fail (the ongoing quest for artificial intelligence arguably failed by the year 2000, the deadline set by Alan Turing for computers to have passed the Turing Test), but that does not mean to say that it will not persist in some way. At the least it is generally agreed that the way in which we talk about and imagine technological forms is directly related to the ways in which they are constructed and implemented. To acknowledge such prospects as intelligent media means to ask pertinent philosophical, political, economic and methodological questions about the meaning and instrumentalisation of 'intelligence' and 'life', and the ways in which those meanings and instrumentalisms might be challenged and contested. Such engagement is characteristic of doing technoscience, so doing technoscience as 'new' media is important in that, quite simply, it offers a means of responding to what some media are becoming, or rather to how some media are evolving.

What are new media and what are they not?

> Those methods and social practices of communication, representation, and expression that have developed using the digital, multimedia, *networked*, computer and the ways that this machine is held to have transformed work in other media: from books to movies, from telephones to television.
>
> (Lister *et al*. 2003: 2)

This is the reasonably uncontroversial definition offered in an important new text that thoroughly problematises and historicises the concept of newness in new media, otherwise characterised through: digitality, interactivity, hypertextuality, dispersal and virtuality.[1] Having acknowledged that 'the newness of new media is, in part, real' (Lister *et al*. 2003: 3) in that there has been and continues to be rapid change and development in the kinds or types of media technologies in circulation, the authors of *New Media: A Critical Introduction* necessarily question the explicit distinction between the 'new' and 'old' media that persists despite increasing familiarity: the no-longer-newness of the new. What, they ask, accounts for the persistence, the seduction of newness in new media? In part, it is regarded as an ideological device, part of the narrative of progress in the West. It is also associated with the designation of a particular, post-1980s PC world of media and communications, and with a general post-1960s world characterised by the transition from modernity to postmodernity, intensifying globalisation and decentralisation, and with the transition from an industrial to a so-called information age (Lister *et al*. 2003: 10). In order to critically assess the qualitative, even epochal transitions attendant upon the quantitative changes wrought by computerisation or more specifically digitisation (Poster 1995),[2] it is necessary to adopt a historical perspective that is non-linear, non-teleological (Bolter and Grusin, 1999).[3] It is also necessary to examine questions of technological power and agency that have been framed within the rather polarised discourses of technological and social determinism (or constructionism). Questions of determinism revolve around 'how far new media and communications technologies, indeed, technologies in general, do actually determine the cultures that they exist within', and conversely, 'how cultural factors shape our use and experience of technological power' (Lister *et al*. 2003: 4). In order to illustrate and explore these positions, Lister *et al*. make effective, dramatic if somewhat reductive use of the work of Marshall McLuhan and Raymond Williams and their debate with each other over questions of technological power during the 1960s and 1970s.[4] This debate is presented as being relevant now to a consideration of new media, foundational to the division between technological determinism and social constructionism in theories of media and technology, and synonymous with the celebratory versus cynical approaches to anything new in media and technology. So, while McLuhan was wholly concerned with identifying the major cultural effects that he saw new technological forms ... bringing about, Williams sought to show that there is nothing in a particular technology which guarantees the cultural or social outcomes it will have.

(Lister *et al.* 2003: 72)

My aim is neither to valorise nor criticise the restaging of this old drama, which I regard primarily as a device, a means to making what for me is a crucial, highly pertinent point pertaining to what new media are not (but arguably should be). The apparent victory of the Williams position on technology and/as cultural form and the establishment of this position within mainstream media and cultural studies, has had the effect of preempting any serious discussion of the role of technology *itself* in cultural change (Lister *et al.* 2003: 74). In other words, technology is deprived of any agency (in the Williams-inspired discourse of social constructionism) having been assigned too much (in the McLuhan-inspired discourse of technological determinism). Certainly, where the question of technological agency is addressed outside of the terms of all or nothing, such as in Actor Network Theory[5] and other aspects of science and technology studies, the question has not been readily integrated within (new) media studies. Lister *et al.* ask whether Williams's humanism should not be critically examined along with McLuhan's determinism (Lister *et al.* 2003: 74). They ask what implications distributed human/machine agency might have for our understanding of both culture and nature (Lister *et al.* 2003: 90). Donna Haraway (1991) explored precisely those implications through her concept of the cyborg or cybernetic organism,[6] regarded by Lister *et al.* as a recurrence of McLuhan's thesis of media technologies as extensions of the human senses. For them, the biological or 'physicalist' emphasis in McLuhan is 'precisely what humanism in cultural and media studies has been unable to address' (Lister *et al.* 2003: 90) and it potentially reopens the question of the relation between biological and technological things. For me, doing this would seem to be fundamental to an adequate analysis of aspects of new media such as: the development of electronic agents or avatars;[7] evolutionary computer games;[8] evolutionary robotics;[9] computer simulation and synthesis of biological forms and processes (such as online virtual ecosystems complete with artificial life forms).[10] These are examples of the metaphoric and material evolutionism that has recently characterised some media form and content, but if we are to take seriously the seemingly endless dispersal of media technology into everyday life, and if 'life' is to be recognised in terms that are not merely cultural, but rather 'naturecultural' (Haraway 2000), then how is it possible to conceive of developments in, for example, mobile technology outside of the terms of biotechnology? If a mobile phone held to the ear is not to be regarded as a biotechnology (and a hands-free set isn't either) then what if/when it is worn inside the ear as a rather sophisticated earplug and is no longer visible externally? At what point, at which boundary, does it become possible to address the relationship between the body and media, between biology and technology? This relationship is central to studies in technoscience.

Why technoscience?

Where, for Lister *et al.*, 'new conceptions of the biological body's relationship to technological media' (Lister *et al.* 2003: 12) is already a concern for an inclusive field of new media, for me it is not, yet Media studies, including new media studies is, as the authors in fact demonstrate in their analysis of the debate between McLuhan and Williams, actually very shy of the biological and of science in general. Donna Haraway, an influential figure in many related fields but a rather marginal one in media studies, employs the concept of 'technoscience' (1997)[11] in order to refute the false distinction between science and technology, but it seems to me that within the current field of new media this concept is not fully accepted, and that this is a vital error, not least considering the huge cultural significance of biotechnology (as a technoscience) in the late twentieth and twenty-first century. Some of the most important political, ethical, social and economic issues are currently converging under the banner of biotechnology, and in a recent interview Haraway validates the argument that biology, or the new biology 'woven in and through information technologies and systems ... is one of the great "representing machines" of the century, superseding film – or literature in the 19th century' (Haraway 2000: 26). From health and food industries to environmentalism, management and intellectual property law, 'there is almost nothing you can do these days', she says, 'that does not require literacy in biology' (Haraway 2000: 26).

Part of what this turn to biology signifies socially and culturally is a return to Darwin, or what is more broadly characterised as 'neo-Darwinism' or 'ultra-Darwinism'. Neo-Darwinism generally refers to post-1953 genetically informed Darwinism[12] where ultra-Darwinism refers to a particular and controversial type often termed 'fundamentalist' and associated with genetic determinism.[13] For Segal, the goal of ultra-Darwinism 'is a return to the allegedly more rigorous authority of the biological sciences of much that has recently been understood as cultural' (Segal 1999: 78). Ultra-Darwinism seeks to root gender and other aspects of identity (and indeed politics) in the biological rather than the social, in nature rather than culture, and so it seeks to close down on possibilities for change (the biological and the natural are regarded here as fixed essences). A key factor in the science wars between academic feminists and academic physicists, post-structuralist cultural theory and scientific realism, ultra-Darwinism flourished while Marxism faded, seeking to supplant a utopian with a tragic vision of the human condition. The tragic vision 'recognises that humans are "inherently limited in knowledge, wisdom and virtue, and all social arrangements must acknowledge those limits"', whereas the utopian vision presents human limitations as 'artefacts that come from our social arrangements' and as surmountable (Malik 2002: 47). Kenan Malik extrapolates the tragic political vision in Steven Pinker's most recent contribution to the cause of ultra-Darwinism, *The Blank Slate*:

> Science has revealed the primacy of family ties, the limited scope of communal sharing, and the universality of violence, dominance and ethnocentrism. It has shown human nature to be fixed, human beings to be flawed and human politics to be constrained by the inadequacies of the human psyche. Since 'our moral sentiments, no matter how beneficent, overlie a deeper bedrock of selfishness', Pinker suggests, 'we should not aim to solve social problems like crime or poverty, because in a world of competing individuals one person's gain may be another person's loss. The best we can do is to trade off one cost against another'.
>
> (Malik 2002: 47)

More than a turn to the right, this represents a turn away from history to biology in the conceptualisation and formation of politics. It is a new, or renewed form of social Darwinism that is mitigated only by the extent of internal as well as external dissent (see Andrew Brown's *The Darwin Wars*) and which is a factor not just 'in' but 'of' the media. Darwinism, particularly ultra-Darwinism, has not just featured significantly in the media content of recent years, it is also a factor in the development – or evolution – of media technologies themselves. Moreover, this evolutionism of media and technologies is more than metaphoric, or even productively metaphoric. It is also technical, material. One such technique is connectionism, a form of computer modelling that is based on the function of neurones in the brain, and hence sometimes referred to as neural networking. Connectionism works through a network or system of interconnected units that function simultaneously. It demonstrates the process of self-organisation and contributes to the problematic evolutionism of the Internet (Kember 2001). Self-organisation is one of a number of biological properties that has been used to describe and develop technologies. Others include self-replication, evolution, emergence and autonomy, all of which are attributed to particular forms of computerisation: cellular automata[14] and genetic algorithms.[15] These are central to the simulation and synthesis of artificial life forms and worlds that underlie sophisticated computer games, telecommunications research and development, military and medical research and development, the concept of intelligent media and even more banal commercial problem-solving applications such as routing and scheduling (Kember 2003).[16] The convergence between biology (particularly molecular and evolutionary biology) and technology underlies the condition of virtuality and is a characteristic of new media. It is dominated and driven by three related discourses: artificial life, evolutionary psychology and genomics. What follows is a brief outline of these three discourses and an indication of existing methodological approaches within technoscience studies that might provide some parameters or suggestions for how to do technoscience as new media.

Which technoscience?

Artificial life is a development of artificial intelligence that is based on a more biological, less psychological approach to the creation of intelligent machines. The aim here is not merely to simulate but to synthesise intelligent life forms – to 'grow' them from the bottom-up rather than to persist with arguably failed attempts to programme them from the top-down. The premise of this particular narrative is that in order to understand life (or intelligent life) it is necessary to put it together rather than take it apart, and so artificial life is presented as an anti-reductionist, anti-rationalist discourse in its turn to, or return to, the body. Intelligent artificial life forms are then characterised as being embodied, autonomous, self-organised, emergent, evolving. Evolutionary psychology constructs an evolutionary theory of mind such that human behaviour is regarded as a facet not (so much) of learning and the environment but of processes of natural selection operating on our genes during the long period of evolutionary history covering the Pleistocene era of hunters and gatherers (Barkow *et al.* 1992). This era determined to a degree the gender roles and rules of psychosocial and sexual engagement that are manifested today and are posited within this framework as being universals (such as masculine dominance, heterosexual normativity and the privileging of hereditary and family ties over others). Genomics is the multidisciplinary field surrounding the Human Genome Project that is engaged in the thorniest debates of the moment: the relative influence on human behaviour and identity of learning and inheritance, genes and the environment, plus the bioethical implications of genetic screening, manipulation and inter-species transfer (transgenesis). It is interesting that, as it enters its second decade and the new millennium, artificial life's agenda-setters are strengthening the association between these three fields such that software artificial life forms are seen to 'exist', or come to life in virtual worlds or ecosystems that operate according to neo-Darwinian principles and are designed to rapidly re-produce then supersede the evolutionary history that produced human intelligence. So the concern here is with the accelerated evolution of new artificial species, replete, at their most advanced, with simulated neural networks, biochemistries and genomes. Artificial life, like genomics (incorporating genomics), operates at the interface between biology and technology, nature and culture, human and machine – raising questions about what *post*-human life *is*, and what it might/*ought* to be.

In *Our Posthuman Future*, Francis Fukuyama argues – in defence of a liberal democracy supposedly threatened by the development of biotechnology – that it is necessary to focus more on the current 'is' of human life than on the 'ought' of a life that is in increasing danger of becoming post-human (2002). The danger, for him, lies in the increasing separation between human nature and human rights. His sense of the threat posed to human nature by the advent of biotechnology is reminiscent of a scene from Samuel Beckett's *Endgame* involving two unfortunate creatures whose humanity, if not 'post', is certainly in question:

HAMM: Nature has forgotten us
CLOV: There's no more nature
HAMM: No more nature! You exaggerate

(1964 [1958]: 16)

Fukuyama, like Clov, exaggerates for effect. The effect in his case is to legitimise US state intervention and control over a global multinational industry that appears to have almost evolutionary autonomy, and to underscore the liberal humanism that informs modern democracies. The side-effect of Fukuyama's intervention, his privileging of 'is' over 'ought', nature over culture, ontology over (ethico)epistemology, is a (side) entrance into the science wars where all aspects of the new biology – including artificial life, evolutionary psychology and genomics – become part of the battle between left and right, academic feminists and academic physicists, constructivists and naturalists. Fukuyama aligns himself with the naturalists, with those concerned with what human life is, in order to resist what he perceives as being the political menace of a post-human future.

The science wars, or more specifically what Andrew Brown terms the 'Darwin Wars' (1999), are a phenomenon of the mid-1990s (arguably sparked by the publication of Gross's and Levitt's *Higher Superstition: The Academic Left and its Quarrels with Science*, 1994) that rehearse arguments for and against the sociobiology of the 1970s, and which echo C.P. Snow's 'Two Cultures' debates of the late 1950s. Those who, in the 1970s, were opposed to biological explanations of human social divisions and relations argued that they were effectively naturalised, and the voice of opposition came not just from outside the field of biology but also, and perhaps most convincingly, from within. Andrew Brown suggests that biologist Steven Rose and geneticist Richard Lewontin were among the most effective critics of sociobiology and that most of their objections were incorporated into the evolutionary psychology project, which is then constituted as being 'revisionist' (Rose and Rose 2000). This revisionism does indeed appear to be the aim of John Ashworth who, as director of the

LSE in the mid-1990s, added his authority to the EP-based Darwin@LSE programme. Introducing a special issue of *Demos Quarterly* (1996), Ashworth calls for a 'sensitive' repackaging of the old sociobiological conflict between altruistic behaviour and the doctrine of the selfish gene. Where E.O. Wilson in the 1970s lacked a sufficiently sophisticated genetics and was too 'assertive' in his claims, the new Darwinists, says Ashworth, can afford to adopt a more conciliatory tone that 'might now lead to something other than a dialogue of the deaf' (Ashworth 1996: 3). This new sensitivity and conciliation produces an apparently non-deterministic, morally corrected Darwinism in which genetic programming does not quite preclude social conditioning, and in which universality is mediated by small degrees of variation. The way things are is then not *necessarily* synonymous with the way things should be. That evolutionary psychology is a sanitised form of sociobiology and both economically (Nelkin 2000) and politically (Segal 1999) expedient is beyond serious doubt, and Lynne Segal responds with understandable scepticism to an invitation to dialogue from a field that clearly seeks to subsume cultural into biological explanations of human behaviour, and which has been described as 'fundamentalist' (Rose and Rose 2000; Gould 2000). The problem as I see it is that lack of alternative to dialogue as a strategy for engaging with fields in which the voices of resistance and opposition have already been assimilated. Evolutionary psychology engages in great detail with, and defines itself according to, feminist and social scientific criticism that therefore cannot be effective simply by being repeated. Artificial life incorporates anti-Cartesian philosophy in its quest to re-embody artificial intelligence. It is defined against the rationalist, masculinist, reductionist tendencies of physics-based artificial intelligence, and is, like evolutionary psychology, a revisionist discourse. Genomics is organised precisely around the conflict between nature and nurture that has long preoccupied feminist and cultural theory suggesting that there might be a need for a closer engagement. By this I don't mean to advocate the kind of 'scientific literacy' that is often demanded of 'humanists' in the science wars, but rather to align with calls for new languages, new forms of communication (Stengers 1997) that visibly cross the great nature/culture divide. The dissent within the new biology certainly, as Steven and Hilary Rose put it, 'demands a reply' (Rose and Rose 2000: 8). The question, then, is what kind of reply? This of course is a question of methodology, but, more than that, a reply or response to the complex dynamics of contemporary biotechnology potentially opens out the political and ethical sphere to include not just other humans but other, non-human agents (animals, machines) networked, connected or spliced together in novel and challenging ways.

Methodologies and more

I have argued, in effect, that resistance or opposition to the new biology is futile. This is not to say that critique is futile and consent inevitable. Dialogue is, rather, one strategy for change – one that might be indicative, for example, of the recent exchanges between feminism and biology – as well as a more adequate reflection of the increasingly complex 'intra-action' (Barad 2000) or 'trafficking' (Franklin *et al.* 2000) between all of the terms of nature and culture (including biology and technology). The effectiveness of this and allied approaches is contingent upon the risks taken, and for Isabelle Stengers risk-taking is vital to a renewed and responsible 'good' science as well as to meaningful cultural analysis. Risk-taking involves the depolarisation of knowledge and the world itself, of epistemologies and ontologies, constructionism and naturalism, and it constitutes the framework for a new alliance-based scientific method capable of approaching the 'undreamed of objects' of contemporary technoscience. Such undreamed of objects have also long been at the centre of Donna Haraway's attention to technoscience, and have been represented through various figurations ranging from the cyborg, vampire, oncomouse, femaleman and modest witness. The modest witness is Haraway's key figuration for science studies and is a direct challenge to the duality of science and nature, subject and object installed within conventional positivistic notions of method. The modest witness embodies a methodology in which all knowledge is situated and therefore partial, not universal. Partial knowledge, like risky science, does not surrender to relativism any more than to a naïve realism but is primarily a more responsible, ethical way of producing knowledge about emergent entities. Within this methodology, subjects encounter other subjects, humans encounter other agents (animal, machine) to which they are connected by new kinds of family ties or kinship.

A methodology for doing technoscience necessarily contains these connections between entities in the world and between the previously distinct, albeit unstable (Latour 1993) categories and concepts (human/machine, human/animal, nature/culture, body/technology and so on) used to organise them. For Karen Barad it is necessarily an 'ethico-epistem-onto-logy', and one that she terms 'agential literacy' as distinct from scientific literacy. Not concerned with the transfer of pristine privileged knowledge to the masses or with the linear cause-and-effect impact of 'nature' on 'culture' or vice versa, agential literacy is both a pedagogy and methodology that reflects and realises the shifting terrain of knowledge itself. This is knowledge no longer clearly demarcated by a knower and a known, a subject and an object and by distinct disciplinary boundaries. The shifting is characterised by Barad not as inter-action (as between separate and fixed realms and entities) but as intra-action (as between connected and fluidly defined realms and entities). Agential literacy is about ethical intra-actions where the notion of dialogue also extends towards the political. Both are strongly influenced by Haraway's formulation of situated knowledge.

In a recent issue of *New Formations*, Phillip Tew and Wendy Wheeler speak, perhaps a little prematurely, of a '*rapprochement* between the two old sparring partners' of the science wars/two cultures debate. It may well be, however, that:

those changes currently underway – especially the widening scientific rejection of positivism, and the renewed phenomenological turn to the lived body and to the complexities of human (and non-human) experience of the lifeworld – hold the promise of theoretical and practical re-engagements in a political and theoretical world of late grown ever more cynical and tired and empty of hope.

(Tew and Wheeler 2003: 7)

The methodological, epistemological and ontological challenge to humanism in media studies as elsewhere, the integration of technoscience and the recognition of human/machine agency that operates outside of the terms of linear cause and effect (genetic, technological, social, economic) determinism and within the realms of complexity opens out or rejuvenates ethical and political questions. These questions are founded on the kinds or types of intra-action, kinship, connectivity and community that are or might be made possible in contemporary technoscientific culture. Neither utopian nor tragic, futuristic nor nostalgic, this nascent politics is informed by both history and biology, and has been spearheaded by a multi- (or trans-) disciplinary feminist and cultural theory concerned with: the rearticulation of matter and discourse in subjectivity (Butler 1993; Grosz 1994; Kirby 1997; Wilson 1998; Fraser 2002); cyborg politics and subjectivity (Haraway 1991; Hables Gray 2002; Braidotti 1994); the articulation of post-humanism (Hayles 1999; Wolfe 1995); evolutionary psychology beyond the science wars (Gray 1997) and the various cultural facets of biotechnology (Haraway 1997; Franklin and Waldby 2000; Kember 2003; Helmreich 1998; Doyle 2003). I have argued elsewhere (2002) that cyborg- or cyberfeminism, rooted as it is in the military, industrial, technoscientific history of cybernetic human/machine systems and equipped with its own complex history of biology and society, is uniquely positioned to adapt strategically to the newly adaptive or evolutionary environment of the new biology. In advocating the kinds of methodologies signalled above, particular dialogic, situated or agentially literate ways of doing technoscience, I am also signalling a kind of history plus biology that would do much to enliven if not repoliticise debates on new media.

By way of a concluding comment I'd like to return to McLuhan, or rather clarify the idea that doing technoscience as new media does not necessarily entail a return or revisionist approach to McLuhan. It is clearly important to revise the dichotomy of determinism/constructionism and to open out questions of agency and the relation between biological and technological things. But McLuhan's fatalism remains a problem for me ('In the history of human culture there is no example of a conscious adjustment of the various factors of personal and social life to new extensions except in the puny and peripheral efforts of artists' etc. [McLuhan 1964: 64]) and what is offered here is not a counsel of either hope or despair in the face of the convergence between biology and media technologies. I have sought to outline more effective strategies than either acceptance or dismissal (both can prove tempting) in the face of, for example, intelligent media and I have begun to outline some of the conceptual and methodological challenges posed to a new field already in need of new alliances.

Notes

1   Digitality in this context refers to 'media that use computers' (Lister *et al.* 2003: 14), where interactivity has been understood as 'the creative management of information', 'consumer choice technologically embodied', 'the death of the author', 'human–computer interaction' and so on (Lister *et al.* 2003: 40). Hypertextuality, similarly difficult to define, 'has come to describe a text which provides a network of links to other texts that are "outside, above and beyond" itself', and dispersal 'recognises the way in which both the production and distribution of new media have become decentralised, highly individuated and woven ever more closely into the fabric of everyday life' (Lister *et al.* 2003: 30). Virtuality here is understood as an abstraction of virtual reality, jointly applied to different forms of imaging and media technologies, and to 'the very character of everyday life in technologically advanced societies' (Lister *et al.* 2003: 34). See also Pierre Levy's *Becoming Virtual*, Plenum Trade, 1998 and N. Katherine Hayles 'The condition of virtuality', in P. Lunenfeld, *The Digital Dialectic*, MIT Press, 2001. For Hayles, 'Virtuality is the cultural perception that material objects are interpenetrated by information patterns' (p. 68).
2   Poster, writing in the first half of the 1990s, asserts that: 'The digital encoding of sound, text and image, the introduction of fibre-optic lines replacing copper wire, the ability to transmit digitally encoded images and the subsequent ability to compress this information, the vast expansion of the frequency range for wireless transmission, innovations in switching technology and a number of other advances have so enlarged the quantity and types of information that may soon be able to be transmitted that a qualitative change, to allude to Engel's dialectical formula, in the culture may also be imminent' (Poster 1995: 81).
3   Bolter and Grusin reject teleological accounts of new media in which they are regarded as the direct outcome of a linear historical process that is constitutive of progress. New media and technologies within this kind of history are necessarily an improvement on old media and technologies from which they are distinguished by virtue of novelty and to which they are related by virtue of a shared essence.
4   This debate is addressed in detail in the Lister text, which also presents a comprehensive bibliography.
5   For Mike Michael, 'What ANT provides is a conceptualisation of interaction that captures the range of exchanges between heterogeneous actors, say the typically human and non-human' (*Reconnecting Culture*, Routledge, 2000: 21) and Alison Adam states that 'ANT researchers see the possibility of including machines alongside other entities not usually accorded the status of agents … for sociological analysis' (*Artificial Knowing*, Routledge, 1998: 60).
6   Haraway's cyborg is conceived of as a hybrid or boundary creature, agential not in the sense of having a subjectivity but in refiguring the contours of the body and technology, nature and artifice.

7 The development of electronic agents or avatars is widespread in entertainment, military and commercial contexts. See Kember 2003.

8 See for example the 'Sim' games, especially *SimLife* and also *Creatures*.

9 Robotics and the history of automata illustrate the long legacy of the convergence between biology and technology, and are finally brought into the new media framework by Lister *et al.*

10 Again, there is a well-rehearsed history ranging from John Conway's *The Game of Life*, to Thomas Ray's *Tierra*, Richard Dawkins's *Biomorph* and Jane Prophet, Gordon Selley and Mark Hurry's *TechnoSphere*.

11 For Haraway, 'Technoscience extravagantly exceeds the distinction between science and technology as well as those between nature and society, subjects and objects, and the natural and the artifactual that structured the imaginary time called modernity' (Haraway 1997: 3).

12 Watson and Crick's 'discovery' of the structure of DNA put Darwin's theory of evolution by natural selection on a surer footing since the mechanisms of inheritance were elucidated.

13 From being one aspect of the behaviours and characteristics upon which natural selection operates, genes become the sole aspect and from being one mechanism in the process of evolution, natural selection becomes the only one (see Gould 2000).

14 John von Neumann's original 1953 model for a self-reproducing automaton was imagined as an infinitely large checkerboard on which the squares represented cells. He drew an ancestor creature on the board and represented different cell states or activities with colour. The box-shaped creature reproduced by colonising territory, cell by cell. The process was ongoing such that the cellular automaton would eventually model not only self-reproduction but also evolution. Von Neumann's idea was realised by Conway's *The Game of Life* during the 1960s and 1970s (see Steven Levy, *Artificial Life*, Jonathan Cape, 1992).

15 Genetic algorithms are evolutionary computer programs designed to solve computational problems. They were first described by John Holland in the 1960s.

16 Genetic algorithms have become a successful means to solve computational problems through the reproduction, mutation, selection and evolution of 'populations' of possible solutions represented as 'chromosomes' or 'organisms'. See Mitchell and Forrest, 'Genetic algorithms and artificial life', in C. Langton (ed.) *Artificial Life. An Overview*, MIT Press, 1997.

References

Ashworth, J. (1996) 'An "ism" for our times', in O. Curry and H. Cronin (eds) *Demos Quarterly. Matters of Life and Death: The World View from Evolutionary Psychology* 10.

Barad, K. (2000) 'Reconceiving scientific literacy as agential literacy. Or, learning how to intra-act responsibly with the world', in R. Reid and S. Traweek (eds) *Doing Science and Culture. How Cultural and Interdisciplinary Studies Are Changing the Way We Look at Science and Medicine*, New York and London: Routledge.

Barkow, J.H., Cosmides, L. and Tooby, J. (eds) (1992) *The Adapted Mind. Evolutionary Psychology and the Generation of Culture*, New York and Oxford: Oxford University Press.

Barthes, R. (1980) *Camera Lucida*, London: Flamingo.

Beckett, S. (1964 [1958]) *Endgame*, London: Faber & Faber.

Braidotti, R. (1994) *Nomadic Subjects: Embodiment and Sexual Difference in Contemporary Feminist Theory*, New York: Columbia University Press.

Bolter, J. and Grusin, R. (1999) *Remediation: Understanding New Media*, Cambridge, MA, and London: MIT Press.

Brown, A. (1999) *The Darwin Wars: The Scientific Battle for the Soul of Man*, London: Simon & Schuster UK Ltd.

Butler, J. (1993) *Bodies That Matter: On the Discursive Limits of 'Sex'*, London and New York: Routledge.

Doyle, R. (2003) *Wetwares: Experiments in Postvital Living*, Minneapolis and London: University of Minnesota Press.

Dyson, G. (1997) *Darwin among the Machines*, London: Penguin Books.

Franklin, S. Lury, C. and Stacey, J. (2000) *Global Nature, Global Culture*, London: Sage.

Fraser, M. (2002) 'What is the matter of feminist criticism?' *Economy and Society* 31(4), November.

Fukuyama, F. (2002) *Our Posthuman Future: Consequences of the Biotechnology Revolution*, London: Profile Books.

Gray, R. (1997) '"In the belly of the monster": feminism, developmental systems, and evolutionary explanations', in P.A. Gowaty (ed.) *Feminism and Evolutionary Biology*, New York and London: Chapman & Hall.

Gould, S.J. (2000) 'More things in heaven and earth', in H. Rose and S. Rose (eds) *Alas, Poor Darwin: Arguments against Evolutionary Psychology*, London: Jonathan Cape.

Gross, P.R. and Levitt, N. (1998 [1994]) *Higher Superstition. The Academic Left and Its Quarrels with Science*, Baltimore and London: The Johns Hopkins University Press.

Grosz, E. (1994) *Volatile Bodies: Toward a Corporeal Feminism*, Bloomington and Indianapolis: Indiana University Press.

Hables Gray, C. (2002) *Cyborg Citizen*, New York and London: Routledge.

Haraway, Donna J. (1991) *Simians, Cyborgs and Women*, London: Free Association Books.

—— (1997) Modest_Witness@Second_Millennium.FemaleMan©_Meets_OncoMouse™, London: Routledge.

—— (2000) *How Like a Leaf: An Interview with Thyrza Nichols Goodeve*, New York and London: Routledge.

Hayles, N. Katherine (1999) *How We Became Posthuman: Virtual Bodies in Cybernetics, Literature and Informatics*, Chicago and London: The University of Chicago Press.

Helmreich, S. (1998) *Silicon Second Nature: Culturing Artificial Life in a Digital World*, Berkeley and Los Angeles: University of California Press.

Kember, S. (2001) 'Resisting the new evolutionism', *Women: A Cultural Review* 12(1).

—— (2002) 'Reinventing cyberfeminism', *Economy and Society* 31(4), November.

—— (2003) *Cyberfeminism and Artificial Life*, London and New York: Routledge.

Kirby, V. (1997) *Telling Flesh. The Substance of the Corporeal*, New York and London: Routledge.

Latour, B. (1993) *We Have Never Been Modern*, New York: Harvester Wheatsheaf.

Lister, M., Dovey, J., Giddings, S., Grant, I. and Kelly, K. (2003) *New Media: A Critical Introduction*, London and New York: Routledge.

McLuhan, M. (1964) *Understanding Media: The Extensions of Man*, London: Routledge and Kegan Paul Ltd.

Malik, K. (2002) 'Human conditions', *Prospect*, October.

Nelkin, D. (2000) 'Less selfish than sacred? Genes and the religious impulse in evolutionary psychology', in H. Rose and S. Rose (eds) *Alas, Poor Darwin: Arguments against Evolutionary Psychology*, London: Jonathan Cape.

Pinker, S. (2002) *The Blank Slate*, London: Penguin Books.

Poster, M. (1995) 'Postmodern virtualities', in M. Featherstone and R. Burrows (eds) *Cyberspace, Cyberbodies, Cyberpunk: Cultures of Technological Embodiment*, London, Thousand Oaks and New Delhi: Sage Publications.

Rose, H. and Rose, S. (2000) 'Introduction', in H. Rose and S. Rose (eds) *Alas, Poor Darwin. Arguments against Evolutionary Psychology*, London: Jonathan Cape.

Segal, L. (1999) 'Genes and gender: the return to Darwin', in *Why Feminism?* Cambridge: Polity Press.

Snow, C.P. (1998 [1959]) *The Two Cultures*, Cambridge: Cambridge University Press.

Stengers, I. (1997) *Power and Invention: Situating Science*, Minneapolis and London: University of Minnesota Press.

Tew, P. and Wheeler, W. (2003) 'Introduction', *New Formations. Complex Figures* 49, spring.

Waldby, C. (2000) *The Visible Human Project: Informatic Bodies and Posthuman Medicine*, London and New York: Routledge.

Williams, R. (1974) *Television, Technology and Cultural Form*, London: Fontana.

Wilson, E.A. (1998) *Neural Geographies: Feminism and the Microstructure of Cognition*, New York and London: Routledge.

Wolfe, C. (1995) 'In search of post-humanist theory: the second-order cybernetics of Maturana and Varela', *Cultural Critique*, spring.

Chapter 17

Synthespians among us

Rethinking the actor in media work and media theory

Jonathan Burston

'Seamless integration' has long been the Holy Grail of the visual effects world, but now it's within our grasp.

(Edlund 1998: 413)

Where is it? Where *is* it?! They *stole* it from us! My precioussssssss. ...

(Gollum)

Digital stars, digital journeymen, and the military industrial media complex

'For years, Hollywood's f/x community had proclaimed that it was only a matter of time before computer-generated characters played larger roles in major studio productions,' announced veteran industry journalist Marc Graser in *Daily Variety* during a recent run-up to the Oscars. 'That time came in 2002' (Graser 2003). The arrival of computer-generated (CG) actors and a connected boom in special effects (f/x) more generally are now both ubiquitous industry talking points: formerly a town of luvvies, Hollywood is turning into a town of nerds, as f/x talent from Silicon Valley moves southward to Los Angeles in search of new employment opportunities now available there in abundance and 'Siliwood' becomes the newly united movie and video game industry's twenty-first century moniker.

This change in geographical nomenclature signals a profound change at the level of the cinematic text. As is lavishly apparent in blockbusters like *The Lord of the Rings* (*LOTR*) and *Harry Potter* films, but also discreetly evident in films like *Road to Perdition*, f/x work is now so thoroughly woven into contemporary movie-making that it actually makes little sense to speak about 'special effects' anymore. 'What we are witnessing now,' writes Wheeler Winston Dixon, 'is nothing more nor less than the dawn of a new grammar, a new technological production and delivery system, with a new series of plots, tropes, iconic conventions, and stars' (Dixon 2001: 366). Like a rumble in the fault line, Old Hollywood's epistemic ground is shifting, and the fact that the town's new stars are often digital is among the most obvious, though strangely, least theorized components of this new cinematic grammar.

Digital stars aren't the only digital actors getting work, however. 'Gollum' from Peter Jackson's *LOTR* trilogy, 'Stuart Little', and *Harry Potter*'s 'Dobby', each human–software hybrids whose personalities are largely reliant upon the talents of carbon-based actors (Andy Serkis, Michael J. Fox, and Toby Jones, respectively), are perhaps the most prominent examples from 2002. But as Industrial Light and Magic (ILM) senior executive Jim Morris puts it, 'It's a given that major movies don't get made now without digital characters', large or small (Graser 2003). Indeed, digital characters, also known as 'synthespians', come in sundry shapes and sizes, and possess varying degrees of functionality, autonomy, and human–machine hybridity. Humanoid synthespians have been active as extras, bit players, and stunt stand-ins for the stars for a few years now (*Gladiator*, *The Patriot*). Though some are entirely computer-generated, they profit year by year from an ever-amplifying realism, thanks to advances in software. Others benefit from increasingly sophisticated motion-capture technologies, often deploying the recorded movements of human actors to fantastical ends. Similar ends often seem less fantastical, strangely enough, when synthespians take 'alien' forms in movies like the *Men in Black* and *StarWars* features.

But in what can only be understood as a benchmark moment, the human creators of digital actors have recently bestowed upon their offspring the gift of artificial intelligence (AI), and with it the coterminous appellation of 'autonomous agent'. This effectively evacuates from the term 'synthespian' any and all of its coyness or prematurity. Consider Stephen Regelous's justly famous 'Massive' software program, which generated the extraordinary fighting hordes at the Battle of Helm's Deep in *LOTR: The Two Towers*. One day early on in Massive's development, director Jackson and programmer Regelous watched in awe as several thousand characters at Helm's Deep, deploying a variable, 'fuzzy' rather than simple 'binary' logic, 'fought like Hell while, in the background, a small contingent of combatants seemed to think better of it and run away' (Koeppel and Sillery 2002: 44).

Synthespians are becoming less of a novelty in the daily lives of their human counterparts than such whimsical stories suggest. Whimsy, in fact, may be entirely out of place, given how regularly Hollywood's journeymen actors rely on stand-in and extra work to stay fed. Less whimsically still: much AI and synthespian technology originates deep inside the martial precincts of what can now justifiably be termed the military industrial media (MIM) complex, an emerging macro-political formation inside of which Siliwood–Pentagon collaboration has lately been increasing prodigiously. Even before Arnold Schwarzenegger's election to the California governorship, this was evident everywhere: in the growing sophistication of motion simulators doing double duty at theme parks and on air force bases; in computer games like *Quake 3* and *Counter-strike*, which also function as military training platforms; and in TV mini-series like NBC's 1997 *Asteroid*, wherein production access to military hardware and personnel resulted in the spectacular promotion of weapons being developed by NBC parent, General Electric, as part of the 'Star Wars' initiative (Down 2001). That such collaborations take place is ultimately unsurprising. What warrants attention is the ubiquity and the intricacy that has lately come to characterize them. Consider the popularity of computer games developed expressly for recruitment purposes like *America's Army*; recall the perennial successes of Pentagon-assisted Hollywood blockbusters like *Behind Enemy Lines*; and ponder, finally, the growing number of AI innovations coming out of places like the disingenuously named Institute for Creative Technologies (ICT), an army-funded Hollywood–Pentagon think tank and laboratory at the University of Southern California, and myriad 'synergies' between the military and media sectors emerge, unprecedented in their clarity and complexity (Burston 2003).

Although this potentially rich area of research ought to be of paramount interest to media studies, it remains troublingly under-examined. Though popular writing exists on the computer and video game industries, most of it is of limited use as it often eschews critical approaches to its subject matter. Important work closer to home is likewise available (Levidow and Robins 1989; Virilio 1989), but, conversely, much of this material is held too tightly by the reins of theory to pull out the emerging particulars of the MIM complex. Media studies generally seems happy to leave critical examination of synthespianism to the largely textual preoccupations of either cyborg studies (Balsamo 1997) or cinema studies (Flanagan 1999), while handing off Pentagon–Siliwood collaboration to international relations and security studies (Der Derian 1998, 2001). Although the gap in media research on the MIM complex is slowly being addressed (Burston 2003, Kline *et al.* 2003), more still needs to be done.

This presents media studies with an opportunity to prevail over what remains, despite important exceptions (McRobbie 1998; Negus 1999; Dean and Jones 2003), one of its most debilitating blind spots: the workaday experiences of entertainment labour. While political-economic analysis shedding light on the interconnections between entertainment capitalism, the military, other techno-industrial sectors, and government constitutes a necessary component of any media research agenda for the MIM complex, in order to meet the challenges such an agenda really presents we must resolve to go further. Media studies needs to heed repeated calls among many of its most reflexive practitioners (Born 1993; Golding and Murdock 2000; Deacon 2003) and finally refuse its inclination toward 'the evacuation of meaning, agency and historical contingency' inside its own political economy tradition by way of its propensity to reduce social actors 'to the 'objective' categories of buyer and seller of labour power' (Du Gay 2002: 293). Examining actors' changing working conditions in a newly digital Hollywood seems a good place to begin this endeavour; and in beginning, not so much reject, but build on what nonetheless remains an extremely valuable mode of enquiry.

Working actors in the new Siliwood

Not long ago, Susan Christopherson (1996) promoted the term 'virtual integration' to describe the current and, in some respects, only nominally post-Fordist terrain of Hollywood production, and today Los Angeles remains a city of semi-autonomous sub-contractors tied firmly to the studios by means of minority investments and licensing agreements. This new but sturdy corporate pattern poses new challenges for entertainment unions: even as the quasi-dispersed, 'virtually' integrated industrial paradigm aids – somewhat paradoxically – the success of independents in a climate of increasing conglomeration, it hinders unions' capacities to negotiate effectively with a burgeoning number of new, affiliated, yet legally separate entities. Entertainment unions, both above and below the line, are fighting a greater number of uphill battles on matters pertaining to fragmentation, casualization, and compensation (Gray and Seeber 1996: 184–5). That Hollywood labour faces this situation while the industry goes digital should come as no surprise. 'The movie business ... is undergoing its greatest period of change since the talkies' (Gray and Seeber 1996: 182) and digital technologies pose real threats to some unions' continued viability (Magder and Burston 2001).

Hollywood's most prominent talent union, the Screen Actors Guild (SAG), is not yet among those on the front lines, but, as the gaming sector expands, there are signs of strain. 'We're remaining flexible in our approach with interactive producers to keep the work under union contracts,' SAG National Executive Director Ken Orsatti offered obliquely in 2001. He was likely aware that in the first few years of the SAG Interactive Agreement (governing members' work in video and computer games), SAG signed up over a hundred interactive productions and earned its members over $2 million (Koseluk 2001). Considerably more impressive, interactive gaming revenues in the USA outstripped movie revenues in 2002 by more than a billion dollars: $9.3 billion to $8.1 billion (Snider 2002). Yet convergence still remains the buzzword in the new Siliwood, and synergy the big brass ring. The profit potentials of movie–game crossovers such as the *Tomb Raider* series have most top agents advancing quickly on the gaming sector, working hard 'to bring name talent to video game titles and to pave a two-way street for the hottest gaming creative talent in movies and television' (Gaudiosi 2003).

These efforts aside, the majority of interactive work goes to journeymen actors, often called in for only two or three days over what is normally an eighteen-month production cycle. This strongly suggests actors' relative unimportance in inter-active production environments – a regular subject in computer-generated imagery (CGI) discourse. Many digital animators are dismissive of human performance labour, referring to non-digital actors as 'meat puppets' and 'blood actors' in an effort to patrol their own emerging creative terrain (Burston 2000). 'At its core,' says Hollywood software developer Allen DeBevoise,

> acting is not about the physical. It's understanding the moment you're in and connecting that moment with your audience. A good animator can be an actor because it's still the mood and emotion they bring to it – it's not the computer doing that.
>
> (*Hollywood Reporter*, 2000)

That this is certainly true, and that human artistry thus remains alive and well and living in the digital studio, in no way diminishes the significance of this departure from Hollywood's historical conception of the role, constitution, and phenomenology of the actor: at actors' expense, animators appear to be gaining higher artistic ground in the digital studio. This is as it should be in many instances, given the wonderment CG artists regularly produce, and given CG animators' mastery in shaping the final cinematic product. 'There is something wonderful,' says ILM's Bill George, 'about being able to see a performance and being able to go over and over it and get exactly what you want' (*Hollywood Reporter*, 2000).

Others clearly feel similarly. In mid-2003, CGI artists found themselves in the midst of an unprecedented hiring boom. The *Hollywood Reporter* reported rumours of 'extreme recruiting methods', 'sensational signing bonuses', and 'feeding frenzies' as the industry geared up for next season's slate of big-budget movies and games (Robertson 2003). Meanwhile, in its employment forecasts for the film and television sector to 2010, the US Department of Labor (DOL) began estimating smaller employment growth percentages for actors than for CGI and other digital workers. The DOL predicts a 63 per cent positive change for computer specialists, an astonishing 75.1 per cent positive change for multi-media artists and animators, and a deflating 26 per cent positive change in employment numbers for actors over the period (DOL 2002–3). Human *star* performers probably have nothing to fear, however. As a SAG interactive execu-tive explained it to me in Los Angeles, stars are in little danger of seeing their livelihoods reduced as audiences will likely continue identifying powerfully with carbon-based Tom Cruises and Russell Crowes on screen. But there are fewer reasons why the actors who pour the stars their drinks, open their doors, and sell them their newspapers need to be real (Weingartner 1999). Since the late 1990s, f/x producers have been able to create 'directable, digital characters whose performance can be shaped on a set just like any actor's' (Edlund 1998: 417), and the SAG executive anticipated a nearby day when falling costs of simulation mean falling demand for journeyman performers. He likewise anticipated new dynamics of stratification among the SAG membership as the employment gap between stars and journeyman actors grows larger (Weingartner 1999).

The synthespian subject

None of this is to suggest that whenever human actors *do* get the chance to ply their craft in digital environments the experience is invariably disappointing or compromised. On the contrary, in optimal circumstances, actors participating in the creation of new synthespian entities are superlative expressions of the new cyborg episteme. Just as the cyborg subject position 'can be a place to learn a new conception of agency' (Gray and Mentor 1995: 232), computer-generated imagery can provide actors with entirely novel, radically empowering environments in which to work. While creating 'Gollum' in *LOTR*, Andy Serkis worked extensively with motion capture technology, setting new methodological standards about which he is justly excited.

> I've been really evangelizing about CG acting. For me, there's no difference. It's liberating because you can play any number of different characters that are not dependent on what your own physicality is. You're an actor. You can embody any character. ... [CGI is] like watching really good puppetry, you know, where there's a magical quality and a greater truth.
>
> (Ain't It Cool News 2003).

Comparing CGI techniques to puppetry works well, because acting is not a monadic process in which an individual interprets text from inside the exclusivity of his or her own 'natural' body. Acting is a profoundly social practice: actors' 'magical qualities' and 'greater truths' depend on a host of objects in the form of sets, costumes, props, and prosthetics – not to mention musicians, directors, 'techies', and other actors. Whether they do so in real or in digital time and space, acting subjects deploy the gamut of these organic and inorganic objects to create liminal meaning, even while these same objects invariably and necessarily contain the possibilities of performance in certain ways. In providing Serkis with a new set of objects with which to interact, the digital studio also provided a new place to exercise 'an instituted practice in a field of enabling constraints' (Haraway 1991: 135). That is, it provided an important new site for the social construction of his postmodern agency.

Serkis wasn't the only one happy with the results. The *Village Voice* proclaimed

The Two Towers to be 'stolen by a cyborg performance of the highest order. ... [T]he pitiful Gollum ... is the soul of the movie – particularly after his consciousness begins to fissure' (Hoberman 2002). 'Gollum is a computer-generated creation and as fully realized a character as can be found in "Towers" – perhaps the most fully realized,' said the *New York Times*. 'Gollum is torn by his nature, and Mr Jackson allows him to be conflicted in a way none of the other characters in the film are' (Mitchell 2002). It is testament to the artistry and dedication of the people who produced him that we witness how thoroughly 'torn by his nature' Gollum actually is. But what repays attention here is precisely how this collaborative spirit between actors and CGI artists is generally *absent* in both cinematic and interactive instances of digital production: in the run-up to the Oscars in 2003, industry and critical opinion pronounced Dobby, Stuart Little, and the latest incarnation of Yoda nothing more than voiced-over 3D cartoons, dwarfed by Gollum's digital shadow (Fleming 2002).

We also need to contemplate a disturbing correspondence between widespread critical praise for Serkis's representations of Gollum's 'fissured consciousness' and a less easily celebrated underside of cyborg disembodiment: those moments when the radically fragmented subject descends into schizophrenic incoherence. Serkis also had this to say about preparing for Gollum, a role that his physical body would originate while never being seen to do so:

> Serkis: 'I actually began to imagine that the state of being a CG character was part of the state of the way that the ring affected you, if you like. So that was the final stage of the [acting] process.'
> Interviewer: 'Sort of a removal of humanity?'
> Serkis: 'Yeah, exactly. Exactly.'
>
> (IGN Filmforce 2003)

These remarks do not contradict Serkis's earlier ones so much as they describe labour conditions in the new Siliwood in another register altogether. Trapped in tortuous relationships with a metaphysically powerful ring on screen and a metaphysically powerful technology in the studio, Serkis is a *torn subject* both within the text and within the context of its production. We return to Marx to rediscover why.

Acting, dialogical labour, and species being

Media studies has historically considered actors' work experiences somewhat tangential to its concerns. 'Part of the problem,' explain Deborah Dean and Campbell Jones, 'is that acting ... "looks like fun" ... and, given the common distinction between work and pleasure ... it can be difficult to think of acting as work' (Dean and Jones 2003: 530). And it's especially easy to devalue the work of 'stars' because of the way they themselves, and entertainment capitalism more generally, bestow upon all mention of acting such abiding tones of self-congratu-lation. But embedded within the actor's nearly insatiable desire for attention is a distinctly non-neurotic desire fundamental to progressive politics. This is the desire for unalienated labour; for work in which each of us may fully apprehend the linked dimensions of our individuality and our sociality:

> Supposing that we had produced in a human manner; each of us would in his production have doubly confirmed himself and his fellow men. I would have: 1) objectified in my production my individuality and thus ... have had the pleasure of realizing that my personality was objective ... 2) In your enjoy-ment ... I would have had the direct enjoyment of realizing that I had satisfied a human need ... 3) I would have been for you the mediator between you and the species and thus acknowledged ... by you as ... a necessary part of yourself ... 4) In my expression of my life I would have fashioned your expression of your life, and thus in my own activity have real-ized my own essence, my human, my communal essence.
>
> (Marx 1971: 202)

Labouring to produce the world in such an auspiciously unalienated fashion, humanity is able to discover its own 'species being' (Marx 1973). Though I have no wish to promote Marx as the ultimate arbiter on matters of human subjec-tivity, I do wish to suggest that such dialogical figurations of human happiness stretch along our onto-historical timeline both prior to Marx and following him, signalling their central place in the way even postmodern subjects understand ourselves. Within the actor's discourse, this is everywhere evident. Indeed, as communications workers of the first (and most earnest) order, actors often desire applause and publicity because of a deep-rooted need to enter into dialogical rela-tions with their audiences in the unalienated modality that Marx here describes (see Burston, forthcoming).

As members of those audiences, we do more than identify with the given part an actor plays. We also identify with *the actor who is playing the part*. As Barry King explains it, we associate ourselves with the *agency* of particular stars; that is, 'with the star *per se* rather than with the narrative functions (characters) he or she represents' (King 1987: 149). Consequently, Danae Clark points out, 'as social subjects who must navigate the gendered, racialized and otherwise politicized space of cultural practices', actors and spectators alike 'come to occupy similar positions and to experience similar struggles in terms of labor power and subject identity' (Clark 1995: 123–4). But crucially, Serkis cannot derive any sense of satisfaction or solidarity from the moment of actor–audience cross-identification Clark has rightly recognized. This is because *as an actor labouring on a text* Serkis is no longer visible. As *Variety* described Gollum, 'The performance is signature Serkis – even though the actor was erased from every scene' (Fleming 2002). Despite the profound physicality that Serkis's working body provided Gollum, the 'star' himself has neither body nor biography on screen. Serkis *qua* Serkis has vanished, and, with him, his primary dialogical strategy for attaining species being.

Such acts of erasure are neither *necessarily* odious nor inevitable. The separation of actors' voices from their bodies has failed to provoke existential crisis inside animation to date, and CGI technologies *can* be employed toward ends more constructively transparent than those currently ascendant. But what is taking place inside the moment of digital cinema is an order of magnitude larger than a new way to make cartoons. The power and ubiquity of Siliwood's latest offerings, in the words of one industry executive, raise the CG bar so high that 'there is no bar anymore' (Graser 2003). And our own everyday movie-watching experience easily confirms what this chapter's opening quotation, from a popular CG practitioners' manual, likewise suggests: under corporate-transnational entertainment capitalism, Siliwood cinema's aesthetic conventions do not bear the marks of Brechtian transparency so much as they do Baudrillardian seamlessness. Though it needn't theoretically be so, mainstream deployments of digital cinematic technology have historically worked to narrow all gaps between appearance and reality, making the 'seam between the screen and actual experience less visible, but not less important' (Scheuer 2001: 115). Robbed of the dialectical play of the actor/character binary, the actor discovers that his/her principal tool for producing species being has likewise gone missing. Gollum's legendary split personality stands as a perfect metaphor for the actually existing dilemma of digital actors who, even in the most favourable circumstances, are deprived of their own best means of creating dialogically enfranchised conditions of production and forever teeter on the brink of traumatic dysfunction.

Researching the MIM complex

Media research must respond quickly to the formidable changes afoot in the new Siliwood by investigating any number of its moments, including the synthespian moment adumbrated here. Even if the far-reaching phenomenological, aesthetic-ideological, and economic implications of the new digital grammar did not now demand it, inquiries into the daily experience of popular performance labour merit specific endorsement as a propitious (if peculiarly underused) means to cut paths into the MIM complex's still largely uncharted territory. That is to say, we really need to hear more from *working* cyborgs. If we did, we might then begin to determine which conditions pertain when actors are engaged in groundbreaking creative labour and which ones hold when, more typically, the material and cultural circumstances of cyborg subjects, despite 'the indeterminacy of their hybrid design', continue operating quite comfortably inside 'concrete relations of power and domination' (Balsamo 1997: 11, 40).

Cultural studies has an important role to play in this budding MIM complex research agenda, though under the sign of the synthespian, textual analysts also might find it productive to consider how *actors themselves* are positioned by the tele-filmic text: how embedded discourses of labour and technology, for example, seek 'to position actors' labor and subjectivity in the field of commodity exchange' (Clark 1995: xiv). *Mutatis mutandis*, this is Clark's project, and it is no idle exercise. Not if we concur with Dean and Jones, who remind us that the moment when an actor 'presents herself in front of the camera, in an assemblage that is always already culturally mediated, is critically important to the reproduction and contestation that is the politics of cultural production' (Dean and Jones 2003: 537). This enduring argument, weirdly inaudible within media and cultural studies, leads back to textual analysis by way of another iteration: screen actors, 'as subjects caught between their positions as labourers and commodity images', are involved in a perpetual conflict 'over the very terms of their representation' (Clark 1995: 119) – a situation that generates any number of questions cultural studies is very well positioned to address. How, for instance, does the romantic spectacularization of virtual realms in films like *The Matrix*, or Spielberg's *AI*, render opaque the emerging power struggles between old-fashioned 'blood actors' and the virtuoso creators of their digital counterparts at firms like ILM, Pixar, and elsewhere? Such questions need asking not least because so many *different kinds* of artists are buffeted on a daily basis between the oscillating subject positions of labourer and commodity image. Across the new cultural economy, we need to deploy closer analysis of the ways artists' work is represented in the texts on which they labour in order to understand how this perpetual oscillation serves both to restrain and to empower their agency. It is here, where star studies meets labour studies, that we can see a new field of inquiry surfacing for both media and cultural studies. One that, in refocusing the analytical lens on the cultural labourer as subject rather than object, forces new thought along lines extrinsic to our conventional concerns; breaking down barriers between our various specializations at a time when media and cultural studies' holistic expansion appears more and more necessary to so many of its own theorists (see Deacon 2003).

Such a project takes on an even greater urgency inside the MIM complex, where new epistemologies of virtual entertainment are blurring boundaries between subject and object, between human agent and machine agent, at breathtaking speed (Morse 1998), and where any available Harawayan cyborg poetics is quickly overwritten by the dubious aesthetics of corporate seamlessness. If we want to see the radical potential inherent in such circumstances emerge in real time and not merely in theory, we need to register media workers' experience of the real-time conditions currently morphing subject–object relations so spectacularly. For at the end of the day, the struggles underway in the new Siliwood are neither theoretical, nor are they distant from our immediate concerns. As outlined at the outset, in the age of Governor Schwarzenegger, digital scabs are not our worst nightmare: 'the Terminator' is. Aiming to account for at least some of the many valences of digital entertainment work inside the MIM complex, media and cultural studies can finally begin to 'facilitate that dialogue in which theory may inform practice, and vice versa' (Born 1993: 242). We can try to generate a wider discussion with entertainment workers whose professional circumstances are increasingly tied up with things *other* than entertainment: circumstances whose disturbing specifics we now urgently need to understand.

References

Ain't It Cool News (2003) 'Mr Beaks sits down with Andy Serkis', www.aintitcool.com/display.cgi?id_14337. Accessed on 26 August 2003.

Balsamo, Anne (1997) *Technologies of the Gendered Body: Reading Cyborg Women*, Durham and London: Duke University Press.

Born, Georgina (1993) 'Against negation, for a politics of cultural production: Adorno, aesthetics, the social', *Screen* 34(3): 223–42.

Burston, Jonathan (2000) 'Synergy, spectacle and megamusicals: the global-industrialisation of the live-entertainment economy', in James Curran (ed.) *Media Organisations in Society*, London: Arnold, pp. 69–83.

—— (2003) 'War and the entertainment industries: new research priorities in an era of cyber-patriotism', in Daya Thussu and Des Freedman (eds) *War and the Media: Reporting Conflict 24/7*, London: Sage, pp. 163–75.

—— (forthcoming) *Corporate Broadway: Media, Megamusicals and the Theater*, Durham and London: Duke University Press.

Christopherson, Susan (1996) 'Flexibility and integration in industrial relations: the exceptional case of the US media entertainment industries', in Lois Gray and Ronald Seeber (eds) *Under the Stars: Essays on Labor Relations in the Arts and Entertainment*, Ithaca, NY: ILR Press/Cornell University Press, pp. 86–112.

Clark, Danae (1995) *Negotiating Hollywood: The Cultural Politics of Actors' Labor*, Minneapolis and London: University of Minnesota Press.

Deacon, David (2003) 'Holism, communion and conversion: integrating media production and consumption research', *Media Culture and Society* (25)2: 209–31.

Dean, Deborah and Jones, Campbell (2003) 'If women actors were working ... ', *Media Culture and Society* 25(4): 527–41.

Der Derian, James (1998) 'All but war is simulation', in Gearóid Ó Tuathail and Simon Dalby (eds) *Rethinking Geopolitics*, New York: Routledge, pp. 261–73.

—— (2001) *Virtuous War: Mapping the Military–Industrial–Media Entertainment Network*, Boulder: Westview.

Dixon, Wheeler Winston (2001) 'Twenty-five reasons why it's all over', in Jon Lewis (ed.) *The End of Cinema as We Know It: American Film in the Nineties*, New York: New York University Press, pp. 356–66.

DOL (Department of Labor, Bureau of Labor Statistics, United States Government) (2002–3) 'Motion picture production and distribution', in *Occupational Outlook Handbook and Career Guide to Industries*, www.bls.gov/oco/cg/cgs083.htm. Accessed July 2003.

Down, John (2001) 'The song machine', www.openDemocracy.net, 23 October, www.opendemocracy.net/debates/article.jsp?id=1&debateId=67&articleId=369. Accessed January 2003.

Du Gay, Paul (2002) 'Organizing identity: Making up people at work', in Paul Du Gay (ed.) *Production of Culture/Culture of Production*, London: Sage, pp. 285–344.

Edlund, Richard (1998) 'Seamlessness', in Clark Dodsworth Jnr (ed) *Digital illusion: Entertaining the Future with High Technology*, Boston: Addison-Wesley, pp. 413–23.

Flanagan, Mary (1999) 'Mobile identities, digital stars, and post-cinematic selves', *Wide Angle* 21(1): 76–93.

Fleming, Michael (2002) 'Oscar hopeful Serkis "Towers" over CGI brethren', *Variety*, 21 November, www.variety.com/index.asp?layout=print_story&articleid=VR1117876425&categoryid=390. Accessed on 23 July 2003.

Gaudiosi, John (2003) 'Top agencies bid for vid game business', *Hollywood Reporter*, 20 February, http://hollywoodreporter.com/thr/search/searh_display.jsp?vnu_content_id=1820524. Accessed on 7 July 2003.

Golding, Peter and Graham Murdock (2000) 'Culture, communications and political economy', in J. Curran and M. Gurevich (eds) *Mass Media and Society*, 3rd edn, London: Edward Arnold, pp. 70–92.

Graser, Marc (2003) 'The clone wars: artificial characters steal scenes from human counterparts', *Variety*, 21 January, www.variety.com/index.asp?layout=print_story&articleid=VR1117879205&categoryid=1390. Accessed on 23 July 2003.

Gray, Chris Hables and Steven Mentor (1995) 'The cyborg body politic and the new world order', in Gabriel Brahm Jnr and Mark Driscoll (eds) *Prosthetic Territories: Politics and Hypertechnology*, Boulder, CO: Westview, pp. 219–47.

Gray, Lois and Seeber, Ronald (1996) 'Looking ahead', in Lois Gray and Ronald Seeber (eds) *Under the Stars: Essays on Labor Relations in the Arts and Entertainment*, Ithaca, NY: ILR Press/Cornell University Press, pp. 181–91.

Haraway, Donna (1991) '"Gender" for a Marxist dictionary: the sexual politics of a word', in *Simians, Cyborgs and Women: The Reinvention of Nature*, London: Free Association Books, pp. 127–48.

Hoberman, J. (2002) 'Vice city', *Village Voice*, 18–24 December, www.villagevoice.com/issues/0251/hoberman.php. Accessed on 28 September 2003.

Hollywood Reporter (2000) 'Perspectives: are virtual actors a viable threat to real actors?' 20 July, http://hollywoodreporter.com/thr/search/searh_display.jsp?vnu_content_id=579556. Accessed on 6 July 2003.

IGN Filmforce (2003) 'An interview with Andy Serkis: the man behind Gollum in *The Lord of the Rings* discusses his career', 27 January, http://filmforce.ign.com/articles/383/383888p1.html?fromint=1 Accessed on 29 August 2003.

King, Barry (1987) 'The star and the commodity: notes towards a performance theory of stardom', *Cultural Studies* 1(2): 145–61.

Kline, Stephen, Dyer-Witheford, Nick and de Peuter, Greig (2003) *Digital Play: Technology, Markets, Culture*, Montreal: McGill-Queen's University Press.

Koeppel, Dan and Sillery, Bob (2002) 'Massive attack', *Popular Science* 261(6): 38–44.

Koseluk, Chris (2001) 'Digital acting: new performing opportunities on the horizon', Screen Actors Guild website, http://www.sag.org.dgtlacting.html. Accessed on 23 June 2003.

Levidow, Les and Robins, Kevin (eds) (1989) *Cyborg Worlds: The Military Information Society*, London: Free Association Books.

McRobbie, Angela (1998) *British Fashion Design: Rag Trade or Image Industry?* London: Routledge.

Magder, Ted and Burston, Jonathan (2001) 'Whose Hollywood? Changing relations and changing forms in the new North American entertainment economy', in Dan Schiller and Vincent Mosco (eds) *Continental Order: Integrating North America for Cyber-capitalism*, New York: Rowman & Littlefield.

Marx, Karl (1971) *Early Texts*, ed. and trans. David McClellan, Oxford: Basil Blackwell.

—— (1973) *Grundrisse*, Harmondsworth: Penguin.

Mitchell, Elvis (2002) 'Soldiering on in epic pursuit of purity', *New York Times*, 18 December. E1. http://query.nytimes.com/gst/fullpage.html?res=9E01E3DB153DF93BA25751C1A9649C8B63. Accessed on 28 September 2003.

Morse, Margaret (1998) *Virtualities: Television, Media Art, and Cyberculture*, Bloomington: Indiana University Press.

Negus, Keith (1999) *Music Genres and Corporate Cultures*, New York: Routledge.

Robertson, Barbara (2003) 'Extreme recruiting', *Hollywood Reporter*, 25 July, www.hollywoodreporter.com/thr/search/search_display.jspvnu_content_id_=1942523. Accessed on 27 August 2003.

Scheuer, Jeffrey (2001) *The Sound Bite Society: How Television Helps the Right and Hurts the Left*, New York: Routledge.

Snider, Mike (2002) 'Where movies end, games begin', *USA Today*, 23 May, www.usatoday.com/tech/techreviews/2002/5/23/e3.htm. Accessed on 12 September 2003.

Virilio, Paul (1989) *War and Cinema: The Logistics of Perception*, London: Verso.

Weingartner, Allen (1999) Personal interview, Los Angeles, 5 March.

Chapter 18

Digital film and 'late' capitalism

A cinema of heroes?

Janet Harbord

'Unfortunately, the only thing "late" about capitalism is that it has rather inconveniently failed to disappear on schedule.'

(D.N. Rodowick 2001: 206)

'A certain nostalgia for cinema precedes its "death". One doesn't – and can't – love the televisual or the digital in quite the same way.'

(Mary Ann Doane 2002: 228)

'Cinema's hundred years appear to have the shape of a life cycle: inevitable birth, the steady accumulation of glories, and the onset in the last decade of an ignominious, irreversible decline.' So starts Susan Sontag's impassioned, polemical essay 'A century of cinema'. According to this account, cinema and its attendant sensibility, cinephilia, are lost objects.[1] The tone of Sontag's account is stirring, mournful and nostalgic, leaving a sense of the present as simply inadequate. The essay leaves open the possibility that new films may inspire, yet such objects will be 'heroic violations of the norms and practices which now govern moviemaking everywhere in the capitalist and would-be capitalist world'. The valiant heroic, according to Sontag, is our only stand against a system of production that has transformed the art of cinema into a culture propelled by corporate profit, with the blockbuster film and its cynical franchise of serial films the most obvious example. Sontag's is a criticism of fatigue in the face of so-called 'late capitalism', yet notable for its own predictable narrative of restitution, whereby the critic restores order through courageous acts of commentary. In so doing, cultural criticism becomes a peculiarly protectivist practice where the polarities (of good–bad, noble–cynical) stay firmly in place. The more complex and contradictory aspects of film culture in the present are paradoxically lost in this heroic struggle, along with questions of what cultural criticism can achieve, and how it might define and approach an object of study at a moment of rapid transformation.

Sontag is not the only commentator to reach for the sententious, and nor is 'late' capitalism the only threat to cinema on the critical horizon. A similar sense of cinema reaching an end is found most notably in a parallel (and overlapping) discourse whose focus is technology. The arrival of the digital age for cinema has, as John Belton argues, been a slow inauguration (Belton 2002). Emerging in the cinema of the 1970s in special effects, digitalisation has leaked into various areas of film production, distribution and exhibition in barely discernable ways. It is only in a wave of millennial anxiety that digitalisation has come to be positioned as the anti-hero about to slay the collective experience of film viewing. Belton sounds a cautious note about what digitalisation may signify, but other commentators tread less circumspectly. With the uptake of digital distribution systems streaming films straight into the home, it is argued, for example in the collection of essays edited by Jon Lewis, the direct distributor–consumer relationship has repositioned cinema as an optional mediation of these positions. And with the refurbishment of home-view technologies to create an ambient viewing space in the front room (the scale and dimension of screens, surround sound, additional and interactive DVD features) the particular experience of cinema-going is potentially eclipsed. As Lewis comments, 'We can now envision a not so distant future in which we will never have to leave our houses to see a movie' (Lewis 2001: 3).

The peculiar convergence of technological and economic development at the end of the twentieth century provides a situation where the prognosis, for both film and cinema, is unclear. Interpretations of the 'condition' of filmmaking in this moment vary widely. On the one hand, there is a sense in which the transmutation of a studio system of film production into a vertically and horizontally integrated web of multinational corporations is the final phase in an exhausted capitalist cycle. In an article that echoes Sontag's fatigue in the face of such cynicism, Christopher Sharrett declares the contemporary an epoch of 'hyperinflation', characterised by 'the endless repetition of narrative formulas' which lay bare the 'wasteland' of the entertainment industry (Sharrett 2001: 319). In a further intertextual twist, Paul Arthur argues that the emergence of apocalyptic disaster films signifies 'the most resonant and deeply ambivalent expressions of the studio system's looming obsolescence' (Arthur 2001: 342). Within this genre, and this historical moment, what is most feared is also mostly vividly imagined and expressed. On the other hand, the ability of the film industry to transform, to adopt a new corporate presence, or corporeality in the manner of the Terminator, characterises the present. Hollywood as a global enterprise has, according to Miller et al., manœuvred, shifting its focus from material production to virtual control through attention to copyright (Miller et al. 2001). In this account, the demise of the cinema and the emergence of new technologies are not threats to the industry, but conversely opportunities to permeate new markets (through the facilities of digital distribution), and engender new film cultures in the provision of software and content for home-view.

Within these competing accounts of the life and potential death of cinema, however, is an elision of the different film cultures that exist. Whilst most accounts concern themselves with the texts of global Hollywood, it is erroneous to generalise the condition of a dominant film industry for all film production. In addition to global Hollywood, a European tradition of art house filmmaking (mourned by Sontag), troubled by its dependent relationship to nation states, provides a different form of film culture. There is also a tradition of cinema from outside of the West, framed by Paul Willeman historically as Third Cinema and now marketed euphemistically as World Cinema, providing another facet. In addition, independent cinema, a convergence of avant-garde and new-wave filmmaking, exists largely outside of cinematic culture, utilising the space of the gallery and/or websites. Each of these forms of film culture exist alongside each other, providing competing definitions of what cinema is and how it can be practised. It is a competition of physical resources, a struggle over visibility played out through marketing, distribution and sites of exhibition. And each film culture connects us to a different sense of scale and space: Hollywood trades in the epic (in terms of story, screen image, diegetic world), offering a connection to a global, transcendental cinema. World Cinema connects us to the space of the nation, with fictional constructs set in recognisable locations. Art house and avant-garde cinema is often located in the realm of the subjective. These distinctions between film cultures and their relationship to space and scale are crude mappings, which are in many instances more nuanced and complex. Yet in posing questions about change, the concept of plural film cultures offers a schematic way of thinking about individual films within specific traditions, and of film cultures acting inter-relationally.

This chapter provides an analysis of how digital technology has been used variously to further the distinctions between film cultures, to emphasise particular features and further demarcate cinematic traditions. Here, technology is precisely not a determining force inevitably operating on film, nor a temporal marker that spells the end of cinema. Rather, digital technology is more usefully envisaged as part of the material condition of cinema that affords opportunities for innovation. In a climate in which the new and the distinct are key factors in a competitive marketplace, digitalisation facilitates the development of film cultures as different from one another. The demarcation of difference most obviously resides in the film text itself, and what follows is an analysis of film cultures and their relationship to change via textual features. Yet, I want to suggest that textual differences are connected to the circuits of distribution and the sites of consumption of each culture. The digital facilitates historical differences between such cultures, and throws into relief the diverse trajectories that films, as objects, travel.

Epic film

To conceive of the present as a moment of change immediately creates a repression of the ongoing unfolding of time and the concomitant everyday transformation of objects and practices. The epic cinema of the present, which has attracted attention partly through its sheer exuberance of scale, was itself a reaction to the emergence of television in the 1950s and the decline in cinema attendance in the late 1960s. Reflecting back to this moment, cinema was reinvented as a theatre of spectacle in order to better distinguish its culture from that of the living room.[2] This form of cinema has slowly evolved as an experiential practice, a visceral experience of spectacle and bodily involvement. Alongside the development of the cinematic theatrical experience in the 1970s and 1980s, the site of the cinema was reconfigured through the lens of consumer choice: the multiplex pluralised film choice within one location (Friedberg 1993), aligned cinema with other consumer practices and positioned it at the margins of city life (Harbord 2002).

The relocation of cinema and the simultaneous redefinition of the scale of film are changes facilitated by digital technology. The transformation of scale has impacted on the narratives and formal structures of the films themselves: the digital has furthered a culture of spectacle and immediacy through the creation of fantastical worlds and the effects of super-human efforts. The narrative structure is characterised by the mythic quest, a journey that involves the hero overcoming obstacles, encountering key archetypal characters, and returning with the elixir, the prize of a precious object or a metaphysical reward such as self-knowledge. As Sean Cubitt remarks of these films, 'Narrative is diminishing in importance (hence the ubiquity of the mythic quest), while diegesis, the imaginary worlds created by films, becomes more significant' (Cubitt 2002: 26). The epic spectacle film is characterised either by revisiting an historical world or creating an imaginary future, temporal locations that allow other diegetic worlds to be constructed. Scott Bukatman refers to the synergy of the science fiction genre and digital technology as an obvious partnership at a moment in which film becomes 'a multimedia, global consciousness' (Bukatman 1998: 249). Digital special effects are key to the creation of projected worlds, whilst science fiction lends a reflexive edge to the discourse of technology. *The Matrix* is a film that illustrates this eloquently, set in the future in 'a world where anything is possible' (Morpheus). In *The Matrix*, it is not only the fabric of the world that is facilitated by the digital, but also the identity of the hero. Neo is a character whose power resides in the super-human abilities of fighting. Synthesising styles of martial arts and conventional (Western) fighting skills, Neo is a creation of digital effects, of mid-air kicks, passages of flight and wall-walking. As Leon Hunt has noted, where martial arts films relied on a notion of authenticity of performance, *The Matrix* offers pleasure in the performance of the virtual, the artificial, the technologically mediated body (Hunt 2002: 195).

Digital technology has profoundly impacted on the process of production, not always in an economy of production but also in large budget films, creating another dimension to post-production. Over one hundred digital artists were employed in the production of *The Matrix* to work on action sequences. As a text, it is a hybrid of analogue and digital formats, a hybridity that thoroughly permeates the film: the text is a *mélange* of East/West cultural influences, and works across the binaries of human/machine, the real/the virtual. Located in a virtual world where humans are deceived into thinking that this is 'real', the protagonists are our doubles; just as the film is a constructed world that we enter, suspending disbelief, so the characters enter a virtual world to play out the fight for humanity. Yet, despite the reliance on digital form, the film exercises a paradoxical relation to technology. The virtual world within the film (the matrix itself) is a clinical place, governed by a rationality best signified by the computer code. Pat Mellencamp comments on the meta-textual relationship to technology thus: '*The Matrix* enacts the contradictions of contemporary technology – it decries the effects of technology on humanity, while at the same time deploying the most advanced technologies to make its point in dazzling, moneymaking images' (Mellencamp 2002: 85). Whilst global Hollywood constantly triumphs the human over the machine in narrative terms, its transformation of film production into a system of virtual ownership (through copyright and the integration of film production and distribution) in fact mimics the matrix more closely than might be imagined.

History in one breath

If the digital is used to create fantastical worlds in a mythic past or fantastical future in global Hollywood film, it is put to another use in the tradition of art house film. Alexander Sokurov's *Russian Ark* uses the properties of digitalisation to evoke a sense of a nation, and equally to create a formally innovative film: *Russian Ark* is a film without an edit. Located and literally shot within the Hermitage museum in St Petersburg, *Russian Ark* is a rendering of history situated in place. Here, the museum itself is a time capsule, an ark having weathered time to preserve cultural artefacts of past ages. The film is shot in one long take; a steady cam travels through an assortment of rooms (35 in total) to return to specific historical moments. History is presented in tableau form, a series of set pieces of 'great' historical moments spanning four centuries. Unlike the epic historical film, in *Russian Ark* the individual is largely absent from the frame. We ostensibly follow a French aristocrat through the opulent halls in a discovery of all that has endured of Russia's post-Renaissance culture. Yet, character is insignificant; the continuous movement of the camera comes to stand in for an embodied point of view. This is cinema travelling, through time and space. Where montage offers and controls a range of perspectives, reactions, exchanges, *Russian Ark* pursues a slow contemplative gaze.

In many ways, *Russian Ark* has been constructed on principles opposing those of Hollywood. It denies the centrality of character, of plot, of a narrative structure punctuated by obstacles and culminating in triumph over adversity. It is a film that meanders without a sense of purpose. Its subject matter resides in a particular historical context, a reflexive return to a time that is pre-revolutionary Russia, forging lost connections with a European culture, with a past that is both buried and preserved. If, as Cubitt argues, history as a discursive text is foreclosed in spectacle film, *Russian Ark* unlocks the past as ill-fitting moments, resistant to a cohering narrative of progress or a determining social fatalism. Here, history is a series of hieroglyphic set pieces, jumbled together; the perpetual motion of the camera as it enters yet another room stumbles upon another scenario, creates the experience of history as dream. And in the haunting quality of a dream, another history is summoned by the film, of Eisenstein, a 'master' of Russian cinema. Eisenstein's fascination with cinematic form was located in the cut, the montage of attractions, a concept that was defined and redefined throughout his life.[3] If *Russian Ark* recalls the filmic past through its negation of montage, it is not simply a project in opposition to Eisenstein. Montage in *Russian Ark* is eliminated as a cut, an act of splicing and forging new relations dialectically with the material of film. Yet the edit returns spatially as each room entered situates the viewer in a different context; this 'spatial edit' requires the viewer to make links between the various tableaux rather than between shots.

The duration of the film as a single take, producing history as an act of exhalation, distinguishes *Russian Ark* from its predecessors. It also marks it out in the contemporary as technologically innovative work. Shot with the Sony high-definition camera, the F900, the film was launched as 'the first high definition Russian movie' (producer Andrey Deryabin). The F900, launched at Cannes 2000, created a shift in digital production, providing the first image to compare in quality to 35-millimetre film. Thus digital stock, like video before it, provided extended duration of shooting. But unlike video the quality of image was sustained. Recorded straight onto hard disc, there is a suggestion that the film somehow returns to a *cinéma vérité*, the product of one shoot located in real time and space, and with real actors (over 4,500 people participated in the shoot). However, in post-production the film was considerably altered with special effects: the effect of candlelight, for example, was added to scenes. *Russian Ark* was then transferred to film for distribution and exhibition.

Digital technology in this context provides a novelty, an innovative filmic experience, which allows Sokurov to make it new. Whilst in interviews the director has stated repeatedly that the project of the film was to engage with art and not technology (the computer still hasn't come up with anything of its own), reviews and marketing materials foreground the technological as breathtaking innovation. The facilities of digital production have allowed this film to define a niche in the marketplace. Receiving major funding from the Russian Federation Ministry of Culture, *Russian Ark* is a national film, concerned with a specific past and located in a national context.[4] It reflexively returns us to questions of Russian identity, culture, heritage, and to a certain extent invites us on a disembodied tour of a tourist site. The première of the film in Russia took place in May 2003, during the celebration of St Petersburg's 300th anniversary, with a parallel link celebration taking place in Paris. In the USA, the premiere was held in Washington at the National Arts Gallery, and was attended by the Russian ambassador. Clearly, the film had an ambassadorial role, promoting Russian culture of a pre-revolutionary era. Its circuit of distribution included major festivals of key global cities following its spectacular premiere at Cannes, including Delhi, Helsinki, Milan, New York, São Paolo, Tokyo and Toronto. If we see the film as an object with a life of its own, defined by a trajectory through these global centres, we begin to see how aesthetics, technology and film cultures are imbricated. The distinction of the text's aesthetics (here facilitated by a particular use of digital technology) ties it to its path of circulation and to certain sites of reception.

The use of digital technology facilitates a particular type of film culture, its textual specificities putting it in dialogue with a tradition of formally innovative filmmaking. Moreover, the innovative dimension of the film, relying on digital technology, facilitates a sense of national cinema. In contrast to the epic scale of Hollywood spectacular films, *Russian Ark* is marketable through its relationship to place and history. Its success therefore is embedded in the conditions of late capitalism where the monopoly on film distribution and exhibition dominates the market, yet a national, state-funded project finds a specialised circuit of distribution.

Digital storytelling in 4/4 time

The final example of the effects of digital technology on film cultures comes from the independent sector, an ill-defined culture of filmmaking, which draws on traditions of formal experimentation and avant-garde practice. The term 'independent' contains many of the paradoxes of a tradition that perceives itself to be separate. In the current climate it is unclear whether independence in filmmaking is attained through a separation from state funding or commercial sponsorship. It raises the question of how culture can be independent from its material conditions of production. Yet it also signals a consciously fierce rejection of filmmaking being put to the service of other interested bodies or other uses (such as a film's relationship to other media texts or products). In so doing, it places critical emphasis on the process of filmmaking itself, an independence from concerns other than the material form of film and its practices.

Timecode is a film of four simultaneously run stories each filling a quarter of the screen. The film is given coherence by spatial location, a map of a part of a city where events take place. Shot with four mobile camera units, *Timecode* borrows from video surveillance and documentary *vérité*, yet its structural composition defies a realist aesthetic. The grammar that is forged in this film is one of simultaneity, the ability to see events, situations and characters impacting on each other. Where the conventional three-act structure creates ellipses in the narrative, sustaining the linear structure of story by moving between narratives, removing the surplus ineffectual material so that the film moves toward moments of enlightenment, *Timecode* reduces this emphasis on moments of knowledge. In a chaos of complex happenings, the effort for the spectator is to track events in the various windows. The director, Mike Figgis, articulates the structural properties of the film in terms of music, a conceptualisation of the script that prioritises the synchronicity of events rather than the unfolding of story: 'I had to have four separate stories going at the same time. I decided to use paper, a string quartet format where each bar line represented one minute of real time.' Where scriptwriting manuals teach a craft of plotting, of placing events and active questions in ways that will 'pay off', here there is a sense of sparseness of structure and an accumulation of significant detail. In *Timecode* we are presented with a surplus of information and detail that culminates in moments of collision. In place of progression in the three-act structure we have co-existence; instead of the sequential the simultaneous; in place of influence and enlightenment we have collision and conflict. Where the mythic quest leads purposefully toward conclusion, *Timecode* creates a grammar of images and sounds that defy clarity of purpose or outcome.

Critical attention to the innovative qualities of *Timecode* have focused on two aspects: its continuous take (like *Russian Ark*), and to its split-screen format. Lev Manovich places *Timecode* neatly into his theory of new media reproducing old media (Manovich 2001, 2002). Here *Timecode* repeats the original distinction between a cinema of spectacle (Méliès) and a cinema of realism (Lumière brothers), by providing an aesthetic of realism to counter the fantasy world of Hollywood film. Yet this conceptualisation refuses both the textual detail of the film, and the extra-textual dimensions that impact on its form. To take the textual features first, *Timecode* is not an unmediated representation of reality, but a film that constructs a particular form of parallel narratives, a visual interface of simultaneous events and a sound text that steers attention through the audial. These features are not merely a reproduction of a tradition of documentary or reality TV aesthetics, but a construction of fictional worlds where the inter-relationship of people, and their impact on one another, is the subject of the film. In many ways, *Timecode* has a meta-relationship to the technical means of its representation: in the film, technology is implicated in the nature of human interaction. Whilst the split screen images present a world of increasingly proximate lives, and technology masters the distances that exist, the film communicates a profound failure of communication between characters. Despite our networks of sophisticated contact, face-to-face encounters are brutal, language obfuscates rather than enlightens characters and communication misfires.

There are two scenes in the film where technology mediates relationships to obfuscate communication. In one scene, a sound device (a bug) is placed in the bag of a character, ostensibly to act as a surveillance mechanism. Her partner suspects that she is having an affair. Listening to events from the distance of her car, what she hears is the soundtrack of a pornography film playing in the background of a meeting between the two characters she suspects. We are privy to the visual information that her partner is indeed having an affair, and about to engage in sex, yet the sound here is from another film. The scene complicates our notions of the real, of what is being communicated and simultaneously miscommunicated: her suspicions are confirmed but through the relay of misinformation. A second moment of disjunction occurs in the final moments of the film when a woman calls her partner on a mobile phone. The conversation is about a reunification, and a meeting is planned for that evening. Yet her partner has been shot and lies bleeding to death. Thus, mobile technologies facilitate an immediacy of communication, but not clarity. Technology is not simply a tool for communication across distance; it creates possibilities for particular relationships where partial knowledge is the result, leading to obfuscation rather than enlightenment.

In addition to the textual reflexivity to technology, the form of the film experiments with the relationship between viewer and text. Sound is deployed in the film to structure our relationship to the text; in the cinematic version of the film, the volume of each window moves up and down as the dramatic tension rises within that particular frame. Despite the fantasy of watching four frames simultaneously, sound is used to control our vision. It is a directorial device, yet it also presents the more philosophical proposition that to comprehend the simultaneity of events and their inter-relationship is beyond possibility. At moments the film allows a leaking of sound from different windows creating something like white noise, sounds competing for a form of address and tipping over into aural assault. In contrasting moments, non-diegetic music rides over the sound from all four windows, relieving the spectator of the task of bringing together the narrative segments. Where, in the tradition of filmmaking, sound is sublimated to the image, in *Timecode*, sound is our means of orientation, of navigation. This feature of the film becomes more pronounced in its version as a DVD. Here, the potential for the viewer to select which story to follow, and the tantalising prospect of the four windows of images, is opened out. In digital format, sound becomes a selection, a choice for the viewer to make, to move between the different stories by tuning in to any of the four sound channels.

Once again, technology needs to be connected to material conditions of circulation, of the life of film as an object. The use of digital technology in *Timecode* transforms the conventional features of film: the single screen, the language of editing, the primacy of the image are conventions radically challenged. But the life span of *Timecode* also stakes out the transformation of the object as it moves through various release windows, as it becomes embedded in other contexts. In a phenomenological sense, film does not simply stay the same, but is transformed by its life as a DVD. The film is situated alongside other intertextual material, is one object on a menu of related choices, and takes film viewing into a more inter-active sphere. This suggests that we need to attend to the various ways in which we engage with film in its various stages of life. To frame the debate simply as innovation or stasis, cinema or home view, polarises the field as inflexible and exclusive positions. Just as there is more than one form of cinema, there are various forms of viewing/using film in a range of locations. This pluralisation of cinema cultures, sites of viewing and viewing practices, however, undoubtedly threatens the powers of critical analysis. Rather than resort to the heroic, we may need to trace more particularly the lives of objects, and their trajectories through the networks that constrain and enable them.

Declining the heroic

Bruno Latour, an anthropologist of science and technology, writes, 'The moderns have a peculiar propensity for understanding time that passes as if it were really abolishing the past behind it' (Latour 1991: 68). Latour's project is to establish the error of thinking about change in linear terms, of dividing time into neat periods (modernism, postmodernism, 'late' capitalism), and placing objects within each historical configuration. For Latour, such divisions are acts of purifi-cation, whilst objects, such as films, are hybrid forms, constituted by a mix of resources drawn from different moments. Film, for example, draws on Greek traditions of drama, Renaissance notions of perspective, nineteenth-century tradi-tions of spectacle. Digitalisation does not affect a radical break or aesthetic disjunction from earlier forms. Rather, the digital contributes to new hybrids of cinematic culture, which might return to earlier cultural traditions in the forging of the 'new'. Interactivity, to offer another example, is an ancient cultural rela-tionship between 'creator' and 'audience' in the tradition of oral storytelling. The 'new' in new media is then the realisation of a particular mix of components, which in turn shape and are shaped by the particular traditions of film cultures. Rather than polarise the past and present, and to create radical disjunctions of an epic scale, our understanding of the digital is more fruitfully traced through local details of emergence, in smaller textual features and film cultures. What we are experiencing is less than a technological revolution and more of an incremental cultural shift and remix.

   In place of an analytical discourse of heroism, a more useful term for thinking through such developments might be the emerging ecologies of film, a term used by O'Regan and Goldsmith to think the relationship between old and new media. Ecology suggests a shift in scale from a distant panoramic view of change, like the opening establishing shot of a film, to a more local investigation of particular forms. To think of film cultures as emerging ecologies signals an approach to cultural change that regards the object in the context of its environment. That is, the study of film in its interaction with and on other objects. Cinema is, as Sontag notes, undergoing a transformation as a set of practices (both production and consumption) that were largely set down a century ago. Yet it is also experiencing reassembly in perhaps less predictable and not totally mournful ways. If Thomas Elsaesser is right, 'the digital is not only a new technique of post-production work and a new delivery system or storage medium, it is the new horizon for thinking about cinema' (Elsaesser 1998: 227). How we think that horizon remains a critical task.

Notes

1   For further discussions of cinephilia and its significance in the end of cinema debate, see Paul Willeman (1994) and Mary Ann Doane (2002). Doane writes, 'It is arguable that cinephilia could not be revived at this conjuncture were the cinema *not* threatened by the accelerating development of new electronic and digital forms of media' (228).
2   *Star Wars* in 1977 is credited in many accounts as the emergence of large-format special effects cinema. The evolution of effects under digitalisation can be measured in both quality and quantity. Lucas's company, Industrial Light and Magic, returned to the 'original' *Star Wars* text and digitally remastered it to radically upgrade effects quality (1997). The latest component in the franchise, *The Phantom Menace*, is comprised of 95 per cent digitally written frames.
3   Eisenstein's essay 'The montage of film attraction' appears in *Selected Works*, vol. 1, *Writings 1922–34*, ed. and trans. Richard Taylor, London: BFI, 1988.
4   Russian Ark was funded also by ARTE, the German–French channel, Filmboard Berlin Brandenburg, Filmforderung Hamburg, among others; there were around fifty financial partners. The state Hermitage retained authorship rights.

References

Arthur, Paul (2001) 'The four last things: history, technology, Hollywood, apocalypse', in J. Lewis (ed.) *The End of Cinema as We Know It*, London: Pluto Press, pp. 342–55.

Belton, John (2002) 'Digital revolutions?' *October* 100: 98–114.

Bukatman, Scott (1998) 'Zooming out: The end of offscreen space', in J. Lewis (ed.) *The New American Cinema*, Durham: Duke University Press, pp. 248–68.

Cubitt, Sean (2002) 'Spreadsheets, sitemaps and search engines: why narrative is marginal to multimedia and networked communication, and why marginality is more vital than universality', in M. Rieser and A. Zapp (eds) *New Screen Media: Cinema/Art/Narrative*, London: BFI, pp. 3–13.

Doane, Mary Ann (2002) *The Emergence of Cinematic Time: Modernity, Contingency, the Archive*, Cambridge, MA, and London: Harvard University Press.

Eisenstein, Sergei (1988 [1924]) 'The montage of film attraction', in *Selected Works*, vol. 1, *Writings 1922–34*, ed. and trans. R. Taylor: London: BFI, pp. 39–58.

Elsaesser, Thomas (1998) 'Digital cinema: delivery, event, time', in Thomas Elsaesser and K. Hoffman (eds), *Cinema Futures: Cain, Abel or Cabel?* Amsterdam: University of Amsterdam Press, pp. 210–29.

Friedberg, Anne (1993) *Window Shopping: Cinema and the Postmodern*, Berkeley: University of California Press.

Harbord, Janet (2002) *Film Cultures*, London, Thousand Oaks, Delhi: Sage.

Hunt, Leon (2002) ' "I know Kung Fu!" The martial arts in the age of digital reproduction', in G. King and T. Krywinska (eds) *ScreenPlay: Cinema/Videogames/Interfaces*, London and New York: Wallflower Press, pp. 194–205.

Latour, Bruno (1991) *We Have Never Been Modern*, trans. Catherine Porter, Cambridge, MA: Harvard University Press.

Lewis, Jo (ed.) (2001) *The End of Cinema as We Know It*, London: Pluto Press.

Manovich, Lev (2001) *The Language of New Media*, Cambridge, MA, and London: MIT Press.

—— (2002) 'Old media as new media: cinema', in D. Harries (ed.) *The New Media Book*, London: BFI, pp. 209–18.

Mellencamp, Pat (2002) 'The Zen of masculinity – rituals of heroism in *The Matrix*', in J. Lewis (ed.) *The End of Cinema as We Know It*, London: Pluto Press, pp. 83–94.

Miller, Toby, Govil, Nitin, McMurria, John and Maxwell, Richard (2001) *Global Hollywood*, London: BFI.

O'Regan, Tom and Goldsmith, Ben (2002) 'Emerging global ecologies of production', in D. Harries (ed.) *The New Media Book*, London: BFI, pp. 92–105.

Rodowick, D.N. (2001) *Reading the Figural, or, Philosophy after the New Media*, Durham and London: Duke University Press.

Sharrett, Christopher (2001) 'End of story: the collapse of myth in postmodern narrative film', in J. Lewis (ed.) *The End of Cinema as We Know It*, London: Pluto Press, pp. 319–31.

Sontag, Susan (2001) 'A century of cinema', in *Where the Stress Falls*, New York: Picador USA, pp. 117–22.

Willeman, Paul (1994) *Looks and Frictions: Essays in Cultural Studies and Film Theory*, Bloomington and Indianapolis: Indiana University Press.

Wyatt, Justin (1994) *High Concept: Movies and Marketing in Hollywood*, Austin: University of Texas Press.

Chapter 19

Internet transformations

'Old' media resilience in the 'new media' revolution

Des Freedman

Introduction

The death – or at least the decay – of the established mass media has been long predicted. Confronted by the challenge of dynamic new media technologies like cable, satellite and especially the Internet, newspapers, broadcast television, recorded music and consumer magazines have seen the erosion of their well-established domination of popular consumption habits (see Table 19.1). During the life of the World Wide Web, the three main US broadcast networks have seen their share of prime-time viewing plummet from 55 per cent in 1992 to 33 per cent in 2002; the top five consumer magazines have lost 18 per cent of circulation since 1995 while the circulation of the five main US daily newspaper titles has dropped 7.4 per cent since 1993 (Dawley 2003). European broadcasters and newspaper publishers have experienced similar declines. A combination of technological innovations (concerning digitization) and cultural shifts (towards a more individualistic consumer society) appear to have handed new media technologies a competitive advantage over their predecessors.

This is an analysis proposed by a number of technology theorists in the 1990s who, galvanized by the promise of a 'new economy' driven by a rapidly expanding Internet, argued that the business models and industrial structures of the traditional media would eventually be superseded by the more streamlined and fluid character of the digital universe. Nicholas Negroponte, Alvin Toffler, Esther Dyson and George Gilder all championed the logic of 'bits' over 'atoms', celebrated the wave of creativity unleashed via the Internet, predicted a shift of power

Table 19.1 Hours per person per year using consumer media

	Broadcast TV	Daily newspaper	Consumer magazines	Pay TV	Consumer Internet
1996	988	92	125	575	8
2001	815	177	119	846	134
2006	726	169	112	892	213

Source: Veronis Suhler, 2003

Note: Figures for 2006 are estimated.

from media bureaucracies to digital networks, and spoke in rather apocalyptic terms of the future of the 'old media'. 'Moving authority from elites and establishments,' wrote Gilder, 'the new technologies drastically change the cultural balance of power.' Everyone else 'will have to change or crash' (Gilder 1994).

Despite the fact that it was the 'dotcoms' and not the 'old media' that crashed in 2000, this assumption has not disappeared and indeed underpins much recent thinking about the media. The British government's justification for liberalizing media rules, ultimately enshrined in the 2003 Communications Act, is based on the 'communications cornucopia' facilitated by the widespread use of mobile and digital technologies that epitomize the ongoing 'communications revolution' (DTI/DCMS 2000: 7). The Federal Communications Commission (FCC) agreed to relax restrictions on broadcast ownership in June 2003 on the basis that the old rules had no place in a media landscape dominated by the multiple sources and cultural diversity of the Internet (see Martin 2003; Powell 2003). It is a position summed up by the CEO of Forrester Research, George Colony, who speaks of the 'inexorable factors that are changing the equation for entertainment' and calls on the captains of the old media industries not to stand in the way of digital progress. 'End the denial. Get over it, get on with it, figure it out. Or end up in the dustbin of history with sheet music publishers' (Colony 2003).

This argument depends on a deterministic definition of new media that assumes that technological transformations in and of themselves make regulatory, corporate and consumer change necessary and inevitable. This chapter examines the actual impact of the Internet on existing mass-media industries, largely in the USA, which has the world's largest media market and one of the most mature Internet populations, and assesses the extent to which particular media sectors have been or are likely to be transformed by 'network logic'. It then analyzes how Internet communication is being shaped by traditional business models and highlights the continuing importance of the existing media in the contemporary communications landscape.

The impact of the new on the old

The revolutionary potential of the Internet as a communication tool (and a threat to 'old media') springs from a more general new-media paradigm that is derived from specific technical capacities associated with particular technological systems. The competitive advantages attributed to Internet communication are the consequence of the unravelling of these defining characteristics (often referred to as the 'principles' or 'essential features' or 'general tendencies') of new media (see Lister et al. 2003: 13–37; Manovich 2001: 27–48; Packer and Jordan 2001: xxx–xxxi; Rogers 1986: 4–6). If we follow this model, we can identify a whole host of key (and interconnected) new-media paradigms including:

- *Interactivity*: the ability of the user to react back on and participate in the communications process (Lister *et al*. 2003: 19–23; Negroponte 1995: 63; Packer and Jordan 2001: xxx; Rice 1984: 35; Rogers 1986: 4). Sparks (2002) refers to the dialogic structure of the Internet in contrast to the 'essentially monologic' structure of traditional mass media.
- *Hypertext* and *hypermedia*: 'the linking of separate media elements to one another to create a trail of personal association' (Packer and Jordan 2001: xxx; see also Castells 2001: 203; Lister *et al*. 2003: 23–30; Manovich 2001: 40–2).
- *Non-linearity* and new strategies of narrativity (Manovich 2001: 225–8; Packer and Jordan 2001: xxxi).
- *Virtuality* and *extraterritoriality*: the respatialization of media flows particularly along a more global axis (Castells 1996: 373–5; Lévy 2001; Lister *et al*. 2003: 34–7).
- *Digitality* or, as Manovich (2001: 27) calls it, 'numerical representation' (see also Lister *et al*. 2003: 14–19; Negroponte 1995: 14–19).
- *Acceleration of time/space compression* (Harvey 1989) with the related emphasis on immediacy (Bolter and Grusin 1999) and decreasing relevance of barriers of physical distance (van Dijk 1999: 17).
- *Modularity*: the assembling of discrete units into media objects (Manovich, 2001: 30–2) that facilitates new media's 'permanent state of flux' (Lister *et al*. 2003: 16) and its 'variability' (Manovich 2001: 36–45).
- *Remediation*: the revising and refashioning of older media forms (Bolter and Grusin 1999). Manovich (2001: 45–8) calls this 'transcoding' and discusses the 'cultural reconceptualization' facilitated by new media.
- *Demassification* and related trends towards individualization, customization, personalization and decentralization (Castells 1996: 340; Lister *et al*. 2003: 30–4; Negroponte 1995: 229; Rogers 1986: 5) that supersede the traditional one-to-many flow of the 'broadcast media' model.
- *Asynchronicity*: 'the ability to overcome time as a variable affecting the communication process' (Rogers 1986: 5).
- *Convergence*: the tendency for hybrid forms and technologies to integrate (Baldwin *et al*. 1996; Castells 1996: 62; Packer and Jordan 2001: xxx).

While all of the above tendencies and processes connect to new-media technologies in significant ways, there are problems with this 'defining characteristics' approach to new media. First, given that this is only a partial selection, the list of new-media paradigms may be so long as to render it analytically useless. Second, these characteristics are not necessarily new: a point made by many of the theorists who employ these classifications (in particular Bolter and Grusin 1999: 21; Lister *et al*. 2003: 37–44; and Manovich 2001: 49–61). There are clear historical precedents for attributes such as interactivity, time/space compression and non-linearity. Third, the processes themselves are far from transparent and need to be contested to reveal underlying meanings. For example, the interactivity celebrated by bulletin board users is not the same as the more commercially understood one used to generate income for reality television and game show programmes via text messaging. Similarly, the 'fact' of media convergence has been used to justify particular corporate transactions (for example the merger of Time Warner and America Online in 2000) and regulatory shifts even though it is now widely acknowledged that it 'has not taken place at the speed expected' (ABN AMRO 2002: 11). Finally, this is a very deterministic approach in that the actual uses of media technologies are read off from their technological capacities, ignoring or marginalizing questions of culture, economics and power.

However, it is also clear that the Internet *has* presented individuals with real possibilities for self-expression, conversation and creative work. The rise of 'blog-ging', the exchanges facilitated through peer-to-peer (P2P) networks, the multiplication of information sources and extension of previously restricted mediated spaces (for example accessing local newspapers from thousands of miles away) are just some of the examples of symbolic activity opened up by the Net. The result, according to some theorists, is the beginning of a thriving and demo-cratic media culture in direct opposition to the traditional mass media. For Howard Rheingold in 1994, the significance of the computer-mediated communi-cation that was emerging in online communities lay 'in its capacity to challenge the existing political hierarchy's monopoly on powerful communications media, and perhaps thus revitalize citizen-based democracy' (Rheingold 1995: 14). Manuel Castells also counterposes the sociality of online media to the passivity of traditional entertainment-dominated mass media and argues that Internet communication has its own logic and language. 'It is open source, free posting, decentralized broadcasting, serendipitous interaction, purpose-oriented commu-nication, and shared creation that find their expression on the Internet' (Castells 2001: 200).

Just as Internet communication is conceptualized as intrinsically democratic and diverse in contrast to the deformities of 'one-to-many' communication, it is also the case that it offers both significant advantages and challenges to traditional media interests. In his analysis of the latter's online strategies, Colin Sparks (2002) discusses the various ways in which the Internet affects the existing processes of production and distribution, and causes problems for long-estab-lished business models. These include the following trends and tendencies:

- The Internet significantly lowers the cost of production and distribution. The huge expense of distributing newspapers, magazines or music across territo-ries is virtually abolished by online distribution and the cost of accessing the content (paying for a computer and an Internet Service Provider) is borne by the consumer. Production costs remain high but savings can be made as the need for physical resources (like ink, paper, plastic and so on) is reduced. This also has the effect of lowering the entry barriers to media markets and allowing for new players to challenge entrenched interests. This does not apply to all media sectors – interactive advertising and marketing, for example, is more expensive than traditional forms and raises the barriers to market entry (see ABN AMRO 2001: 11).

- The Internet 'erodes advantages based on physical space' and on 'time of production and distribution'. Online media can be consumed from anywhere in the world where there is access to a suitable computer and a phone line, transcending both national (print and terrestrial broadcast) and international (satellite, short-wave radio) media circuits. They can also be constantly updated and consumed thus disrupting traditional time-based classifications (for example the morning paper or the evening bulletin) and stimulating a more fluid, 'rolling' form of media culture.

- The Internet facilitates the 'disaggregation of editorial and advertising material'. For much of the media, editorial content is provided as the means of luring consumers to the newspaper, magazine or broadcast programme where they are then exposed to the advertising that funds the content in the first place. Sparks argues that the searchable nature of the Internet allows advertisers to reach selected audiences (and vice versa) without the need of the editorial 'meat' thus jeopardizing the existence of print publications that depend on advertising revenue. For example, the British government has announced that it intends to place advertisements for public sector workers on websites from 2005, a move that led the *Guardian* newspaper to talk of publishers' fears that 'readers will turn to [the] internet and stop buying their titles when looking for job ads' (Byrne 2003).

- The Internet also facilitates a much more direct and specific relationship between different participants in the communications process. Rather than the diffuse and general model of broadcasting, individuals can go straight to a variety of news sources instead of relying on the newspaper or bulletin; music fans can go straight to their favourite band's website or to a P2P service like KaZaA or Gnutella to download music instead of tuning into a radio programme or buying a CD. Similarly, bands and news sources can now target particular consumer profiles with desirable information. This form of disintermediation is of particular concern to record companies and newspapers as they consider their role and their business models in an online era.

- The Internet competes with offline media for both audiences and revenue. A Pew Internet study of online behaviour in 2002 found that 25 per cent of Internet users in the USA were watching less television with 14 per cent reporting a decline in newspaper reading because of time spent on the Internet (Pew 2002: 4). The Net's share of spending on media is modest at the moment: US consumers, for example, spent $990 million on Internet content in 2001 as compared to $9 billion on magazines (Veronis Suhler Stevenson 2003: 64–5). However, the Internet's presence is felt more acutely in some media sectors than others. While Internet advertising accounts for only 2.1 per cent of the total ad spend in the USA (NAA 2003), online classifieds make up nearly 6 per cent of total classified advertising (IAB 2003; NAA 2003) and are predicted to reach 19 per cent of the classified market by 2010 (ABN AMRO 2001: 159) presenting a genuine threat to many newspapers and trade magazines.

- Finally, the Internet allows for the provision of highly specific, customized content (as selected by the consumer) as opposed to the diverse material to be found in broadcast television or in your daily newspaper. Generalist outlets in press and broadcasting have long been challenged by niche products (consumer magazines, cable channels) but the Internet accentuates the problem. If you are interested in celebrity gossip or foreign news but not both, then the *Daily Mirror* during the war on Iraq would be less appropriate than a website that is focused on one but not the other. Online media provide for a much more individualized experience than the 'one-to-many' structure of the traditional mass media.

Sparks concludes that these tendencies do not threaten all media systems to the same extent and that the scale of disruption is related to two issues. First, there is the need to develop a suitable revenue model for exploiting the advantages presented by the Internet. Thus far, the Internet has not generated the expected windfall for media companies as, with a number of important exceptions like pornography, *Big Brother* and financial information, consumers have been reluctant to pay for media accessed through the net. This has led to much frustration in the industry. The former head of broadband at cable company Telewest, David Docherty, has criticized the 'cookie monsters' who 'want everything for free. They think the net is an anarchistic space and that anything intended to commercialise it is to be fiercely resisted' (Docherty 2002). Peter Chernin, the chief operating officer of News Corporation, famously commented at a new-media conference that there was 'no viable business model that works' for commercial media on the Internet (quoted in Pesola 2002). Possibilities presented by the Internet have thus not always been realized because no one has figured out how to make them profitable, ameliorating the Net's impact on existing media.

The other relevant factor concerns the amount of bandwidth required to shift particular media online. Sparks proposes a 'working hypothesis that the greater the informational content of a class of media artefacts, the more difficult and

protracted will be the task of transforming it into an Internet based medium'
(Sparks 2002). This suggests that the migration of film and television to the Net is
not likely to be as immediate as that of music and print, which require less bandwidth and which have both seen a significant number of online innovations (see
Table 19.2).

Given that the Internet has not had a uniform impact across the existing
media, it is worth discussing the industry that it has affected the most: the music
industry. A series of headlines in the last several years have drawn attention to the
catastrophic state of record sales across the world that fell 19 per cent (in value)
between 1995 and 2002 with a 7 per cent decline in 2002 alone (IFPI 2003). The
record companies have put the blame firmly on illegal Internet downloads facilitated by the growing number of file-sharing networks, the most famous of which,
Napster, was sued successfully and shut down by the Recording Industry
Association of America in 2001. The industry has since escalated its attempts to
prevent Internet piracy by threatening to sue not just Internet Service Providers
but individual users as potential copyright infringers. This has failed to curb the
enthusiasm for P2P networks and a Pew Internet survey in July 2003 found that
35 million US adults were still downloading music files online with 26 million
sharing them with other users (Pew 2003a: 1). Only a tiny minority of those
downloads are licensed due to the inability – or the reluctance – of the record
companies to develop attractive, legal online music services. Even the highly
successful launch of Apple's iTunes service in April 2003 is not expected to plug
the gaps caused by declining sales (Gibson 2003).

P2P networks are perhaps the clearest embodiment of many of the characteristics discussed earlier that contribute to the revolutionary character of the
Internet. They are highly interactive, dialogic and decentralized, and have helped
to create thriving and 'authentic' fan communities in opposition to the perception
of the record companies as bureaucratic, conservative and profit-led. They are an
example of a workable business model (at least for the users) and a new paradigm

Table 19.2 The impact of the Internet on existing media businesses

	Bandwidth	Data-gathering potential	Point of threat	Commercial threat
Theatrical Film	Very High	`Moderate	Distant	Low
Video	High	Moderate	Distant	Low
TV	High	High	Present	Medium
Radio	Low	Moderate	Present	Medium
Press	Low	Very high	Present	High
Magazines	Low	Very high	Present	High
Music	Low	Moderate	Present	Very high

Source: Adapted from Sparks (2002)

for music distribution that has shaken up the record industry in the last few years (see Alderman 2001).

Yet the argument that illegal downloads are the unique, or even the major, cause of the decline in sales needs further examination. This is not the first severe decline in record sales – indeed, throughout its history, the music industry has been subject to cycles of boom and slump, none of which have been caused by one identifiable factor such as piracy. For example, the end of the 'rock boom' in the late 1970s witnessed both a substantial fall in sales, some 40 per cent in the USA and 20 per cent in Europe between 1978 and 1983 (Frith 1987a: 59), and the identification of a new villain: home-taping using new audiocassette recorders. Simon Frith argues that there was a far more complex bundle of reasons than home-taping. 'The rock business faced a crisis at the end of the 1970s not because of punk or the cycle of business competition but because of "outside" technological and social changes' (Frith 1987b: 70) including a fall in the number of teenagers, rising youth unemployment and an increase in the number of home-base leisure activities (e.g. computer games, VCRs as well as cassettes). 'What home taping signifies,' Frith concludes, 'is the changing place of music in leisure generally. Records are being replaced not by tapes as such but by other leisure activities; music is being used differently and in different, more flexible forms' (Frith 1987b: 73).

This is particularly true today when music is consumed in a growing number of contexts (from TV commercials and films to clubs, elevators and shopping malls) and via an ever-changing array of technologies (including mobile phones, PCs, MP3 players, iPods, as well as traditional hi-fi). Simplistic narratives of technological succession – that Internet technologies will necessarily undermine hard carrier sales – is as misplaced as previous assertions that film would kill off photography or that television would kill off film.

There is no single explanation for the recent decline in global record sales. To place the burden wholly or partly on illegal downloads from the Internet is to ignore a host of other reasons, including:

- A slowing global economy;
- The maturing of the CD market and consumer perception of the high cost of CDs;
- The popularity of rival leisure activities such as video games and DVDs;
- The continuing 'corporate concentration' of the music industry leading to a reliance on formulas and a reluctance to invest in new artists;
- A lack of major musical innovations.

The willingness of the industry as a whole to identify P2P services as the major cause of declining sales suggests that the record companies are reluctant to investigate their own responsibility and eager to use the threat of Internet 'piracy' as a justification for securing new, corporate-friendly copyright legislation for the digital age. A few major hits, a more proactive engagement with the distributional and marketing possibilities offered by the Internet, and, above all, an economic upturn are far more likely to produce a reverse in the fortunes of the music industry than its current strategy of criminalizing Internet users. We may therefore conclude that even in an area in which the Internet has had a significant impact on the existing media, the nature of this relationship is far from clear, predictable or irreversible.

The resilience of old media

Much critical attention has focused on the impact of the Internet on the existing media; less has been devoted to assessing the ways in which the old media have impacted on the particular uses and forms of Internet communication. In order to do this, it is necessary to provide a snapshot of the extent to which traditional media still have a grip on the consumption habits and market structures of the media industries in general. In overall terms, the two largest US media sectors are that of entertainment (films, video games, DVDs, etc.) and pay television followed by newspapers and broadcast television (see Table 19.3). While the consumer Internet sector is larger than that of magazines and radio, it is important to stress that the bulk (some two-thirds) of this spending is on access fees (payable to Internet Service Providers and telecommunications companies) rather than on advertising or original content. Furthermore, while the growth of the Internet has been and continues to be particularly impressive (in relation to other sectors), it is still not expected to match the revenues of broadcast television, the epitome of 'old' media.

How can it be the case that, despite all the talk of a communications revolution, Internet communication is not likely to be the dominant media form, at

Table 19.3 Communications industry sectors ranked by size (US)

	2001	2006
	$ billions	$ billions
Entertainment	74,011	97,382
Pay Television	70,212	106,322
Newspapers	61,942	79,418
Broadcast Television	38,665	46,695
Consumer Internet	21,537	39,111
Consumer Magazines	20,911	24, 494
Radio	17,892	24,143

Source: Adapted from Veronis Suhler Stevenson 2003

Note: Figures for 2006 are estimated.

least for the foreseeable future? Of course this is partly a technical issue: that as soon as bandwidth questions are resolved and high-speed Internet access is readily available, there is an increased likelihood of existing media migrating to the Internet. But there are also two other important factors in explaining the continuing domination of 'old media'.

First, the cost of Internet access is likely to remain a significant factor in making 'free' media more attractive, both in richer countries in the West and in the poorest countries where access to electricity – let alone a computer – is some way off. Second, the very characteristics that make the Internet so attractive and innovative – its capacity to provide customized communication along decentralized networks – raises the premium on its counterpart: the mass audience. Although mass-circulation newspapers may continue to lose readers and free-to-air broadcast networks may carry on haemorrhaging viewers, their ability to reach mass audiences is likely to reap dividends. According to global banking group ABN AMRO:

> We believe that advertisers will continue to use the traditional TV networks as they will remain the most efficient medium to reach a mass audience. Price increases for their airtime will more than offset viewing share losses and advertising revenue will continue to grow.
>
> (ABN AMRO 2001: 65)

This explains the enormous premiums attracted by, for example, the Super Bowl in the USA where traditional brands turn to traditional means to reach target viewers. In 2002, the cost for a 30 second television spot during the programme was $2.2 million; Budweiser spent $22 million on 300 seconds of exposure, AT&T and Pepsi spent $8.8 million on 120 seconds while a truly 'old' brand, Cadillac, spent $6.6 million on a mere 90 seconds of advertising (Nielsen 2003).

This resilience emerges even when we look at news, an area of media use in which the Internet has attracted significant audiences and has made an important contribution through expanding the number of sources available and facilitating a constantly 'updateable' approach to news production and consumption. A British survey of news habits in 2002 found that 65 per cent of the British public claimed they regard television as their main source of news compared to 16 per cent for radio, 15 per cent for newspapers and 2 per cent for the Internet (Hargreaves and Thomas 2002: 44). A large-scale survey conducted for the FCC in 2002 found similar results: 85 per cent of respondents claimed to have turned to television in the last seven days to find out about local news as against 63 per cent for newspapers, 35 per cent for radio and 19 per cent for the Internet. The figures for national news were 84 per cent, 50 per cent, 30 per cent and 21 per cent respectively (FCC 2002: 1 and 9). During the war in Iraq when there was an added incentive for individuals to broaden their range of sources, online news consumption increased massively. However, a Pew research project concluded that 'TV still rules the news world' and, when asked how they were getting most of their news about the war, 89 per cent of respondents answered television, 24 per cent newspapers and 19 per cent radio. The figure for Internet consumption was negligible (Pew 2003b: 2).

In the context of the continuing importance of the offline media, let us examine some of the key features of Internet media use (see Table 19.4). Clearly, the most common uses of the Internet are informational, to seek out data on specific topics (travel, weather, shopping, etc.) or to communicate electronically with other individuals. While the figures for downloading music are almost certainly understated (perhaps the result of the illegal nature of file-sharing), the low levels of 'creative' behaviour are more surprising and do little to support the notion that the Internet is an intrinsically more sympathetic environment for mediated activity. Blogging and online discussions are undertaken vigorously but, thus far, only by a minority of enthusiasts rather than the general online population. The figures demonstrate that the Internet is more commonly used as a tool of individual research and connection rather than as a site of mass-mediated production and interaction.

How does this proposition sit with uses of the Internet that are specifically media-related, for example news? If we return to the example of online activity during the war on Iraq, we find that according to Pew research some 77 per cent of online Americans specifically used the Internet in connection with the war. However, only 17 per cent of these online respondents reported that they got most of their information about the war from the Internet as opposed to 87 per cent who turned to television, virtually the same figures as the offline population (Pew 2003b: 2). More disturbing for those who speak of the Net's innate diversity, when these users were online 32 per cent of them turned to US network

Table 19.4 Selected uses of the Internet (per cent)

	US (2002/3)	UK (2002)
E-mail	52	64
Get news	32	11
Look for information	29	58
Shopping	N/A	24
Sports information	12	12
Play a game	9	3
Internet banking	7	3
Download music	4	2
Create internet content	4	N/A
Take part in an online group	4	<0.5

US source: Pew 2003c
UK source: Towler 2002

television sites, 29 per cent to newspaper sites and 15 per cent to US government sites – far more than those who turned to alternative sources like weblogs, alternative news organizations or political campaign groups (Pew 2003b: 5). Detailed FCC research about media consumption in 2002 found that of those who get their news from Internet sites, the vast majority choose websites where news is gathered from traditional news suppliers. 22.4 per cent turn to MSN.com where news is supplied by US network NBC, 19.1 per cent to CNN.com, and 17.9 per cent and 13.3 per cent respectively to Yahoo and America Online where news is provided mainly by the large news agencies, Associated Press and Reuters (FCC 2002: 20).

A similar pattern emerges in the UK. Online news is becoming increasingly popular with 10.6 million people accessing news-related sites, approximately one-sixth of the population (Hargreaves and Thomas 2002: 42). By far the most popular news site is the BBC's followed by the *Guardian*, Channel Four, Sky and ITV – all established broadcasters or publishers. The majority of Internet news use, therefore, appears to be parasitic on traditional news suppliers. For a minority, however, the Internet provides an opportunity to bypass mainstream sources and access alternative or specialist voices. Hargreaves and Thomas argue that this particularly applies to young and ethnic minority audiences, and conclude that the Internet

> appears to be emerging as the news home for those who feel under-served by conventional mass media. It is also, however, a medium used chiefly by the better off: 20 per cent of ABC1s use it against only 10 per cent of C2DEs, confirming the concerns of those worried about a digital divide.
>
> (Hargreaves and Thomas 2002: 46)

This demonstrates both the potential diversity offered by the Net and also the danger of its institutionalizing inequalities of media access.

Internet diversity is often characterized by the range of voices and sources that it offers. Yet here too it appears that actual online use is rather different from what is possible. A survey conducted for the British consumer watchdog, Which? Online, found that out of the many millions of unique websites on the Internet the average user only visits thirteen in an average week. Indeed 42 per cent of users pass through five or fewer sites a week, the same number of free-to-air television channels available to them (Which? Online 2002: 9). Furthermore, the list of the most popular entertainment sites is dominated by either familiar names or non-media activities: the BBC has three sites and Microsoft one in the top ten with the rest largely consisting of weather, sports, betting and mobile telephony gateways (Netimperative 2003).

US online users demonstrate a more promiscuous engagement with the

Internet, perhaps reflecting the lower access costs and amount of content designed for Americans. In June 2003, the average Internet user visited fifty-four unique sites – a much healthier diet of consumption that their British counterparts. However, the proportion of time that they spend with only a handful of sites appears to be increasing. Research conducted by Jupiter Media Matrix found that the number of companies controlling half of all time online had fallen from 11 in March 1999 to only four in March 2001, the most popular of which were AOL Time Warner Network, Microsoft sites, Yahoo! and Napster. The conclusion of senior analyst Aram Sinnreich was that the data shows 'an irrefutable trend toward online media consolidation' (Jupiter Media Matrix 2001). By June 2003, the order was different but the companies – and thus the voices – dominating Internet traffic were the same (with the exception of the now-defunct Napster).

Trends towards consolidation, the control of distribution networks by familiar multinational companies and the relatively narrow media consumption patterns of the majority of the online population suggest that the technological possibilities of the Internet are being constrained by the economic imperatives of the media business. Online media are just as subject to market pressures as offline media and display many of the same distinctive characteristics as the 'older' cultural industries analysed by theorists like Bettig (1996) and Garnham (1990). They argued that, in response to the unpredictability and high production costs of the cultural commodity, cultural industries are forced to adopt strategies to minimize risk and maximize returns. This may involve attempts to create scarcity, to secure domination of distribution channels, to engage in horizontal integration or to deliver audiences as commodities to advertisers and sponsors. The attempts by mass-media and Internet companies to lobby for more stringent copyright legislation, to pursue the logic of mergers and acquisitions, to develop increasingly sophisticated and intrusive ways of delivering users' attention to advertisers and to tie up exclusive deals between content providers and distributors – all of these are evidence of a traditional economic logic being applied to corporate efforts to develop a profitable business model for Internet media. Old priorities remain but confront new situations: reflecting on the uncertain future of the advertising industry, one senior US media analyst argues that 'the new media paradigm is gone. What you have is the old idea that where people are spending time is an opportunity to sell to them – but they are spending time in new places' (quoted in Harmon 2001).

Conclusion

The Internet has had a definite but uneven impact on the existing mass media. For a variety of technological, economic and cultural reasons, the music and publishing industries have been particularly affected although even in these cases there is no uniform or irrevocable pattern of influence. It is quite probable that newspapers and record companies will be able to leverage (as the investment bankers like to say) their offline power into the online sectors in which they have an interest. Indeed many large print titles are already doing just this while the major record labels are moving slowly but surely towards a recognition that the Internet may not be the threat they have rather hysterically proclaimed it to be but a complementary way of doing business.

Just as the Internet has not destroyed traditional media industries, regular use of the Internet has not replaced the consumption of other media forms. Recent studies indicate that more people are consuming media simultaneously and that the idea of a 'silo' mentality is out-of-date. In the USA, one study found that 59 per cent of men and 67 per cent of women watching television 'regularly or occasionally go online at the same time' (Cuneo 2002). European viewers are slightly more focused: only 33 per cent of men and 36 per cent of women watch television when online while approximately 20 per cent of both men and women regularly watch television at the same time as reading their emails (Greenspan 2003). This is not the multimedia convergence long predicted by technologists and futurologists but media compatibility that points to the emergence of a new, varied and complex media environment co-habited by offline and online, mobile and fixed, visual and text-based technologies.

In this changing environment, the 'old' – in the shape of the corporations, voices, brands and economic imperatives that dominate offline – is just as likely to affect the 'new' as the 'new' is likely to make life difficult for the 'old'. Perhaps from the evidence gathered here, the 'old' is set to exert a stronger influence on the structures, content and consumption patterns of new digital media – at least for the foreseeable future. The impact of the Internet on traditional media forms and institutions should not be ignored or underestimated but evaluated within the context of the material forces that dominate the production and consumption of all media. For those people who are committed to the possibilities of media fostering a more democratic, diverse and critical culture, there is little point in addressing 'new' issues if we have not yet resolved some very old problems concerning the concentration, commercialization and marketization of the media that surround us.

References

ABN AMRO (2001) *Mediaspace 2001: Sub-sector Analysis*, London: ABN AMRO.
——— (2002) *Pan-European Media: The Next Move*, London: ABN AMRO.
Alderman, J. (2001) *Sonic Boom: Napster, P2P and the Battle for the Future of Music*, London: Fourth Estate.
Baldwin, T., Stevens McVoy, D. and Steinfield, C. (1996) *Convergence: Integrating Media, Information & Communication*, London: Sage.

Bettig, R. (1996) *Copyrighting Culture: The Political Economy of Intellectual Property*, Boulder: Westview Press.

Bolter, J. and Grusin, R. (1999) *Remediation: Understanding New Media*, Cambridge, MA: MIT Press.

Byrne, C. (2003) 'Magazines under threat from government ad plan', MediaGuardian.co.uk, 9 June. Available online at http://politics.guardian.co.uk/egovernment/story/0,12767,973781,00.html (accessed 24 June 2003).

Castells, M. (1996) *The Rise of the Network Society*, Cambridge, MA: Blackwells.

—— (2001) *The Internet Galaxy*, Oxford: Oxford University Press.

Colony, G. (2003) 'Digital denial', CNET News.com, 13 January. Available online at http://news.com.com/2009–1122–980364.html (accessed 27 January 2003).

Cuneo, A. (2002) 'More consume multiple media simultaneously', AdAge.com, 8 October. Available online at www.adage.com/news.cms?newsId=36250 (accessed 15 October 2002).

Dawley, H. (2003) 'Dispelling myths about newspaper declines', *Media Life Magazine*, 4 June. Available online at www.medialifemagazine.com/news2003/jun03/jun02/3_wed/news3wednesday.html (accessed 15 August 2003).

Docherty, D. (2002) 'Why I quit', MediaGuardian.co.uk, 2 December. Available online at http://media.guardian.co.uk/mediaguardian/story/0,7558,852024,00.html (accessed 19 August 2003).

DTI/DCMS (2000) *A New Future for Communications*, government white paper, London: HMSO.

FCC (Federal Communications Commission) (2002) *Consumer Survey on Media Usage 8*, conducted by Nielsen Media Research, Washington, DC: FCC.

Frith, S. (1987a), 'Copyright and the music business', *Popular Music* 7(1): 57–75.

—— (1987b) 'The industrialization of popular music', in J. Lull (ed.) *Popular Music and Communication*, London: Sage, pp. 53–77.

Garnham, N. (1990) *Capitalism and Communication*, London: Sage.

Gibson, O. (2003) 'Legal downloads won't make up for drop in CD sales, record labels told', MediaGuardian.co.uk, 30 July. Available online at www.guardian.co.uk/business/story/0,3604,1008594,00.html (accessed 1 August 2003).

Gilder, G. (1994) 'Life after television updated', *Forbes ASAP*, 23 February.

Greenspan, R. (2003) 'Many channels surfers are web surfers', *CyberAtlas*, 29 April. Available online at http://cyberatlas.internet.com/markets/advertising/article/0,1323,5941_2198711,00.html (accessed 15 August 2003).

Hargreaves, I. and Thomas, J. (2002) *New News, Old News*, London: Independent Television Commission/Broadcasting Standards Commission.

Harmon, A. (2001) 'Fusing old and new in a media strategy', *New York Times*, 6 December.

Harvey, D. (1989) *The Condition of Postmodernity: An Enquiry into the Origins of Cultural Change*, Oxford: Basil Blackwell.

IAB (Internet Advertising Bureau) (2003) *IAB Internet Advertising Report*. Available online at www.iab.net/resources/pdf/IAB_PwC_2002final.pdf (accessed 15 August 2003).

IFPI (International Federation of the Phonographic Industry) (2003) *The Recording Industry: World Sales 2002*, London: IFPI.

Jupiter Media Matrix (2001) 'Rapid media consolidation dramatically narrows number of companies controlling time spent online', press release, 4 June. Available online at www.jup.com/company/pressrelease.jsp?doc=pr010604 (accessed 10 June 2001).

Lévy, P. (2001) *Cyberculture*, London: University of Minnesota Press.

Lister, M., Dovey, J., Giddings, S., Grant, I. and Kelly, K. (2003) *New Media: A Critical Introduction*, London: Routledge.

Manovich, L. (2001) *The Language of New Media*, Cambridge, MA: MIT Press.

Martin, K. (2003) 'Opening remarks by Commissioner Kevin J. Martin', *FCC Hearing on Media Ownership*, Richmond, VA, 27 February. Available online at hraunfoss.fcc.gov/edocs_public/attachmatch/DOC-233244A1.doc (accessed 1 August 2003).

NAA (Newspaper Association of America) (2003) 'Total US advertising volume'. Available online at www.naa.org/artpage.cfm?AID=1573&SID=147 (accessed 15 August 2003).

Negroponte, N. (1995) *Being Digital*, New York: Alfred A. Knopf.

Nielsen Media Research (2003) *TV and Advertising Trends surrounding the Super Bowl*, press release, 23 January. Available online at www.nielsenmedia.com/newsreleases/2003/pre-superbowl_2003.htm (accessed 18 August 2003).

Netimperative (2003) *Top Ten: United Kingdom 'Entertainment' Sites*, 11 August. Available online at www.netimperative.com (accessed 14 August 2003).

Packer, R. and Jordan, K. (2001) 'Overture', in R. Packer and K. Jordan (eds) *Multimedia: From Wagner to Virtual Reality*, New York: W.W. Norton & Company, pp. xiii–xxxi.

Pesola, M. (2002) 'Media chiefs reject internet business model', Ft.com. Available online at http://news.ft.com/ft/gx/cgi/ftc?pagename=View&c=Article&cid=FT3XNV0EEYC&live=true (accessed 13 March 2002).

Pew Internet Project (2002) 'Getting serious online'. Available online at www.pewinternet.org/reports/toc.asp?Report=55 (accessed 15 August 2003).

—— (2003a) 'Music downloading, file-sharing and copyright'. Available online at www.pewinternet.org/reports/pdfs/PIP_Copyright_Memo.pdf (accessed 15 August 2003).

—— (2003b) 'The Internet and the Iraq war'. Available online at : www.pewinternet.org/reports/pdfs/PIP_Iraq_War_Report.pdf (accessed 1 August 2003).

—— (2003c) 'Daily Internet activities'. Available online at www.pewinternet.org/reports/chart.asp?img=Daily_Internet_Activities.htm (accessed 1 August 2003).

Powell, M. (2003) 'Should limits on broadcast ownership change?' *USA Today*, 21 January.

Rheingold, H. (1995) *The Virtual Community: Surfing the Internet*, London: Minerva.

Rice, R. (1984) 'New media technology: growth and integration', in R. Rice and Associates, *The New Media: Communication, Research and Technology*, London: Sage, pp. 33–54.

Rogers, E. (1986) *Communication Technology: The New Media in Society*, New York: The Free Press.

Sparks, C. (2002) 'The impact of the Internet on the existing media', from proceedings of a seminar on 'The Internet and Modern Communications', Nicosia, 29 March 2002.

Towler, R. (2002) *The Public's View*, London: Independent Television Commission and Broadcasting Standards Commission.

Van Dijk, J. (1999) *The Network Society*, London: Sage.

Veronis Suhler Stevenson (2003) *Communications Industry Report: Forecast Summary*, New York: Veronis Suhler Stevenson.

Which? Online (2002) *Annual Internet Survey 2002*. Available online at www.which.net/surveys/key.html (accessed 10 August 2003).

Index

ABN AMRO 284

Aboriginal communities 39

academic context: dismantling of feminism 59–60, 60–1, 61–2; media and cultural studies in Britain 131, 132

academic disciplines 19–20

Actor Network Theory 238

actors: creating synthespian entities 251, 255–6, 259; dialogic relationship with audience 256–8; working in new Siliwood 253–5

Adorno, Theodor 10, 115, 119, 153, 197, 197–9, 203, 207

advertising: culture industry 199; history of language in 118; HSBC's 'glocalisation' campaign 35–6; influence on media and culture 127, 154; Internet 279, 280; niche media 51; pressures to exploit Internet media 287; as promotional culture 149, 150, 151, 152, 154, 156, 157–8; use of traditional networks 284; Wonderbra image 63–4

aesthetics: Becker's view of conventions 203–4; and cultural value 7, 195; melodrama in films 224; melodramatic modes in *EastEnders* 226–8; popular cultural forms 10–11, 196; production of *Russian Ark* 269; and state influence 207

Afghanistan 77

Africa: presence in Peckham 105, 109–10; *see also* West African music

African Americans in USA 79

agency: and determinism/constructionism debate 237, 245; effects of media 188–9

Agre, Phil 48

AI (film) 259

Ain't It Cool News 255

Aksoy, Asu 7, 8, 10, 16, 71–2

Alberoni, Francesco 181

Alexander, Jeffrey 180–1

Ally McBeal (TV series) 17, 67, 217

Alsop, Will 106

alternative media 183, 189

America Online 278, 286

American Revolution 79

Americanisation 31, 41

Ang, I. 135

animators 254

anthropology: functionalism 178; structuralism 24

AOL Time Warner Network 287

Appadurai, Arjun 40, 72

Apple: i-Tunes service 281

area studies 3

Aristophanes 125

Arledge, Roone 118

Armstrong, Gary 101, 107

Arnot, M. 61

art forms: Bourdieu's insight 205–6; commodification and cultural production 198–9

'art house' film production 11, 265

art worlds: Becker's perspective 202–4; Bourdieu's view 206

Arthur, Paul 264

artificial intelligence (AI) 236, 251

artificial life 236, 241, 241–2, 243

artists: Adorno's concerns 200, 201;